T0315140

LONDON RECORD SOCIETY
PUBLICATIONS

VOLUME XXIX
FOR THE YEAR 1992

TWO TUDOR SUBSIDY
ASSESSMENT ROLLS
FOR THE CITY OF LONDON:
1541 AND 1582

EDITED BY
R. G. LANG

LONDON RECORD SOCIETY
1993

© LONDON RECORD SOCIETY

The publication of this volume has been made possible by grants from the Twenty-seven Foundation and the Marc Fitch Fund

Unaltered reprint 2015

ISBN 978-0-90095-229-6

Distributed for the London Record Society by
Boydell & Brewer Ltd,
PO Box 9, Woodbridge, Suffolk, IP12 3DF, UK
and of Boydell & Brewer Inc.
668 Mt Hope Avenue, Rochester, NY 14620, USA
Website: www.boydellandbrewer.com

Printed and bound in Great Britain by
4edge Limited

CONTENTS

Contents

Contents

Contents

Contents

Contents

ABBREVIATIONS USED IN FOOTNOTE REFERENCES IN THE INTRODUCTION

(Abbreviations used in the edited subsidy rolls are listed in the section on Editorial Practice.)

Beaven	Beaven, Alfred B., *The Aldermen of the City of London temp. Henry III –1908* (2 vols., 1908, 1913)
G.L.	Guildhall Library
Letters and Papers	*Letters and Papers, foreign and domestic, of the reign of Henry VIII*, ed. J. S. Brewer, James Gairdner, and R. H. Brodie (21 vols. and Addenda, 1862–1932)
Schofield, dissertation	Schofield, R. S., 'Parliamentary Lay Taxation 1485–1547' (unpublished Ph.D. dissertation, University of Cambridge, 1963)
Statutes	*Statutes of the Realm,* ed. A Luders, T. E. Tomlins, J. Raithby, et al. (11 vols., 1810–28)
Tudor Royal Proclamations	*Tudor Royal Proclamations,* ed. Paul L. Hughes and James F. Larkin (3 vols., 1964–69)

MANUSCRIPTS IN THE PUBLIC RECORD OFFICE

C.60	Chancery, Fine Rolls
C.66	Chancery, Patent Rolls
C.212	Chancery, Petty Bag Office, Miscellaneous Rolls
E.159	Exchequer, King's Remembrancer, Memoranda Rolls
E.179	Exchequer, K. R., Subsidy Rolls, etc.
E.208	Exchequer, K. R., *Brevia Baronibus* (Writs under the great seal or privy seal to the Treasurer and Barons of the Exchequer)
E.359	Exchequer, Pipe Office, Enrolled Accounts of Subsidies, Aids, etc.

E.371	Exchequer, Lord Treasurer's Remembrancer, Originalia Rolls
S.P.12	State Papers Domestic, Elizabeth I
S.P.14	State Papers Domestic, James I
S.P.46	State Papers Supplementary

MANUSCRIPTS IN THE CORPORATION OF LONDON RECORDS OFFICE

Jour.	Journals [of the Common Council]
Letter Book	Letter Books
Rep.	Repertories [of the Court of Aldermen]

INTRODUCTION

The documents published in this volume are the assessment rolls for the City of London of 1541,[1] for the second payment of a lay subsidy granted by parliament in 1540,[2] and of 1582,[3] for the second payment of a lay subsidy granted in 1581.[4] They are the earliest and latest of only six complete surviving assessments for the subsidy in Tudor London, the others being the assessments of 1547, 1549, 1564, and 1577.[5] These two documents give the names of 3,433 residents of London valued and assessed for the subsidy in 1541 and 5,900 in 1582, listed by ward and parish. They give the names of a further 652 aliens and denizens taxed *per poll* in 1541 and 1,358 in 1582; these were 'strangers' above a certain age whose wealth fell below the threshold for assessment.[6] The subsidy acts required valuation and assessment of companies as well as individuals, and 35 companies in 1541 and 40 in 1582 paid toward the subsidy in London.[7] Finally, in 1541, but not in 1582, the estates

1. E.179/144/120.
2. *Statutes*, 32 Hen. VIII c.50.
3. E.179/251/16.
4. *Statutes*, 23 Eliz c.15. There are two earlier publications of Tudor subsidy assessments for London: *Returns of aliens dwelling in the city and suburbs of London from the reign of Henry VIII to that of James I*, ed. R.E.G.Kirk and Ernest F. Kirk, Publications of the Huguenot Society of London, X (1900, 1902), and Queen's College, Oxford, MS 72, ff.143-162, 'a copy of a subsidy roll or assessment of the city of London made in 1589', in *Visitation of London 1568 with additional pedigrees 1569-90; the arms of the city companies; and a London subsidy roll, 1589*, ed. by H. Stanford London and Sophia W. Rawlins, The Publications of the Harleian Society, 109 and 110 for 1957 and 1958 (1963). The latter is not a complete assessment roll. It may be what was called a 'high book'. See below, xxvii–xxix.
5. The 'official' copies of the subsidy assessment rolls comprise part of the records in the Public Record Office class E.179 (Exchequer, King's Remembrancer, Subsidy Rolls, etc.). The Exchequer copies of the subsidy rolls together with subsidiary documents in the same class are listed in five List and Index Society volumes: vols. 44, 54, 63, 75, and 87. By complete I mean that all membranes or rotulets of the assessment certificates for all wards are extant, not counting Bridge Without, which was taxed as part of the borough of Southwark in Surrey. Some of the documents are in imperfect condition, with some loss of names and assessments. This is especially the case with the assessment roll of 1549. Versions of subsidy assessments are to be found in the State Papers Domestic and in local record offices, libraries, and private collections. All such 'unofficial' assessment rolls that I know of for London happen to be incomplete and were never intended to be complete; they are either documents preliminary to the compilation of the rolls in Exchequer or they are selective extracts made for other uses, such as the raising of military harness. The document erroneously described as 'Transcript of Second Payment of Lay Subsidy granted 18 Elizabeth' (P.R.O. Round Room, Press Mark 10/63) is a partial list of subsidymen and their valuations for the purpose of assessing lance and light horse for a muster. It omits persons valued at less than £15 in goods, at less than £10 in lands and fees, and strangers taxed per poll.
6. See below, Tables IA and IB. The subsidy rolls for both years listed a few people for whom there were no entries of assessments; they are not included in these tables.
7. See below, Table II.

of orphans of citizens of London were liable to the subsidy. These orphans' estates were valued and assessed in a separate, single, city-wide assessment certificate that is included in this volume following the 1582 assessment roll.

The depth of the stratum of the population liable to assessment (other than strangers taxed *per poll*) and, therefore, the number of people and companies whose names appear in the subsidy rolls, was determined first of all by the exemption levels set in each subsidy act. These exemption levels varied from one Tudor subsidy to another up to 1563; thereafter they remained constant. The number of persons assessed depended secondly on the quality of the administration of the subsidy. There is much contemporary comment and circumstantial evidence to indicate that by the later sixteenth century the administration of the subsidy had become routine and negligent, two consequences of which were a progressive undervaluation of movables and income and a decline in the proportion of the population assessed for the subsidy (even at constant exemption levels).

Partial and fragmentary survival of the subsidy rolls, exemption levels that may provide a view of only a shallow, top stratum of society, and valuations of dubious reliability are obvious problems that anyone using these documents has to be concerned with. There are other less obvious problems. These records have a formal simplicity that can mislead. They do not always mean what they seem to tell us. But because they list large numbers of people in a way that seems to be meaningful and because of the scarcity of comparable sixteenth century records providing such broad and yet detailed and quantifiable data, the subsidy rolls will continue to have an enticing charm to historians of the social and economic structure of communities as well as to those who want to locate individuals in their social and economic milieu.

The purpose of this introduction is to assist scholars in the interpretation of these records of subsidy assessment for the City of London. The subsidy rolls are not records of collection, and collection will be considered only when it bears on the record of assessment. Questions of the subsidies' yield and the place of the subsidy in government finance are not treated.

THE SUBSIDY

The subsidy was a relatively new tax in 1541. The principal and normal form of parliamentary taxation from 1334 to the sixteenth century was the fifteenth and tenth. The crown and parliament developed and brought to maturity a new form of parliamentary subsidy in legislation of 1512-15 and 1523.[8] The 1512 act for a subsidy levied in 1513 (4 Hen. VIII c.19) was a graduated poll tax assessed on the basis of rank and wealth. It did, however, introduce several of the principles of the Tudor subsidy: an open yield; assessments on

8. Roger S. Schofield, 'Parliamentary Lay Taxation, 1485-1547' (unpublished Ph.D. dissertation, University of Cambridge, 1963), pp.198-214. I am obliged to Dr. Schofield for permission to cite his dissertation, which remains the basic study of 15ths and 10ths and subsidies of the early Tudor period. See also his 'Taxation and the political limits of the Tudor state' in *Law and government under the Tudors: essays presented to Sir Geoffrey Elton*, ed. Claire Cross, David Loades, and J.J.Scarisbrick (Cambridge,1988), pp.227-255.

valuations of two distinct forms of wealth – movable goods and annual income – and then charging taxpayers according to whichever assessment yielded the most; and administration of assessment and collection by local commissions with supervisory powers over local assessors and collectors. The 1514 act (5 Hen. VIII c.17) for a subsidy to be levied in that year revived the principle of a directly assessed tax. Instead of a graduated poll tax as in 1513, the assessments for the 1514 levy were based directly on the valuations of individuals' wealth in goods and annual income. The 1514 act also provided, as subsequent subsidy statutes did, for the resolution of uncertainty that would arise if a person were assessed in more than one place; a certificate of assessment obtained from the commissioners in one place and presented to the commissioners in another would serve to exonerate that person from payment in the second place. If, however, of two or more assessments one was higher than the other(s), the person was liable to payment of the higher assessment. The crown and commons intended the 1514 tax to raise £160,000. The valuations and the rates set on them produced a yield that fell nearly £110,000 short. Parliament passed the first 1515 subsidy act (6 Hen. VIII c.26) to make up the shortfall and when that levy also failed, passed the second 1515 act (7 Hen. VIII c.9) for a subsidy and a fifteenth and tenth to be levied in 1516. The second subsidy act of 1515 removed overriding control of the administration of the subsidy that the acts of 1514 and the first of 1515 (and to a lesser extent the act of 1512) vested in the commons (or a committee of the commons) and royal officials, and placed control of the subsidy commissioners in the exchequer. The 1523 act (14 & 15 Hen. VIII c.16) introduced one last, fundamental feature of the subsidy, the separate assessment of peers and commons, by taking the assessment of peers out of the hands of the subsidy commissioners and putting it under the supervision of the lord chancellor and other senior officers of the crown. From 1512 to the death of Elizabeth parliament enacted 26 subsidy statutes providing for 58 separate payments, each based, ostensibly (except for the payment of 1516 under the second act of 1515) on fresh valuations and assessments. The Stuart parliaments passed nine subsidy acts, the last in 1663.[9] Parliament continued to grant fifteenths and tenths to the crown after the introduction of the subsidy

---

9. This count includes the act of 1553 (7 Edw. VI c.12) whose two payments Mary remitted by letters patent confirmed by statute. All but one of the subsidy acts are printed in *Statutes*, but they are not all indexed nor are they all easily recognized as subsidy acts by their titles. A printed copy of the one act not printed in *Statutes* (18 Jac. I c.1) is in P.R.O. S.P.46. The act of 1670-71 (22 and 23 Car. II c.3) applied the name subsidy to a basicially different kind of tax. In the following list of the Tudor lay subsidy acts the number of payments each statute required is given in brackets followed, from 1589 (when parliament began to grant more than one subsidy in a single act), by the number of subsidies: 4 Hen. VIII c.19 (1 payment); 5 Hen. VIII c.17 (1); 6 Hen. VIII c.26 (1); 7 Hen. VIII c.9 (1); 14 & 15 Hen. VIII c.16 (4); 26 Hen. VIII c.19 (2); 32 Hen. VIII c.50 (2); 34 & 35 Hen. VIII c.27 (3); 37 Hen. VIII c.25 (2); 2 & 3 Edw. VI c.36 (3); 3 & 4 Edw. VI c.23 (1); 7 Edw. VI c.12 (0) – Mary remitted the act's two payments by letters patent confirmed by statute, 1 Mar. St.2. c.17; 2 & 3 Phil. & Mar. c.23 (2); 4 & 5 Phil. & Mar. c.11 (1); 1 Eliz. c.21 (2); 5 Eliz. c.31 (2); 8 Eliz. c.18 (2); 13 Eliz. c.27 (2); 18 Eliz. c.23 (2); 23 Eliz. c.15 (2); 27 Eliz. c.29 (2); 29 Eliz. c.8 (2); 31 Eliz. c.15 (4 payments – 2 subsidies of 2 payments each); 35 Eliz. c.13 (4 – 2 subs. of 1 payment and 1 sub. of 2 payments); 39 Eliz. c.27 (3 – 3 subs. of 1 payment); 43 Eliz. c.18 (7 – 1 sub. of 1 payment and 3 subs. of 2 payments each).

(the last three were voted in 1624), but always, from 1512, in the company of one or more subsidies.

THE TERMS OF THE SUBSIDY ACTS

The assessment of every subsidy rested on a specific subsidy act. Most of the clauses of these exceptionally long statutes (around 15,000 words in their mature form) were drafted before the beginning of the parliamentary session in which a subsidy bill was introduced. The administrative sections of the bill were fashioned closely on previous statutes. Although some of the additions and deletions of administrative provisions in the subsidy acts of 1548 to 1563 were of considerable consequence, most of the differences between one subsidy act and another from 1515 to the end of Mary's reign are related to the exemption levels, tax rates, number of payments, and the timetable for valuation and collection. The Henrician and Edwardian acts show royal officials and parliaments shifting the exemption levels from one subsidy to the next, changing the rates, varying the ratios between rates applied to valuations of goods on the one hand and annual income on the other, experimenting with progressive rate structures (as in 1523, 1543, 1545, and 1553), and treating in various ways the liability to a poll tax of aliens and denizens not otherwise charged. This *ad hoc* approach to drafting the variable terms of a subsidy gave way in the acts of 1558 and later to the application of a fairly consistent view of what a 'subsidy' was. From the last subsidy act of Mary's reign (4 & 5 Phil. & Mar. c.11) to the last of Elizabeth's (43 Eliz. c.18) a subsidy normally was, in respect to rates, a tax on native subjects of 2s. 8d. in the £ on the value of goods and 4s. in the £ on annual income from lands, fees, etc., and a tax on aliens and denizens at double those rates.[10] The exemption levels or thresholds of liability were £5 (1558 and 1559) and then £3 (from 1563 on) in goods or £1 in income from lands, etc. for native subjects, and for aliens and denizens £1 in goods or £1 income. Aliens not otherwise liable were subject to a poll tax.[11] The subsidy could be levied in a single payment or it could be spread over two payments. The notion of a subsidy was so firm by the 1580s that neither declining levels of valuation nor huge expenditures on defence could alter it. When bigger tax revenues were needed they were not achieved by higher rates or lower exemption levels (nor by tighter administration of the subsidy acts), but by voting multiple subsidies. The subsidy in London did not become settled in the manner of the fifteenth and tenth, however; the nominal yield from the divisions of assessment and collection did

---

10. The rates under the 1566 act (8 Eliz. c.18) were an exception: 1s.10d. in the £ on the value of goods and 2s.8d. on lands, etc., for English, and double those rates for aliens and denizens.
11. From 6 Hen. VIII c.26 through 2 & 3 Edw. VI c.36 all the subsidy acts but two imposed a poll tax on aliens and denizens above a certain age (ranging from 12 to 16) who were not otherwise liable to assessment for the subsidy. Aliens and denizens were not taxed per poll by the acts of 1534 (26 Hen. VIII c.19) and 1545 (37 Hen. VIII c.25). From the 1553 act (7 Edw. VI c.12) through the 1566 act (8 Eliz. c.18) all aliens and denizens were taxed *per poll* regardless of age. The 1571 act (13 Eliz. c.27) limited the poll tax to strangers 14 years of age or older. The 1576 act (18 Eliz. c.23) imposed the poll tax on strangers 7 years old and above. Seven years remained the age threshold in subsequent acts.

not become fixed, nor did the obligation to pay the subsidy come to rest upon the community of the city, ward or parish.

The subsidy act of 1540

The subsidy act of 1540, under which the 1541 assessment certificates were drafted, followed the standard language of the Tudor subsidy statutes in levying a tax on 'everye person of what estate or degree he be of, according to the tenor of this Act'.[12] That is, peers, clergy, women, and children as such were not exempted from the lay subsidy; anyone who owned property, real (in lay fee) or personal, could be liable. While the assessments of peers are in separate rolls, spiritual persons who held lay fees of substantial income could appear in the lay subsidy rolls as well as in the clerical subsidy rolls produced under the concurrent acts of the convocations of Canterbury and York as confirmed by parliamentary statutes. How many clergy appear in the lay subsidy rolls as holders of real property by descent or purchase cannot be determined from the subsidy rolls and related documents alone, but there are certainly some as the subsidy acts anticipate there should be.[13] Only problem cases come to light. John Leyland, for example, was valued at £100 in goods in Cornhill Ward in 1541 (**80**) without any indication that he was a member of the clergy, rector of a parish church in Guisnes in the Marches of Calais and prebendary of Newington in the diocese of Salisbury. It is only because of his successful suit to the barons of the exchequer for disallowance of the assessment of 50s. in London that we know of his clerical status and spiritual promotions. His discharge rested, apparently, on the argument that his benefices were subject to the clerical disme, subject also, therefore, to the clerical subsidy, and that he had no land, tenements or other lay hereditaments whereby he could be taxed as a lay person.[14] The statute law, contained in the clerical as well as lay subsidy acts, governing the liability of clergy in 1540 and 1581 to the lay subsidy may be simply summarized: any spiritual person possessing real property held in lay fee yielding an income at or above the exemption level set down in the lay subsidy act was liable to an assessment on that income for the lay subsidy; no person holding an ecclesiastical promotion subject to the clerical disme and assessed for the clerical subsidy on the income from that promotion or preferment should be liable to assessment on that income for the concurrent lay subsidy; and no person chargeable for the clerical subsidy should be made contributory to the concurrent lay subsidy by an assessment on movables.[15] Married women, if English, were not assessed

12. The language of the 1581 act was: 'every person Spirituall & Temporal, of what estate or Degree he or they be of...'.
13. The 1540 act states that 'every spirituall person ... shalbe rated and set according to the rate abovesaid, of and for every pounde that the same spiritual person ... hath, by discent bargayne or purchase ... in any manor landes tenementes rentes services or hereditamentes, after the trew just and clere yerely valew thereof ...; so that it extende to the valew of xx^li or above' (32 Hen. VIII c.50, sect.viii).
14. E.359/44, 2nd payment of subsidy granted 32 Henry VIII, r.19; E.159/321, *communia* Easter 34 Henry VIII, r.59.
15. The last point is not explicit in either the clerical or lay subsidy acts of 1540, but it is implied. It had been explicit in the preceding lay subsidy act of 1534 (26 Hen. VIII c.19, sect.xvii).

for the subsidy it would appear;[16] probably all of the English women assessed in London were widows or spinsters. Infants, who could acquire and own property under common law, were not exempted by any specific provisions of the subsidy acts, but in practice children with living fathers do not seem to have been liable and only the estates of orphans were assessed.[17]

The 1540 act provided for a subsidy to be paid in two payments, one to be assessed in 1540 and the second in 1541. In standard form, it set rates and exemption levels for two sorts of people: those born under the king's 'obeysance' (native subjects) and those not (strangers who had been granted letters of denization and aliens). The London subsidy commissioners commonly identified these two groups as 'English' and 'strangers' or 'aliens'. The statute set the tax threshold, or exemption level: English who had to their use any 'Honours, Castells, Manors, Landes, Tenementes, Rentes, Servyce Hereditamentes, Annuities, Fees, Corrodies, profites of the true juste and clere yerelye value of xxli or above . . . (Landes and Tenementes chargeable to the Disme with the Clergye onelye except)' were to be taxed at the rate of 12d. in the £ for each of the two payments of the subsidy. The commissioners abbreviated these sources of annual income as 'lands' or 'fees', or 'lands and fees'. English who had goods to the value of £20 and upward were to pay at the rate of 6d. in the £. Goods liable to valuation for assessment included coin, plate, stocks of merchandise, harvested crops, household goods, 'all other goods movable' whether in England or not, and all sperate debts. Apparel (other than gold, silver, and jewels) were excluded from the valuation for assessment, and debts owing could be deducted. As it applied to native born English, this subsidy of 1540 and 1541 was a tax on the relatively rich. The exemption levels for Englishmen's goods and lands were never again set so high. Strangers were assessed on the same bases – 'lands and fees' and 'goods' – but the threshold of liability was set at an annual income of £1 from lands and fees and a valuation of £1 in goods. The rates at which the annual income and goods were taxed were double those applied to English. Moreover, all strangers 12 years of age and above and not otherwise taxable were liable to a poll tax of 4d. at both of the two yearly payments. Oddly, and apparently incorrectly, 33 strangers in five wards were assessed in 1541 on the yearly value of their wages.[18] The last subsidy act to make wages explicitly a basis for assessment was the statute of 1523.

Corporations and non-corporate religious fraternities, gilds, and mysteries were also assessed. They were taxed at the same rates as strangers, but only above the English thresholds for the value of goods or income (£20). Goods of churches and chapels, or goods otherwise dedicated to the service of God, were exempted.

The subsidy act of 1581
The 1581 act also granted a subsidy in two payments. The rates were higher for the first payment (1581) than for the second (1582). For the first payment

16. Schofield, dissertation, pp.247-250.
17. Schofield, dissertation, p.250. There is no explicit reference to the taxation of orphans' estates prior to the statute of 1540. The act of 1548 (2 & 3 Edw. VI c.36, sect.i) and all later subsidy statutes exempted orphans' estates.
18. Below, **29, 30, 33, 34, 58, 84, 133, 135,** and **136**.

(1581) the rates were 1s.8d. in the £ on the valuations of Englishmen's goods and 2s.8d. on annual income from lands, etc., 3s.4d. on strangers' goods and 5s.4d. on strangers' lands. For the second payment, the assessment certificates of which are published here, the rates were 1s. in the £ on valuations of Englishmen's goods, 1s.4d. in the £ on annual income from land, etc., 2s. in the £ on strangers' goods, and 2s.8d. in the £ on strangers' lands. The liability threshold had by this time been settled at a valuation of £3 for Englishmen's goods and £1 for Englishmen's annual income from lands and fees and valuations of £1 of strangers' goods and lands. Under the 1581 act, all strangers of the age of seven or above and not otherwise assessed were subject to a poll tax of 4d. at each payment of the subsidy. The estates of orphans were specifically exempted from the subsidy as they had been since the act of 1548 (2 & 3 Edw.VI c.36). Companies were taxed at the same rates as individual Englishmen as they had been since 1548.[19]

THE SUBSIDY COMMISSION: APPOINTMENT AND COMPOSITION

The levying of every subsidy payment began with the appointment of the subsidy commissioners for each county and for specified cities, boroughs, towns, and royal households. The commissioners had direction of the entire administration of the subsidy from the appointment of assessors to payment into the exchequer; and not direction only, for the commissioners bore ultimate responsibility for the payment or discharge in exchequer of the tax assessed in their divisions. If collectors defaulted in payment and the crown could not make good its loss through distraint or attachment on the collectors themselves, the Lord Treasurer could, and did, initiate process against the commissioners who appointed them.[20]

The subsidy acts of 1512 and 1514, the first act of 1515, and the act of 1523 empowered members of the House of Commons to appoint the commissioners. Cromwell's subsidy act of 1534 gave the king power to appoint commissioners 'at his pleasure'. From 1540 the Tudor subsidy acts usually assigned appointment to the lord chancellor (or lord keeper of the Great Seal), the lord treasurer, the lord president of the council and the lord privy seal or two of them, the lord chancellor (or lord keeper) to be one.[21]

The subsidy assessment rolls appear to give the names of the commissioners, but the lists they give are commonly incomplete. In the post-Henrician years, particularly, the names of many of the commissioners are not included in the indented certificates of assessment – the subsidy rolls. The names of all the London commissioners do appear in the 1541 subsidy roll, but in 1582 fewer than a third of the commissioners were party to the indentures. For complete lists of commissioners one must look elsewhere.

19. In the subsidy act of 1545, however, English, strangers, and companies were all taxed at the same rates.
20. See, for example, E.179/282 Pt.2, 'A Booke of all olde Collectors debts' (not foliated), probably compiled in 1602, covering outstanding debts from as early as 1581, *passim*, for notes of process against subsidy commissioners.
21. Appointment in 1581 and 1582, however, rested with the lord chancellor or lord keeper, the lord treasurer, the steward of the queen's household, the lord admiral, and the lord chamberlain of the queen's household, or two of them, with the lord chancellor or lord keeper to be one (23 Eliz. c.15, sect.ix).

The subsidy commissioners received their appointment and charge under letters patent, relatively few enrolments of which survive. The commissions were generally entered in the Fine Rolls and copies were sent to the exchequer by means of the Originalia Rolls. Taken together, these sources still do not provide a complete record of the subsidy commissions,[22] and in sets of commissions that appear otherwise to be complete the commissions for London are sometimes omitted.

From about the beginning of Edward VI's reign the Fine Roll copies of the subsidy commissions were entered on rolls separate from the main Fine Roll series. Some of the surviving separate rolls of subsidy commissions continue to be classed as Fine Rolls through Mary's reign; others, and all of the Elizabethan survivals that have been located, are classed as Chancery Petty Bag Office Miscellaneous Rolls (C.212).[23]

In terms of membership, there appear to have been three distinct, successive types of subsidy commissions for London in the period 1512 to 1603. The commissions that the commons named in 1512, 1514, and 1515 had as their members the mayor, aldermen, and recorder of London, giving a direct civic control over the levying of the subsidy. The commons provided for the same civic control in the commissions of 1523 and 1524. The crown continued to appoint commissions comprised of aldermen in 1535 and 1536.[24]

Complete civic control gave way in 1540 and 1541 to government control, or, more exactly, control by the privy council. Cromwell had complained of under-valuation for the subsidy granted in 1534. In fact, he reassessed the City of London himself at two and a half times the assessment returned by

22. Schofield, dissertation, pp.220-21 and Appendix II, Chancery Enrolments of Commissions, pp.475-77. Dr. Schofield gives references to known sets of commissions to 1546. To his list may be added the commissions for the first of the two payments under 26 Hen. VIII c.19 (C.60/345).
23. Only one Edwardian and two Marian sets of commissions survive in the class C.60 (C.60/367B; C.60/370, pt.2; and C.60/372, pt.2). The twenty-three rolls of subsidy commissions in the records of the Petty Bag Office, C.212/22/1-23 (Edward VI to James I), some of them containing commissions for Wales only or England only, are listed in P.R.O. Round Room, Press 22, no.94B, Chancery Petty Bag Miscellaneous Rolls (C.212), where they are described as supplementary to the Fine Rolls.
24. The names of commissioners in 1512, 1514, and 1515 are in lists appended to the subsidy acts: *Statutes*, 4 Hen. VIII c.19; 5 Hen. VIII c.17; and 6 Hen. VIII c.26. There were no new commissions under second subsidy act of 1515. The commissions of 1523 and 1524 for the two payments under the 1523 act were recorded in C.66/642, m.13,d, dated 30 Aug. 1523 (calendared in *Letters and Papers*, v.III, Part II, no.3282) and C.66/645, m.1d-8d, dated 1 Aug. 1524 (*Letters and Papers* v.IV, Part I, no.547). The commissions of 1523 and 1524 omitted the recorder, the prior of Holy Trinity Aldgate (who served as aldermen of Portsoken ward) and alderman Thomas Mirfyn, who died very shortly after the 1523 commission was issued. The commission of 1524 was simply copied from that of 1523 with the curious result that Thomas Baldry appears twice, once by name and once by title, 'the mayor', and John Munday, mayor at the time of the 1523 commission, was thereby omitted. Neither was John Cawnton, who replaced Mirfyn as alderman of Bishopsgate, included in the 1524 commission. Although no complete list of commissioners appointed under 26 Hen.VIII c.19 has been located, it is clear from the names of the commissioners who were party to the indentures or certificates for the second of the two payments (1536) that the character of the commission remained civic; they included the names of five aldermen and the recorder. See, for example, E.179/144/99, indenture between the commissioners and the petty collectors for the ward of Cheap, 20 April 1536. The names of aldermen may be obtained from Beaven.

the commissioners.[25] When the commission for the first payment of the grant of 1540 was issued in the autumn of that year, the privy council directed the chancellor to hold back on the schedule of aldermen's names that had previously been delivered to him and to name to the commission instead Robert earl of Sussex, great chamberlain (the member of the commission to whom the chancellor was to deliver the letters patent); John Lord Russell, lord admiral; Cuthbert Tunstall, bishop of Durham; Stephen Gardiner, bishop of Winchester; Edmund Bonner, bishop of London; Sir Richard Rich, chancellor of augmentations; Sir John Baker, chancellor of first fruits and tenths; and the mayor of London. Ultimately, the recorder of London, Sir Roger Cholmely, was added to the commission. The council decided that aldermen other than the mayor were to be merely assessors.[26] The larger commission of 1541, for the second payment of the same subsidy, shows at least an equal determination to keep the administration of the subsidy under government control; it included the archbishop of Canterbury and two other bishops, ten officers of state and royal officials, the mayor of London and the recorder of London.[27] This placement of control of the London subsidy commission in the hands of royal officials came shortly after the crown had intruded its nominees into the mayoralty in at least three successive years: 1535, 1536, and 1537, and possibly in 1538.[28] The membership of these commissions of 1540 and 1541 was not entirely consistent with the intention of the 1540 act, which gave two qualifications for commissioners: that they be 'persons as ... shalbe thoughte suffycyent for the sessyng and leving [*sic*] of the same Subsidie' and that they be inhabitants of the places where they were put in commission.[29] While the commissioners were all 'sufficient' within the meaning of the act, they were not all residents of London; one may note specifically Sir Ralph Sadler, Sir Edward Northe, and William Whorewood as lay commoners in the commission in 1541 who were not assessed for the subsidy in London. The privy council's intervention, although possibly pushing aside some legal niceties, had the desired effect; the level of subsidy valuations in London peaked in 1541.

As though to emphasize the change in control, the mayor was removed in 1540 and 1541 from his usual place at the head of the commission and given precedence over the other commoners only. When the lord chancellor, Sir Thomas Audley, repeated this affront to civic pride in the commission of 1544 the court of aldermen reacted sharply. 'Not contentyd for that my lorde mayer was not fyrste named in the seid commyssyon', the aldermen ordered the town clerk to name the mayor first in the public reading of the commission. Subsequently, the court minutes note with satisfaction, 'all the seid

---

25. Schofield, dissertation, pp.327-28. The residents of London did not pay on Cromwell's assessments, however.
26. *Letters and Papers*, XVI, no.112, Privy Council to Lord Chancellor, 2 Oct. 1540; Jour. 14, f.223,b, precept from subsidy commissioners to the sheriffs of London, 12 Oct. 1540.
27. C.60/353B, m.13. The list of commissioners given in the fine roll does not include Sir Richard Pollard, who is named as a commissioner in the 1541 assessment roll (below, 1).
28. Guy L. Gronquist, 'The Relationship between the City of London and the crown, 1509-1547' (unpublished Ph.D. dissertation, University of Cambridge, 1986), pp.17-19.
29. *Statutes*, 32 Hen. VIII c.50, sect.vi.

lordes [of the commission] with one assente att all their severall sessyons ... causyd hym [the mayor] to sytt & kepe the chief place'.[30]

The appointment of the commission for the first payment of the first subsidy of Mary's reign restored a significant aldermanic element to the panel.[31] From this time until 1603 or after, the London commission had a substantial numerical preponderance of councillors, officials, judges and law officers of the crown to whom were joined the lord mayor and a number of the senior aldermen. Mary's first London commission included four alderman who had passed the mayoralty among its 27 members. The commission that administered the subsidy in London in 1582 was essentially the same as the commission of 1555. It had 29 members: the lord mayor, 15 councillors and royal officials, the bishop of London, three judges, the two principal law officers of the crown, six aldermen who had passed the chair, and the recorder of London.[32] Only the mayor, five of the aldermen, and the recorder were party to the certificates of assessments returned into the exchequer.[33] Possibly the actual administration of the subsidy was as much in the control of the aldermen in 1582 as it had been before 1540, but we know far too little about the operation of the commissions to be sure of that.

THE SUBSIDY COMMISSION: DUTIES

The short and formal letters patent appointing a subsidy commission merely required those named in the commission to levy the subsidy according to the provisions of the statute. They could divide themselves, as they considered expedient, into smaller groups for the execution of the act, but the London commissions did not. However, most of the actions required of the commission could legally be performed by as few as two of its members.

The statutory procedures for administering the subsidy were basically the same in 1540-41 and 1581-82. The 1540 act required the commissioners for each payment first to summon a number of 'substauncyall, discrete and hon-

---

30. Letter Book Q, ff.97b-98, court of aldermen, 29 January 1544.
31. C.60/37, commission dated 10 Dec. 1555. For lists of commissioners, possibly incomplete, for the first and second payments under 34 & 35 Hen. VIII c.27, see E.179/144/123 and, for example, E.179/147/634. There are neither enrolments of London commissioners nor assessment certificates for the last subsidy of Henry's reign, 37 Hen. VIII c.25. For the commission for the third payment under 2 & 3 Edw. VI c.36, see *Calendar of the patent rolls . . . Edward VI*, vol.V, pp.360-61.
32. C.212/22/8, commissions dated 3 July [1582], for the second payment under 23 Eliz.c.15. The London commissioners were: Sir James Harvey, lord mayor; Sir Thomas Bromley, lord chancellor; William lord Burghley, treasurer; Edward earl of Lincoln, high admiral; Thomas earl of Sussex, chamberlain of the queen's household; Henry earl of Northumberland; Henry earl of Huntingdon; Robert earl of Leicester; John Aylmer, bishop of London; Thomas lord Wentworth; Sir Francis Knolles, treasurer of the household; Sir James Croftes, comptroller of the household; Sir Christopher Hatton, vice-chamberlain of the household; Sir Francis Walsingham, principal secretary; Sir Christopher Wray, chief justice of queen's bench; Sir Ralph Sadler, chancellor of the Duchy of Lancaster; Sir Walter Mildmay, chancellor of the exchequer; Sir Gilbert Gerard, master of the rolls; Sir Edmund Anderson, chief justice of common pleas; John Southcote, justice of queen's bench; John Popham, attorney-general; Sir Thomas Offley, ald.; Sir Rowland Hayward, ald.; Sir Lionel Duckett, ald.; Sir John Ryvers, ald.; Sir Thomas Ramsey, ald.; Sir Nicholas Woodroffe, ald.; Thomas Egerton, solicitor-general; and William Fleetwood, serjeant at law and recorder of London.
33. Below, **166**.

est ... inhabitants' and constables and other local officials to a meeting where they were to be sworn as presenters, or assessors, of the various places within the limits of the commission. The assessors were to return at a second meeting to present to the commissioners in writing the names and values of the residents and fraternities, guilds, and corporations of those places. The commissioners were then to begin work on the compilation of the certificates, or subsidy assessment rolls. They were to examine on oath those whom they suspected of being of greater wealth than reported by the assessors; to examine on oath, also, those who claimed to be of less wealth than the assessors had set down; and to assess each other. This done, they were to put the certificates of assessment in final form as indentures on parchment between themselves and the collectors whom they appointed for each of the divisions within the limits of their commission; to deliver signed and sealed estreats or copies of the certificates to the collectors; and to deliver other signed and sealed copies – the subsidy assessment rolls – into the receipt of the exchequer. The few changes made in these basic steps between 1540 and 1581 related mostly to the oaths for obtaining true valuations.

THE TIMETABLE FOR ASSESSMENT AND COLLECTION

The subsidy acts set a series of deadlines for the commissioners that established the basic timetable for assessment and collection of each subsidy payment. The timetable for the two payments of 1540 and 1541 under the 1540 act were the same. The commissioners were to appoint assessors between 1 September and 20 October, presumably early rather than late in the period, for the assessors were to complete their task by 20 October. The London commissioners in 1541 apparently assembled the assessors, took oaths of them, and gave them their charge on 5 October. On 2 October, 13 of the commissioners ordered the alderman of each ward to summon two of the 'most honest, substancyall and dyscrete' citizens of the ward to appear with the aldermen before the commissioners at Guildhall on 5 October to receive directions for the taxation and assessment of the subsidy.[34] Although the precept of 2 October does not mention 'assessors' or 'presenters' it contains language that seems to mark it as an order requiring attendance of prospective assessors. If the two citizens from each ward were, indeed, to serve as assessors, they did not comprise the whole body of assessors. This is evident from the 1541 assessment certificate for Queenhithe Ward, where six taxpayers are identified as the 'presenters' or assessors of the ward (below, **146**). Possibly the commissioners themselves nominated some of the assessors for each ward while requiring the aldermen to nominate two. At this meeting on 5 October the assessors from each ward presumably took the statutory oath to enquire of and certify the values of the inhabitants of their wards; listened while the commissioners read to them the tax rates on English, strangers, lands and goods; and received instructions on the form in which they were to make their returns to the commissioners. This business concluded, the commissioners set another day and time when the assessors, or 'presenters' as the statute terms them, were to attend with their written returns of valuations and tax assessments. The commissioners could at this time examine the assessors

34. Jour. 14, f.277,b

on their valuations.[35] Because the commissioners' final certificate of assessment superseded the assessors' returns, the latter have not been found to survive, at least for the Henrician subsidies.[36] We lack, therefore, the evidence they may have given on methods of valuation and on the extent of the commissioners' contribution to the final assessment certificate. Just when this second gathering of assessors before the commissioners took place in 1541 is not known, but it should have been on or by 20 October, which was not only the deadline for completion of the assessment, but also the deadline (within three weeks of the Feast of St. Michael, according to the statute) by which the commissioners were to appoint collectors for each of the wards (the petty collectors) and give them copies of the final, revised version of the assessments.[37]

There probably was, then, a legal maximum of 16 days (5 to 20 October) for the assessors to do their valuing and assessing, for the commissioners to hear appeals from those who claimed to be overvalued, and for the estreats for the petty collectors to be drafted. The indentures between the commissioners and the petty collectors were actually dated 24 October 1541,[38] which may have extended the entire assessment procedure to a maximum of 20 days.

The commissioners next appointed high collectors, as required by statute, probably two for each of four groups of wards into which the city was divided for collection purposes. Their division into pairs to collect from four groups of wards seems probable from known practice on other occasions – in 1544, 1547, and 1582, for example.[39] The high collectors were bound by indentures with the commissioners to receive the ward collections from the petty collectors (two for each ward) and to pay the sum collectable in each ward into the receipt of the exchequer by 6 February 1542. Copies of the indentures between the London commissioners and the high collectors do not survive for 1541, but the names of the eight high collectors are given in the indentures between the commissioners and the petty collectors and in the Exchequer Enrolled Accounts.[40]

Finally, before 16 November, the commissioners were to return into exchequer estreats of their indentures with the petty collectors and the high collectors, that is, the subsidy assessment rolls as we have them.

The statutory timetable and basic procedures for administering the two payments under the 1581 act were similar to those for 1540-41. In 1582, the commissioners were to appoint assessors by 28 August, the assessment was to be completed and certified into exchequer by 20 September, and payment was to be made into exchequer by 20 November. The main difference from 1541 was the much shorter time allowed for collection. Most of the adminis-

---

35. *Statutes*, 32 Hen. VIII c.50, sect.viii.
36. Schofield, dissertation, pp.273-74. However, some of the London 'high books' and 'low books' of the later sixteenth and seventeenth centuries, discussed below, may be copies of assessors' original returns.
37. *Statutes*, 32 Hen. VIII c.50, sect.x.
38. Below, **1**.
39. E.179/144/123, m.57-64; E.179/145/151; and below, **166**.
40. E.359/44, 2nd payment of subsidy granted 32 Hen. VIII, r.19. For the names of the eight high collectors in 1541, see below, **11**.

trative procedures set down in the 1581 act were essentially the same as those of 1540. Some significant changes – the elimination of oaths for obtaining true valuations and changes in the clauses governing the resolution of multiple assessments of the same person – are discusssed below.[41]

HIGH ASSESSORS AND PETTY ASSESSORS IN LONDON: AN ELABORATION OF THE STATUTORY ASSESSMENT PROCEDURES

The assessment procedures actually followed in London from the mid-sixteenth century on were somewhat more elaborate than those set out in the statute. They involved valuation and assessment at two levels. By the middle of the sixteenth century it was the practice for the London commissioners to appoint two groups of assessors: a panel of high assessors for the entire city (customarily six aldermen and six commoners by the second half of the century) and panels of low assessors or petty assessors for each of the twenty-five wards. The high assessors valued the city's richest inhabitants on the basis of returns from the aldermen and the petty assessors in each ward valued the rest. The two panels of assessors presented to the commissioners two separate books of valuation and assessment, the 'high book' and the 'low book'. There may have been two groups of assessors as early as the payments of 1540 and 1541.

The earliest clear evidence for this two-tiered method of assessment is a precept of 1549 that the mayor issued as subsidy commissioner. In it, he commanded the aldermen to 'sesse all the inhabitauntes within your said warde beinge of the valewe of x li in gooddes & upward unto the some of L li and to certyfie the high Sessors of the said Relief within the said Citie thereof in writinge at the Guyldhall betwixt this & Wednesdaye next comming'.[42] References to high assessors follow in precepts of 1555 (the aldermen required to certify to the high assessors the names of inhabitants of their wards worth £40 and upwards in goods), 1557 (the aldermen required to certify the names of inhabitants worth £50 and upwards in goods), 1559 (the aldermen required to do the same and also to certify the names of inhabitants worth £5 to £50), 1563 (the aldermen required to certify to the high assessors the names of inhabitants worth £30 and upwards in goods and £20 and upwards in lands), and 1571 (the aldermen required to furnish the high assessors with a book of the names of the inhabitants of every ward and to order the petty assessors to give their last indentures to the high assessors).[43]

Circumstantial evidence strongly suggests that some kind of two-tiered assessment system existed in London in 1540 and 1541. It has already been observed that the council ordered in 1540 that aldermen other than the mayor be removed from the subsidy commission and serve instead as assessors. There is a recorded precept of October 12, 1540, from the commissioners for the first payment (1540) under the act of 32 Hen. VIII c.50 ordering five aldermen and five commoners to appear before the commissioners the following day to be told what they were to do concerning the 'taxation and

---

41. See below, pp. xlvi–xlvii, lv–lvii.
42. Jour. 15, f.413,b. This precept concerns the first payment of the relief under 2 & 3 Edw. VI c.36.
43. Jour. 16, f.364,b; Jour. 17, ff. 25,b, 133,b; Jour. 18, f.152,b; Jour.19, f.356.

assessing' of the subsidy.[44] The later panels of high assessors we know also to have comprised equal numbers of aldermen and commoners, and it is hard to imagine what role these ten men were to perform in the taxation and assessing of the subsidy if it were not closely comparable to that of the high assessors. At the same time, however, we are aware of the existence of 'presenters' or ward-level assessors for the second payment in 1541, and there were, presumably, such ward assessors in 1540 also. It seems likely, then, that there was a two-tiered system of assessment in London as early as 1540.

Copies of precepts concerning the subsidy that were entered into the Journals of the Common Council constitute much the largest body of evidence on the peculiarities of assessment in London, but their brevity and the irregularity of their entry make it impossible to draw from them alone a coherent account of assessment procedures. Two documents of the early seventeenth century, however, do provide descriptions of the assessment process and a key to interpreting the terse and scattered precepts in the sixteenth-century journals: one is a short, general account of the administrative framework for assessing a subsidy in London, the other is a formulary of 1621 for assessing the subsidy in Bassishaw ward.[45]

The commissioners in 1621 first summoned all the aldermen, their deputies, the common councilmen and others of chief rank to the number of about 200 to a meeting before the commissioners sitting at the Guildhall. There the commission was read and the commissioners appointed 12 men, six aldermen and six commoners, to be high assessors.[46] An analogous meeting appears to have been held in 1550, when the sheriffs directed the aldermen, 14 persons named, and the most substantial inhabitants from every ward to gather before the commissioners.[47] The commissioners, through the sheriffs, summoned a similar meeting for the single-payment subsidy voted in 1558, when six aldermen and six commoners named, the rest of the aldermen, and the most substantial persons from every ward were required to appear before them.[48]

Second, in 1621 the mayor as commissioner issued a precept to the aldermen requiring them to give to the high assessors at at Guildhall a list of the inhabitants of their wards and a copy of the last assessment list.[49] In 1550, the commissioners issued an apparently analogous precept to the aldermen requiring that they deliver in writing the names of persons deceased or

---

44. Jour. 14, f.223,b. The five aldermen were Sir John Allen, Sir Ralph Warren, Sir Richard Gresham, Sir William Forman and Ralph Allen. The commoners were Sir John Gresham (who was elected alderman of Aldgate 25 Oct., 1540), Edward Worth, esquire, Stephen Vaughan, William Gonson, and John Malt.

45. S.P. 14/23/28, f.70, 'Notes for Taxacion of Subsidye in London', [1606]; G.L. MS 3505, Bassishaw Ward, Record and Assessment Book, 1610-63, ff.42-44, 'The Orderly proseding and manner of the taxacion & assessment of one intire subsedy graunted to his Majestie in the 18 yere of his highnes reigne of England etc. from the first Summons unto the Collexcion thereof'.

46. G.L. MS 3505, f.42,b. The 'Notes for Taxacion of Subsidye' (SP 14/23/28, f.70) state that 'The high Sessors for the citie of London and liberties thereof have allweys bene in nomber xii, whereof vi Aldermen & vi of the most suffycient Commoners being suche whoe are thought to be best acquaynted with the wealth and abilitye of the Citizens.'

47. Jour. 16, f.49.

48. Jour. 17, f.65,b.

49. G.L. MS 3505, f.42,b.

departed who had been assessed for the previous payment and those of like value who had moved into the ward.[50] Similar precepts of 1555, 1557, 1559', 1563, and 1571 are noted above, all of them requiring the aldermen to furnish the high assessors with lists of potential taxpayers in their wards.[51]

At this point, the high assessors could begin their work, which was to assess all inhabitants of the city whose goods or annual income from lands, etc. were above a specified level and to deliver their presentment of valuations and assessments to the commissioners 'in a booke fayre wrytten, subscribed withe their owne handes'.[52] The earliest known high assessors' book is one of 1559 compiled for the first payment of the subsidy granted that year.[53] It contains about 1,029 assessments of people valued at £50 or more in goods or in lands and fees, grouped by ward and by parish within the ward, and the assessments of 44 companies. It was signed by six aldermen and six commoners – the high assessors. A high assessors' book of 1572 also survives.[54] The high assessors on this occasion appear to have dealt with Englishmen and strangers valued at £20 and above in goods or lands, giving a total of about 1,074 assessments. Again the book was signed by the 12 high assessors. Neither of these surviving high books of assessments, unfortunately, is for a subsidy payment for which the exchequer copies of the subsidy assessment rolls are extant; one cannot, therefore, compare the high books with the final certificates returned by the commissioners. There are extant what may be copies of other Elizabethan high assessors' books for London, but as they are not explicitly identified as such, and lack the high assessors' signatures, they could be merely compilations of the names and values of wealthy taxpayers extracted for other purposes from the subsidy certificates. One of these has been published as a London subsidy assessment roll of 1589.[55]

50. Jour. 16, f.49,b, precept 8 March, 1550.
51. There are later precepts of 1576, 1581, 1582, 1585, etc. for the same purpose that refer merely to 'assessors', not the 'high assessors'. (Jour. 20 (2), f.286; 21, f.111,b; 21, f.212,b; 21, f.427.) This is only a change in style; the assessors in these later precepts are high assessors. Similarly, the 12 high assessors in the subsidy assessment roll of 1582 were all called simply 'assessors'. (See below, **226**, **233**, **267**, **278**, **354**, **394** (aldermen) and **210**, **277**, **292**, **300**, **354**, **358** (commoners).
52. S.P. 14/23/28, f.70. The threshold for assessment by the high assessors was not the same for every subsidy.
53. G.L. MS 2859, 'The first Assesment of the subsedy in the first yeare of Quene Elizabeth Sessed the xx day of June 1559 taxed by the highe Collectors [*recte* assessors] of the Citie of London'. This book has marginal additions in another hand of assessments for the last subsidy of Mary's reign and for the second payment under the 1559 act.
54. G.L. MS 2942, 'The Booke of the Names of all ye Citizeins and Inhabitantes within the Cittie of London, And the Suburbis of the same, Ceassid by the Hyghe Ceassors ffor the Seconde Paymente of the Subsedye graunted to our Soveraigne Lady Quene Elizabeth...', headed 'The boke wryten by the hy sesors for London 1572' and endorsed 'Subsedie for London made by the highe Sessors A° 1572'.
55. S.P. 12/96, 'Matters of State and Force in the Kingdom. Anno 1575', contains a list by ward and parish of Englishmen valued at £50 and above in goods for an unspecified subsidy. S.P. 12/109/43 is another version of this document, endorsed 'London. The particular valuation of the citizens in London in everie ward there for the subsidie for 50ᵗ and upwards'. It includes the same errors in internal headings as the preceding document. It has an added section of strangers assessed by the high assessors. S.P. 12/109/44 is a third version, endorsed 'London. Taxacion in Subsidie at 50ᵗ et ultra', that includes all that is in the first two versions and assessments in lands and fees at £50 and upwards. These documents can be identi-

When the high assessors had completed their valuation and assessment of the rich, the commissioners appointed petty assessors in each ward to value the rest of the inhabitants.[56] In 1621, the mayor, as commissioner, issued precepts commanding the aldermen to appear before the commissioners at Guildhall with ten or more of the most substantial inhabitants of each ward, all of them persons (if there were enough) who had been assessed in the high book. At least four of them were to be persons who had served as petty assessors or petty collectors for the last subsidy payment. The commissioner appointed some or all of these people to be petty assessors.[57] A similar precept had been issued in 1550.[58] Often the commissioners themselves named the petty assessors in the precepts of summons sent to the aldermen;[59] less frequently they instructed the aldermen to nominate persons to be appointed.[60] The commissioners charged the petty assessors with the valuation and assessment of the inhabitants of their wards whose goods or income from lands, etc. were below the high assessors' threshold and of inhabitants whom the high assessors had 'omytted, forgotten or left out of their bookes'.[61] All of the low books that have been found are of the early seventeenth century; there are low books of 1610 and 1621 for Bassishaw ward,[62] and 1626, 1629, and 1641 for Aldersgate ward.[63] A curious case of double assessment in London in 1582 was that of William Gosnold or Gosnall who was assessed twice in the same ward: by the low assessors on a valuation of £5 in goods, yielding an assessment of 5s. **(320)** and by the high assessors on a valuation of £20 in lands, yielding an assessment of 26s.8d. **(316)**. He paid the higher assessment.[64]

fied either as versions of high books or as extracts from the assessment certificates for the first subsidy payment under 18 Eliz. c.23. A similar document, Queen's College Oxford MS 72, is published in *Publications of the Harleian Society*, vols. 109 and 110, *Visitation of London 1568 with Additional Pedigrees 1569-90*, ed. H. Stanford London and Sophia W. Rawlins (1963), pp. 148-164. This contains assessments for the first payment of the first subsidy levied under 31 Eliz. c.15.

56. S.P. 14/23/28, f.70.
57. G.L. MS 3505, f.43.
58. Jour. 16, f.49,b.
59. The commissioners nominated the petty assessors in 1550, 1555, 1557, 1568, 1571, 1572, 1577, and 1581 (Jour. 16, ff.49,b, 364,b; 17, f.26; 19, ff.92,b, 356; 20 (1), f.10; 20 (2), f.363; 21, f.111,b). In 1581, the commissioners named some of the petty assessors and gave the aldermen the choice of the rest.
60. In 1546, 1582, 1587, and 1589 (Jour. 15, f.219,b; 21, f.215; 22, ff.117 and 318,b).
61. S.P. 14/23/28, f.70.
62. G.L. MS 3503, f.4,b, 'A coppie of the Sessment of the second parte of the third subsedi granted to his Majestie', i.e. under 3 Jac. I c.26. This has two lists of names and assessments, one designated 'the high booke' (17 people and 4 companies) and the other 'the lowe booke' (36 people). The same MS, f.43, has a similar entry for the payment of the first subsidy under 18 Jac. I c.1, with 25 inhabitants and 4 companies assessed by the high assessors and 33 inhabitants by the low assessors.
63. G.L. MS 1503/2, 'Aldersgate. Second Subsidy. 1ᵐᵒ Car.I', containing 155 low book assessments and names of the eight petty assessors for the second subsidy under 1 Car. I c.6. G.L. MS 1503/3, 'Aldersgate Ward. The Lowe bookes. The 18th of April 1629', containing 74 assessments for St. Botolph's parish only and the names of thirteen petty assessors, under 3 Car. I c.8. G.L. MS 1503/4 is a similar document, undated. G.L. MS 1503/5, 'Aldersgate Ward. The Lowe bookes for the subsedyes seased the xxixᵗʰ of Aprill 1641', a complete inhabitants list, apparently, with assessments on fewer than half those listed.
64. E.359/52, r.14, 2nd payment of subsidy granted 23 Elizabeth.

Vestiges of both high and low books are conspicuous in some of the completed assessment certificates. In 1582, the high assessors made presentments of English valued at £50 or more in goods and £10 *per annum* or more in lands, etc. and of strangers valued at £10 or more in goods or lands. In Aldgate ward, for example, the assessments in each parish are given first for the English and strangers valued by the high assessors and then for the English and strangers valued by the petty assessors (**185-196**). The certificate for Broad Street ward has generally the same arrangement, as does that for Tower ward, where, however, there is no breakdown of taxpayers by parish (**233-240, 373-387**). The petty assessors in Aldgate and in Coleman Street wards, gave taxpayers occupational identifications that were retained in the commissioners' certificates while the high assessors did not (**186-196, 261-265**). So consistently are valuations within the respective ranges of the high and petty assessors bunched separately, those of the high assessors always coming first, that one may fairly confidently go through the certificates and draw a line between the last name on the high assessors' presentment and the first name of the low book. There are a few outliers that may represent commissioners' adjustments of assessors' valuations.

Another artefact of this two-tiered system of valuations and assessments is a bi-modal distribution of valuations in London for the later sixteenth-century subsidies. This needs to be taken into account in any use of the subsidy rolls for analyzing distribution of wealth. In 1582, for example, the petty assessors valued 319 English residents at £20 to £49 in goods, while the high assessors valued 348 at exactly £50 in goods, the threshold for valuation and assessment by the high assessors. In the absence of any extensive revision by the commissioners, this system resulted in valuations and assessments that possess integrity only within the two separate ranges of the petty and high assessors.

Contemporaries came to see the two-tiered system of valuation and assessment as a reason for the decline in the number and level of subsidy assessments in London. One critic observed early in James I's reign that the assessors seldom advanced anyone whose wealth had greatly increased from the low book to the high book.[65] The numbers assessed at or above the threshold of the high assessors thereby diminished over time.

The further steps in the assessment procedure in London apparently corresponded to the administrative clauses of the subsidy acts, and they were the same in 1582 (and 1621) as they had been in 1541 (except that in 1582 the commissioners valued and assessed the assessors, as they had done since 1548). The commissioners made their revisions in the assessors' presentments, appointed petty collectors for each ward and two high collectors for each of the four groups of wards, drafted the estreats of the indentures between themselves and both sets of collectors, and returned their signed and sealed copies of those indentures into the receipt of the exchequer. The exchequer copies of the indentures with the high collectors happen to have survived for 1582, making the record of the commissioners' certification of assessment complete.

---

65. S.P. 14/23/28, undated [early James I], 'The Causes of the abasement of the subsedy'.

THE WARD AND PARISH AS DIVISIONS OF ASSESSMENT

The commissioners returned into the exchequer in 1541 and 1582, as on other occasions, assessment certificates for 25 wards. Bridge Ward Without, the twenty-sixth ward, created in 1550, was included in Surrey for tax purposes. In 1541, the commissioners also submitted a separate city-wide certificate of the assessments of the estates of orphans. Beginning with the act of 1548 orphans' estates were exempted from the subsidy. The only London 'orphans' books' apparently extant, however, are those for the payments of 1541 and 1544.[66]

The ward was the basic division of assessment and collection, but within the ward the assessments of individuals were usually listed under subheadings of parish or part-parish. Only in Cornhill, Lime Street and Tower wards in 1541 and in Lime Street and Tower wards in 1582 did the assessors not present their returns with some sort of parochial subdivision.

The parochial subdivision of the subsidy certificates was probably a practice carried over from the manner of levying fifteenths and tenths in the city. The sum owing from each ward for the fifteenth and tenth (commonly called the 'fifteenth') was fixed, and this sum was itself the total of what had become fixed payments from each parish or part-parish within a ward.[67] The sum actually levied in the the parish could differ from the sum owed, for parishes might aim at a surplus in the assessment in order to relieve the poorest inhabitants from payment.[68] In some entire wards charity provided relief from the fifteenth.[69] In general, however, parochial assessment and collection was basic to the levying of a fifteenth in the city. Ordinarily, when a fifteenth was levied the commissioners for the fifteenth or the mayor commanded the alderman of each ward to call together the inhabitants of the ward and at that time to oversee the election of assessors from the parishes of the ward and appoint parochial collectors.[70] The parochial collectors of the fifteenth (the

66. For the certificate of orphans' assessments in 1544, in the form of an indenture between the commissioners and the petty collectors of the 'subsidy of orphanage', see E.179/144/123, m.65-71.
67. This can be illustrated by a table of parochial charges for a fifteenth in Broad Street ward set down in the vestry minute book of the parish of St. Bartholomew by the Exchange (G.L. MS 4384/1, p.66).
68. As, for example, in the part of the parish of St. Margaret Lothbury in Coleman Street ward in 1585 (G.L. MS 4352/1, ff.53-54) and St. Mary Aldermanbury in 1591 (G.L. MS 3570/1, vestry minutes 3 October 1591).
69. The bequest of Sir William Taillour, mayor 1468-9 (d.1483) provided relief for anyone assessed 12d. or less for a fifteenth in Cordwainer ward (Rep. 14, f.87b). All residents of the wards of Aldgate, Billingsgate, and Dowgate were relieved of parliamentary fifteenths by the charity of John Reynwell, mayor 1426-7 (d.1445) (John Stow, *A Survey of London*, ed. C. L. Kingsford, 2 vols. (Oxford, 1908), I, p.207; Letter Book P, f.16b; Betty R. Masters, ed. *Chamber Accounts of the sixteenth century*, London Record Society Publications, 20, for 1984 (1984), xxv-xxvii; Guy L. Gronquist, 'The Relationship between the City of London and the crown, 1509-1547', (unpublished Ph.D. dissertation, University of Cambridge, 1986), pp.187-192).
70. Of the few such precepts recorded, see, for example, that of 20 Dec. 1540 for levying the first of four fifteenths that parliament granted in 32 Henry VIII (Jour. 14, f.238). A precept (25 April 1581) to the aldermen for levying the first fifteenth that parliament granted in 23 Elizabeth was essentially the same, except that it came from the mayor rather than the commissioners (Jour. 21, f.111).

fifteenth's petty collectors) paid the sum owing from the parish or part-parish directly to the high collectors, who, like the high collectors for the subsidy, had responsibility for the sums owing from groups of wards. Although it made no difference to the officials of the exchequer how much came from one parish and how much from another, so long as the ward totals were accounted for, within the city itself parochial accounting was essential to levying a fifteenth and tenth in the customary manner.

In assessing a subsidy, the listing of the taxpayers by parish in the commissioners' certificates conformed in a familiar way, but only superficially, to the parochial assessments for the fifteenth. Because the parish was not an essential administrative unit for the subsidy it could be treated with frustrating casualness.

Just over half of the city's parishes (55 of 108 in 1582) lay in more than one ward: forty-one in two wards, nine in three wards, and five in four wards.[71] The subsidymen in two or more part-parishes in a ward are often listed together under a single heading, making it practically impossible to distinguish the parishioners of one part-parish from those of another. When this is the case, one cannot combine the assessment lists from the parts of parishes lying in two or more wards to make up an assessment list of subsidymen for the whole parish.

Adding to the difficulty of parish-level analysis of the subsidy assessments rolls is the fact that some parishes are simply not mentioned in the subsidy certificates. For example, in 1541 there were strangers but no English listed as of the parish of St. Mary Mounthaw, which lay entirely in Queenhithe ward. It is possible, of course, that no English in that parish met the high threshold for assessment. St. Mary Mounthaw does not appear at all, however, in the assessment roll of 1582. Altogether there were 23 other parishes in 1541 and 24 in 1582 (all of them lying in more than one ward) that were not designated in the assessment certificates for one or more of the wards in which they lay. Either there were no residents of these part-parishes liable for the subsidy, or they were included with the residents of other parishes under incomplete headings. In 1541, for example, the subsidymen in the part of Allhallows Staining in Aldgate ward were subsumed under other parochial headings. The householders of the parish are known from the assessment for the parish clerk's wages for 1541-42.[72] At least three of the householders of this part-parish were listed under the heading of St. Olave Hart Street, three others were listed under St. Katherine Coleman, and probably two can be identified with subsidymen listed under St. Katherine Creechurch. Allhallows Staining is again missing from the Aldgate ward subsidy assess-

71. On the wards into which parishes extended I have followed John Smart, *A Short history of the several wards, precincts, parishes, &c. in London* (London, 1741). Smart gives the number of houses in 1741 in every precinct and ward, in every parish, and in all the parts of the the same parish in different wards. The parishes that I have taken as existing in 1582 are those which Stow describes in the 1603 edition of the *Survey of London*. I have included in my count Holy Trinity Minories which Stow treats as of Portsoken ward though it was later recognized as situated in the county of Middlesex. For a map and list of parishes with dates of abolition or merger, see Derek Keene and Vanessa Harding, *A survey of documentary sources for property holding in London before the Great Fire*, London Record Society Publications, 22, for 1985 (1985), xvi-xix.

72. G.L. MS 4958/1, churchwarden's accounts, 1539-72, ff.7-9.

ments in 1582. On that occasion, all of the subsidymen of the part-parish in Aldgate ward were listed under the double heading of St. Andrew Undershaft and Allhallows London Wall.[73]

There was at least one case in 1582 of a large number of subsidymen being shifted in the final compilation of the assessment roll from the listing of the parish in which they were actually resident to that of a neighbouring parish. In Bishopsgate ward, those householders in the parish of St. Helen Bishopsgate who were assessed by the high assessors were placed under the heading of St. Ethelburga.[74] The indifference of the assessors and commissioners to accuracy in the parochial headings means that parochial designations must be accepted with caution. Uncertain or disputed parish boundaries may compound the problem.

One cannot be certain that a person was resident even in the ward in which his or her name was entered for the subsidy. Ward boundaries could be unclear or the subject of controversy. The aldermen appointed a commission in 1533, for example, to determine whether dwellers within the precincts of the Blackfriars ought to be treated as residents of the ward of Farringdon Within or of Castle Baynard ward.[75] In 1543 the inhabitants of Castle Baynard and Queenhithe wards both claimed contributions toward the fifteenth from the house of Hughe Loft.[76] Whether the Smiths' hall and adjoining houses were in Queenhithe or Castle Baynard ward and whether the long shop in the Poultry was in Cheap or Broad Street were at issue in 1558.[77] In 1559 the aldermen had to order an inquest to determine whether the Haberdashers' hall was in Aldersgate ward or Cripplegate.[78] Such uncertainty may explain some of the double assessments for the subsidy that occurred. In 1541 Hugh Loft was assessed in Castle Baynard ward (par. of St. Benet Paul's Wharf, below, **54**) and in Queenhithe ward, adjoining (par. of St. Peter Paul's Wharf, below, **146**). William Pettyngall and John Bendles were assessed in Cordwainer ward (parishes of Holy Trinity the Less and St. Thomas Apostle, below, **78**) and in Vintry ward (par. St. Thomas Apostle, below, **161**). Anthony Coley (or Coole) was assessed in St. Leonard Eastcheap in Bridge ward and in the same parish in Candlewick ward (below, **46**, **64**); Sebastian Bony was assessed in the adjoining wards of Billingsgate (St. Margaret Pattens, below, **28**) and Langbourn (St. Gabriel Fenchurch, below, **136**); Robert Byrkham or Byrcham was assessed in Aldersgate (St. Botolph without Aldersgate, below, **5**) and in Cripplegate (St. Giles

---

73. In fact, all of the taxpayers under that heading from Emanuell Franckline to widow Bloys (below, **192**) were parishioners of Allhallows Staining (G.L. MS 4958/2, ff.40-42, Allhallows Staining, assessments for parish clerk's wages for 1582-83).

74. This statement is based on an examination of lists of receipts and arrearages of payments toward parish clerk's wages in St. Ethelburga for 1581-82 (G.L. MS 4241/1. pp.67-68) and names occuring in the churchwarden's accounts of St. Helen Bishopsgate between 1581 and 1585 (G.L. MS 6836, ff.34-40 and p.282). Of the 20 people assessed by the high assessors and listed under St. Ethelburga, I believe that the only actual residents of that parish were Matthew Harrison, Mr. John Cowper, and Elizabeth Stevens.

75. Letter Book P, f.22.

76. Guy L. Gronquist, 'The Relationship between the City of London and the Crown, 1509-1547', (unpublished Ph.D. dissertation, University of Cambridge, 1986), p.185.

77. Rep. 14, ff.45, 94b.

78. Rep. 14, f.205.

Cripplegate, below, **88**); and Roger Nowyes or Newys was assessed in Castle Baynard (St. Gregory by St. Paul's, below **59**) and in Farringdon ward Within (St. Michael le Querne, below, **103**). It is probable, of course, that the premises of some of these men did cross parish and ward boundaries.[79]

One cannot place complete confidence even in the assessors' and commissioners' treatment of the city's boundaries with Middlesex. The most obvious case of confusion in either 1541 or 1582 occurred in Farringdon ward Without in 1582 when the petty assessors of the ward carried their assessment up Chancery Lane 'above the field gates and in the Fields' (below, **319**). While this area was part of the parish of St. Dunstan in the West, it was not within the liberties of the city. In the event, none of the 20 people valued and assessed in this neighbourhood paid the subsidy as residents of Farringdon Without. Twelve of them paid as residents of Ossulstone hundred, four paid in other counties where they were also resident and were discharged in Middlesex as well as in the city, where one paid is uncertain (but it was not in Farringdon Without), and three others were reported by affidavits from the collectors to have no distrainable property in Farringdon Without.[80]

THE NUMBERS OF ASSESSMENTS IN 1541 AND 1582: ENGLISH, STRANGERS, ORPHANS, AND COMPANIES

In 1541 the commissioners' certificates presented 2,762 valuations and assessments of English, 671 of strangers, and 35 of companies. There were, in addition, 652 strangers assessed *per poll*. Not all of these assessments signified actual liability, as we shall see. In 1582, with the lower threshold of liability and a bigger population, the number of valuations of English was almost twice as large: 5,418. These totals do not include those few people in both years whose names were listed without any valuation and assessment: notably, in 1582, the earl of Northumberland (**175**), who would have been assessed with the peers, Sir Christopher Wray (**178**), Sir Francis Walsingham (**193**), Sir Walter Mildmay (**330**), and Sir Christopher Hatton (**342**). In 1541, 157 (5.7% of the assessments of English) were of women; 229 English women were assessed in 1582 (4.2% of all assessments of English). In both years, the certificates identify well over half of the women assessed as widows.

The number of strangers assessed on valuations was lower in 1582 than in 1541, despite identical thresholds of liability for strangers. This probably indicates a reduction in the size of the alien merchant communities whose members accounted for a large proportion of the strangers liable to valuation for the subsidy in 1541. The number of aliens taxed *per poll*, on the other hand, was in 1582 twice what it had been in 1541 (see Tables IA and IB). This was partly a consequence of the lower age threshold for the poll tax (7 years instead of 12), but it also reflects the larger number of alien craftsmen, artisans, and small traders resident in the city in the later sixteenth

79. That these double entries are assessments of the same person and not of two people with the same name is evident from the Lord Treasurer's Remembrancer's Enrolled Accounts (E.359/44, r.19, 2nd payment of the subsidy granted in 28 Henry VIII) which record the discharges from payment in all but one place in cases of assessment in more than one place.
80. E.359/52, r.14, 2nd payment of the subsidy granted 23 Elizabeth.

century, many of them religious refugees. The 1582 subsidy certificates record altogether 1840 aliens aged seven and above in the 25 wards, a total that is reasonably consistent with figures in the April 1583 return of aliens.[81]

The certificate of assessment of the estates of orphans in 1541 contains the names of at least 160 deceased citizen fathers and possibly as many as 175. The 206 mostly legible entries in the certificate give the names of 160 fathers. The names of the fathers in another 15 entries are illegible. By the custom of London the orphans of deceased citizens were entitled to one-third of their fathers' estates in goods, and for enforcement of this custom city officials acting as the court of orphans inventoried and divided estates and took recognizances of sureties nominated by the executors for payment to the orphans of their portions when they came of age. The entries in the certificates of assessment of orphans' estates give the names of the recognitors, the names of the deceased and the sums payable by the recognitors to the orphans. These sums are the values on which the tax assessments were calculated (at the rate for Englishmen's goods). Because the total of the portions of a single family of orphans was often spread among several groups of sureties, the number of entries in the orphans' book is larger than the number of estates they represent.[82] Many of the orphans' fathers had, by 1541, been dead for several years. Some of their children, in some cases, had been advanced before their deaths, others had since come of age and received their portions, and other children not yet of age had been partially advanced by their guardians – through payment of apprenticeship premiums for example. Therefore, even if the valuations of these citizens' personal estates at the time of death were accurate, the total of the sums in 1541 still payable to the orphans of a late citizen by the sureties do not in themselves provide a basis for the calculation of the wealth of the deceased.

Religious fraternities (in 1541) and city companies or guilds (in 1541 and 1582) were the only companies assessed for the subsidy. Although other corporations and non-corporate companies possessing movables or lands would seem by the terms of the subsidy acts to have been liable to assessment they were not, in fact, assessed. Except for Jesus College – a college for priests with lodgings and library in Dowgate ward – neither was any other sort of corporate body taxed in the more comprehensive (because of the low exemption level) subsidy assessment roll of 1544.[83]

The number of active parish fraternities in 1541 is unknown. The chantry certificates of 1546 and 1548 describe about 20, but this includes only those with landed endowments. Others financed themselves from quarterage pay-

---

81. The April 1583 return gives a total alien population of 2443 in the 25 wards, a figure that includes those in the liberties of Blackfriars (Farringdon Within), St. Martin le Grand (Aldersgate), and Whitefriars (Farringdon Without) (S.P.12/160/27, printed in R.E.G.Kirk and E.F.Kirk, eds., *Returns of aliens dwelling in the city and suburbs of London from the reign of Henry VIII to that of James I*, Publications of the Huguenot Society of London, 10, Pt.1 (1900), pp.376-377.)
82. For an account of the city's involvement in the estates of orphans, see Charles Carlton, *The Court of Orphans* (Leicester, 1974), especially pages 34-37 and 42-54.
83. E.179/144/123, r.31 for Jesus College.

ments.[84] Most of them were undoubtedly too poor to be assessed given the high threshold of the 1540 act. The three wealthy enough to be assessed in 1541 were the brotherhood of the Trinity in the parish of St. Botolph Aldersgate and the two parochial brotherhoods of St. Dunstan in the West and St. Bride (below, **11, 114, 117**). Only five more fraternities, eight in all, were taxed in 1544, however, for the second payment under the 1543 act, when the exemption level was £1 in goods or lands.[85]

The guilds or city companies assessed in 1541 and 1582 are listed in Table II. The total number of companies that the city recognized in either year is unknown. In 1540, the city assessed 68 companies for cressets for the mid-summer night watch.[86] Sixty-eight may actually represent what at least one city official took to be the total number, for four of the poorest (the Turners, Glaziers, Tapissers, and Longbowstringmakers) were included without any cressets being required of them, suggesting a desire for completeness.[87] Also, the number of companies furnishing cressets for the 1540 midsummer watch was larger than the number (60) attending the lord mayor's feast at Guildhall in 1531[88] and the number (61) rated for payment of 500 marks for the poor of St. Bartholomew's Hospital in 1548,[89] which are the other two most extensive lists of city companies of the 1530s and 1540s. Thirty-two, about half, of the city companies were assessed for the subsidy in 1541. Forty, or about three-quarters of the city companies, were assessed in 1582.[90] In 1580 and in 1585 the city assessed 52 companies for furnishing soldiers and in 1586 the same 52 for providing gunpowder.[91] There were 26 occasions between 1570 and 1590 when lists of companies assessed for furnishing men, military harness, grain, or gunpowder were entered into the Journals of the Common Council

84. Caroline M. Barron, 'The Parish fraternities of medieval London' in *The Church in Pre-Reformation society: essays in honour of F.R.H. Du Boulay*, ed. Caroline M. Barron and Christopher Harper-Bill (Woodbridge, Suffolk, 1985), p. 21.
85. E.179/144/123. The five were the brotherhoods of St. George in St. John Zachary (Aldersgate ward), St. Giles (Cripplegate), Our Lady and St. John the Baptist (Billingsgate), Our Lady in St. Magnus (Bridge), and Jesus and Our Lady, St. Mildred (Queenhithe). It is surprising that the fraternity of St. Giles, whose goods were valued at £52. 2s. 10d. in 1544, was not assessed in 1541.
86. Letter Book P, f.217.
87. Letter Book P, f.217. The other companies assessed for cressets in 1540 and not assessed for the subsidy in 1541 were, in the order in which they were listed: Plumbers, Painters, Pewterers, Waxchandlers, Girdlers, Curriers, Cordwainers, Bowyers, Fletchers, Poulters, Pastillers, Tilers, Masons, Joiners, Woodmongers, Plasterers, Blacksmiths & Spurriers (joined in assessment), Fruiterers, Bottlemakers & Horners (joined in assessment), Greytawyers, Farriers, Marblers, Paviors, Founders, Weavers, Minstrels, Cartetakers [Cardmakers ?], Linen-Drapers, Loriners, Foisters, Parish Clerks, Stationers, Upholsterers, and Brown Bakers. One company, the Cooks, was assessed for the subsidy in 1541, but not for the midsummer cressets in 1540.
88. John Stow, *A Survey of London*, ed. C. L. Kingsford, 2 vols. (Oxford, 1908), II, pp.190-92.
89. Jour. 15, f.399b.
90. Of the 52 companies assessed by the city in 1580, 1585, and 1586, the following were not assessed for the subsidy in 1582: Saddlers, Barber Surgeons, Butchers, Woodmongers, Fruiterers, Brown Bakers, Broderers, Poulters, Upholders, Minstrels, Turners, Basketmakers, and Glaziers. One company, the Fletchers, was assessed for the subsidy but not for the city levies in these three years. I am obliged to Miss Betty Masters, former Deputy Keeper of Records of the Corporation of London, for sending me typed copies of 1579 and 1586 company lists at a time when I did not have access to the originals.
91. Jour. 21, f.19; 21, f.426; 22, f.37b.

and only in 1572 and 1587 were more than 52 companies assessed: 60 in 1572 to furnish men and arms to make a show before the Queen at Greenwich[92] and 55 in 1587 to raise money for the purchase of 10,000 quarters of wheat.[93]

In 1541 several companies appeared twice in the assessment certificates. An entry at the end of the Tower ward certificate is headed 'Corporacions & felyshippes whiche were not presentyd this yere ne assessyd at the Ingrossing of the bookes, and therfor writen heere in this warde bycause of most rome for the wryten of them' (**157**). There follow the names of seven companies – Ironmongers (crossed out), Merchant Taylors (livery and bachelors listed separately), Scriveners, Woolpackers, Carpenters, Butchers, and Leathersellers – all but the Butchers actually entered and assessed identically in their proper wards. The double assessment of these companies obliged the commissioners to submit into exchequer certificates of payment in one place in order to secure discharge in the other.[94] The Scriveners paid in Cripplegate and were discharged in Tower. The others paid in Tower ward. The Woolpackers were discharged in Coleman Street and the Merchant Taylors, Carpenters, and Leathersellers were discharged in Broad Street ward.

It is notable that in both 1541 and 1582 there were 'lesser' companies that paid more toward the subsidy than a number of the twelve 'greater' or 'principal' companies. In 1541, the Brewers, Barbers, Leathersellers, Saddlers and Carpenters all paid more than the Salters, Haberdashers, Clothworkers, and Ironmongers. In 1582, the Cutlers and Brewers paid more than the Haberdashers and Vintners, while these and 12 other lesser companies paid more than the Ironmongers.

Only a few hundred of the people assessed for the subsidy in either 1541 or 1582 are identified in the subsidy rolls by their occupations or company memberships. The entries of such information in 1541 are so infrequent and irregular (except in the orphans' book) that they are probably not susceptible to any significant analysis. In 1541 about 30 aliens and 25 English taxpayers were identified by craft or trade. In most cases this information was probably given to help the collectors in distinguishing between like-named people in the same neighbourhood. For example, two persons named John Marten (both aliens) were assessed for the subsidy in the precinct of St. Martin le Grand; one was identified as a shoemaker, the other as a leather dyer (**9, 10**). No one else in the precinct was identified by occupation. The three Robert Clerks assessed in the part parish of St. Sepulchre in the ward of Farringdon Without were distinguished as a woodmonger, a haberdasher, and a joiner (**120, 122**). Again, these were the only people in this part parish identified by trade. The two John Johnsons in Tower ward were distinguished as a brewer and a cooper (**150, 154**). Why all of the assessed residents of Mugwell Street in the detached part of Farringdon ward Within (**101, 102**), or all of the strangers in the parish of St. Ann Blackfriars (**110**) should have been identified by occupation (or as servants) is a puzzle.

In 1582 as in 1541, craft and trade designations were scattered through the

92. Jour. 19, f.407.
93. Jour. 22, f.130.
94. E.359/44, r.19, 2nd payment of the subsidy granted in 32 Henry VIII.

certificates, probably to provide distinguishing identifications, but in a few areas of the city the petty assessors' returns to the commissioners gave occupational identifications of taxpayers that were retained in the commissioners' certificates for the exchequer. In Aldersgate ward, occupations are given for nearly all of the strangers assessed by the petty assessors (**171-174, 176, 183**); in Aldgate ward the petty assessors gave occupations of nearly all Englishmen and nearly all strangers whose estates were valued, but not of those assessed *per poll* (**185-186**); in Coleman Street ward the occupations of nearly all English people valued by the petty assessors are given, but not of strangers (**261-265**); in the parish of St. Ann Blackfriars in Farringdon ward Within strangers taxed per poll are identified by occupation, but not those who were assessed on a valuation (**313-314**); and in the parishes of St. Bartholomew the Less and St. Bartholomew the Great in Farringdon Without occupations are given for most of the low book English. Significant analysis of the occupational structure of even these limited areas is difficult without knowing the occupations of the taxpayers in the high book and of those English not included in the subsidy at all.

The title 'doctor' distinguishes the leading members of the professions of civil law and medicine in the subsidy certificates; unfortunately it is almost always used with a surname only. There were in 1541 probably six doctors of law and nine doctors of physic assessed for the subsidy in London. There was one 'doctor' whose profession has not been ascertained.[95] In 1582, at least 23 doctors of law and 19 doctors of medicine were assessed. There were four unidentified 'doctors'.[96] Most of the civilians lived in or near Doctors'

---

95. The doctors of law can be identified from G.D.Squibb, *Doctors' Commons: a history of advocates and doctors of law* (Oxford, 1977), Appendix III, a register of members of Doctors' Commons. The doctors of medicine can be identified from William Munk, *The Roll of the Royal College of Physicians of London*, vol. I, 1518-1700, 2nd ed. (London, 1878) and Sir George Clark, *A History of the Royal College of Physicians of London*, vol. I (Oxford, 1964). The doctors of law assessed in London in 1541 were: William Coke (**106**), Thomas Legh (**51**), Sampson Michell (**51**), William Peter (**5**), John Storye (**107**), and John Tregonwell (**107**). The doctors of medicine were: Agostino de Angostini (assessed as Dr. Augustyne, **133**), Richard Bartelett (**124**),Thomas Bylle (**124**), John Clement (**71**), Walter Cromer (**86**), Nicholas Encolius (assessed as Dr. Nicholas, **13**), Dr. Morres (**16**), George Owen (**86**), and Edward Wotton (**86**). 'Mr. Doctor Broddowe' (**13**) has not been identified.

 Three subsidymen were designated physicians, but not doctors: Mr. John (**102**), John Ruston (**140**), and William Freeman (**164**).

96. Identifications are based on the sources cited in the preceding note. The doctors of law assessed in 1582 were: William Awbrey (**252**), John Becon (**245**), William Bingham (**305**), Matthew Carew (as Carye, **319**), Julius Caesar (**304**), Bartholomew Clerke (as Dr. Clark, Dean, **246**),William Clerke (**246**), Thomas Creake (**248**), Valentine Dale (**248**), William Drurye (**251**), William Farrand (**248**), Robert Forthe (**250**), John Hammond (**286**), John Hone (**304**), Lawrence Hussey (**306**), Henry Jones (**246**), William Lewen (as Lowen, **261**), David Lewes (**246**), Thomas Martin (**246**), William Mowse (**246**), Robert Salisburye (**321**, see Joseph Foster, *Alumni Oxoniensis ... 1500-1714, S-Z* (Oxford, n.d.), p.1304, D.C.L. 1579), Thomas Skevington (**247**), Edward Stanhope (**246**).

 The doctors of medicine were: Edward Ateslowe (**284**), William Barnesdale (**331**), Richard Cawdwell (**246**), Edward Doddinge (**317**), Thomas Fryer (**178**),William Gilbert (**251**), Thomas Hall (**331**), Christopher Johnson (**316**), Roger Marbecke (**280**), Richard Master (**284**), Thomas Muffet (**346**), Hector Nonnez (**375**), Thomas Penny (**362**), Robert Preyst (**276**), John Synynges (**369**), Richard Taylor (**358**), Peter (or George?) Turner (**329**), John Vulpe (**368**, see John Venn and J.A.Venn, *Alumni Cantabrigienses ...*, Part I, vol. IV (Cambridge, 1927), p.306), and George Walker (**338**).

Commons and in the neighbourhood of the courts in which they practiced, close to St. Paul's. By 1582, Doctors' Commons having moved from Paternoster Row to Mountjoy House in Knightrider Street in 1568, the civil lawyers comprised the parochial élite in St. Benet Paul's Wharf and St. Gregory by St. Paul's in Castle Baynard ward.[97] The residences of the doctors of medicine were more dispersed, as was the practice of medicine, although only five of the doctor physicians in 1582 lived east of Walbrook. The front part of Stone House in Knightrider Street, which Thomas Linacre had conveyed to the Royal College of Physicians, provided accomodation for meetings and a library (and an anatomical theatre from 1584), but no lodging or commons for the college's members.[98]

THE PROPORTION OF HOUSEHOLDERS ASSESSED FOR THE SUBSIDY

In general, heads of households comprised the population at risk in assessment for the subsidy based on valuations of wealth. The exceptions to this were the companies and (prior to 1548) the estates of orphans. However encompassing the language of the statutes may have been, it is clear that servants, wives, and children were not subject to valuation for assessment, though the servants, wives and children of strangers could be liable to a poll tax.

Rappaport has estimated that about 25 per cent of the heads of households in London were assessed in 1582.[99] In 1541, the threshold of liability to assessment was, as we have seen, exceptionally high; although strangers valued at £1 or more in goods or income were taxable, only English valued at £20 or more in goods or in income from lands, etc. were assessed. Even with this high threshold, perhaps as large a proportion of the heads of households was assessed in 1541 as in 1582.[100]

The proportion of heads of household assessed varied considerably from one neighbourhood to another. While there are no ward lists or counts of

Two people designated 'Doctor Smith' were assessed in 1582 (**280** and **307**); who they were and whether they were civilians or physicians is not established. There were probably two medical doctors named Richard Smith in London at this time (Munk, *op. cit.*, pp.67-68) and a Dr. Simon Smith, a civilian (Squibb, *op. cit.*, p.162). Doctors Daniell (**201**) and Bartlet (**248**) have not been identified.

97. Squibb, *op. cit.*, pp.2, 56-60; Brian P. Levack, *The Civil lawyers of England, 1603-1641* (Oxford, 1973), pp.3-29, 36.
98. Clark, *op. cit.*, vol.I, pp.52, 63, 70, 150.
99. Steve Rappaport, *Worlds within worlds: structures of life in sixteenth-century London* (Cambridge, 1989), p.166. His calculations are based on an estimated population for the city, excluding Southwark, of 102,600, and an average household size of four or five people.
100. There were 2691 assessments of English and 671 assessments of strangers, not counting the 652 strangers assessed per poll. Assuming that the population of London, which was about 50,000 in 1500 and 70,000 in 1550 (Roger Finlay, *Population and metropolis: the demography of London 1580-1650* (Cambridge, 1981), p.51), was about 66,000 in 1541, and (following Rappaport) that the average household size was 4.5, about 23 per cent of householders were assessed. If one makes the further assumption, as Rappaport does, that 10 per cent of London's population throughout the sixteenth century lived in Southwark, reducing the nominal 1541 population within the jurisdiction of the London subsidy commission to 59,400, about 25 per cent of householders were assessed.

householders for this period, there are parochial lists of occupiers around 1582 in the form of assessments for the fifteenth and tenth and for parish clerks' wages from which one can make rough calculations of the proportion of householders assessed in a number of parishes.

Wherever there is evidence for the levying of a fifteenth or for assessing parish clerks' wages in the city, it points to a general practice of imposing a charge on the occupier of every property in a sum associated with the property. The same practice seems to have held in the levying of beadles' wages, scavengers' bills and tithes. It can be illustrated from the vestry minutes of several parishes.[101]

From parochial assessments of around the year 1582 one can calculate roughly the proportion of householders assessed for the 1582 subsidy payment in 12 parishes. The results are set out in Table III. The proportion of householders assessed varied from a high of about 90% of all householders in St. Mary Magdalen Milk Street (mostly in Cripplegate ward) to about 40% of the householders in St. Ethelburga the Virgin (Bishopsgate ward). This sample is surely biased in favour of wealthier parishes. All 12 were among the 70 parishes considered able in 1598 to take care of their own poor and beyond that to contribute to poor relief in other parishes.[102] No parish in the city stands out as likely to rank much above St. Mary Magdalen Milk Street in its proportion of subsidy-paying householders, but if there were data available making it possible to include in the sample the large extramural parishes and some of the poorer parishes along the riverfront, we should probably find in them a smaller proportion of subsidymen than in St. Ethelburga.

There was in the second half of the century, a time in which London's population doubled, a continuous decline in the proportion of London householders assessed for the subsidy, and a decline in the actual number of assessments, even though the threshold of liability remained the same from 1563. Excluding aliens taxed *per poll* there were 7,123 residents assessed for the subsidy in 1564 for the first payment under 5 Eliz. c.31 (only a year after Elizabethan England's deadliest outbreak of plague), 6,463 in 1577 for the second payment under 18 Eliz. c.23, 5,900 in 1582 in the assessment roll published here, and 4,968 in 1606 for the first payment under 3 Jac. I c.26.[103]

By the end of the sixteenth century to be taxed at all for the subsidy was a mark of substance. So, for example, when Richard James, a London brewer, sought to put up five or six houses contrary to restraints on building, he argued that they would be dwellings for 'honest persons of competent wealthe able to pay subsidie to hir majestie'.[104] The poor law of 1597 required that appointment of overseers of the poor should go first to 'substan-

101. G.L. MS 1311/1, St. Martin Ludgate vestry minute book from the year 1568 to 1715, 27 Sept. 1594; G.L. MS 3570/1, St. Mary Aldermanbury vestry minute book, 1569-1609, ff.40b, 53; G.L. MS 943/1, St. Botolph Billingsgate orders of vestry, 1592-1673, f.2.
102. On the 1598 survey of the poor and assessment of relief, see Rappaport, *Worlds within worlds*, pp.168-172. Although only 21 parishes were net receivers of poor relief, they included about half the total area of the city (Rappaport, p.172, fig.6.1; Finlay, *Population and metropolis*, pp.168-171).
103. S.P.14/28/55 for 1564; E.179/145/252 for 1577, based on count; Table IB for 1582; S.P.14/26/89, f.191 for 1606.
104. S.P.12/138/34, James to the council, May (?), 1580.

tiall Howsholders ... beinge Subsidy men'.[105] In *Westward Ho*, Monopoly, when arrested for debt, complained that it was 'a most treacherous part to arrest a man in the night, and when he is almost drunk, when he hath not his wits about him to remember which of his friends is in the Subsedy'.[106] In *Michaelmas Term*, Shortyard, disguised as a sergeant, said to Master Easy, who had been arrested for defaulting on a bond: 'what say you to us, if we procure you two substantial subsidy citizens to bail you...?'[107]

THE ASSESSMENT FIGURES: APPARENT AND ACTUAL LIABILITY TO PAYMENT

The sums in the assessment certificates do not represent what the collectors were obliged to pay into the receipt of the exchequer, nor do the individual assessments present an accurate statement of what every taxpayer was obliged to pay to the collectors. The subsidy acts allowed the high collectors a discharge of 6d. in the £ for pains taken in administering and collecting the subsidy payment: 2d. in the £ to go to the high collectors, 2d. to the petty collectors, and 2d. to the commissioners according to their actual involvement in the business of administering the subsidy and with particular regard to their clerical expenses.[108] Most users of the subsidy assessment rolls will be more interested in the discrepancy between the apparent and the actual liability of individual taxpayers.

In order to get a complete picture of the tax liability of individuals one must use the Exchequer Enrolled Accounts: Subsidies, P.R.O. Class E.359.[109] There one will find the entries of exonerations of the collectors for specific assessments: exonerations for the assessments on people who received discharge in a London ward because of an assessment in another place for which they remained liable; exonerations for the assessments on people who successfully contested their liability before the barons of the exchequer; for assessments on individuals who received exoneration by writ of privy seal directed to the treasurer and barons of the exchequer; and for assessments on people who were declared by the collectors to have no distrainable goods within the limits of their collection divisions (which may signify either default or non-residence).

A significant feature of the 1582 London assessment roll is the presence in its margins of marks and notations that, when examined in conjunction with the Exchequer Enrolled Accounts, are seen to distinguish those entries of assessments for which the collectors received exoneration from payment into exchequer. These marginalia are listed and explained in the section on editor-

---

105. *Statutes*, 29 Eliz.c.3, sect.i.
106. Dekker and Webster, *Westward Ho*, III, ii, lines 101-103. First performed in 1604.
107. Middleton, *Michaelmas Term*, III, iv, lines 88-90. First performed 1605-6.
108. *Statutes*, 32 Hen. VIII c.50, sect.xiv; 23 Eliz. c.15, sect.xxiv. The assessors did not receive compensation; they bore no risk of loss, as collectors did, and they did not have the administrative expenses of drafting indentures and so on that the commissioners incurred.
109. I am deeply obliged to Sybil M. Jack of the University of Sydney for informing me of the significance of these records. Her help was crucial. She is, of course, in no way responsible for errors that I may have made in use of them.

ial practice, below.[110] The 1541 assessment roll lacks such distinguishing marks and notations, but from the Exchequer Enrolled Accounts one can still identify the individual assessments for which the collectors received exoneration.

Apparent and Actual Liability in 1541

The subsidy acts made elaborate and sometimes confusing provision for discharging individuals assessed in more than one place from all but one assessment. And when people received such discharges, the collectors had to be exonerated for the sums rendered uncollectable.

The 1540 act required, as earlier subsidy acts had done, that every person liable to be taxed for the subsidy should be assessed 'in such place where he at the tyme of the said certyfycathe to be made shall kepe his house or dwelling, or where he then shalbe most conversant abiding or resiant, or shall have his most resort, and shalbe best knowen at the tyme of the certificathe to be made, and no where elles'. No person was to be 'doble charged for the said subside nether set or taxed at several places'.[111] The act goes on to provide for those who were assessed in two or more places, generally persons who had two or more places of residence or who were members of a royal or noble household and who also had separate places of residence. Those who were double charged could present certificates under the hands of two or more of the commissioners in one place declaring their assessment and liability to payment in that place. This certificate would serve to discharge them against the collectors in the other place. This certificate would serve also to discharge the petty collectors of payment to the high collectors, and to exonerate the high collectors when they settled their accounts in exchequer.

Prior to the subsidy act of 1558, people assessed in more than one place had no choice as to which of two or more assessments they would pay; they had to pay the highest assessment.[112] Usually, therefore, they presented certificates from the commissioners in the place of higher assessment to the collectors in the place of lower assessment. To proceed in the opposite direction, which sometimes happened, complicated matters by compelling the taxpayer to make partial payments of assessments to the collectors in two places. The sum of the two payments equalled the higher assessment. The early Tudor certificates testifying to assessment or payment should be distinguished from the certificates of residence made under the Elizabethan subsidy acts of 1563 and after, which are discussed below.

None of the certificates of assessment or payment presented to the London collectors in 1541 has been located, but a record of them and of all other exchequer exonerations of collectors from payment exists in the exchequer

---

110. Several previous editors have called attention to the existence of such marginalia in Elizabethan subsidy rolls: Alfred Ridley Bax, ed., 'The lay subsidy assessments for the county of Surrey in 1593 or 1594', *Surrey Archaeological Collections . . . published by the Surrey Archaeological Society*, 18 (1903); G.D.Ramsay, ed. *Two sixteenth century taxation lists, 1545 and 1576*, Wiltshire Archaeological and Natural History Society, Records Branch, 10 (1954); and T.L.Stoate, ed. *Dorset Tudor subsidies granted in 1523, 1543, 1593* (1982).
111. *Statutes*, 32 Hen. VIII c.50, sect.ix.
112. *Statutes*, 32 Hen. VIII c.50, sect.x.

Enrolled Accounts: Subsidies (E.359). These accounts, filed by subsidy payment and grouped by place within each file, record the name and assessment of every person or company of whose payment collectors were discharged and the sum and place of the assessment for which every such person or company remained answerable.

In 1541/42, the London high collectors received complete discharge of 120 assessments of individuals and 6 assessments of city companies on the basis of certificates of assessment or payment. Most (67) of the London assessments entirely discharged were those of officers or servants in one of the royal households who were liable for payment there: 52 in the king's household or chamber (but only 51 assessments, for two people were assessed jointly), 10 in the queen's household (one of them the widow of a member of that household), 5 in the prince's household, and one in the household of Anne of Cleves. Thirty-one of these 120 people and the 6 city companies were actually assessed twice in London itself. Twenty-two of the 120 putative London taxpayers of 1541/42 received discharges because they were liable for payment of a higher assessment in some other county, city, or borough.

A further 16 people assessed in London presented certificates of assessment or payment from the commissioners in a place where they had a lower assessment that only partially discharged them from payment in the city: 6 of the king's household, 1 of the queen's household, and 9 assessed in other counties, cities, or boroughs. These were people who had made payment of assessments that were lower than those for which they were chargeable in one of the city wards. They received discharge in London only for what they had already paid elsewhere, and they had to pay the London collectors the difference between the high and low assessments.

There were, then, 142 exonerations of payment in London wards in 1541/42 based on certificates of assessment or payment under the hands and seals of commissioners in other places.[113]

This is not the sum total of multiple assessments among those appearing in the London subsidy roll of 1541. A further 41 people paid their assessments in London and presented certificates from the London commissioners to collectors in other places for their discharge – 37 in the country and 4 in one of the royal households.[114]

Twelve of the 1541 London assessments were wholly or partially remitted by process before the barons of the exchequer, resulting in further exonerations of the collectors for payment. John Leyland, as we have seen, was taxed as a spiritual person and argued successfully that he had no lay estate whereby he could be taxed in the lay subsidy. John Lucas, esq. (**110**), Sir Christopher More (**110**), Sir John Raynefford (**12**), and Sir Brian Tuke (**52**) all protested assessment in London on the ground that they were commissioners for the subsidy payment in other places (Kent, Surrey, Essex, and Essex respectively) and that by the terms of the subsidy act anyone appointed a commissioner should be assessed within the limits of his commission by his

113. E.359/44, r.19, 2nd payment of subsidy granted 32 Henry VIII.
114. E.359/44, roti.1-18, 2nd payment of subsidy granted 32 Henry VIII.

fellow commissioners.[115] John Wellesborne (**109**) also argued that he should not be assessed in London on the ground that as a gentleman of the privy chamber he was assessed in the king's household and, more to the point, that he had no residence in the city.[116] The barons discharged the collectors of an assessment on Alen Haute (**32**), whose goods and chattels were all in the hands of Sir Brian Tuke, and of an assessment on Dame Katherine Edgecombe (**114**), who paid part of her tax in Cornwall and part in London.[117] The barons also discharged in part or entirely assessments on three aliens; the three had presented a writ from the king commanding the treasurer and barons of the exchequer to allow the said aliens to appear before them to certify by oath the value of their goods and merchandise. The aliens were then to be assessed on the value so certified. Except by such exercise of the king's grace one was essentially without remedy in getting an assessment revised once the commissioners had returned the assessment certificate into exchequer. These three, Anthony James (**49**), John Reconger (**62**), and Roger de Prate (**165**), swore that their goods and chattels were worth less than their valuations in the subsidy certificates; their assessments were reduced and the collectors discharged accordingly.[118] The enrolled accounts also record the barons' judgement discharging the collectors of a joint assessment on Laurence Burlyns and Matthew Bowe, aliens, in Langbourn ward, but their names do not appear in the assessment roll.[119]

There were a further 61 uncollectable assessments in 1541/42 for which the collectors were exonerated. These were cases in which the petty collectors swore before the commissioners that at the time they first received their copies of the assessment certificates certain subsidymen had no property in the ward from which the tax could be recovered by distress. The commissioners then drew a certificate addressed to the barons of the exchequer testifying to that oath, which the petty collectors used for their discharge with the high collectors and the high collectors for their discharge in the receipt of the exchequer. The language in the exchequer enrolled accounts implies that 60 of the 61 defaults in 1541 resulted from people having moved from the city before the beginning of the collection,[120] and that may actually have been the

---

115. E.359/44, r.19, 2nd payment of subsidy granted 32 Henry VIII; E.159/321, *communia* Michaelmas 34 Henry VIII, r.69, *communia* Easter 34 Henry VIII, r.48, *communia* Michaelmas 34 Henry VIII, r.68, *communia* Trinity 34 Henry VIII, r.24.
116. E.359/44, r.19, 2nd payment of subsidy granted 32 Henry VIII; E.159/321, *communia* Trinity 34 Henry VIII, r.24.
117. E.359/44, r.19, 2nd payment of subsidy granted 32 Henry VIII.
118. E.159/321, *communia* Easter 34 Henry VIII, r.66; E.359/44, r.19, 2nd payment of subsidy granted 32 Henry VIII.
119. E.359/44, r.19, 2nd payment of subsidy granted 32 Henry VIII. A 'Lawrence Burgon' was assessed in Langbourn (**131**), possibly the same person, but the name of Matthew Bowe does not appear.
120. 'The said collectors remain exonerated by reason of the act of parliament concerning the granting of the said subsidy because the said [persons named] ... withdrew from the said city before the subsidy certificates came into the hands of the collectors, leaving nothing wherefrom they could levy the said amounts or any part of them, as the said collectors say on oath' (E.359/44, r.19, 2nd payment of subsidy granted 32 Henry VIII). [Translated from Latin.] One of the defaulters in 1541 – Edmund Cockerell, assessed in Vintry ward (**160**) – clearly had personal property in the city that the collectors were unable to distrain.

case. Few of the commissioners' certificates of the petty collectors' oaths for the Henrician subsidies seem to survive. One of 29 May 1546 for Farringdon ward Without for the third payment of the subsidy granted under 34 & 35 Hen. VIII c.27 distinguishes between the seven people who had departed 'into other places' and the three who remained in the ward but had no distrainable goods and chattels.[121] The threshold of liability for this subsidy was low, however, (£1 in goods or income from lands, etc.) and there would have been more subsidymen of marginal ability. London certificates of uncollectable assessments for the Edwardian and Marian subsidies, however, state in more general terms only that the petty collectors have deposed on oath that defaulters 'have not nor at any time since the coming of their estreats to their hands for the said collection have had ... any manner of lands or tenements goods or chattels within their said limits whereby they might have received or levied by distress the several sums ... to them severally estreated'.[122]

Apparent and Actual Liability in 1582
The subsidy assessment rolls in 1582 represented actual liability even less closely than in 1541/42. There are three main explanations for this. First, by 1582 the subsidy acts provided a new way of dealing with multiple assessments that enabled many people who were assessed in more than one place to pay the lower assessment, and that was commonly an assessment outside London. Secondly, the crown came to exercise more generously its prerogative to free individuals and classes of people from being taxed for the subsidy. Finally, the proportion of uncollectable assessments had increased.

The subsidy act of 1558 eliminated a feature of the subsidy that had been fundamental since the act of 1514: that if people were valued and assessed in two places at different figures they should remain liable to payment of the higher assessment and be discharged of the lower.[123] The subsidy act of 1548 first compromised the principle of payment of the higher assessment by providing that subsidy commissioners be taxed only where they were commissioners.[124] This gave statutory force to earlier decisions of the barons of the exchequer in favour of persons who claimed that their being commissioners in one place was ground for discharge anywhere else. The tacit exemption of commissioners in the 1548 act from the general obligation to pay the highest assessment was made explicit in 1553.[125] Then, in 1558, the commons dropped the entire clause requiring payment of the higher assessment.[126]

The provision for payment of the higher assessment, originating in the 1514 act and dropped in 1558, had never set well with the provision included in all subsidy acts from 1512 on that people should be taxed for the subsidy

121. E.179/144/127.
122. See the collection of such certificates in E.179/382/4.
123. *Statutes*, 5 Hen. VIII c.17, sect.iii. The statute reads that 'yf eny happen to be sett in ii places, upon certefycat therof made the best and moste somme uppon hym so taxed to be taken and abide, and the other to be discharged'.
124. *Statutes*, 2 & 3 Edw. VI c.36, sect.xv.
125. The drafters of the act accomplished this by inserting the words underlined: 'And yf any other then Comyssioner happen to be sett in two places, upon Certificat thereof made...' etc. (*Statutes*, 7 Edw. VI c.12, sect. xiii). No tax was actually levied under this act, however.
126. *Statutes*, 4 & 5 Phil. & Mar. c.11.

in the place where they were most resident,[127] for the drafters took inadequate account of the possibility that the higher of the two assessments might not be in the place where a person was most resident. With the elimination of the requirement that people pay the higher assessment, the principle that governed in cases of multiple assessment was that one pay the assessment made in the place where one was most resident. The 1563 act gave administrative clarity to the determination of place of most residence by providing for certificates of residence. These certificates were to be obtained from the subsidy commissioners in the place where one claimed to be most resident and presented in the place where one sought discharge.

> 'And that every person taxed in anny Countie or Place other then where he is moste ressyaunt or hath his Famylye, or in anny Countie or Place other then where he is a Commyssioner for this Subsedie, yf he be a Commyssioner, upon certificate made to the sayde Corte of Excheaquer, under thandes and Seales of Three Commyssioners for the Subsedye in the same Countie or Place where suche persone is moste ressiaunt or hath his Famylye, or where he is a Commyssioner . . . testifyinge suche his most Ressyancy, havinge of Famyly or beinge a Commyssioner, shalbe a sufficient Dyscharge for the Taxaccion of that persone in all other Places . . . ; And that suche Certificate withoute any Plee or other Cyrcymstance shalbe a sufficient Warraunt, aswell to the Barrons and Awdytors of the saide Corte of Escheaquer as to all and every other Officers to whome the Allowances therof shall apparteyne; payinge for suche Discharge and Allowance only iis. and no more.'[128]

An effect of these changes was to make payment on the lower of two assessments common.

Of the 5900 assessments on valuations in the London subsidy roll of 1582, 385 were discharged by certificate of payment or assessment (the older way of dealing with assessment in more than one place) or by certificate of residence (the newer way of handling multiple assessment): 73 of these were discharges for people who paid in the queen's household or chamber, 16 were discharges for people who paid a second assessment in London itself, and the remaining 296 were discharges in London for people who paid in the country.[129] A further 88 people assessed in two or more places paid their London assessments and received discharge by presenting certificates from London commissioners to collectors in the country. Altogether, 473 (6.5%) of the people assessed for the subsidy in London in 1582 were assessed in a second place. A few of those were assessed in three places.

While all of the Londoners assessed in two or more places in 1541 remained answerable for the higher assessment or one of two or more identical assessments (except for those who could use their appointments as commissioners in one place to get the barons to vacate a higher assessment in another), in 1582 over half of those in London with multiple assessments (264 of 473) arranged that they should be liable for payment of the lower

---

127. *Statutes*, 4 Hen. VIII c.19, sect.xi.
128. *Statutes*, 5 Eliz. c.31, sect. xiii.
129. E.359/52, roti. 7, 13, 14, 2nd payment of subsidy granted 23 Elizabeth.

assessment.[130] It was even easier to obtain a certificate of residence in 1581-82 than it had been in 1563; only two commissioners instead of three were required to sign it and it cost only 6d. instead of 2s.[131] Sixpence was a small price for alderman Sir Nicholas Woodroffe, lord mayor 1579-80, to pay to be discharged of £13 10s. in Lime Street ward (**362**) on payment of £5 in Ratcliffe, Middlesex; for alderman Sir John Branche, lord mayor 1580-81, to pay for discharge of £13 in Candlewick ward (**241**) on payment of £3 6s. 8d. in Ongar, Essex; or for Mr. John Barker for discharge of £15 in Tower ward (**373**) on payment of £3 6s. 8d. in Ipswich.[132] Woodroffe, incidentally, was a subsidy commissioner in London at the time. However, 117 of the London subsidymen who were assessed in two or more places do appear to have remained answerable for the higher assessment.

It was not long before the widespread use of these new-fangled certificates of residence came to be seen, no doubt correctly, as one important cause of the decline in the yield of the subsidy in London.[133] Burghley apparently hoped, in 1593, to reintroduce a statutory provision for payment on the highest assessment, but the act that parliament passed (35 Eliz. c.13) contained no such remedy.[134] Many of these certificates of residence survive in the P.R.O. class E.115, but as their archival integrity has been lost through rearrangement according to the initial of the surname of the person assessed, an examination of the certificates pertaining to a particular subsidy payment from a particular division of collection is impracticable. There are in the 462 bundles in this collection, besides certificates of residence, many certificates of the earlier form, testifying to assessment or payment.

Writs of privy seal granting exemption from payment of the subsidy and directed to the treasurer and barons of the exchequer further eroded apparent obligation. Such writs were unknown in 1541, but common in 1582. By 1582, the classes of persons who could expect to receive exoneration from payment of the subsidy by privy seal included the musicians and trumpeters of the queen's household, the yeomen of the queen's chamber, the grooms and riders of the queen's stable, the gentleman porter and yeomen waiters of the Tower of London, the officials of the mint, the officers of the College of Arms, and alien merchants who were born as subjects of the king of Spain in Antwerp and the Low Countries. In addition, aliens and denizens who held positions in the queen's household and chamber were exonerated from payment at the rate for strangers and charged as English. Sometimes writs grant-

---

130. Sixty-three remained liable for one of two or more identical assessments, 117 remained liable for the high assessment, and in 29 cases it is not known whether the assessment outside London was higher or lower than that in the city.
131. *Statutes*, 23 Eliz. c.15, sect.xiii.
132. E.359/52, roti.7, 14, 2nd payment of subsidy granted 23 Elizabeth.
133. 'The Causes of Abasement of the Subsedy I find to be these: ... 2. many citizens of good value having country dwellings are taxed where theyre houses and land is and also taxed heere, but finding themselves under chardged there to that they be heere cessed procure themselves to be discharged heere and pay there' (S.P.14/23/28, undated [early James I]).
134. S.P. 12/244/51, notes by Burghley, 27 February, 1593, proposing that if a person be assessed in two places he should pay in the place of the higher assessment provided that he had habitation there any time in the preceding year.

ing exoneration from payment were issued in favour of individuals: ambassadors or military commanders resident abroad, for example.[135]

Forty-six alien merchants born in Antwerp and other places in the Low Countries as subjects of the king of Spain were exonerated of both payments under the 1581 act by writ of privy seal dated 16 October 1581. The writ itself did not name the eligible merchants, but required that a certificate of their names be prepared by the lord mayor or the governor of the Company of Merchant Adventurers and be directed to the lord treasurer, the chancellor, and the barons of the exchequer. The certificate for the first payment of the 1581 subsidy (that for the second payment has not been found) is actually under the hands of the lord mayor and the governor and deputy governor of the Merchants Adventurers, who state that the list was compiled after consultation with 'diverse substancial and credible merchauntes of the saide Companye'. Merchants from Antwerp had enjoyed regular exoneration from payment since 1556, at least, in reciprocation for the freedom of English merchants from any similar tax in the Low Countries.[136] French and Italian merchants had received privy seals exempting them from the subsidy in 1556, but that exoneration may have been exceptional; certainly they had to pay in 1581 and 1582.[137] Merchants of the Hanse, who seem to have been exempted from valuation and assessment for the subsidy early in the sixteenth century without royal writ, under the conditions of their privileged status in the Steelyard, do not seem to have retained their uniquely favoured position after the revocation of their privileges in 1552, 1555, and 1556.[138]

135. E.208/25, collection of original writs sent to exchequer. See, for example, writs of privy seal of 5 July 1581 and 10 August 1581 exempting 35 of the queen's musicians and trumpeters from both payments under the 1581 subsidy act.

136. The 1581 writ and 1581 certificate are in E.208/25. The writ of 1556 (first payment under the 1555 act) is in E.208/24. The late Henrician (post 1541) or Edwardian enrolled accounts might reveal earlier grants to the Antwerp merchants. The Marian and earliest Elizabethan writs name the merchants who are to benefit. Certificates of names are attached to later writs. The names of the beneficiaries of the 1581 writ in 1582 (second payment) are given in the enrolled accounts. This exoneration extended only to merchants, not craftsmen, who resorted to London only for trade of merchandise and who were not denizens. The merchants of the Low Countries exonerated in 1582 were: Anthonie Anthonison (**374**), Walter Artson (**207**), Andreas Bircrofte (**284**), Fraunces Bishop (**257**), Augustine Bolle (**374**), Fraunces Boules (**185**), Gyles Bowntenacle (**245**), Peter Bowtell (**398**), Giles Bultiel (**383**), Peter Buskell (**363**), Peter de Coster (**352**), Nicholas Delanoy (**355**), Emanuell Demetris (**355**), John and Fraunces Dingins (**233**), Pierre Drumes (**383**), Joice van Erpe (**201**), Martyn de la Falia (**243**), widow Fortre (**374**), John Fortrye (**383**), Nicholas Founteyne (**191**), Erasmus della Founteyne (**192**), Jaques and John Garbye (**375**), Jaques Garrett (**375**), Nicholas Haunsman (**383**), Peter Hubline (**192**), John Hublone (**191**), Jacob Johnson (**185**), Mathew Lulles (**203**), Guilliam ver Maiden (**206**), Michael Mannet (**355**), Alexander Myllyn (**355**), John Papworth (**237**), Charles van Payne (**296**), Adrian de Porter (**363**), Jaques de Rewe (**384**), John Rosier (**201**), Balthezar Ruttes (**374**), Joyce Vanbush (**352**), Abraham Vandelon (**355**), Joyce Vandenstene (**243**), Peter Vandewall (**352**), Abraham Vanharwick (**357**), Haunce Walters (**344**), Jaques Whitfrongell (**233**), William Whytebread (**355**), Haunce Wonters (**203**), and Jaques Yeoman (**243**).

137. Writs of 3 December 1556 and 4 December 1556 exonerated, respectively, about 16 French merchants and 20 Italian merchants (11 of them from only part of their assessments) from the first payment under the 1555 act (E.208/24).

138. Michael Edwin Bratchel, 'Alien Merchant Communities in London, 1500-1550' (unpublished Ph.D. dissertation, University of Cambridge, 1975), p.24; E.179/397, recognizance dated 17 November 1564; G.D.Ramsay, *The City of London in international politics at the accession of Elizabeth Tudor* (Manchester, 1975), pp.62-70, 158-162.

Officers of the College of Arms also benefitted from a privilege of exemption from payment of the subsidy under the terms of Edward VI's grant of letters patent to the heralds.[139] A writ of privy seal to the treasurer and barons of the exchequer at the time of each subsidy payment listed the officers of arms and, citing the patent of 1549, ordered their discharge.[140] Ten of the 13 officers were assessed and discharged in London in 1582.[141] The officials of the mint, by their office, similarly received exoneration of payment effected by writs of privy seal based on letters patent; four of them were discharged in London in 1582.[142] Finally, Balthesar Sanches (the queen's comfit maker), an alien assessed in Walbrook ward (**395**), was one of nine strangers, all personal servants of the queen, who benefitted from a writ granting them the privilege of paying the subsidy at the rates for English.[143] Strangers who were servants of the monarch had received such partial exemptions from at least the first subsidy of Mary's reign.[144]

Uncollectable assessments for which the collectors swore that the persons assessed had no distrainable property within their collection divisions numbered 426 in London in 1582, 212 of them assessments on strangers taxed *per poll*. That is 5.9% of all individual assessments – by number, not by value. Sixty-one, 1.5%, had been uncollectable in 1541/42.

There were fewer discharges on process before the barons of the exchequer in 1582 than there had been in 1541/42. Two doctors of civil law, Dr. William Mowse and Dr. Edward Stanhope (**246**), were discharged upon process on the ground that Mowse, as rector of East Dereham in the diocese of Norwich, and Stanhope, as prebendary of Botevant in the diocese of York, were liable to payments for the clerical subsidy that exceeded their assessment for the lay subsidy and, therefore, exonerated by the terms of the subsidy act.[145] A claim to discharge on similar grounds by another civilian, Dr.

139. Anthony Wagner, *Heralds of England: a history of the office and College of Arms* (1967), pp.100-101.
140. There are some later Elizabethan original writs exonerating the officers of arms in E.208/25.
141. The ten were the three kings of arms – Sir Gilbert Dethick (Garter), Robert Cooke (Clarenceux), and William Flower (Norroy); four of the six heralds – Edmund Knight (Chester), John Cooke (Lancaster), Hugh Cotgrave (Richmond), and Sir William Dethick (York); and three of the four pursuivants – Richard Lee (Portcullis), Ralph Brooke (Rouge Croix), and Nicholas Paddy (Rouge Dragon). The enrolled accounts erroneously treat Edmund Knight, assessed in Aldersgate and Castle Baynard wards, as two people. There is a list of the officers in *The College of Arms, Queen Victoria Street, being the sixteenth and final monograph of the London Survey Committee*, by Walter H. Godfrey, C.B.E., F.S.A., F.R.I.B.A., assisted by Sir Anthony Wagner, K.C.V.C., D.Litt., F.S.A., Garter King of Arms, with a complete list of the officers of arms, prepared by the late Stanford London, F.S.A., Norfolk Herald Extraordinary (1963).
142. Richard Martyn, alderman and master of the mint, Anthony Bere, William Doddington, and Thomas Dowsing (E.359/52, roti. 7, 14, 2nd payment of subsidy granted 23 Elizabeth). They are identified in the margins of the subsidy roll as officers in the Tower of London.
143. E.359/52, r.7, 2nd payment of subsidy granted 23 Elizabeth; E.208/25, privy seal dated 4 July 1581, for both payments granted in 1581.
144. A number of original writs exonerating royal servants who were strangers are scattered among E.208/24 and E.208/25.
145. E.359/52, r.14, 2nd payment of subsidy granted 23 Elizabeth. They are identified as civilians in *D.N.B.* and in G. D. Squibb, *Doctors' Commons: a history of advocates and doctors of law* (Oxford, 1977), p.153, 160.

Henry Jones (**246**), who occupied two rectories in the diocese of St. Asaph, failed. Also rejected were the claims of Lionel Duckett (**283**) and William Patten (**279**) to exoneration from payment on the ground of their being founder shareholders of the Company of Mines Royal.[146] Finally, Thomas Herdson (**373**) received discharge in 1582 as a resident of Folkestone, a member of the port of Dover, whose inhabitants enjoyed the exemption from payment of the subsidy that the statute granted to all residents of the Cinque Ports.[147]

In sum, the London collectors received entire or partial discharges for 209 (5%) of the 4085 assessments in the 1541 subsidy roll and for 874 (12%) of the 7258 assessments in 1582 on the basis of certificates of assessment or payment, certificates of residence, writs of privy seal, certificates of default, and decisions of the barons upon process in the court of exchequer. All of these kinds of exoneration or discharge that the collectors received resulted in an actual yield for the subsidy that was less, and by the end of Elizabeth's reign much less, than what contemporaries called the 'first charge', that is the totals of the assessments for each ward in the subsidy rolls.[148] Very few people in London with high assessments on annual income from lands or fees actually paid their London assessments. Of the 31 people valued in London at £100 a year or more in lands and fees in 1582, only one, John Roche, gent. (**216**), paid in London. The collectors received discharges for the assessments on all the rest: 26 discharges on the basis of tax liability elsewhere (either by certificate of assessment or certificate of residence) and 4 on the basis of the collectors' affidavits that the person assessed had no distrainable property in their collection divisions. The subsidy rolls are seen to be a record of assessment, not a final record of tax liability, still less of what individuals actually paid.

SUBSIDY VALUATIONS AND ACTUAL WEALTH

There is no time at which London valuations for the subsidy can be taken as representing actual worth in goods or income, or even as an index of actual wealth. They can probably be taken as an indication of wealth rank order as that was widely perceived to be within a particular assessment division and within the distinct groups of high book and low book taxpayers.

---

146. E.359/52, r.14, 2nd payment of subsidy granted 23 Elizabeth. On Duckett and Patten in the Company of Mines Royal, see M.B.Donald, *Elizabethan copper: the history of the Company of Mines Royal, 1568-1605* (1955), pp.46, 60-62. On the question of exemption of shareholders from the subsidy, see Donald, pp.99-100 and Helen Miller, 'Subsidy assessments of the peerage in the sixteenth century', *Bulletin of the Institute of Historical Research*, 28 (1955), p.22, n.2.
147. E.359/52, r.14, 2nd payment of subsidy granted 23 Elizabeth. Herdson's residence in Folkestone was certified by Sir William Brooke, Lord Cobham, a subsidy commissioner for Kent and Lord Warden of the Cinque Ports.
148. S.P. 14/26/89, a comparison of subsidy paid in London in 5 Elizabeth and 3 James. Discharges came to 22% of the first charge for the payment of 1564 and 51% of the first charge for the payment of 1606. In 1606, only 29 people in London were valued at £100 or more. Of those, only 7 actually paid in London. The collectors received discharges for the assessments of the remaining 22: 15 by certificates of payment or residence, 5 by writs of privy seal, and 2 upon collectors' oaths that the persons assessed had no distrainable goods in their collection divisions.

Some historians who have worked with the subsidy rolls have suggested that assessment certificates of the 1520s to 1540s may have presented valuations that approximated the actual worth of taxpayers. It is doubtful that valuations were realistic even in Henry's reign. Dr. Schofield, by comparing a small sample of subsidy valuations with independent and more nearly realistic valuations made for other purposes (feodaries' surveys and probate inventories) found that in Henry VIII's reign subsidy assessments based on annual income from land were 'tolerably realistic' while those based on valuations of goods were less so. In a sample of 39 cases the subsidy valuations based on annual income from land averaged 68 per cent of the valuations of annual income in the feodaries' surveys. In a sample of 20 cases in the period 1524-42, subsidy valuations based on goods averaged 48.7 per cent of probate valuations. The gap between subsidy and probate valuations widened thereafter.[149]

London is not represented in Schofield's samples, but as he showed in his earlier work, there is strong circumstantial evidence of undervaluation in London in Henry VIII's reign. There was probably undervaluation in 1516, for there was a drop from the 1515 subsidy yield that can most simply be explained by undervaluation. Wolsey was so concerned with undervaluation of the rich, at least, that he summoned the mayor and seven aldermen before the council in Star Chamber, and threatened that if they did not pay on the difference between their assessments in 1515 and those of 1516 he would assess them on oath 'upon the true value of their substance within the sum of C markes'. They paid the difference rather than submit to assessment on oath.[150] There is also evidence of undervaluation for the subsidy granted in 1523; it appears from a comparison of the valuations of the aldermen for the city's £20,000 loan to the crown in 1522-23 with their valuations for the Anticipation of the first payment of the 1523 subsidy. The valuations of 19 aldermen were lower for the subsidy than for the loan, one remained the same, and two rose. Setting aside Sir Lawrence Aylmer, who, at the time of the loan, 'his debtes payd is skant worth xl[li]', the average valuation of the goods of 21 aldermen for the loan was £1,815; the average valuation of the goods of the same twenty-one aldermen for the Anticipation was £869, a drop of over 50 per cent.[151] This evidence bears on undervaluation of the rich, however, and one of the strongest conclusions reached by Schofield's statistical analysis is that the rich were on the average much more undervalued than the poor.[152] There was probably widespread undervaluation, though, for the subsidy granted in 1534. Cromwell's complaints of undervaluation in London appear well-grounded in view of the great increases in the 1541 valuations. In Cornhill ward, 21 people were assessed in 1537 for the second payment

149. Roger Schofield, 'Taxation and the political limits of the Tudor state', in *Law and government, under the Tudors: essays presented to Sir Geoffrey Elton*, ed. Claire Cross, David Loades, and J.J.Scarisbrick (Cambridge, 1988), pp.243, 252-253.
150. Schofield, dissertation, pp.335-336.
151. E.179/251/15B, the loan books of 1522-23; E.179/144/83, a single membrane schedule of the valuations and assessments of the mayor, aldermen and sheriffs of London for the Anticipation, dated 25 Nov., 1523.
152. Schofield, 'Taxation and the political limits of the Tudor State', in *Law and government under the Tudors: essays presented to Sir Geoffrey Elton*, p.253.

under the 1534 act and again in 1541 for the second payment under the 1540 act. Nineteen of their valuations were higher in 1541, one was lower, and one remained the same. The valuations of 13 of these 21 residents had more than trebled while five others had doubled.[153] Increases of this magnitude in five years can scarcely be attributed to individual prosperity or inflation; they are more likely the consequence of the wholesale replacement of aldermen by royal officials in the subsidy commissions for London in 1540 and 1541.[154]

Valuations in London probably peaked in 1540 or 1541, as suggested in Table IV by the distribution of the valuations of English residents assessed on goods in all of the extant subsidy certificates of three wards – Bassishaw, Coleman Street, and Cornhill – from 1536 to 1582. The number of people valued at £20 and above in these wards was greater in 1541 than for any other subsidy payment for which the assessment certificates have survived.

Valuations at the top of the scale fell markedly after 1541, despite the fact that the years 1542-51 saw a currency debasement, a price rise in London of more than 75 per cent, and an increase in wages of 50 per cent or more.[155] There were 65 Londoners assessed for the subsidy in both 1541 and 1544 who were valued at £1000 or more in one of those years. The valuations of 4 of the 65 were higher in 1544 than in 1541, the valuations of 15 stayed the same, and the valuations of 46 fell. (See Table V.) In 1544, the total of the valuations of this group of London's richest inhabitants was 16% below what it had been in 1541.[156] It is unreasonable to suppose that valuations in 1541 were unrealistically high, for it was a simple matter to get an excessive valuation reduced upon oath before the commissioners prior to the return of the certificates into exchequer.

While valuations were higher in London in 1541 than for any other subsidy payment for which there are certificates, and higher probably than for any payment with the possible exception of 1540, one cannot conclude that individual valuations were reasonably accurate even then. What makes one doubt their accuracy is the differences between the valuations of individuals who were assessed in more than one place. In 1541, 171 residents of London were assessed for the subsidy in a second place, and, as shown in Table VI, valuations often differed. The valuations that are relevant to this issue are those that the assessors in the two or more places made independently of each other, without the taxpayer as the common source. So, we can exclude from consideration valuations that differed by only a pound of so, resulting in assessments that varied by only six pence or so. Twenty-six of the taxpayers had such proximate valuations and assessments. In these cases the difference between the valuations seems generally to have been contrived by the taxpayer in order to ensure liability for payment in one place rather than another. Members of royal households, in particular, seem to have been willing to pay the extra six pence in order to avoid payment as residents of London. For

153. E.179/144/102; E.179/144/120.
154. Rappaport found a gradual 22 per cent rise in prices in London from the last decade of the fifteenth century through the early 1540s (Steve Rappaport, *Worlds within worlds*, p.130).
155. Ibid., p.130-135, 145.
156. James Tait also found the assessments of 1541 to be 'clearly much stricter than usual' in Salford hundred (James Tait, ed., *Taxation in Salford hundred, 1524-1802*, Chetham Society, new series, 83 (1924), xxvi).

example, the movables of John Alelye were valued at £400 in Broad Street ward (**51**) and at £401 in the king's household. The higher valuation increased his assessment by six pence, and exonerated him in London. Similarly, the goods of John Dale were valued at £300 in Farringdon Without (**119**) and at £301 in the king's household; those of John Heathe at £100 in Bishopsgate ward (**34**) and at £101 in the king's household. We can discount these 26 multiple assessments as not having been made independently.

We can probably exclude another 43 cases from consideration. These were persons whose valuations in two or more places were identical. It is extremely improbable that assessors in two places would independently arrive at identical valuations.

This leaves 102 cases in which the assessors probably made independent valuations. In almost two-thirds of those cases (66 out of 102) the higher valuation was more than 1.5 times the lower valuation. In almost one-third of the cases (33 of 102) the valuations were at least twice as high in one place as in the other. The differences between valuations were sometimes extreme. Thomas Taylor was valued at £40 in goods in Southwark ('country' in Table VI) and at £250 in goods in adjoining Bridge ward (**43**). He paid the higher assessment, as the law required, and received discharge on the lower. Even within London there could be great differences in valuations. John James was thought by the assessors of Farringdon Within to be worth £30 in goods (**110**), while the assessors of Farringdon Without valued him at £100 (**111**). Hugh Loft was assessed in three places, two of them in London. The assessors in Willesden, Middlesex, valued him at £100, the assessors in Queenhithe ward at £200 (**146**), and the assessors in adjoining Castle Baynard ward at £300 (**54**). Assessors valued William Munday at £20 in Cripplegate (**84**) and at £66 13s. 4d. in neighbouring Aldersgate (**5**).

It is fairly certain that in cases of double assessment the higher assessment reflects a more accurate valuation than the lower, for an excessive valuation could easily be reduced upon oath. But the differences between valuations in the cases of double assessments cast into doubt the ability of the assessors to evaluate. The valuation of worth in goods may have been particularly difficult.

How the assessors and commissioners valued a person's estate is uncertain. The subsidy acts are almost silent on the procedures to be followed in valuation, but the general methods stipulated and implied are direct enquiry of the person being valued (sometimes on oath, sometimes not) and estimation. There is no hint in the statutes, in the exchequer records, in the council's orders, or in correspondence relating to valuations for the subsidy (or for any other Tudor assessments) of reliance upon direct inspection or the examination of rentals or inventories (except indirectly in valuing orphans' estates). In the middle decades of the century there appears to have been a shift of emphasis from valuation by direct enquiry to valuation by estimation and a concurrent change in the object of valuation from obtaining realistic appraisals of goods and income to obtaining valuations that were equitable in relation to other valuations in the same community.

The assessors and the commissioners both had responsibility for valuations; the assessors made the initial valuations of everyone except the commissioners and the commissioners valued each other and revised the asses-

liv

sors' valuations. The statutes gave little positive direction to the assessors. The acts of 1512 (4 Hen. VIII c.19) and 1514 (5 Hen. VIII c.17), simply required the 'presenters' or assessors to present to the commissioners the names and values of taxable persons. The commissioners could examine the assessors on oath and call before them for examination on oath as many other persons as they deemed expedient. From 1515 to 1559, the acts required the presenters or assessors to take an oath before the commissioners to 'inquire with my fellows that shall be charged with me...of the best and most value of the substance of every person dwelling or abiding within the limits of the places that I and my fellows shall be charged with'[157]. How they were to enquire is not specified. Although the commissioners continued in 1563, and after, to charge the assessors in these same terms, the subsidy act of 1563 dropped the requirement of the assessors' oath before the commissioners and it was never restored. More tellingly, the subsidy act of 1563 also began the proscription against assessors using corporal oaths in their enquiries into values.[158] This would seem to imply that assessors in the past had, at least occasionally, examined on oath.

The commissioners also made valuations of wealth – of fellow commissioners, of the assessors (from the act of 1548 on), of persons whom they suspected of being undervalued in the assessors' presentments (except under the act of 1534, which contained no such provision), and of persons who claimed that they had been overvalued by the assessors – and the acts are more specific on the methods the commissioners were to follow.

The acts of 1512 to 1515 required that each commissioner be valued upon his oath, certificate, or 'otherwise' by at least two other commissioners.[159] Subsequent acts dropped the oath, but maintained the method of direct enquiry. From 1523 to the 1545 act commissioners were 'valued and rated...by examynacion' of at least two fellow commissioners,[160] and under the 1548 act by a majority of their fellow commissioners.[161] From the act of 1552-53 on, the statutes dropped the provision for examination and stated simply that the commissioners should 'sett taxe and sesse every other Commyssyoner joyned withe them in every suche Commyssion'.[162] This represents an early and significant shift from valuation on direct enquiry to valuation on estimation by social peers.

Those whom the commissioners suspected of being undervalued in the assessors' returns they could summon, and, from 1515, examine upon a prescribed oath. If for good reason a person summoned could not appear, the commissioners examined on oath people acquainted with that person's affairs.[163] Until 1543, the statements on oath of people suspected of being

---

157. *Statutes*, 6 Hen. VIII c.26, sect.vi; Quote from 32 Hen. VIII c.50, sect. viii.
158. *Statutes*, 5 Eliz. c.31, sect.xi.
159. *Statutes*, 4 Hen. VIII c.19, sect.viii; 5 Hen. VIII c.17, sect.iii; 6 Hen. VIII c.26, sect.viii.
160. *Statutes*, 14 & 15 Hen. VIII c.16, sect.vii; 37 Hen. VIII c.25, sect.xvi. The latter act required that they be valued by two or three fellow commissioners who had themselves been valued by the lord chancellor, the lord treasurer, the lord president of the council or two of them or such other two or three persons as the king should appoint.
161. *Statutes*, 2 & 3 Edw. VI c.36, sect.xvii.
162. *Statutes*, 7 Edw. VI c.12, sect.xiv; quoted from 23 Eliz. c.15, sect.xvi (1580-81).
163. *Statutes*, 6 Hen. VIII c.26, sect.vi.

undervalued were decisive; they were 'rated and charged accordyng to the value and substaunce shewed by his or their disposicyon or his or ther oathes made and none otherwyse'.[164] This language, which would appear to bind the commissioners to accept the word of such deponents, was dropped from the act of 1543. How the commissioners were to proceed thereafter is not clear. This language binding commissioners to accept statements of worth on oath applied also to those who appeared before the commissioners to complain of overvaluation. From 1514, persons who considered themselves overvalued by the assessors could, prior to the return of the assessment certificates into exchequer, appear before the commissioners for revaluation on oath.[165] Up to 1543, they could count on this determination of taxable value by oath. The 1543 statute, however, gave the commissioners great latitude in the cases of those claiming to be overvalued; 'upon the othe of the saide persone so complaynyng', the commissioners 'maie abate defalke increase or enlarge the same Assessment according as it shall appeare to them juste upon the same examinacion'.[166] It is not clear that they had such leeway with the undervalued, but as the statute did not require the commissioners to administer the oath, they may have proceeded by direct enquiry without oath in cases of suspected undervaluation. These provisions remained in effect until the act of 1558, which dropped all reference to the set oath for persons suspected of being undervalued.[167] The 1559 act introduced an actual proscription, included in all subsequent subsidy acts, against the commissioners' use of any corporal oaths in their examination of underassessment.[168]

In the rejection of the oath as a tool for getting at 'the best and most value of the substance' of taxpayers there appears to have been an implicit acknowledgement of the fictitious nature of the valuations. This was a significant consideration in the drafting of the 1563 act, which dropped the oath that the assessors had previously taken and proscribed the use of oaths by assessors in setting valuations. Robert Atkinson, in a 1563 speech in the commons against a bill to widen the obligation to take the oath of supremacy, referred to the deletion of the assessors' oaths: 'In the bill of conveyinge over [exporting] of horses there was a clause that whosoever should convey over any horse and would sweare that it was for his necessarie travaile, it was lawful; and because that men sticked not at such a trifle to forsweare themselves that clause was repealed, and upon like consideracion by the grave advice of this House was the oathe left out of the subsedie book.'[169]

The deliberate prohibition, beginning in 1559, against commissioners examining under oath those whom they suspected of being undervalued, the deletion from the 1563 statute and all subsequent subsidy acts of the oath formerly administered to the assessors, and the prohibition, beginning in 1563, against assessors using examinations under oath in making valuations not only point to the awareness of the decline in subsidy valuations, they indicate

---

164. Quoted from *Statutes*, 6 Hen. VIII c.26, sect.vi.
165. *Statutes*, 5 Hen. VIII c.17, sect i.
166. *Statutes*, 34 & 35 Hen. VIII c.27, sect.vii.
167. *Statutes*, 4 & 5 Phil. & Mar. c.11, sect.x.
168. *Statutes*, 1 Eliz. c.21, sect.x.
169. *Proceedings in the parliaments of Elizabeth I*, ed. T. E. Hartley, I (Leicester, 1981), p.100. That it is unclear exactly to which oath Atkinson refers does not much matter.

that neither the council nor parliament expected that assessors and commissioners should any longer try to discover the best and most value of the substance of every person.[170] As Sir Ralph Sadler put it in 1566, the ideal in assessing the subsidy was that people should contribute 'according to our porcions, according to our habilities'.[171] In this spirit, the council instructed the subsidy commissioners in 1576: 'Where heretofore persons of very great possessions and wealthe have ben assessed at very meane sommes, and persons of the meanest sorte have ben enhanced to paye after the rate of the uttermost value of their substaunces, you shall now have good regarde to order the said taxacions more indifferentlie, so as the greatest burden beinge laid upon the most welthie, the poorer sorte maie in propocion be the more easied.'[172]

The government did not give up trying to ascertain true values for various purposes, but recognized from the beginning of Elizabeth's reign the uselessness of the subsidy books in doing so. In enforcing the Marian statute for maintaining horses and furnishing armour and weapons, the queen and council regularly instructed the lieutenants or the county commissions for musters that they were to base the statutory military assessment not on wealth as set in the subsidy books but as it was in deed.[173] The government also sought to obtain true valuations of the worth of recusants, and when the council in 1577 ordered the bishops to certify the names and worth of recusants, it stipulated that their lands and goods should be valued as 'you thinck they are in deed and not as they be valewed in the subsidye booke'.[174] The commissioners for piracy in the coastal counties received letters in 1578 requiring them to make returns of the values of offenders, 'not after the rates that they have ben set in subsedie, but according as, in dede, they maie spend in landes and be worth in goodes'.[175] Except for the musters in 1569, when the council ordered commissioners to be severe in trying the value of goods and lands on oath,[176] the government largely left local officials to their own devices in making valuations. In practice, this meant relying on estimation or common opinion. The council in 1574 instructed the lieutenants of the counties to determine for the purpose of furnishing horses, armour and weapons, 'the trewe & most probable value ether in landes or goodes of every person (as ether by their open doynges in the world, or by other probable meanes shall appeare likely)'.[177] For valuing the estates of recusants in 1577, the council sent to the bishops

---

170. General undervaluation was recognized as a problem in Mary's reign (S.P.12/4/21), but not yet acknowledged as an irremediable one.
171. *Proceedings in the parliaments of Elizabeth I*, ed. T.E. Hartley, I (Leicester, 1981), p.143.
172. S.P.12/107/97, printed in G.D.Ramsay, ed., *Two sixteenth century taxation lists, 1545 and 1576*, Wiltshire Archaeological and Natural History Society, Records Branch, 10, for 1954 (Devizes, 1954), pp.161-62.
173. 4 & 5 Phil. & Mar c.2; S.P.12/12/11, directions to county lieutenants, 20 April 1560; S.P.12/13/3, Sir Edward Unton, commissioner for musters in Berkshire, to Sir Thomas Parry, lieutenant of Berkshire, 12 July 1560. For other instruction to base military assessments on true worth, not subsidy valuations, see S.P.12/51/8; S.P.12/54/6; S.P.12/58/18; S.P.12/76/38; S.P.12/80/63; S.P.12/97/1; S.P.12/136/38; S.P.12/136/52; S.P.12/137/50.
174. S.P.12/116/15.
175. S.P.12/122/18.
176. S.P.12/49/65.
177. S.P.12/97/1.

the names of gentlemen in each county 'who, we thinck, can well informe your lordship of their [recusants'] partyculer valewes'.[178] The diocesan returns to Westminster explain the valuations in such phrases as these: 'by common reporte of publique fame', 'we do esteme to be worthe', 'as they are thought to be in the common opynion of men', 'accordinge to ... Common fame and beleef of neighbours adjoynauntes', 'our opinions for the value of their landes & goodes', and values of lands and goods 'as they are taken'.[179] Lord North and other commissioners for musters in Cambridgeshire summed up the matter of valuation when they informed the council in 1580 that 'wee have non other meane to knowe the truth of mens' habilities but by the Creditt we give to the gentlemen themselves'.[180]

Whether estimation or common opinion could produce realistic valuations is questionable, but the distinction that the council constantly made between real worth and the subsidy valuations in the context of other valuations implies its resigned acceptance of consistently low assessments for the subsidy. Undervaluation for the subsidy was, as Sir Walter Mildmay said in 1575, 'a matter now drawn to be so usual that it is hard to be reformed'.[181]

There were efforts to reform the subsidy, but they were aimed at more equitable assessments, as in 1576, or at improved rather than realistic valuations. Proclamations of 1559, 1574, and 1580 linked the enforcement of the statutes of apparel of 24 Henry VIII and 1 & 2 Philip and Mary to valuations for the subsidy in an effort to raise them without attempting to bring them up to realistic levels. The contrivance that the government employed was simple; either people should dress according to their subsidy valuations or their subsidy valuations should be raised to meet their level of apparel. But in so using vanity to squeeze out tax yield, the government cannot have intended to get realistic valuations. People needed to prove only £200 in goods or £200 *per annum* in lands in 1559 and £500 in goods or £200 *per annum* in lands in 1580 to enjoy all clothing and fashion to which wealth (as distinct from status) could give licence.[182] If this scheme was implemented, it seems to have had limited success. No one was valued in the London subsidy rolls at £500 in goods in 1582, and only three people (John Cowper, Sir William Damsell, and Sir Rowland Hayward) were valued at £400. There were only four valuations of £200 *per annum* in lands or fees (Dame Anne Gresham, Sir Thomas Kitson, Sir John Peter, and Sir Thomas Ryvet) and two of them paid on valuations under £200 *per annum* outside London (Peter in Essex and Ryvet in Cambridgeshire).

By the middle years of Elizabeth's reign, the object of valuation for the subsidy was not to obtain true values but to ensure that when a subsidy was levied people paid according to their relative ability as their communities commonly perceived that to be. What was aimed at, Lord North wrote as a subsidy commissioner for Cambridgeshire in 1589, was the contentment of

178. S.P.12/116/15.
179. S.P.12/117/12; S.P.12/117/22; S.P.12/118/11 V; S.P.12/118/32; S.P.12/118/45; S.P.12/119/5 I.
180. S.P.12/142/6.
181. Quoted in Stephen Dowell, *A History of taxation and taxes in England from the earliest times to the year 1885*, vol.I, 2nd. ed. (London, 1888), p.146.
182. *Tudor royal proclamations*, v.2, pp.137-38, 384-386, 456-62.

all men, not accurate assessments, not even assessments that bore some fixed relation to wealth. In a letter often cited, he informed Burghley that 'There is no man assessed before me but is known to be worth at the least in goods 10 times as much as he is set at, and 6 times more in lands than his assessment; and many be 20 times, some 30, and some much more worth than they be set at, which the commissioner cannot without oath help.'[183] That the community perception of assessment according to ability was a central concern of subsidy commissioners is evident from the outcome of Sir Horatio Palavicino's appeal to the subsidy commissioners in Cambridgeshire in 1598 for a reduction in his valuation. It was twice that of any other gentleman in the county, and that, he said, gave a false and inconvenient impression of his relative wealth. The commissioners in the end defended their valuation, according to Palavicino, on the ground that it was consistent with common opinion.[184]

One might think common opinion a poor guide to ability to contribute to the public charge when it could lead to some being valued in the subsidy certificates at one-tenth and others at one-thirtieth or less their real worth. Aside from the problem of finding a better alternative, this is not necessarily the case. Common opinion could redress a basic structural flaw in the subsidy – the payment of an assessment on the value of goods or on income from land, etc., but not on both. This feature of the subsidy favoured those who possessed a balanced estate in real and personal property.[185] Common opinion could also redress the probable inequity, favouring landowners, of the relationship between rates on goods and rates on lands; indeed, this may be why Lord North and the other commissioners in Cambridgeshire apparently thought it desirable to undervalue goods more than lands.[186] No doubt common opinion was informed by impressions rather than evidence of wealth systematically gathered – observations of the size of house and household, the quality of entertainment and public appearance – so 'he that had a cup of red wine to his oysters was hoisted in the Queen's subsidy book',[187] and the only virtue of a well-dressed wife was 'to improve my credit in the subsidy book'.[188]

183. Historical Manuscripts Commission, *Calendar of the Manuscripts of the Most Hon. the Marquis of Salisbury*, part III (1889), p.429.
184. Historical Manuscripts Commission, *Calendar of the Manuscripts of the Most Hon. the Marquis of Salisbury*, part VIII (1899), p.547-48.
185. Julian Cornwall observes the point in respect to the 1523 act in *The Subsidy rolls for the county of Sussex, 1524-25*, Sussex Record Society, 16, for 1956-7 (n.d.), xxxiii. If it is assumed that generally the rich were most likely to benefit from the principle of payment on goods or lands (whichever assessment was higher) the act of 1523, which provided for additional payments in 1526 by those valued at £50 and above in income from lands, etc. and a payment in 1527 by those valued at £50 and above in goods, and the acts of 1543, 1545, 1553 and 1555, which had progressive rate structures, may be considered more equitable than later subsidy statutes.
186. W.R.B.Robinson discusses the likely inequities in respect to the 1543 act in 'The First subsidy assessment of the hundreds of Swansea and Llangyfelach, 1543', *Welsh History Review*, 2 (1964-5), 125-145 (pp.131-132).
187. Lyly, *Mother Bombie*, II, v, lines 8-12. *The Complete works of John Lyly*, ed. R. Warwick Bond, vol. III (Oxford, 1902), p.193.
188. Middleton, *Anything for a quiet life*, I, i, lines 61-63.

THE FORMATION OF THE COMMON OPINION OF WORTH IN ELIZABETHAN LONDON

In London, the common opinion of a person's wealth was formed in the close communities of ward, parish and precinct where there was by 1582 a tradition of taking stock of neighbours' abilities. Frequent and various enquiries into the numbers and affairs of all or large classes of the city's inhabitants, wide participation in the assessment and collection of several kinds of local taxes, and the public scrutiny given these assessments in popular meetings all contributed to making the evaluation of one's neighbours a habit of mind.[189]

In the parishes and precincts neighbours assessed each other for the wages of the parish clerks, beadles, scavengers, rakers; for city and parliamentary fifteenths and tenths; and for a wide range of occasional levies. The mayor and aldermen and the privy council commanded many city-wide surveys of inhabitants, with increasing frequency after 1558. There were surveys of those who possessed military harness or who were able for military service; enquiries, usually at the instigation of the privy council, into the number and condition of the foreign born; censuses of 'foreigns', Englishmen resident in but not free of the city, often because of government concern with the number of gentlemen residing in the city; censuses of the poor made in response to increasing vagrancy and almost as a matter of course in the administration of the poor law; searches of houses converted into tenements or lodgings; searches to find out how many lodgers there were in the city (including their names and occupations); and in 1573 an extensive census to produce a record of the names, trades, and occupations of the inhabitants of every parish, together with the names of the owners of every tenement.

Large numbers of people were involved in this frequent, officially sponsored scrutiny of their neighbours' condition. Parishioners in vestry commonly elected assessors for fifteenths and tenths; for the bills for the clerk's, scavenger's, and raker's wages; and for levies to meet occasional parochial charges. In the parish of St. Bartholomew by the Exchange at least 13 parishioners had experience as assessors for parochial levies in the fifteen years preceding the assessment of the subsidy payment of 1582.[190] St. Bartholomew by the Exchange is probably exceptional only in the fullness of its vestry minutes and their survival from an early date. In St. Alban Wood Street, the vestry elected nine parishioners during the years 1585 to 1588 to serve as assessors.[191] St. Margaret Lothbury favoured larger panels of assessors: eight in 1578 to assess the parish for repairs to the church and for defacing windows with images, eight in 1581 to increase the levy for the clerk's wages, and eight in the same year to make a new assessment for the fifteenth.[192]

189. On the broad participation of householders in the general political life of the city, see Valerie Pearl, 'Social Policy in early modern London', in Hugh Lloyd-Jones, Valerie Pearl and Blair Worden, eds., *History and imagination: essays in honour of H.R. Trevor-Roper* (1981), pp.116-117. On the precinct (a subdivision of the ward) and parish as units of local administration, see Alice E. McCampbell, 'The London parish and the London precinct, 1640-1660', *Guildhall Studies in London History*, 11 (1976), pp.107-124.
190. G.L. MS 4384/1, St. Bartholomew by the Exchange, Vestry Minutes, 1567-1643.
191. G.L. MS 1264/1, St. Alban Wood Street, Vestry Minutes, 1583-1676.
192. G.L. MS 4352/1, St. Margaret Lothbury, Record Book, 1571-1677, ff.32, 41, 49, 57.

The people chosen in the parishes to assess their neighbours represented a limited range in the social spectrum – householders of the sort whom their fellows also chose to serve as constable, churchwarden, member of the wardmote inquest, and common councilman – but the wider group of substantial parishioners who attended vestry meetings could, and did, approve and disapprove the work of the assessors or even make the assessments then and there.[193] After six parishioners of St. Mary Aldermary, elected by a general vestry, had assessed a fifteenth and tenth, the assessment was 'openlye read and published and by the hole Assemblye ther gethered ratified and allowed to continewe as a perpetual president'.[194] Assessors did not always perform their tasks to such general satisfaction. In St. Margaret Lothbury in 1591, a small group of six or eight parishioners who disapproved the existing assessment for the poor of Christ's Hospital made their own assessment of the parish and apparently tried to enforce it, to the great confusion of parochial taxpayers. In vestry, 'The question beinge moved which of the asseasments they would have to stand in effect yt was agreed by erectinge of hands that the fyrst asseasment ... should stande.'[195] The majority of the parishioners of St. Martin Ludgate became so incensed with assessors for the fifteenth and tenth who had 'raised and pulled down at their discrecions' the assessments of divers parishioners that they appointed 22 people to reassess the parish and to produce an assessment list that 'should remaine for ever as a president'.[196] Sometimes the parishioners in vestry constituted themselves assessors. In assessing a fifteenth and tenth in St. Bartholomew by the Exchange in 1594, all of the 18 parishioners in attendance at the vestry meeting joined in the valuation and together set down what everyone should pay.[197] In St. Botolph Billingsgate in 1593, 'The common counsell of this parish..., the churchwardens, and most of the parishe dyd mete and assemble themselves together not only for the ceasing of every man, but also to apoynt collectors for the gathering therof.'[198]

The subsidy differed in principle from most parochial and ward levies in being assessed on valuations of wealth rather than on the occupation of property. The only more or less regular local levies in London based on valuations of wealth were those for poor relief. The subsidy also differed in its administration in having assessors formally appointed by commissioners who were not responsible to the wardmote, vestry, or whole body of parishioners. Still, the assessors for the subsidy were people who had been assessors in their

193. The city's large extramural parishes had select vestries by Elizabeth's reign. It is not known how many of the intramural parishes had them. But even as late as 1638, when 59 of London's 109 parishes had select vestries, many parishes with select vestries also had general vestries that met to elect precinct and parochial officers and to assess charges. See Ian Archer, 'Governors and governed in late sixteenth-century London, c.1560-1603: studies in the achievement of stability' (unpublished D.Phil. thesis, University of Oxford, 1988), p.52, and Valerie Pearl, 'Change and stability in seventeenth-century London', *The London Journal*, 5, no.1 (1979), p.15 and note 33.
194. G.L. MS 6574, St. Mary Aldermary, Churchwardens' Accounts, 1576/7-1664/5, 20 May 1599, at end of volume.
195. G.L. MS 4352/1, St. Margaret Lothbury, Record Book, 1571-1677, f.63.
196. G.L. MS 1311/1, St. Martin Ludgate, Vestry Minutes, 1568-1715, 27 Sept. 1594.
197. G.L. MS 4384/1, p.141.
198. G.L. MS 943/1, St. Botolph Billingsgate, Orders of Vestry, 1592-1693, ff.1-2.

parishes; people who knew the occupations, number of servants, quality of dwellings, and rents paid by their neighbours; and people who were likely in turn to be assessed by their fellow parishioners on another occasion.

The number of assessors at work for most payments of the subsidy is uncertain. We need not accept the statement of the author of the 'Notes for Taxacion of Subsidye' that the number of high assessors had always been 12,[199] but it does appear that their number was settled at 12 by the early subsidies of Elizabeth's reign. Little is known about the petty assessors, but their numbers probably varied from one subsidy to another and from ward to ward. In Queenhithe ward in 1541, a ward that had 57 English and 18 stranger subsidymen, there were six 'presenters' or assessors, mostly from the middle ranks of the ward's taxpayers. Only in the assessment certificate for this one ward are they identified (**146**). In 1546, 1568, and 1572 the commissioners would seem to have ordered four men from each ward to appear before them to be charged as assessors.[200] In 1550 and 1558 some account seems to have been taken of ward size, for there were six persons summoned from the wards of Farringdon Without and Cripplegate; two each from Lime Street, Bassishaw, Portsoken and Aldgate; and four men from all of the rest.[201] In 1555 and 1571, the commissioners summoned eight men from Tower ward in what seem to have been exemplars for precepts to all of the aldermen requiring them to have men in attendance to be charged as assessors, but there is no way of knowing whether there were to be eight from every ward.[202] More certain is the evidence for Bassishaw ward in 1610 and 1621. The eight petty assessors appointed in 1610 assessed only 34 inhabitants; the eleven petty assessors in 1621 assessed 33.[203]

In 1582, a precept in the form of one for appointment of assessors required the aldermen to have 16 people from Farringdon Without and Cripplegate wards and 12 from all of the rest appear before the commissioners. If all of those summoned were actually appointed, the panels of petty assessors would probably have been larger in 1582 than for any other sixteenth-century subsidy payment, and would have given the city as a whole 308 petty assessors.[204]

There is likely to have been the same level of community concern for the equity of subsidy assessments as there was for the equity of parochial and ward levies, and if it seems that something like the common opinion of the parish eventually prevailed in assessing clerk's wages it is not too much to expect that common opinion should have been satisfied in assessing the subsidy. The two-tiered system of valuation and the large number of petty assessors would have contributed to this outcome.

The likelihood that the subsidy assessments were widely accepted as reasonably equitable within the local community gains support from the use that the mayor and aldermen and the common council made of the subsidy valua-

---

199. S.P. 14/23/28, f.70, 'Notes for Taxacion of Subsidye in London', [1606].
200. Jour. 15, f.219,b; Jour. 19, f.92,b; Jour. 20 (1), f.10.
201. Jour. 16, f.49; Jour. 17, f.65,b. These precepts seem to have provided for a meeting at which both high assessors and petty assessors would be charged.
202. Jour. 16, f.364; Jour. 19, f.356.
203. G.L. MS 3505, ff.4,b and 43.
204. Jour. 21, f.212,b.

tions in imposing civic levies. The city of London seems to have first used the subsidy valuations for the purpose of rating other levies in 1578 at the instigation of the central government. The privy council ordered the city to equip and train 2,000 soldiers for the queen's service. Along with its detailed instructions on the selection, mustering and training of the troops, the council sent its recommendation on the way to finance the soldiers: 'It is thought mete that the charge to be levied within the Cittie ... shalbe onely extended and levied upon such of thinhabitantes as are taxed in the subside booke, everie one pro rata, and the reast not to be any waie burdened therwith.'[205] Customarily, the mayor, aldermen, and common council had allocated the burden of raising and furnishing men among the livery companies and city fellowships, and for the greater part of the charge in 1578 they did so again. When the charge was borne by the companies, however, it was borne only by citizens, freemen of London, and not by the residents of the city in general. To extend the burden broadly among substantial residents the corporation followed the privy council's recommendation in part by levying a tax, based on valuations for the subsidy, on all foreigns (non-citizen native English), strangers born, and denizens.[206] The privy council, in fact, enjoined the use of subsidy assessments on a national scale at this time for a variety of purposes while clearly dismissing the valuations as statements of actual worth. In 1577, the council made rates on the valuations in the last subsidy book the basis for local levies for the furnishing and training of shot.[207] In 1580, the council made copies of the subsidy assessments available to the county-wide commissions for muster to give them better knowledge of how to direct particular commissioners in the rating of men in their localities.[208] The government itself used subsidy assessments in deciding on the acceptability of sureties nominated by prospective customs farmers.[209]

Although the city raised soldiers on a number of occasions in the decade from 1578,[210] the corporation did not use the subsidy valuations again for a city levy until the spring of 1588. The city did tax non-freemen to raise money toward the cost of large-scale musters twice during that decade (in February 1580 and in April 1585), but in neither instance did the Common

205. Jour. 20 (2), ff.394-395, the queen's letter to the city, 12 March 1578, and the privy council's instructions.
206. Jour. 20 (2), f.404. By a subsequent mayoral precept strangers born in the Low Countries, subjects of the king of Spain, were exempted from this tax as they had also been from payment of the subsidy.
207. Commissioners' returns: S.P.12/112/7, Northamptonshire; S.P.12/112/10, Bedfordshire; S.P.12/112/11, Lincolnshire; S.P.12/113/8, Buckinghamshire; S.P.12/114/6, Oxfordshire; S.P.12/116/8, Essex; S.P.12/116/9, Suffolk; S.P.12/116/10, Norfolk. For details of local variations in setting rates and thresholds of liability, see also Lindsay Boynton, *The Elizabethan militia, 1558-1638* (London and Toronto, 1967), p.94.
208. S.P.12/136/5, note of matters to be contained in the commission for the musters, etc., 18 Jan., 1580.
209. S.P.12/252/39; S.P.12/263/1.
210. The City raised 400 soldiers in August 1579 (Jour. 20 (2), f.505), 300 in July 1580 (Jour. 21, ff.54, 55), 500 in September 1580 (Ibid., ff.69-71), 500 in July 1585 (Ibid., f.454), 60 in April 1586 (Jour. 22, f.24), and 800 in April and June 1587 (Ibid., ff. 98, 104,b, 106), all at the charge of the city companies.

Council make the subsidy valuations the basis of the tax.[211] There were no fresh subsidy valuations available for either of these occasions.

In the ten years from 1588 to 1597, during which time there were new valuations and assessments for a subsidy payment in every year except 1597, the city used the parliamentary subsidy valuations ten times to raise money: on nine occasions to furnish men or ships for the war against Spain and once to secure a supply of grain for the city. Three times in 1588 the common council imposed a levy based on valuations for the subsidy: in March to raise and furnish ten thousand men,[212] to furnish sixteen ships and four pinnaces,[213] and in August 1588 for equipping the ships and pinnaces and training the soldiers.[214] Again in 1589, 1591 (twice), 1594, 1596, and 1597 the city imposed levies based on the subsidy valuations, at varying rates, to raise money for the finance of soldiers and shipping.[215] In January 1597 the city used the subsidy valuations for a local purpose for the first time; in order to keep grain in the city from being sold in the country, the officers of each ward were to call before them the subsidymen to persuade them to buy one bushel of wheat or rye for each pound at which they were valued.[216] In Cripplegate ward, at least, the actual assessment, although based on valuations for the subsidy, devolved upon the parishioners in vestry.[217]

The valuations for the subsidy constituted a tax base particularly appropriate to these years of frequent local taxation, so frequent that in 1596 the common council enacted that a register book of all city subsidies, 15ths and 10ths, and other impositions be maintained in the city chamber to serve as a current record of who had and had not paid toward any particular levy.[218] There were at this time fresh subsidy books frequently at hand, and they had the advantage of spreading the tax burden among foreigns and aliens as well as citizens and of sparing those least able to contribute. There were, however, alternative means of finance available to the city that continued in use in furnishing soldiers, fitting out and victualling ships, buying gunpowder and grain, rebuild-

211. Jour. 21, ff.19, 20,b, 421,b, 427, 454,b. In one case the aldermen and common councilmen of each ward made the assessments and in the other the aldermen, their deputies, and three of the most substantial men of each ward assessed the non-free inhabitants.
212. Jour. 22, ff.144, 161-62, 166-67, 170,b, 171, 173. This was a levy on subsidy valuations of 6d. in the pound. The committees of the common council that had the management of this business also tried to use the subsidy books in the enforcement of the muster itself, punishing by commitment to Newgate anyone valued at £50 in goods or under and of the age of fifty years and under who, being selected, refused to serve (Ibid., f.190). This action, which flagrantly favoured the very rich, was found to cause 'great inconvenience', whereupon the common council ordered that *anyone* who refused to serve in his own person should be committed (Ibid., f.193).
213. Jour. 22, ff.173, 175. This was a levy of 2s. in the £ on those assessed on goods and 3s. in the £ on those assessed on lands, etc. The common council ordered the alderman, his deputy, the constables and common councilmen of each ward to assess those not in the subsidy books.
214. Jour. 22, f.200,b. The rates were the same as those for supplying the ships and pinnaces in the spring.
215. Jour. 22, ff.321,b, 325,b, 329, 339,b, 416, 451, 456; Jour. 23, ff.4, 29, 31, 92, 289, 293; Jour. 24, ff.85, 210,b, 212. As in 1588, the ward officers assessed residents not included in the most recent subsidy books but of sufficient wealth to be assessed for the subsidy.
216. Jour. 24, f.178.
217. G.L. MS 3570/1, St. Mary Aldermanbury vestry minute book, 1569-1609, f.45.
218. Jour. 24, f.144.

ing the city's gates and walls, acquiring civic firefighting equipment, or relieving the city's hospitals. The common council could rate the city companies and limit the use of subsidy valuations to foreigns and aliens, levy multiple 15ths and 10ths on the wards and parishes, raise forced loans on bond, or make rated assessments on wealth valued independently of the subsidy. Had the subsidy certificates not embodied the common opinion of relative ability to pay the city need not have used them.

The frequent use made of the subsidy assessments for levying taxes other than the parliamentary subsidy suggests that within the limits of the local community people regarded the subsidy valuations as tolerably equitable. Moreover, given the large number of assessors and their close ties to their localities it is likely that valuations represent the common opinion of the relative position of householders in respect to wealth. Within their different local contexts, Sir Nicholas Woodroffe's £270 valuation by the high assessors in London and £100 valuation by the assessors of Ratcliffe in Middlesex may both have been consistent with the common opinion of relative wealth. But the differences between the two valuations caution against comparisons across assessment divisions and stand as a clear warning against taking the subsidy valuations as an index of wealth.

NOTE ON EDITORIAL PRACTICE

The subsidy roll for 1541, E.179/144/120, consists of 26 rotulets of no uniform size, some of two or more membranes, filed exchequer-wise and numbered in a modern hand. There is one rotulet for each of the 25 wards and one for the assessments on orphans' estates. Each rotulet is an indenture between the London subsidy commissioners and the collectors for the wards and for the orphans' estates. There is no obvious order to the arrangement of the file.

The roll for 1582, E.179/251/16, consists of 121 single-membrane rotulets. The first four are indentures between the commissioners and the high collectors for each of the four groups of wards into which the 25 were divided. They bear the signatures of the high collectors. Each of the remaining 117 membranes is part of an estreat of indentures between the commissioners and the petty collectors for one of the wards, signed by the petty collectors or bearing their marks. The membranes for the wards within each of the four collection groups are filed together, but within the four groups there is, again, no obvious order to the arrangement of the wards.

This edition of the 1541 and 1582 London subsidy assessment rolls aims to include all of the information of the originals that relates to valuation and assessment, but the form of the presentation departs from the originals in several respects. The wards are here arranged alphabetically. The beginning of each rotulet in the original documents is marked in the printed text by the rotulet number in square brackets. In 1541 and again in 1582, the language of the indentures between the commissioners and the petty collectors is the same for all wards. It is given in full for only the first ward in both years – Aldersgate ward. In the originals, entries of assessments are set down in two or three columns on each rotulet. Omitted here are the parochial or other headings repeated at the heads of the second and third columns when lists of subsidymen from the same parish are carried over. In the originals, the individual assessment is entered in three secondary columns, one each for name, valuation, and assessment. These three columns are here reduced to two: name (with valuation in round brackets) and assessment.[219]

In the originals, language specifying the basis for valuation follows the name: 'in goods', 'in lands', 'in fees', 'in lands and fees'. Most Londoners taxed for the subsidy were assessed on valuations of goods. Here, only if the assessment derived from a valuation of some form of annual income is the language specifying the basis for valuation given. In all other cases it may be taken that the valuation was of goods and chattels. All valuations and assessments (in Roman numerals in the original rolls) are here given in Arabic.

Pound, shilling, and pence signs, omitted from individual entries of assessments, are given here at the head of the pound, shilling, and pence columns into which the assessments have been arranged.

Names and English words abbreviated and contracted in the originals are extended. The extensions follow modern spelling. Latin words are usually extended when there is no doubt about the intended ending. In some cases an apostrophe is given in place of a terminal extension. The original spelling has been retained except that i, j and u, v have been transcribed to conform to modern usage when it is known what that is. There may be errors in the rendering of more unusual surnames. There is also opportunity for error in deciding whether a letter is a u or an n. Some punctuation has been added, mostly commas to distinguish names in series.

The sums of assessments for wards that appear to be incorrect in the originals and discrepancies between valuations and assessments have not been corrected, though attention has been called to the latter by the use of '*sic*' in square brackets. The few words or names that the editor has added are in square brackets, and any words in square brackets are added words. Names are supplied (nearly all of them forenames) only when they have been derived from exchequer records directly related to one or the other of the two subsidy payments represented here, principally the Exchequer Enrolled Accounts: Subsidies (E.359). In every case, the source is noted. The first names of doctors of law and of medicine are given in the Introduction, notes 95 and 96.

The original documents are, generally, in good condition, and their hands are legible. At some points, however, the editor admits uncertainty, even defeat. A question mark in square brackets, [?], means that the reading of the preceding word or name is questionable. Empty square brackets, [ ], common in the printed text of the badly faded 1541 orphans' book, take the place of illegible letters, names, words, or numbers. Square brackets around the word 'blank', [blank], indicate that a name, surname, valuation, or assessment was omitted in the original.

The subsidy roll for 1582 has a variety of marginal marks and notations relating to the actual tax obligation of persons assessed and the actual

---

219. For strangers assessed *per poll*, the 1541 subsidy roll had no entry in the second column, only the 4d. assessment in the third column. The 1582 indentures, however, put 4d. in the valuation column, which was repeated in the assessment column.

accountability of the collectors for particular assessments. In one way or another, these notations all concerned exonerations from payment.[220]

Per bre', per privat sigill', per bre' de privat sigill': of identical significance, any one of these notations to the left of a taxpayer's name in the original document indicates that the taxpayer received exoneration from payment by the queen's writ of privy seal directed to the treasurer and barons of the exchequer.

Aff' or *per affid'*: this notation to the left of a person's name in the original document indicates that the commissioners had declared by certificate or affidavit to the treasurer and barons that the assessment was uncollectable because, as the petty collectors had sworn before the commissioners, the person taxed had no distrainable goods or chattels within the collection division (the ward) at the time the estreats were delivered into the hands of the collectors. This exoneration of the collectors did not extend to the taxpayers.

+ or x: a cross placed to the left of a taxpayer's name in the original document signifies an exoneration, usually because the taxpayer was answerable for an assessment in another place. Sometimes, however, this mark signifies an exoneration by writ of privy seal, an exoneration upon process before the barons of the exchequer, or an exoneration of the collectors by the commissioners' affidavit. Occasionally, but not regularly, the following phrase accompanies it.

Exoneratur hic quia oneratur in com' –: this notation, entered to the right of the assessment figure, means that the taxpayer was exonerated because of an assessment elsewhere for which the taxpayer remained answerable. Not all such exonerations are so noted in the original.

O^a [*oneratur*]: written always in the abbreviated form, usually next to the assessment but occasionally to the left of the name, this notation indicates that the taxpayer had also been assessed in another place, had been exonerated in that place, and remained answerable for the present assessment.

These notations point to more specific information contained in the Exchequer Enrolled Accounts: Subsidies – that is, the ground for exoneration by writ of privy seal; the place and amount of the answerable assessment of persons exonerated by reason of having been assessed also in another place; and the amount and place of assessments exonerated elsewhere. This information is supplied here in an abbreviated form in square brackets following the valuation. The enrolled accounts give evidence in a very few instances of exonerations that are not noted in the 1582 assessment roll. In these cases, the editorial abbreviations of exoneration and specific information are supplied in square brackets as though the subsidy roll did have the appropriate marginal notations.[221] The full statements of place in the enrolled accounts are here reduced to the county or city in order to save space.

Although the 1541 assessment roll does not have such notations bearing on the actual accountability of taxpayers or collectors, there were then, as in 1582, uncollectable assessments of which collectors were discharged and

220. For a discussion of exonerations from payment, see above, pp. xlii–li, 'The assessment figures: apparent and actual liability to payment'.

multiple assessments requiring taxpayers' exonerations. As for 1582, the specific details of these exonerations can be found in the enrolled accounts. The information contained there is supplied in the edited 1541 subsidy roll as for the 1582 roll – in square brackets after the valuations, using the abbreviations that follow.

[a] The collectors were discharged of the assessment upon the commissioners' affidavit that the collectors had sworn that the person assessed had no distrainable goods in the collection division. These entries were denoted by the marginal notation *aff'* or per *affid'* in the 1582 assessment roll.

[ass.] [followed by assessment and place] The taxpayer was assessed and exonerated in another place, remaining answerable for the present assessment. These entries were denoted by the marginal notation O^a in the 1582 assessment roll.

[b] The taxpayer and the London collectors were exonerated by writ of privy seal directed to the treasurer and barons of the exchequer. These entries are denoted in the 1582 original by the marginal notation *per bre'*, *per privat sigill'*, or *per bre' de privat sigill'*.

[b – Antwerp mer.] The taxpayer was a merchant of the Low Countries and subject of the King of Spain. He and the collectors were exonerated by writ of privy seal.

[x] [followed by place and assessment] This signifies that the taxpayer and collectors were exonerated of the present assessment, and that the taxpayer remained answerable in the named county, city or other London ward for the assessment in that place. In 1541, the x is sometimes followed by an editorial note in the form 'owes – amount in the ward of –' when the taxpayer had already paid on a lower assessment in another place and had to make up the difference between that and the higher assessment. A marginal cross, variably + or x, distinguishes such entries in the 1582 original. The marginal notation *exoneratur hic quia oneratur in com'* – sometimes accompanied it. If either the other place or other assessment is not given in the enrolled accounts a question mark follows the x.

[x-K] Exonerated, remaining answerable for an assessment in the household of the king.

[x-Q] Exonerated, remaining answerable for an assessment in the queen's household.

[x-P] Exonerated, remaining answerable for an assessment in the household of the prince.

[x-AC] Exonerated, remaining answerable for an assessment in the household of Anne of Cleves.

[x-Process] The taxpayer was exonerated of the assessment upon process before the barons of the exchequer.

221. Other marginalia in the 1582 assessment roll are given in footnotes.

Table IA. *Valuations of English and Strangers, by Ward, 1541*

Ward	Number of valuations of English in goods £20	£21-49	£50-99	£100-199	£200-499	£500+	total	Number of valuations of English in lands, fees, etc.	Total valuations of English	Number of valuations of Strangers in goods £1-19	£20-99	£100+	in lands	Total valuations of strangers	Total valuations of English and Strangers	Strangers assessed per poll
Aldersgate	32	15	9	5	5	6	72	7	79	75	16	3	0	94	173	158
Aldgate	35	19	11	6	4	0	75	11	86	34	19	1	0	54	140	69
Bassishaw	19	8	3	0	2	6	38	0	38	6	1	0	0	7	45	6
Billingsgate	30	43	14	10	3	12	112	1	113	16	3	0	0	19	132	40
Bishopsgate	35	26	18	12	7	7	105	7	112	12	6	3	3	24	136	8
Bread Street	27	18	30	14	15	22	126	1	127	4	0	0	0	4	131	8
Bridge	52	27	22	15	19	10	145	0	145	1	0	0	1	2	147	10
Broad Street	26	13	9	11	9	12	80	3	83	5	8	6	1	20	103	5
Candlewick	26	29	8	5	6	4	78	0	78	5	3	3	0	11	89	8
Castle Baynard	51	31	12	13	9	3	119	3	122	21	5	0	2	28	150	24
Cheap	46	35	17	23	24	16	161	0	161	3	1	0	0	4	165	3
Coleman Street	16	16	5	3	4	4	48	3	51	2	0	0	1	3	54	1
Cordwainer	30	14	17	12	23	12	108	0	108	0	0	0	0	0	108	0
Cornhill	29	16	12	14	8	3	82	0	82	0	0	0	0	0	82	0
Cripplegate	57	42	25	21	13	15	173	7	180	24	3	3	0	30	210	9
Dowgate	36	21	10	3	1	2	73	0	73	27	1	2	0	30	103	11
Farringdon Within	74	67	46	27	19	18	251	8	259	10	10	2	1	23	282	34
Farringdon Without	126	102	50	36	56	6	376	9	385	39	3	1	0	43	428	74
Langbourn	46	33	15	1	4	8	107	1	108	67	13	7	23	110	218	37
Lime Street	7	7	10	0	4	5	33	2	35	1	1	0	0	2	37	3
Portsoken	12	8	1	2	1	0	24	1	25	39	13	2	4	58	83	74
Queenhithe	15	22	9	7	2	2	57	0	57	7	0	1	11	19	76	7
Tower	34	19	11	18	14	11	107	4	111	38	11	7	0	56	167	59
Vintry	23	12	10	11	8	4	68	0	68	27	0	0	0	27	95	0
Walbrook	27	20	8	8	4	6	73	3	76	1	1	1	0	3	79	4
Total	911	663	382	277	264	194	2691	71	2762	465	118	43	45	671	3433	652

Table IB. *Valuations of English and Strangers, by Ward, 1582*

	Number of valuations of English in goods							Number of valuations of English in lands, fees, etc.				Total valuations of English	Number of valuations of strangers			Total valuations of English and Strangers	Strangers assessed per poll
	£3	£4–9	£10–19	£20–49	£50–99	£100+	Ward total	£1–19	£20–49	£50+	Ward total		£1–49	£50+	Ward total		
Aldersgate	144	108	20	2	13	2	289	12	12	13	37	326	58	0	58	384	151
Aldgate	106	45	7	4	10	6	178	5	9	12	26	204	39	4	43	247	149
Bassishaw	14	14	14	1	8	8	59	1	0	0	1	60	1	0	1	61	2
Billingsgate	60	40	28	16	25	6	175	0	1	0	1	176	27	7	34	210	118
Bishopsgate	54	36	30	12	26	6	164	8	5	6	19	183	30	3	33	216	206
Bread Street	46	45	26	15	35	22	189	0	1	0	1	190	4	0	4	194	2
Bridge	66	44	42	12	28	8	200	0	0	0	0	200	6	1	7	207	8
Broad Street	56	37	30	18	32	17	190	1	2	4	7	197	13	3	16	213	75
Candlewick	52	27	21	13	18	6	137	1	0	1	2	139	9	3	12	151	17
Castle Baynard	96	52	23	21	21	3	216	8	8	8	24	240	2	0	2	242	5
Cheap	64	46	40	12	72	16	250	0	0	1	1	251	1	1	2	253	11
Coleman Street	48	32	16	9	17	9	131	6	10	1	17	148	5	0	5	153	47
Cordwainer	34	36	19	8	37	14	148	0	2	0	2	150	3	2	5	155	6
Cornhill	29	43	20	11	17	2	122	0	1	0	1	123	2	0	2	125	0
Cripplegate	157	85	37	11	44	19	353	9	26	5	40	393	13	0	13	406	48
Dowgate	55	34	24	13	7	4	137	1	0	0	1	138	14	3	17	155	36
Farringdon Within	122	91	73	32	36	18	372	5	16	5	26	398	47	0	47	445	57
Farringdon Without	302	251	115	54	34	7	763	24	43	12	79	842	26	0	26	868	46
Langbourn	77	74	39	17	21	8	236	2	0	0	2	238	35	9	44	282	119
Lime Street	22	15	6	1	7	3	54	1	3	0	4	58	0	2	2	60	18
Portsoken	25	25	6	0	3	0	59	13	2	1	16	75	9	4	13	88	84
Queenhithe	62	42	15	3	9	2	133	2	1	1	4	137	6	1	7	144	13
Tower	87	74	31	15	30	14	251	4	7	1	12	263	74	6	80	343	115
Vintry	61	28	19	10	13	5	136	1	2	0	3	139	6	0	6	145	23
Walbrook	53	33	16	9	28	10	149	0	1	0	1	150	1	2	3	153	2
Total	1892	1357	717	319	591	215	5091	104	152	71	327	5418	431	51	482	5900	1358

Table II. *City Companies assessed in 1541 and 1582*

	1541 tax assessed				1582 tax assessed		
	£	s.	d.		£	s.	d.
Drapers	16	0.	9.	Goldsmiths	10	0.	0. L
Goldsmiths	15	4.	8. L	Fishmongers	6	8.	0. L
Skinners	13	4.	6.	Skinners	5	0.	0.
Merchant Taylors	13	3.	8.¹ L	Clothworkers	4	14.	8. L
Fishmongers	10	13.	8. L	Salters	4	14.	8. L
Vintners	10	0.	0.	Mercers	4	12.	0. L
Brewers	8	11.	2½	Merchant Taylors	3	5.	4. L
Mercers	7	10.	0. L	Drapers	3	1.	4. L
Barbers	5	8.	1.	Grocers	2	15.	0.
Grocers	5	0.	0. L	Cutlers	2	0.	0.
Leathersellers	4	13.	7.	Brewers	1	8.	0. L
Saddlers	4	2.	4. L	Haberdashers	1	8.	0. L
Carpenters	3	14.	10.	Tallowchandlers	1	8.	0. L
Salters	3	3.	8½ L	Vintners	1	6.	8. L
Coopers	3	0.	0.	Dyers	1	1.	4. L
Butchers	2	17.	9.	Armourers	1	1.	0.
Cutlers	2	15.	0.	Bakers	1	0.	0.
Haberdashers	2	14.	2. L	Cordwainers	1	0.	0. L
Clothworkers	2	11.	4. L	Curriers		17.	4.
Innholders	2	2.	0.	Pewterers		17.	4. L
Dyers	2	0.	0.	Leathersellers		16.	0. L
Bakers	1	12.	4.	Carpenters		14.	8. L
Broderers	1	6.	11.	Coopers		13.	4. L
Tallowchandlers	1	5.	6. L	Girdlers		13.	4. L
Woolpackers	1	3.	0.	Scriveners		13.	4. L
Scriveners	1	2.	0.	Ironmongers		10.	8. L
Ironmongers	1	1.	8. L	Waxchandlers		10.	8. L
Armourers	1	0.	0. L	Smiths		10.	0.
Cooks	1	0.	0.	Innholders		8.	0.
Cordwainers	1	0.	0.	Weavers		8.	0. L
Girdlers	1	0.	0.	Stationers		6.	8.
Pewterers	1	0.	0.	Founders		6.	0.
				Painters		6.	0.
				Cooks		5.	4. L
				Tylers & Bricklayers		5.	4. L
				Joiners		5.	0.
				Masons		5.	0.
				Plumbers		5.	0.
				Fletchers		1.	8. L
				Plasterers		1.	4. L

Note
L = assessment on valuation of annual income from lands.
1. This is the sum of separate assessments on the livery (£9.0.4) and on the bachelors (£4.3.4).

Table III. *Percentage of heads of households assessed for the subsidy in 1582 in 12 parishes*

Parish	Approx. no. of households	No. of people assessed	Approx. % of heads of house- holds assessed
1. St Mary Magdalen Milk Street (the part in Cripplegate Ward)	32	29	91
2. Allhallows Honey Lane	32	26	81
3. St. Antholin Budge Row	48	34	71
4. St. Peter West Cheap	59	40	68
5. St. Olave Jewry	51	33	65
6. St. Margaret Lothbury (the part in Coleman Street Ward)	61	31	51
7. St. Mary Aldermanbury	97	49	51
8. St. Bartholomew by the Exchange	86	40	47
9. Allhallows the Great	155	67	43
10. St. Ethelburga the Virgin	63	26	41
11. St. Christopher le Stocks	67	38	57
12. Allhallows Staining	114	54	47

Note

These twelve parishes are the only ones for which there appears to be reasonably tractable evidence of the numbers of households in about 1582 and in which the number of persons assessed for the subsidy can also be determined. The approximate numbers of heads of households are drawn from the following parochial records (all G.L. MSS): 1., MS 2596/1, f. 180, assessment for a fifteenth, 1585; 2., MS 5022, f. 123, assessment for a fifteenth, 1581; 3., MS 1046/1, f. 15, assessment for parish clerk's wages, 1581–2; 4., MS 645/1, ff. 111v–112, collection list for parish clerk's wages, 1583; 5., MS 4415/1, f. 9v, assessment for a fifteenth, 1582; 6., MS 4352/1, ff. 53–4, assessment for a fifteenth, 1585; 7., MS 2500A/1, 'The booke of the Parson and Clerkes wages de Anno domini 1577. . .', erroneously catalogued as St. Michael Bassishaw; 8., MS 4384/1, assessment for a fifteenth, 1582; 9., MS 819/1, pp. 405–10, assessment for clerk's wages, 1586; 10., MS 4241/1, pp. 67–8, collection list for clerk's wages, 1581–2; 11., MS 4423/1, f.14, collection list for clerk's wages, 1581–2; 12., MS 4958/2, ff. 40–2, assessment for clerk's wages, 1582–3;

The number of heads of households in column 1, which includes those dwelling in rents and chambers, is only an approximation. Some of the properties in most if not all parishes were shops, cellars, stables, or warehouses occupied separately from dwellings. In three of the parish lists cited above, such non-residential property is clearly distinguished: in Allhallows Honey Lane it accounted for about 8.5% of the total number of assessments for the fifteenth, in St. Olave Jewry for about 12% of assessments, and in St. Bartholomew by the Exchange for about 8.5%. In the remaining nine parishes, all people the nature of whose property is uncertain have been counted as occupiers of dwellings and heads of households; the figures in column 1 for those nine parishes may therefore be slightly exaggerated. Where one person was charged for two or more houses in one parish, it has been assumed that each of those houses was occupied by a separate household, and counted accordingly.

Inhabitants of the last two parishes listed, St. Christopher le Stocks and Allhallows Staining, were assessed for the subsidy along with people from other parishes or part parishes, so it is not possible to arrive at an exact total for either parish. The figures in column 2 in these cases represent those persons who were listed in the parochial assessment and also, by the same name, assessed for the subsidy. Fortunately the parochial assessments in these two parishes were made within months of the subsidy assessment. In the other ten parishes, no attempt has been made to match names from one assessment to another: the figures in column 2 are simple totals. There was evidently a rapid turnover of householders: in St. Bartholomew by the Exchange, 86 persons were assessed for clerk's wages in July 1579, but only 65 (76%) of them appeared on the next clerk's wages roll in February 1581, 19 months later. The 21 individuals who had disappeared had been replaced by 22 new names (G.L. MS 4384/1, pp. 47–9, 60).

Table IV. *Valuations of English in goods in all extant subsidy certificates 1536–1582 for the wards of Bassishaw, Coleman Street, and Cornhill*

Number assessed at:	1536[1]	1541[2]	1544[3]	1547[4]	1549[5]	1564[6]	1577[7]	1582[8]
£500 and above	0	13	10	4	4	1	0	0
£200 and above	8	27	22	16	13	14	6	3
£100 and above	18	44	40	43	39	25	18	19
£50 and above	33	64	58	54	82	55	65	61
£20 and above	129	168	140	(92)[9]	112	82	75	82
£10 and above			189	(155)	171	135	122	132
£4 and above			267	(223)		195	201	221
£3 and above			298			255	273	312
£2 and above			372					
£1 and above			473					

Notes
1. P.R.O. E.179/144/100; E.179/144/102; E.179/144/107.
2. E.179/144/120.
3. E.179/144/123.
4. E.179/145/138; E.179/145/151.
5. E.179/145/174.
6. E.179/145/218; E.179/145/219.
7. E.179/145/252.
8. E.179/251/16.
9. The valuations of eight inhabitants of Cornhill Ward, probably all of them at less than £50, are lost through damage to the document. The figures in brackets are based on the surviving entries.

Table V. *Changes in the valuations of estates of people assessed in 1541
and 1544 and valued at £1000 or more in one or both years.*

	1541[1]			1544[2]		
	£	s.	d.	£	s.	d.
Allen, Ralph	1333	6.	8.	3333	6.	8.
Altham, Edward	1600			1600		
Barfort, Robert	1000			800		
Barnes, George	1500			1200		
Barons, Bartholomew	1333	6.	8.	1400		
Blanke, Thomas	1000			900		
Bonvyce, Anthony	1333	6.	8.	1333	6.	8.
Bowes, Martin	3333	6.	8.	2000		
Bowyer, Thomas	1000			666	13.	4.
Bridges, Giles	1000			800		
Brown, John	1000			900		
Bucklond, Richard	1333	6.	8.	1200		
Burlace, Edward	1000			700		
Butler, William	2000			1600		
Callard, Richard	2000			1500		
Calton, Thomas	1000			800		
Campane, Bartholomew	1000			666	13.	4.
Chersey, Robert	1000			1333	6.	8.
Cholmley, Sir Roger	1000			666	13.	4.
Chybborne, Christopher	1000			666	13.	4.
Clerke, John	1000			900		
Cottes, John	1333	6.	8.	1200		
Dawbeney, Robert	1000			500		
Dobbes, Richard	2000			1800		
Dormer, Michael	2666	13.	4.	2333	6.	8.
Forman, Sir William	1333	6.	8.	1000		
Franke, John	1000			900		
Gresham, Sir John	5000			3333	6.	8.
Gresham, Sir Richard	2666	13.	4.	1333	6.	8.
Gresham, William	1000			800		
Hamcotes, Henry	1333	6.	8.	1200		
Hill, Rowland	3333	6.	8.	3000		
Hoberthorne, Henry	2000			1500		
Holte, Richard	1000			1000		
Huntlowe, Thomas	1333	6.	8.	1333	6.	8.
Hynd, Austen	2000			1700		
Jenyns, Barnard	1333	6.	8.	1333	6.	8.
Jervys, Richard	3000			3000		
Lathom, Ralph	1000			1000		
Laxton, William	1333	6.	8.	1333	6.	8.
Locke, William	1600			1200		
Malte, John	1333	6.	8.	1000		
May [Mery], William	1333	6.	8.	1000		
Osborne, Richard	1333	6.	8.	1333	6.	8.
Palmer, Robert	2000			2000		
Pargetter, Anne Lady	2000			1700		
Pynchester, Roger	1000			700		
Randell, Vincent	1000			700		

Rede, Richard	1333	6.	8.	1200		
Richmond, John	800			1000		
Roche, Sir William	1333	6.	8.	1333	6.	8.
Sadler, John	1333	6.	8.	1200		
Soutt, John	1333	6.	8.	1333	6.	8.
Spakeman, Nicholas	1000			666	13.	4.
Spencer, Sir James	2000			1200		
Spynnell, Paintellyn	1000			800		
Statham, Elizabeth	2000			2000		
Sukley, Henry	1333	6.	8.	1333	6.	8.
Symondes, Mistress, widow	2666	13.	4.	1200		
Tolowes, John	2000			1400		
Trappes, Robert	3333	6.	8.	2666	13.	4.
Waren, Sir Ralph	4000			2666	13.	4.
Wethypole, Paul	1333	6.	8.	1200		
Whyte, Thomas	2000			2000		
Wolf, Morgan	1000			666	13.	4.
	104,833	6.	8.	88,066	13.	4.

Number of valuations raised: 4
Number lowered: 46
Number unchanged: 15
Overall drop in total valuation, 1541–1544: 16%

Notes

1. There was a total of 89 valuations of £1000 and above in 1541. In addition to the 64 listed above, five people were assessed at £1000 and above in 1541 in Lime Street Ward and seven in Tower Ward. They may also have been assessed in 1544, but the 1544 certificate for Lime Street is missing and that for Tower is incomplete. These were: (Lime Street) William Boyer (£2666 13. 4.), William Browne (£2500), Stephen Kyrvin (£1000), Andrew Judd (£2666 13. 4.), Dennys Lewson, widow (£1000); (Tower) Sir John Alen (£3000), Sir John Champnes (£1333 6. 8.), Sir William Denham (£2000), William Gunston (£1000), John Pope (£1000), William Robyns (£1000), Ambrose Wolley (£1333 6. 8.).

The following people were also valued at £1000 and above in London in 1541: William Daunse (£3000), Sir William Holles (£4000), Lady Margaret Kytson (£1333 6. 8.), Sir George Monnox (£1000), Robert Paget (£1333 6. 8.), Richard Reynold (£1333 6. 8.), George Robynson (£1000), Ralph Rowlett (£3000), Thomas Ryshton (£1000), John Talkerne (£1000), Sir Bryan Tuke (£2000), William Wilkynson (£1333 6. 8.), and John Wylford (£1333 6. 8.). Most of these died before the 1544 assessment, but some may actually have been assessed in 1544 and their names overlooked.

2. From P.R.O. E.179/144/123. The individual certificates for Tower and Lime Street Wards are damaged or missing, as noted above. Apart from these, there was a total of 50 valuations of £1000 and above in 1544.

In addition to the 46 listed above, four estates were valued at £1000 or above, none of which had been listed under the same name in 1541. These were: the widow of William Adyngton (£1333 6. 8.), the executors of William Daunse (£2000), Sir Richard Longe, who married Lady Kytson (£1333 6. 8.), and Lady Holles, widow of Sir William Holles (£1900).

Table VI. *Variations in the valuations of London residents assessed in more than one place in 1541.*

Place of second assessment	London	A Royal household	A Royal household	A Royal household	Country	Country	Country	Total
Place of payment	London	A Royal household	London	London and Royal household	London	London	London and country	
No. of cases	30	65	4	7	22	34	9	171
Identical valuation (1:1)	10	20	0	0	7	6	0	43
Ratio of higher to lower valuation:								
1.001–1.09:1	1	19	0	0	5	1	0	26
1.1–1.19:1	0	2	0	1	0	1	2	6
1.2–1.29:1	3	1	0	2	1	4	2	13
1.3–1.39:1	2	4	0	1	2	4	0	13
1.4–1.49:1	0	2	0	0	1	1	0	4
1.5–1.99:1	10	7	3	1	4	6	2	33
2.0–2.99:1	3	7	0	2	1	4	1	18
3.0–3.99:1	1	1	1	0	1	2	2	8
4.0–4.99:1	0	1	0	0	0	2	0	3
5.0–5.99:1	0	1	0	0	0	1	0	2
6.0–6.99:1	0	0	0	0	0	1	0	1
7.0–7.99:1	0	0	0	0	0	1	0	1

Source

THE 1541 SUBSIDY ROLL FOR LONDON
E.179/144/120

1. [r.7]   ALLDRYCHEGATE WARDE

Thys Indenture made the xxiiiith daye of Octobre the xxxiiith yere of the Raigne of our most dradde Soveraigne lorde kyng Henry the viiith by the grace of God kyng of Ingland Fraunce and Ireland defendor of the fayth and of the Churche of Ingland and also of Ireland in erthe Supreme hedde, Bytwene the Right honourable Thomas Archebysshop of Canterbury, Thomas Audeley lorde Audeley of Wallden and Chauncelor of Ingland, Edward Erle of Hertford, Edmund bysshop of London, Thomas bysshop of Westminster, Androwe lorde Wyndesor, William lorde Seint John, Wyllyam Roche knyght Mayor of the Citie of London, Raulf Sadler knyght, Richard Ryche knyght Chauncelor of the Augmentacion of the Revenues of the kynges highnes Crowne, Thomas Pope knyght, Roger Chamley knyght serjaunt at Lawe, Richard Pollard knyght, Edward Northe knyght and William Horwodde esquier the kynges Attorney generall Commyssioners deputeid by our sayd Soveraigne lorde for the execucion of the Secounde payment of the Subsydy grauntyd unto our sayd Soveraigne lorde in his graceis highe Court of parlyament holden at Westminster in the xxxii yere of his graceis Raigne within the Citie of London on the one partie, And Roger Taylor of the paryshe of Seint Butulphes goldsmyth, And John Maye of the paryshe of Seint Anne letherseller whom the sayd Commyssyoners have deputeid and nameid and by thes presentes do depute and name petycollectors for the same Secounde payment of the sayd Subsydy of the warde of Allderichegate within the sayd Citie of London on the other partye, Wytnessith that the same Roger Taylor and John Maye soo deputeyd and nameid petycollectors for the sayd warde of Allderichegate and Auctorysyd by thes presentes therunto shall Receave unto the kinges highnes use all suche Somes of money as in this extrete ben contayneid and specyfied as hereafter folowyth

		£	s.	d.
2.	SEYNT LEONARD PARYSHE			
	Englyshemen			
Wylliam Elder (£30)			15	
Raphaell Cornyshe (£20)			10	
William Cheven (£40)			20	
Robert Large (£20)			10	
Nicholas Trappes (£100)			50	
Robert Trappes (5000 marks)		83	6	8
	[Aliens]			
Garret Copleman (£20)			20	

1

	£	s.	d
John Pystow (20 marks)		13	4
Gregory Carpinter (20s.)			12
Reke Johnson and Ames Savery his servauntes			8
Maryan Obedd			4
John Horsekeper with Mr Trappes			4
William Orton servaunt with Mighell Thombe			4
Nicholas Dowyk and Isak Bevis servauntes			
with Alen Clerke			8
Summa	90	8	4

3.   SEYNT JOHN ZACHARIES PARYSHE
Englishemen

	£	s.	d
Edmund Lee (£20)		10	
Richard Kynwallmerse (£20)		10	
Henry Forest (£20)		10	
Elys Dyall (£20)		10	
Mastres Stapper (£20)		10	
Roger Younge (£20)		10	
Nicholas Wodcok (£20)		10	
Mistress Elyzabeth Onely wydow (£600)	15		
Alyens			
Domynyk van Ryne (100s.)		5	
John Ofmaster his servaunt			4
Lucas Vering & Fraunceis Vanhed servauntes			
with Hikman			8
Bonadventure Whitman			4
Summa	18	16	4

4.   SEYNT ANNES PERRYSHE
Englyshemen

	£	s.	d
John Maye (£200)		100	
Raulf Caldwall (£80)		40	
William Tylley (£50)		25	
William Morgan (£30)		15	
Thomas Jenettes (£20)		10	
John Morres (£20)		10	
Thomas Went (£40)		20	
John Skynner (£30) [x- Mddx. 15s.]		15	
William Blitheman (£20) [x- Castle Baynard ward			
15s. as 'Blyghman']		10	
William Taylor (£20)		10	
Henry Sutton (£20)		10	
Thomas Edgar (1000 marks)	16	13	4
Alyens			
Peter Boder (20s.)		12	
David Fylde bookebynder, Richard Lambe,			
Jamys Spycer, and Hans within			
John Benson		16	

	£	s.	d
John Westfeling (40s.)		2	
John Johnson his servaunt (20s.)			12
Summa	30	3	8

SEYNT MARY STAYNEING PARYSHE
Englishemen

	£	s.	d
Hughe Egerton (£20)		10	
Thomas Hawes (£100)		50	
William Myrfyn (100 marks)		33	4
Mistress Stafferton (£40)		20	
Mistress Pullet (£20)		10	
Henry Elyet (£20)		10	

Alien

	£	s.	d
Jamys Randy servaunt with Bernerd Langton (20s.)			12
Summa	6	14	4

5. SEYNT BOTULPHES PERRYSHE
[English]

	£	s.	d
Phylypp Lentall in landes and fees (£100) [x - Essex 106s.4d.]		100	
Nicholas Talbot in landes (£40)		40	
John Mynne (£300)	7	10	
Peter Swyft (£60)		30	
Edward Gostwyk in fees & landes (£90) [ass. 50s. in Beds.]	4	10	
William Purdue (100 marks) [ass. 13s.4d. in Herts. as 'Purdy']		33	4
John Wylloughby (£100) [x - K 50s.]		50	
Alyxaunder Chapman (£40)		20	
[Blank] Pyerson (£20)		10	
[Blank] Penyngton (£200)[1]		100	
John Butler in landes & fees (£80) [x - Northants. £4]	4		
Hughe Fuller in landes & fees (£120) [x - Essex £2; owes £4 in Aldersgate]	6		
Thomas Haselop (£20)		10	
Peter Smyth (£20)		10	
William Garter (£20)		10	
John Wotton (£30)		15	
Fulke Pygot (£20)		10	
John Melsham (£60)		30	
[Blank] Kettyll (£40)		20	
John Underhill (£20)		10	
Andrew Bullok (£60)		30	
Roger Taylor (200 marks)		66	8

1. E.359/44, r. 16 gives name as John Pennington.

3

	£	s.	d
William Sewerd (£30)		15	
John Hunt (£20)		10	
Robert Stanfild (£40)		20	
John Lawrence (£30)		15	
Robert Wenham (£20)		10	
Richard Forde (£40)		20	
Richard Eton (£20)		10	
Robert Burton (£20)		10	
Robert Byrkham (£30) [ass. 10s. in			
Cripplegate ward]		15	
John Sylvester (£20)		10	
Mistress Elyzabeth Bewers (£20)		10	
William Munday (100 marks) [ass. 10s. in			
Cripplegate ward]		33	4
Rychard Warren gent in landes (£30)		30	
William Standyshe (£30)		15	
Sir Marmaduke Constable knight in			
landes (£200) [x - Warwickshire £10]	10		
Doctor Peter (£400) [ass. £6 13s.4d.			
in K and £7 in Essex]	10		
William Candyshe (1000 marks) [ass. 100s.			
in Herts.][2]	16	13	4
Thomas Twesell (£600) [x - Q £15)	15		
Sir John Daunsy knight (£800)	20		

6.   Alyens

	£	s.	d
Jasper Brand with William Smert			4
John Stephins ryngmaker (20s.)			12
John Egborne bocher, Henry Nicholas			
shoomaker, John Lacy shoomaker,			
Stephin de Fowe, John de Prye			
& Wyllyam Frysket		2	
John Genyns alias Usheer (20s.)			12
Garret Shomaker and Lambert Waterson			8
Thomas Johnson (£40)		40	
John Clayse			4
Godfray Garland (100s.)		5	
John Florence, Wynkyn the Delf, John			
Johnson with Richard Suthwell			12
John Harford (40s.)		2	
Antony Ayshe (£4)		4	
Garet Baches and Barthillmew Smyth			
servauntes with the said Antony			8
Crystyan Kerver and Roger Weston			8
Summa huius perrochie	137	10	4

2. E.359/44, r. 17 gives name as William Cavendishe.

	£	s.	d
7. PRECYNCT OF SEINT MARTENE LE GRAUNDE BEING IN DYVERSE PARYSHEIS Englyshemen			
Thomas Dowy (£20)		10	
Hughe Payne (£80)		40	
William Sutton (£20)		10	
Emme Tyseman wydow (£100)		50	
John Petit (£20)		10	
Peter Peterson denyzen (£300)	15		
Alyens			
Fraunceys Woddlak (100 marks)		66	8
Nicholas Gelkyn & John Hankyn, his servauntes, John Garrardson and Henry Herman servauntes with Peter Peterson			16
Garrat Williamson (£60		60	
James Baleman & John Baleman his servauntes			8
Albert Peterson (20s.)			12
Henry Ducheman his servaunt			4
Garret Crulle (20s.)			12
Bernarde Vanlangley his servaunt			4
John van Roy (20s.)			12
William Guylham (20s.)			12
John Smyth (20s.)			12
George a Calen (£20)		20	
Herman Coke and John Gally his servauntes			8
Egbert Mason (£10)		10	
Derik Wert and Segar Egbertson his servauntes			8
George Heys (£60)		60	
Selis Ducheman and Richard Gowith his servauntes			8
Nicholas Dewys wydow (20s.)			12
Elen Younge wydow (20s.)			12
Guylham Master (20s.)			12
Augustyne Fagot & John Graundlemare his servauntes			8
Denmarke Frencheman (20s.)			12
Edmund Guylham his servaunt			4
Arnold Willinson (20s.)			12
John Derik (20s.)			12
Cope Helmer (20s.)			12
Peter Grayne his servaunt			4
John Fulmer (20s.)			12
John Smyth and John Mitto			8
Peter Port (40s.)		2	
Rowland Graunt & John Tybo his servauntes			8

5

	£	s.	d
Lenard Peterson (£200)	10		
Symond Nicholles & John Polles			
his servauntes			8
Deryk Hoole servaunt with Elen Younge			4
John Bargayne, Henry Ducheman and			
Richard van Roy servauntes with			
John Grenekyn			12
8. Crepyn Desyrey (100s.)		5	
John Desyrey his servaunt (20s.)			12
Guylbert [Blank] (20s.)			12
Glawlde Toby his servaunt			4
Josyn la Roy (40s.)		2	
Robert Herall his servaunt			4
Antony Tatteletta (40s.)		2	
Peter Tettaletta and Antony de Hamys			
his servauntes			8
William Merschan (20s.)			12
John Hewe			4
Albert Kerst & Lambert Eldrom			8
Nicholas Roy (40s.)		2	
Selven Ewas, Thomas Wight & John Hun			
his servauntes			12
Rumbold Rost (20s.)			12
Henry Wese (£120)	6		
Walter Johnson, Rubell Paylle,			
Deryk Buse & Jamys Watt			
his servauntes			16
Jamys Cremer (£20)		20	
Gosen Antony, Fraunceis Herryson			
& Herman Herryson his servauntes			12
Henry Williamson (£80)	4		
Deryk Fawke and Fraunceis Tylor			
his servauntes			8
Garrett Sclutter £50)		50	
William Clutt and Jakes Ducheman			
his servauntes			8
Henry Garretson (100s.)		5	
Garret Holt & Herman Johnson			
his servaunt			8
Henry [Blank] (40s.)		2	
Garret Brain (20s.)			12
Deryk Ducheman his servaunt			4
Herman Cremer (£4)		4	
John Rynche & Adam Noyle his servauntes			8
Henry Hall (£5)		5	
Leonard Hall & John Pellet			
his servauntes			8

	£	s.	d
Raulf Twyne (100s.)		5	
Edward Twyne & Antony Golencheis			
his servauntes			8
John Dowfet (£40)		40	
Glaud Teshe and Rose			
his servauntes			8
John Symond (40s.)		2	
Fraunceis Ducheman [and] Egbert Ducheman			
his servauntes			8
9. John Myler (20s.)			12
Walter Harryson his servaunt			4
John Leonard (20s.)			12
Jasper Carle (£6 13s. 4d.)		6	8
Denys de Hayes (40s.)		2	
Thomas de Fekmen & Guylham			
Fraunceis his servauntes			8
Arnolde Marcelles (£40)		40	
Nicholas Stokkton & Adryan Johnson			
his servauntes			8
Cornelis Hubert (20s.)			12
Henry Cutton his servaunt			4
Andrew Gaynes (20s.)			12
Lodowyk Stratcher his servaunt, Henry			
Johnson, Tyse Petson, John Albertson			16
Pylgrym Arnold (40s.)		2	
John A. Colen (40s.)		2	
Garret his servaunt			4
Jamys Cole (20s.)			12
Adryan Harryson & Arnold Stekton			
his servauntes			8
Antony Johnson (£4)		4	
John Raynarde and Garret Cornelys			
his servaunt			8
Herman Vyolet (£40)		40	
Frederyk Williams his servaunt			4
Julyan a Poto and Garrat Johnson			
servaunt with Glawd Vycot			8
William Cowbrydge (£20)		20	
Godfray Clayes and Jamys Harryson			
his servauntes			8
John Marten shomaker (20s.)			12
Deryk Keble and Dymon Deveret			
his servauntes			8
Edward Ryssell (£10)		10	
John de Foo and Roger Gyve			
his servauntes			8
Peter Ryckes (£30)		30	

	£	s.	d
Thomas Edmundes Harman Johnson &			
Jamys Raynerdson his servauntes			12
Tyse Tyseman, John Vaneke Bartyllmew			
Johnson and John Tyseman servauntes			
with Emme Tyseman			16
Fraunceis Wodde (100s.)		5	
John Albright and Arres Johnson			
his servauntes			8
Bowen Fayth (£4)		4	
William Johnson his servaunt			4
Garret Mersey (40s.)		2	
Rowland Johnson (100s.)		5	
John de Man and Lukes Leonardes			
his servauntes			8
10. John Brystow (£100)	100		
Marten Williams and John Johnson			
his servauntes			8
Deryk Costerd (£20)	20		
Deryk Harman & Leonard Harman			
his servauntes			8
Mathew Isberd (100s.)		5	
John Lamare his servaunt			4
Stephen Garrard (£4)		4	
Adryan Hert (20s.)			12
Garret Glassy (40s.)		2	
William Peterson & William Garrettes			
his servauntes			8
John Kenter (40s.)		2	
Fraunceis de Garden his servaunt			4
Peter Vyne (20s.)			12
Robert Haylis and John Davylon			
his servauntes			8
Mighell Story (20s.)			12
Jamys Quaplet his servaunt			4
Mighell Geryn (20s.)			12
Nicholas Clary (20s.)			12
Austyn Lawrence his servaunt			4
Peter Cremer (20s.)			12
John Bewry (20s.)			12
Peter de Hew his servaunt			4
John de Rone (40s.)		2	
William Graunt & William Seintgyle			
his servauntes			8
Henry van Oke (20s.)			12
William Vangule his servaunt			4
Peter Govert (£60)	60		
Dennys Pervoy & Gyles Wyttow his servauntes			8

	£	s.	d
John Medy and Vyncent Frenche			
servauntes with Thomas Dewy			8
Jamys Household (20s.)			12
Antony van Campton his servaunt			4
Guylham Pollyn (60s.)		3	
Lewys Cary & Bartyllmew Morgan			
his servauntes			8
John Breme & Garret van Ryne			8
John Marten letherdyer (100s.)		5	
Rowland Belmer his servaunt			4
Symon Overt (£10)		10	
Stephen Baske and Nicholas de Potes			
his servauntes			8

11.　　　　CORPORACIONS HALLES AND FELOWSHIPPES

	£	s.	d
Goldsmythes hall in Landes by			
the yere (£304 12s. 3d.)	15	4	8
Cokes hall (£20)		20	
Brothered of the Trynytie in Seint			
Botulphes paryshe (£20)		20	
Summa	99	8	
Totalis huius ward			
pro parte dominus			
Regis	383		12

All whiche Somes of money so by them Receaveid they shall Content and paye to Thomas Edgar, Guydo Crayford esquyers, John Wyseman gent, John Sturgyon Iremounger, John Scut merchaunt Taylor, Hughe Egleby gent, Thomas Broke merchaunt Taylor, and William Wodlyf mercer, highe Collectors of the same at suche dayes and placeis as the sayd highe Collectors shall appointe unto them Retayneing and Reserveing in ther handes of the sayd Somes by them soo Receaveid fower pence for every pounde, Whereof Twoo pence they shall have for ther labors, and the other Twoo pence they shall paye to the Commyssyoners of the same Accordeing to the Teanor purport and effect of the sayd Act of Subsydy, In witnes whereof to the one parte of thes Indentures Remayneing with the said petycollectors the sayd Commyssyoners have putt ther Seales, And to the other parte of the same Indentures Remayneing with the sayd Commyssyoners the sayd petycollectors have Sette ther Seales the daye and yere fyrst above writen.

	£	s.	d

12. [r.4] ALGATE WARDE
[Petty collectors: Thomas Offle and William Inggram.]

THE PARISSHE OF SAINT KATHERYN CHRISTCHURCHE
[English]

	£	s.	d
Thomas Farlakenden gentilman (£400)			
[ass. £6 in Kent][3]		10	
Richard Duke (£300) [x - Farringdon ward			
Without £10]	7	10	
William Peryns (£50)		25	
William Whytton (£30)		15	
William Damerall (£60)		30	
John Jackeson (£40)		20	
John Gryffyn (£40) [x - K 22s. as 'Gryffyth']		20	
Mastres Dynne (£20)		10	
John Butssey (£30)		15	
Richard Rogers (£20)		10	
Thomas Gonne (£30)		15	
Richard Roodyng (£20)		10	
Thomas Spencer (£20)		10	
John Lake (£20)		10	
William Monckas (£30)		15	
William Davye (£20)		10	
Robert Woodde (£20)		10	
Hugh Appowell [blank]		[blank]	
John Morres (£50)		25	
William Yngeram (£60)		30	
Robert Smyth (£20)		10	
[Blank] Somer (£20)		10	
[Blank] Semar esquyer (£100)		50	
John Ellys (£20)		10	
John Torner (£30)		15	
Nicholas Taverner (£40)		20	
Edwarde Cornewallys [blank]		[blank]	
Thomas Maynard (100 marks)			
[ass. 33s.4d. in Kent]		33	4
Sir John Raynefford in landes (£200)			
[x - Process]	10		
John Wisdom (£20)		10	
Robert Waight (£20)		10	
Robert Todde (£20)		10	
[Blank] Philpot (£20)		10	
John Abbes (£30)		15	

3. E.359/44, r. 10 gives surname as Harlakynden.

		£	s.	d
13.	Straungers within the same parisshe of Saint Kateryn			
Gallion Sopper (40s.)			2	
Andryan Garet servient (4d.)				4
Garard Marten servient (4d.)				4
Mr Doctor Broddowe (£20)			20	
Manewell Farnand servient (4d.)				4
Maryon Nonnes servient (4d.)				4
John Slenes servient to Spencer (4d.)				4
James Johnson (40s.)			2	
Cornelys Royson servient (4d.)				4
William Formarke servient (4d.)				4
William Ravener servient to Sharpe (4d.)				4
Cornelis Joyse (4d.)				4
Doctor Nicholas (£50)			50	
Nicholas Barbor servient (4d.)				4
Peter Cobler alias Andrianson (40s.)			2	
Millis Revelson servient (4d.)				4
Nicholas Cole (40s.)			2	
Peter Evers servient (4d.)				4
Mighell de Reste (200 marks)		6	13	4
Philip Check servient (4d.)				4
Coppen servient (4d.)				4
Mr. Androwe (£30)			30	
Mr. Gabriell (£30)			30	
James Dalte (40s.)			2	
John Crikwell serviens Philpot (20s.)				12
Thomas Hackett (4d.)				4
Fraunces Garret (4d.)				4
Jaques Labonore (£20)			20	
John Edwardes (40s.)			2	
Peter Apreste (4d.)				4
Peter Ansam (4d.)				4
John Angell (4d.)				4
Ellancke widow (4d.)				4
	Summa	66	16	4

		£	s.	d
14.	THE PARISSHE OF SAINT ANDREWE UNDERSHAFTE [English]			
John Chamberlen (£20)			10	
Thomas Dayle (£60)			30	
Richard Pynckard (£20)			10	
Thomas Gedney (£60)			30	
Robert Allyn (£40)			20	
Nicholas Pecke (£40)			20	
John Bullok (£40)			20	
Symon Burton (£20)			10	
Thomas Edon (200 marks) [x - Suff. 70s.]			66	8

	£	s.	d
John Royston (£50)		25	
William Wilson (£20)		10	
John Strete (£20)		10	
[Edward] Brisselley serviens dominus Regis (£100) [x - K 50s.][4]		50	
Sir William Pikeryng in landes (£100)	5		
Thomas Lyce (100 marks)		33	4
Straungers			
Barnardyne Buttessey (£30)		30	
Hauns Holbene in fee (£30)	3		
Gillam de Forde (£10) [x - AC 13s.4d.]		10	
Elizabeth serviens (4d.)			4
Bastian Founder (£20)		20	
Mr Bocher gent [Blank]	[Blank]		
Summa	28	5	4

15. THE PARISSHE OF SAINT KATHERYN COLMANS
[English]

	£	s.	d
Robert Byrde (£20)		10	
John Goose (£20)		10	
John Reppingall (£20)		10	
John Griffith (£20)		10	
John Boshe (£40)		20	
Geffrey Tulle (£20)		10	
Robert Yugleger (£20)		10	
Cristofer Eliott (£20)		10	
William Broughe (£40)		20	
Richard Tilton (£30)		15	
Henry Webbe gent (£100) [x - Q 70s.]		50	
John Edwardes [Blank]	[Blank]		
Straungers			
John Marliart serviens J Boshe (£3)	3		
Nicholas Rossell serviens eiusdem (£3)	3		
Roger Williamson (20s.)			12
Nicholas Jonson (20s.)			12
Henry Skarat (20s.)			12
Oliver Rampas (£10)		10	
John Joson servient (4d.)			4
William Palmer (20s.)			12
John Collins (£10)		10	
Godfrey Lawbori (£5)		5	
Richard Johnson serviens (4d.)			4
John de Broke (20s.)			12
Robynet Grushe serviens (4d.)			4
Piers Santere serviens (4d.)			4
Robynet Cornew (£10)		10	
Summa	11	2	4

4. E.359/44, r. 19 gives Edward as first name.

	£	s.	d
16. Straungers			
Garrett Lessot serviens (4d.)			4
Bartilmew Bell (£10)		10	
Walter Johnson serviens (20s.)			12
Arthur Gynes serviens (4d.)			4
John de la Mara (40s.)		2	
Michell Thomas serviens (4d.)			4
John Pynckard (£5)		5	
Peter Danyell serviens (4d.)			4
Charles Pyot serviens (4d.)			4

THE PARISSHE OF SAYNT OLAVE
[English]

George Sutton gent in landes (£50)			
[x - Mddx 40s.;			
10s. Aldgate]		50	
John Hyde (£50)		25	
William Latheham gent in landes (£20)			
[x - Essex 35s.]		20	
Robert Dartenoll (£40)		20	
Thomas Denton gent (£40)		20	
Margaret Coltman widow (£20)		10	
Mr Doctor Morres (£40)		20	
Thomas Brampston gent (£50) [x - Q £4, as			
Barnardeston]		25	
Sir Thomas Wyat knight in landes (£400)[5]	20		
Sybell Marten widow (£40)		20	
Robert Forde (£20)		10	
Thomas Persevall (£20)		10	
Robert Grace (£20)		10	
Richard Borden (£20)		10	
Peter Lokwood (£20)		10	
John Symondes ynglysshe (£20)			
[x - Q 10s.]		10	
The Iremongers hall in landes			
(£21 14s. 10d.)		21	8

17. Straungers there			
Peter John (£60) [x - K 84s. 2d. as			
Petye John]		60	
Peter Roshet serviens (4d.)			4
Marten serviens (4d.)			4
Margaret serviens (4d.)			4
Johan Pretrell maid servaunt (4d.)			4
Nicholas Pevall (£10) [x - K £3			
as Puvall]		10	

5. This entry is crossed out.

	£	s.	d
Marion serviens (4d.)			4
Philip Weldon gent (£50) [x - K £11 4s. 5d.]	50		
Bastian Rigo (£5)		5	
Mark Anthony in fee (£30) [x - K 51s. 8d.]		60	
Katheryn serviens (4d.)			4
Cornelis Johnson (20s.)			12
Harman Lowkyn (40s.)		2	
Reynold serviens (4d.)			4
Bartilmew Knife (4d.)			4
James Trevison (20s.)			12
Giles serviens Richard Estwood (4d.)			4
Nicholas Garard (4d.)			4
Henry Rutte (£20)		20	
Mr Leonard Dulce (£20)		20	
Peter Brushe serviens (4d.)			4
Marcus Senys (20s.)			12
John serviens (4d.)			4
Pole Behendelen (4d.)			4
Gilbert John serviens (4d.)			4
Giles Mace (£30)		30	
Byrde Carman serviens (4d.)			4
John Gelder serviens (4d.)			4
John Paine (4d.)			4
John Lambert serviens (4d.)			4
Stephyn Grace serviens (4d.)			4
Henry servient (4d.)			4
18. Arnolde Fesaunt (£30)		30	
William A Nowry serviens (4d.)			4
Godfrey Leonard serviens (4d.)			4
Water Johnson serviens			
Richard Garlond (4d.)			4
John serviens eiusdem (4d.)			4
Henry Kacke (40s.)		2	
Swere Pawlen serviens (4d.)			4
Peter serviens (4d.)			4
John Lewkors serviens Mr Barras (4d.)			4
Galiard serviens eiusdem (4d.)			4
Miles Johnson (£30)		30	
Long John (£30)		30	
William Marrowe (40s.)		2	
Nicholas Pinsson (£30)		30	
Peter Mangiard serviens (4d.)			4
John Gilbersson serviens (4d.)			4
Gennynges Hollaund widowe (20s.)			12
Riall serviens (4d.)			4
Fursser serviens (4d.)			4
Michell Lovell (40s.)		2	

14

	£	s.	d
Peter Rome serviens (4d.)			4
Collet Peterlei serviens (4d.)			4
James Gromekin (40s.)		2	
John Grove serviens (4d.)			4
Stephyn Howsbroke now at Barwik in fee (£80)	8		
William Dosheant serviens J. Walman yng-[lish?] (4d.)			4
Giles Close (4d.)			4
John Valmon (20s.)		12	
Henry Trayton serviens Long John (4d.)			4
Henry Pilcher serviens Myles Johnson (4d.)			4
Gennynges Camincle in fee [Blank]	[Blank]		
Summa	43	14	4

19. THE HOUSEHOLDE OF THE LORDE CHAUNCELLOUR
OF ENGLANDE

	£	s.	d
John Eyre in landes by the yere (£20)		20	
Robert Veer in land by the yere (£30)		30	
Richard Cupper in landes by yere (£40)		40	
Roger Horne in landes by yere (£100) [x - Cripplegate ward £6 13d. 4d.]	5		
John Fletewood in landes by yere (£20)		20	
Edward Baynard in landes by yere (£26 13s. 4d.) [ass. 22s. 8d. in Wilts.]		26	8
George Norton in landes by yere (£20)		20	
Edmond Marten (£20)		10	
William Smyth (£200)	5		
Thomas Barbor (£100)		50	
Richard Venables (£20)		10	
Summa	21	6	8
Totalis huius ward pro parte dominus Regis	171	5	

20. [r.11] BASSYNGSHAWE WARDE
[Petty collectors: Humfray Pakington of the parish of St. Michael Bassishaw and John Coke, Clerk of the Staple.]

	£	s.	d
Nicholas Tycheborne (£40)		20	
John Forster gent (£40)		20	
Thomas Stroder (£50)		25	
Edward Grene (£20)		10	
Kynborow Pyknor wydow (£40)		20	
Alys Barlow wydow (£30)		15	
Edmund Style (£60)		30	
William Cloughe (£20)		10	

	£	s.	d
Crystofer Elys (£20)		10	
Roger Marten (£40)		20	
John Norden (£30)		15	
Phylyp Boyes (£50)		25	
William Lyncoln (£20)		10	
John Wallden (£20)		10	
Edward Guylham (£20)		10	
William Botson (£40)		20	
George Bysmor (£40)		20	
Nicholas Sheperd (£20)		10	
Alyxaunder Neveson (£20)		10	
Richard Collyns (£20)		10	
Thomas Bateman (£20)		10	
William Domer (£20)		10	
George Wysedom (£20)		10	
Giles Stroder (£20)		10	
Richard Knight (£20)			
[x - Castle Baynard ward 20s.]		10	
John Travers (£20)		10	
Elizabeth Byrche wydow (£20)		10	
John Forster brewer (£20)		10	
21. Alyn Bygmor (£20)		10	
Thomas Alee (£20)		10	
Lady Yarford (£800)	20		
Edmund Kempe (£800)	20		
Peter Storkey (£400)	10		
William Fernley (£500)	12	10	
Humfray Pakyngton (£500)	12	10	
John Coke (1000 marks)			
[ass. in Castle Baynard £16 13s. 4d.]	16	13	4
Jamys Danyell (£400)	10		
John Maynerde the last yere assessid			
in goodes in this warde and now			
dwellyth in Chepe warde (1000 marks)	16	13	4
Jamys Atwodde Alyen (60s.)		3	
Godfraye Oxe Alyen (60s.)		3	
Adryan Deux Alyen (£20)		20	
Pero le Doulx Alien (£20) [x - K 30s.]		20	
John Oriet Alien (100s.)		5	
Jaques [Blank] Alien (100s.)		5	
Johannes [Blank] Alyen (40s.)		2	
Arnold Fonsaunt, Marten King, Balms			
Skyllams, John Peterson, Garrat			
le Doulx, Fraunce le Doulx Alyens			
& servauntes		2	
Cowpers hall (£60)		60	
Guyrdelers hall (£20)		20	

	£	s.	d
Totalis huius ward pro parte dominus Regis	146	6	8

22. [r.17]   BYLLYNGES GATE WARDE
[Petty collectors: Emanuel Lucar and Humffrey Knyght.]

THE PARYSHE OF SAYNT MARY HILL
[English]

	£	s.	d
Alexander Perpoynt (£25)		12	6
Johanne Morton wedowe (£20)		10	
Thomas Clayton (£300)	7	10	
Roger Chaloner (£60)		30	
Thomas Goodneston (£60)		30	
Freman Overton (£30)		15	
John Daye cordyner (£20)		10	
Woulston Wynne (£100)		50	
John Brydde (£260)	6	10	
John Haynys (£40)		20	
Robert Wheatley (£30)		15	
Thomas Lucas (£25) [x - P 13s. 4d.]		12	6
Richard Leuesham (£30)		15	
John Hale (£25)		12	6
Henry Smythe (£30)		15	
Richard Bradforde (£40)		20	
William Brayfelde (£40)		20	
Thomas Shattesham (£30)		15	
Thomas Lorymer (£100)		50	
William Cawdwyn (£50)		25	
Robert Younge (£66 13s. 4d.)		33	4
William Broke (£60)		30	
William Patten (£30)		15	
uxor Smythe (£60)		30	
John Sampye (£30)		15	
Henry Beattes (£20)		10	
John Austen (£20)		10	
Stephyn Kenall (£20)		10	
William Kelley (£30)		15	
Thomas Mabby (£260)	6	10	
James Quycke (£50)		25	
William Stephyns (£30)		15	
William Pasmere (£40)		20	
uxor Russell (£30)		15	
Gefferey Fraunces (£30)		15	
Rice David (£20)		10	
John Potter (£40)		20	
William Oystridge (£30)		15	
Nicholas Altrope (£25)		12	6
John Thompson (£24)		12	

	£	s.	d
William Burnynghill (£300)	7	10	
Adrian Serle (£30)		15	

23.   Straungers

	£	s.	d
James Johnson servaunt with Thomas Mondye			4
Uxor Goddeffreye basketmaker (£10)		10	
Laurence de Mountffrome			4
John Hayes			4
Peter Nicholas			4
Garret Harryson (£4)		4	
Henry Walterson			4
William Williamson			4
John James with Ryse David			4
Christofer Hadder servaunt with			
William Audeley			4
Walter Lynn (20s.)			12
Peter Iper servaunt William Hasyle			4
Cornelis Harry			4
Roger Jacobson servaunt with Rise Davy			4
William Williamson lyeng with Thomas Stoner			4
John James			4
Summa	64	19	8

24.   THE PARYSHE OF SAYNT BOTULPHE
[English]

	£	s.	d
William Knyght (£40)		20	
Uxor Stodard (£25)		12	6
John Broman (£26 13s. 4d.)		13	4
Richard Horton (£40)		20	
Uxor Collynge (£200)	5		
Thomas Turnburll (£250)	6	5	
John Wennis (£20)		10	
Michell Haward (£100)		50	
Uxor Badelye (£110)		55	
John Sykyllmore (£50)		25	
William Saunderson (£50)		25	
Henry Austen (£66 13s. 4d.)		33	4
Nicholas Ruell (£60)		30	
Richard Clay (£20)		10	
John Tysowe (£66 13s. 4d.)		33	4
Edward Hall (£30)		15	
Thomas Howe (£25)		12	6
Richard William (£25)		12	6
Henry Herdson (£100) [ass. 10s. in Kent]		50	
Richard Lodge (£20)		10	
Robert Rogers (£20)		10	
Richard Maunsell (£50)		25	
Owyn Clune (£40)		20	

	£	s.	d
Richard Phillypis (£40) [x - K 33s. 4d.]		20	
John Bynkes (£120)	3		
Thomas Cooke (£120)	3		
John Tewell (£20)		10	
Humffrey Knyght (£300)	7	10	
John Snowden (£30)		15	
John Dendyshe (£20)		10	
William Fyrmyn (£20)		10	
Sir William Roche knyght (2000 marks)	33	6	8
Emanuell Lucar (£600)	15		
Straungers			
John Johnson			4
Jozephe Woharpe			4
Peter van Senlowe			4
John Besard			4
Summa	101		6

25. THE PARYSHE OF SAYNT ANDROWES
[English]

	£	s.	d
Nicholas Howe (£160)	4		
Robert Wilkyns (£30)		15	
Thomas Clerke (£30)		15	
John Harryson (£200)	5		
John Chowe (£20)		10	
Robert Draper (£100)		50	
Thomas Nykson (£20)		10	
Robert Wood (£25)		12	6
Thomas Surbutt (£25)		12	6
William Hunt (£20		10	
Laurence Bruges (£20)		10	
Thomas Blanke jun (£20)		10	
John Perkyns (£25)		12	6
John Chalderbye (£25)		12	6
John Sponer (£120)	3		
Thomas Palmer gent in fees			
(£46 13s. 4d.) [x - K 46s.8d.]		46	8

26. Straungers

	£	s.	d
Michell Crymer			4
William Smythe servant to Rowland Kendall			4
Michell Mylys (£5)		5	
Fraunces Gralyng			4
Andrewe Peter servaunt with Edward Haysley			4
John Pyteo servaunt with Henry Roff			4
Jasper Arnold (£50)		50	
Harman Williamson			4
Arnold Adrian			4
Mathewe Peterson			4

	£	s.	d
Arnold Gylis (£10)		10	
James Johnson			4
Peter Peterson			4
Cornelis Johnson (£12)		12	
Peter Damyan			4
Hubberd Peterson		▪	4
John Miller (20s.)			12
Mathewe Jacobe			4
Seger Dyrrykson (£3)		3	
John Mychillis			4
John Lyon (20s.)			12
John Dogan			4
Adrianson			4
Elis Cornelis (£25)		25	
William Norwiche (£6)		6	
Jasper Savoye (£25)		25	
Gobert Tilman (20s.)			12
Barthilmewe Johnson			4
Summa	30	11	4

27. THE PARYSHE OF SAYNT GEORGE
[English]

	£	s.	d
James Mountfford (£50)		25	
Edward Hayward (£40)		20	
John Woodman (£20)		10	
Aleyn Creswell (£20)		10	
Richard Gryffyn (£20)		10	
Robert Whytt (£20)		10	
Robert Brigges (£20)		10	
Sir William Forman knyght (2000 marks)	33	6	8
Elisabethe Gale widowe (£400)	10		
John Cherley (£400)	10		
Baptyst Morryson & his			
Compagnyons strangers (£400)	20		
Straungers			
Peter Lyon			4
John Etter servaunt with John Woodoner			4
Olyver Tophardyke			4
Elisabeth servaunt with Morysin			4
Summa	78	3	

28. SAYNT MARGARETES IN PODYING LANE
[English]

	£	s.	d
James Woodcooke (£40)		20	
Nicholas Keyser (£40)		20	
Roger Wellys (£22)		11	
Peter Curyant (£20)		10	
Henry Creade (£20)		10	

	£	s.	d
Richard Gyffordes wedowe (£400)	10		
Straungers			
Frederyke Cornelys (40s.)		2	
John Jonson			4
Summa	13	13	4

THE PARYSHE OF SAYNT MARGARET PATENS
[English]

William Lucas (£20)		10	
Henry Forthe (£20)		10	
Gilbert Lauson (£20)		10	
Edward Rewe (£20)		10	
Rauff Dyer (£20)		10	
Straungers			
Roger Polcoo with Rauff Dyer			4
John Cornelis			4
Bastyanus Bony (£10) [x - K 40s.; ass. 15s. in Langbourn ward]		10	
Robert Sweter (£6)		6	
William Parwell (£5)		5	
Adrian Cornelis (£3)		3	
Summa	3	14	6
Summa istius warde	292	2	6

29. [r.2] BISSHOPPESGATE WARDE
[Petty collectors: John Rowlesley and Robert Wylford.]

THE PARISSHE OF ALHALLOWES [Lombard Street]
[English]

	£	s.	d
Robert Wryght (800 marks)	13	6	8
Henry Fissher (£400)	10		
William Barlowe (£133 6s. 8d.)	3	6	8
John Legate (£160) [ass. 30s. in Mddx.]	4		
William Johnson (£66 13s. 4d.)		33	4
Hugh Churche (£70)		35	
Edmond Cane (£60)		30	
Thomas Pratt (£40)		20	
William Hankes (£30)		15	
Thomas Peterborowe (£25)		12	6
Laurence Underwoode (£20)		10	
Henry Bryght (£25)		12	6
Richard Staverton (£20)		10	
Henry Reade (£20)		10	
John Browne (£20)		10	
Edward Sewarde (£20)		10	
Straungers			
Aregonne Morell widowe (£8)		8	
Jacob servaunt with Wright, his wages (30s.)			18

	£	s.	d
Elizabeth servaunt with Staverton (4d.)			4
Lewys Corraunt all laren merchant (£20)		20	
Summa	42	11	6

30. THE PARISSHE OF SAYNT PETER
[English]

	£	s.	d
John Richemond (£800)		20	
John Hasilwood of the receipt (£500)			
[x - Essex £10; owes £2 10s. in			
Bishopsgate ward]	12	10	
Sir Cristofer Morris knight in landes			
& fees (£140)	7		
Adam Wyntrope (£200)	5		
John Lambe (£120)	3		
John Burwell (£80)		40	
John Taylour (£30)		15	
John Lynsey (£60)		30	
Oliver Edson (£40)		20	
Margaret Buckstone widow (£40)		20	
William Walker (£35)		17	6
Thomas Weller (£35)		17	6
William Mathew (£20)		10	
John Hethe (£30)		15	
John Uxley (£20)		10	
Richard Leycrofte (£20)		10	
John Bell (£20)		10	
John Brysley (£20)		10	
Robert Wryght the yonger (£30)		15	
Robert Grube (£30)		15	
Thomas Lawsee (£20)		10	
William Gurlye (£200) [x - K £5]	5		
William Carden paynter (£20)		10	
Straungers			
Maynerde Sipkynson (£5)		5	
Adryan Michaell in wages (20s.)			12
Thomas George in wages (20s.)			12
Summa	66	12	

31. THE PARISSHE OF SAYNT MARTYN
[English]

	£	s.	d
Edward Altham (£1600)		40	
Robert Wylford (1000 marks)	16	13	4
Henry Polstede (£700)	17	10	
Richard Davye (£66 13s. 4d.)		33	4
Thomas Twyne (£50)		25	
John Hamonde (£50)		25	
Thomas Fermor (£50)		25	
Richard Yarrowe (£25) [x - K 13s.]		12	6

22

	£	s.	d
Robert Kyrke (£20)		10	
Straunger			
Antony Brewse servaunt with Wyllys (4d.)			4
Summa	80	14	6

THE PARISSHE OF SAYNT ELLYN
[English]

	£	s.	d
Sir William Holles knight (£4000)	100		
Sir Richard Crumwell alias Williams			
in landes & fees (800 marks)	26	13	4
Straungers in the same parisshe			
Anthony Bonvyce (2000 marks)	100	marks	
Domynyk Lomlyn denyzen (£500)	25		

32.   Englisshmen

	£	s.	d
Robert Brograve (£200) [ass. 25s. in Kent]	5		
Guy Crayforde (£300)	7	10	
Alen Haute (£133 6s. 8d.) [x - Process][6]	3	6	8
William Crane (£200) [x - K £4 5s.; owes 15s.			
in Bishopsgate ward; ass. 50s. in Essex]	5		
Jamys Jaskyn (£200) [ass. 40s. in Mddx.]	5		
William Shelton in landes and fees			
(£110 6s. 8d.)	5	10	4
Edward Skipwyth in landes and fees			
(£60) [x - K £4]	3		
Edward Paynton in landes and fees (£40)		40	
Jeram Shelton (£40)		20	
Robert Wynsore (£35)		17	6
Robert Owtrede (£20)		10	
Ellys Broke (£30)		15	
Leonard Candeler (£25)		12	6
Richard Kirton (£25)		12	6
Mr [John] Parker the kinges servaunt in landes			
and fees (£20) [x - K 50s.][7]		20	
Laurence Wyllyams (£20)		10	
Straungers			
Balthazer Everyse (£200)		10	
Benedick Canyell (£30)		30	
Adryan Hambythe (£20)		20	
Laurence de Pount (£30)		30	
Steven Mavell (£5)		5	
John Wandon (40s.)		2	
John Credar servaunt (4d.)			4

6. The collectors were exonerated from accounting for the sum of 66s. 8d. assessed on Alan Haute or Hawte by virtue of judgment of the barons. All of Haute's goods had come into the hands of Sir Brian Tuke who was held responsible for payment of Haute's assessment (E.359/44, r. 19).

7. E.359/44, r. 19 gives John as first name.

	£	s.	d
Peter [Blank] servaunt (4d.)			4
Domynyk Polyster servaunt with Antony			
Bonvyce (£10)		10	
Summa	275	8	10

33. THE PARISSHE OF SAYNT ALBOROWE[8]
[English]

	£	s.	d
John Johnson (200 marks)	3	6	8
William Adde (£100)		50	
William Wever (£100)		50	
William Lewys (£50)		25	
Miles Winbusshe (£50)		25	
Robert Kichyn (£50)		25	
Thomas Pette (£50)		25	
Richard Berde (£50)		25	
Johan Tailor widow (£30)		15	
Thomas A Woode (£25)		12	6
Thomas Arnolde (£20)		10	
Roger Foberye (£20)		10	
James Draper (£20)		10	
Rowland Dent (£20)		10	
William Wethersbye (£20)		10	
William Welles (£20)		10	
Agnes Venlenson (£50)		25	
Thomas Wegone (£20)		10	
Straungers in the same parisshe of Saint Alborowe			
John Loberye (£15)		15	
Cornelis Nycolles (20s.)			12
John Cole servaunt (4d.)			4
Fraunces Stevens servaunt (4d.)			4
William Archar servaunt (4d.)			4
Nicholas Pole servaunt in wages (20s.)			12
Arnold George servaunt in wages (20s.)			12
John Nycolles servaunt with Dent (4d.)			4
Summa	21	13	6

34. THE PARISSHE OF SAINT BOTULF
[English]

	£	s.	d
Master [Edward] Vaughan in landes & fees			
(£66 13s. 4d.) [x - K £4 10s.][9]	3	6	8
John Rowseley (£100) [x - K 50s.]		50	
William Parker (£110)		55	
John Gattes (£100)		50	
William Perrye (£66 13s. 4d.)		33	4
John Hethe (£100) [x - K 50s. 6d.]		50	

8. St. Ethelburga.
9. E.359/44, r. 19 gives Edward as first name.

	£	s.	d
John Deryche (£50)		25	
Mr [John] Halles of the spittell (£100)			
[x - Mddx. 60s.][10]		50	
Robert Woode (£50)		25	
My Lady Adams (£40)		20	
Robert Hunt (£26 13s. 4d.)		13	4
Robert Stevyns (£20)		10	
Mathew Wight (£25)		12	6
John Brasier (£25)		12	6
John Stringfelde (£25)		12	6
John Browne (£20)		10	
Rauf Sympson (£20)		10	
John Howell (£20)		10	
George Dutton (£20)		10	
Margaret Lorkyn (£20)		10	
Robert Warner (£20)		10	
Thomas Scawpam (£20) [x - Surrey 24s.]		10	
James Ardyngton (£20)		10	
William Bennet (£20)		10	
William Sherborne (£20)		10	
[Blank] Etton (£20)		10	
Mastres Allen widow (£25)		12	6
[Blank] Edgrave (£20)		10	
Straungers			
Manuell [Blank] (£80)	4		
James Reynoldes (£40)		40	
John Turney servaunt in wages (50s.)	2		6
Garret Clyff servaunt in wages (20s.)			12
Peter Perche (£5)		5	
[Blank] Adam servaunt (4d.)			4
Summa	37	7	2
Totalis huius ward pro parte dominus Regis	524	7	6

35. [r.16]   BREDSTREET WARDE
[Petty collectors: Thomas Dutchefeld and Robert Coxe of the parish of St. Matthew Friday Street.]

ALHALLEU PARYSHE
[English]

	£	s.	d
William Cheball (£120)	3		
Harry Dunce (£20)		10	
Nicholas Clerke (£20)		10	
William Leye (300 marks)	5		
Richard Husbond (£50)		25	
George Dalton (£60)		30	

10. E.359/44, r. 19, gives John as first name.

	£	s.	d
William Crompton in londes (£60)	3		
William Baker (200 marks)	5	marks	
Katheryn Milles wedowe (£40)		20	
Cornelis Borne (£20)		10	
John Juxson (£30)		15	
John Burnet (£60)		30	
Anne Lady Pargetter (£2000)	50		
Richard Rede (2000 marks)	33	6	8
John Cokes (£500)	12	10	
William Tucker (£600)	15		
Robert Mellyshe (£700)	17	10	
William Harper (£600)	15		
Thomas Dytchefeld (£500)	12	10	
Lawrens Wythers (1000 marks)	16	13	4
Thomas Roo (£600)	15		
Henry Hoberthorne (£2000)	50		
The Salters Hall in londes (£68 11s. 7d.)	3	8	8½
Summa	262	15	4½

36. SAYNT JOHN THE EVANGELYST PARYSHE IN
WATLYN STRETT
[English]

	£	s.	d
John Smythe (£100) [x - Essex 102s.]		100	
John Hawes (500 marks)	8	6	8
John Fulwood (£300)	7	10	
John Yerwood (£100)		50	
Edmond Asgue (300 marks)	5		
Elisabeth Whytt (£60)		30	
Nicholas Welber (£100)		50	
William Saddocke (£100)		50	
Robert Holsome (£80)		40	
Ceceley Hall wedowe (£30)		15	
Reynold Hatfeld (£20)		10	
Andrewe Sarre (£20)		10	
Anne Lady Asgue (£800)	20		
John Asgue (£500)	12	10	
John Cannon (£600)	15		
Summa	86		20

SAYNT MATHEWE IN FRYDAY STRETT
[English]

	£	s.	d
William Coxe (100 marks)		33	4
Thomas Porter (£20)		10	
John Kyng (£40)		20	
Humffrey Beche (£80)		40	
John Robertes (£70)		35	
Gregory Nicholas (£20)		10	
Robert Coxe (£200)	5		

	£	s.	d
Thomas Lewes (£20)		10	
Rauff Marshall (£50)		25	
John Chapman (£20)		10	
Rauff Allen Alderman (£1333 6s. 8d.)	33	6	8
John Denyngton (£400)	10		
Richard Dobbes (£2000)	50		
William Mounslowe (£500)	12	10	
Summa	120	10	

37. SAYNT PETER AND MARY MAGDELYN IN CHEPPE
[English]

	£	s.	d
Symond Palmer (200 marks)	3	6	8
William Tyllysworthe (£80)		40	
Robert Browne (£50)		25	
John Gardyner (£80)		40	
Fowke Skydmer & John Ludyngton (£250)	6	5	
Clement Newes (£120)	3		
Thomas Barnes (100 marks)		33	4
Thomas Heys (300 marks)	5		
Roger Horton (£400)	10		
Thomas Trappes (500 marks)	8	6	8
John Wakley (£40)		20	
Bartholomewe Barons (2000 marks)	33	6	8
Summa	77	3	4

PARTE OF THE PARYSHE OF SAYNT AUSTEN
AT PAULLES GATE
[English]

	£	s.	d
John God thelder (£40)		20	
John God the younger (£20)		10	
Christofer Nicolson (100 marks)		33	4
Robert Warren (£60)		30	
Alexander Walker (100 marks)		33	4
Thomas Ackworthe (£60)		30	
Thomas Hilton (£50)		25	
Nicholas Martyn (£50)		25	
John Bridgys (£50)		25	
Richard Robynson (£30)		15	
Richard Gymlett (£300)	7	10	
Richard Crose (£20)		10	
Thomas Rydley (£30)		15	
Richard Hackelett (£30)		15	
Androwe Yerdeley (£30)		15	
William Crokes (£20)		10	
Jervys Hilton (£20)		10	
Thomas Armerer (£20)		10	
Richard Bucklond (2000 marks)	33	6	8
Richard Holte (£1000)	25		

	£	s.	d
John Malte (2000 marks)	33	6	8
John Soutt (2000 marks)	33	6	8
William Hewetson (£600)	15		
Summa	164		20

38. SAYNT MILDREDES PARYSHE IN BREDSTRETT
[English]

	£	s.	d
Robert Colway (£100)		50	
William Boye (£60)		30	
William Becham (£30)		15	
Thomas Langham (£40)		20	
Clement Kyllyngworth (£20)		10	
Thomas Horner (£20)		10	
Richard Wethers (£20)		10	
William Flecton (£30)		15	
Robert Sowle (£20)		10	
Harry Robertes (£20)		10	
Robert Spryngnell (£20)		10	
Richard Beddall (£20)		10	
David Gyttons (£80)		40	
William Hufswayte (£80)		40	
Mastres Symondes wedowe (4000 marks)	66	13	4
Straungers			
Henry Colman (40s.)		2	
Fetheryke of Holse			4
Antony Esterne			4
Edward Haryson			4
Wynkyn Jerves			4
Summa	80	16	8

39. SAYNT MARGARET MOYSES IN FRYDAY STREAT
[English]

	£	s.	d
Walter Myllett (300 marks)	5		
Richard Eddes (300 marks)	5		
Michael Foxe (300 marks)	5		
William Gonne (£100)		50	
Richard Walles (£100)		50	
John Hollond (£50)	3	15	
John Scotte (100 marks)		33	4
William Fletcher (100 marks)		33	4
James Gonter (£20)		10	
Humffrey Felde (£20)		10	
Henry Bushe (£40)		20	
Richard Warner (£400)	10		
The Cordners Hall (£20)		20	
Straungers			
Harry Kenrey (£6)		6	
Dirrycke Dyrryckson			4

	£	s.	d
Peter Collman botcher (40s.)		2	
Gilis Affeld his servaunt			4
Arnold Leade his servaunt			4
John Garrett, Cobler (40s.)		2	
Dyrryke Peterson			4
Summa	40	13	

40.   PARTE OF SAYNT NICHOLAS COLL ABBY
AND MARY MAGDALEN IN FYSSHYSTRETT
[English]

	£	s.	d
Margarett Honnyng (100 marks)		33	4
Mastres Wygmanpole wedowe (£20)		10	
Thomas Otwell (£30)		15	
Mastres Reynoldes wedowe (100 marks)		33	4
Mr Wodford (100 marks)		33	4
Robert Reynoldes (100 marks)		33	4
James Goldsmythe (£40)		20	
William Story (£20)		10	
John Bulloke (£20)		10	
Thomas Beston (£20)		10	
Henry Pemerton (£30)		15	
Edward Hall (£20)		10	
Thomas Williamson (£40)		20	
Robert Harry (£100)		50	
Summa	15	3	4
Summa istius warde	847	5	½

41. [r.9]   BRYDGE WARDE
[Petty collectors: Nicholas Cosen of the parish of St. Benet Gracechurch, merchant taylor, and Thomas Doughtie of the parish of St. Magnus the Martyr, fishmonger.]

PERRYSHE OF SEYNT OLAVE [Southwark]

	£	s.
William Blanck (£100)		50
John Alen (£20)		10
Water Carter (£40)		20
William Haynes (£20)		10
Henry Chamley (£60)		30
Thomas Armeston (£20)		10
John Thomas (£100)		50
Thomas Malagrave (£20)		10
Summa	9	10

42.   SEYNT MAGNUS PARISHE

	s.
Roger Wolhouse (£60)	30
Symond Loo (£60)	30
William Selyard (£40)	20
Antony Caverley (£40)	20

	£	s.	d
Nicholas Luff (£20)		10	
John Hodgekyn (100 marks)		33	4
Hamlet Brasy (£20)		10	
Henry Clokar (£20)		10	
Richard Large (100 marks)		33	4
Henry Buckfold (£20)		10	
John Griffin (£20)		10	
George Briges (£400) [x - Cornhill ward			
£12 10s.]	10		
Richard Flower (£20)		10	
Wydow Curle (£20)		10	
William Temple (100 marks)		33	4
William Uxley (100 marks)		33	4
Richard Braunche (£20)		10	
John Redman (£50)		25	
Richard Hilles (£100)		50	
Richard Huchecok (£30)		15	
John Dowse (£250)	6	5	
Thomas Anselow (600 marks)	8	6	8
William Bukstede (100 marks)		33	4
William Sherman (£20)		10	
Alyxaunder Banxe (£20)		10	
Christofer Cotes (£20)		10	
William Garad (£200)		100	
William Raynoldes (£40)		20	
William Johnson (200 marks)		66	8
Christofer Wykes (£20)		10	
John Proctar (£20)		10	
Richard Abyrford (100 marks)		33	4
William Lyners (£100)		50	
Nicholas Cosen (£200)		100	
43. John Tryse (100 marks)		33	4
Richard Lambard (£20)		10	
William Frestone (£20)		10	
Thomas Carter (£30)		15	
Christofer Bussher (£40)		20	
Thomas Clerke (£40)		20	
Richard Morgan (£20)		10	
John Cowper (£200)		100	
William Turke (£200)		100	
Wydow Bayly (£60)		30	
Thomas Taylor (£250) [ass. 20s. in Southwark]		6	5
Agnes Hamcotes (£40) [x - Southwark 30s.]		20	
George Turke (£20)		10	
Alyxaunder Bele (£20)		10	
John Cartar (£20)		10	
Thomas Goseling (£40)		20	

	£	s.	d
Nicholas Byrche (£20)		10	
Robert Lyners (100 marks)		33	4
Cutbert Prat (£20)		10	
John Lane (£500)	12	10	
Richard Turke (1000 marks)	16	13	4
John Symson (£800)	20		
Henry Brayne (1000 marks)	16	13	4
Thomas Doubty (£400)		10	
John Crouche (£400)		10	
Summa	183		20

44.   SEYNT BENET PARYSHE

	£	s.	d
John Sheperd (£40)		20	
John Sturgyon (£300)	7	10	
Henry Wheler (£20)		10	
William Stanes (£20)		10	
Raulf Clarnes (£100)		50	
Christofer Smyth (£40)		20	
John Starkay (£20)		10	
William Fysher (£20)		10	
Margaret Cony (£20)		10	
Paterik Cornyshe (£60)		30	
Richard Ivet (£20)		10	
John Wylsher (£20)		10	
Richard Fylde (£250)	6	5	
William Bele (£200)		100	
Joanne Byrde (£20)		10	
Nicholas Barkar (£200)		100	
Wedow Sylner (£20)		10	
Jamys Banester (£30)		15	
Vyncent, Philip, Lawrens, petite John, Olyver, John the coke, Hector, Margery, Alyantes & servauntes to Jamys de Mercepeine and his Compaignyon (2s. 8d.)		2	8
Jamys de Mercepaigne and Barthillmew Fortene straungers (£400)	20		
Summa	55	2	8

45.   SEYNT MYGHELL PARRISHE

	£	s.	d
Bryan Screven (£20)		10	
John Bekingham (100 marks)		33	4
William Watson (200 marks)		66	8
John Osborne (200 marks)		66	8
Thomas Palley (£100)		50	
Fowke Conwaye (£40)		20	
Nicholas Brewreley (100 marks)		33	4
Robert Harding (£40)		20	
Henry Gardyner (£40)		20	

	£	s.	d
John Gardyner (£400)	10		
Felyship of fyshemongers in landes			
yerely (£213 17s. 4½d.)	10	13	8
John Perry (1000 marks)	16	13	4
Henry Hamcotes Aldreman (2000 marks)	33	6	8
John Swyngclyf (£400)	10		
Summa	96	13	8

SEYNT MARTEN PARRYSHE

	£	s.	d
Leonard Johnson (£150)		75	
John Hopkyns (£20) [x - K 20s.]		10	
Thomas Browne (100 marks)		33	4
William Shref (£20)		10	
William Coke (100 marks)		33	4
John Crewse Ducheman (£4)		4	
Angell Mynster Wassell Crewse (8d.)			8
Summa	8	6	4

46. SEYNT MARGARET PARRISHE

	£	s.	d
Richard Nese (£20)		10	
George Dodes (£20)		10	
John Bukney (£50)		25	
William Harvy (£40)		20	
Henry Wales (£40) [x - Broad Street			
ward 25s. as 'Wallesse']		20	
John Essex (£80)		40	
John Bereman (£40)		20	
Agnes Mason (£100)		50	
Richard Middellton £20)		10	
John Enderby (£30)		15	
Jamys Bonam (£20)		10	
Robert Wodde (£30)		15	
Robert Browne (£20)		10	
Cutbert Maners (£20)		10	
William Johnson (£20)		10	
John Core (£400)	10		
Summa	23	15	

SEYNT LEONARD PARRYSHE

	£	s.	d
Richard Slowghe (£40)		20	
George Bayly (£20)		10	
Richard Stagge (£60)		30	
John Hayes (£30)		15	
John Pecok (£20)		10	
Antony Coley (£20) [x - Candlewick ward			
20 s. as 'Coole'][11]		10	

11. E.359/44, r. 19 gives surname as Colly.

	£	s.	d
Robert Broke (£100)		50	
John Storley (£30)		15	
Elyzabeth Gurry (£20)		10	
47. William Grene (£100)		50	
Robert Sowthwik (100 marks)		33	4
John Genyns (£20)		10	
John Armestrong (£20)		10	
William Alen (£40)		20	
Richard Hall (£200)		100	
Thomas Medow (100 marks)		33	4
Thomas Blanke (£1000)	25		
Humfray Barons (£600)	15		
Summa	61	6	8

ALHOWEYS PARRISHE

	£	s.	d
John Baker (£150)		75	
Humfray Jonar (£20)		10	
Raulf Foxeley (£800) [ass. £16 13s. 4d.			
in Broad Street ward]	20		
Leonard Richeman (£20)		10	
Edward Bright (£40)		20	
John Harris (£40)		20	
John Farthing (£200)		100	
Robert Warner (£600)	15		
Summa	46	15	
Totalis huius ward pro parte dominus Regis	484	11	

48. [r.3]   BRADSTREATE WARDE

[Petty collectors: Thomas Carmarden of the parish of St. Peter le Poer, scrivener, and Thomas Goodman of the parish of St. Bartholomew the Less, mercer.]

THE PARISSHE OF SAINT BARTILMEW THE LITLE
[by the Exchange]
[English]

	£	s.	d
John Wylforde Alderman (2000 marks)	33	6	8
Cristofer Chybborne (£1000)	25		
Nicholas Wylford (1000 marks)	16	13	4
Water Lambart (£400)	10		
Nicholas Crosswell (£20)		10	
Jasper Fesaunt in landes yerely			
(£100) [x - Mddx. 100s.]	5		
John Wight (£200)	5		
William Laune (£50)		25	
Mathew Philipsonne (£20)		10	

33

	£	s.	d
Richard Plummer (£20)		10	
Thomas Hamsonn (£20)		10	
James Hawle grocer (£20)		10	
John Snarley (£40)		20	
John Phillipes (£30)		15	
Robert Phillipsonn (100 marks)		33	4
Richard Grygge (100 marks)		33	4
William Greneway (£60)		30	
Thomas Godman (£60)		30	
Richard Tulle (£300)	7	10	
Henry Atkyns (£20)		10	
Thomas Knott (£20)		10	
Straungers			
Phillip de Aranda (£100)	5		
Peter Championn (£100)	5		
Peter Anthony (£200)	10		
Vittor Corye (£40)		40	
John Swego (£20)		20	
Mark Phesaunt (£20)		20	
Alexaunder Tonis (£10) [x - Langbourn ward			
10s. as 'Theymor']¹²		10	
John Cocke servaunte with Peter Champion (4d.)			4
Summa	139	17	

49. THE PARISSHE OF SAYNT BENETTES FYNKE

William Wylford jun (1000 marks)	16	13	4
Straunger			
Alvero de Astedelo and Antony Masewelo (£200)	10		
Englisshmen there			
John Bugham (£100)		50	
John Baxter in landes yerely (£20)		20	
Thomas Stacy and John Cowseworth (£120)	3		
Richard Kyng and Antony Payne (£40)		20	
Walter Knyght (£60)		30	
Edmond Johnson (£20)		10	
Michell Atwayte (£60)		30	
Thomas Moltoun (£20)		10	
John Tayler (£20)		10	
John Hichecock (£20)		10	
Thomas Wodhowse (£20)		10	
Straungers within the said parisshe of			
Saint Benettes Fynk			
Anthony James (£100) [Process -			
discharged 50s.]¹³	5		

12. E.359/44, r. 19 gives surname as Tomer.
13. Anthony James swore before the barons that the value of his goods and chattels at the time of taxation did not exceed £50. The barons discharged him and the collectors of 50s. of the 100s. assessed on him (E.159/321, *communia* Easter 34 Hen. VIII, r. 66).

	£	s.	d
Fernando de Barro (40s.)		2	
Thomas Andersonn (4d.) [a]			4
Summa	44	15	8

50.   SAINT MYLDREDES AND [St. Mary] WOOLCHURCHE
[English]

	£	s.
William Tomlinson (£20)		10
Robert Heronn (£100)		50
Edward Rest (£100)		50
George Forthorgile (£20)		10
George Betensonn (£100)		50
Richard Pelter (£100)		50
John Downe grocer (£20)		10
Thomas Mansey (£20)		10
Summa	12	

SAINT CRISTOFERS AT THE STOCKES
[English]

	£	s.	d
Richard Reynold (2000 marks)	33	6	8
Robert Herdes (400 marks)	6	13	4
Robert Bele mercer (£40)		20	
Oliver Richardsonn (£120)	3		
Gelbart Parne £20)		10	
Thomas Armestonn (£30)		15	
Richard Ramsey (£20)		10	
Straungers there			
Bartilmew Campane (£1000) [ass. £50 in			
Tower ward and £50 in Southwark]	50		
Charles Armiccun (£20)		20	
and Sylvester Popoleskerye thorcharkes			
[sic] (£5)		5	
Balletto Magaleytye (£5)		5	
Summa	97	5	

51.   SAINT MARTYNS OUTE WYTCHE
[English]

	£	s.	d
John Aleley (£400) [x - K £10 6d.]	10		
John Kedermyster (£600)	15		
Richard Suthwerk, deade, William and			
Cristofer his sonnes, executors			
(£400)	10		
George Littelcote (£40)		20	
Thomas Lawden (£40)		20	
Antony Cole (£40)		20	
Straungers there			
Alexander Pymenta (£10) [a]		10	
Blanca Denys widowe (4d.) [a]			4
Summa	38	10	4

	£	s.	d
SAINT PETERS THE PORE			
[English]			
Doctor Lee (1000 marks) [x - Mddx. £25]	16	13	4
Rauf Foxley (1000 marks) [x - Bridge			
ward £20]	16	13	4
Robert Palmer (£2000)	50		
Richard Wadyngton (1000 marks)	16	13	4
Jane Lady Lambert (£400)	10		
Thomas Pawlett in landes and fees			
yerely (£40) [ass. 40s. in			
Hampshire]		40	
Edward Canker (100 marks)		33	4
John Smalley (£40)		20	
John Graye (£20)		10	
[William] Abbot serjeaunt of the kinges			
seller (£200) [x - K £5 6d.][14]	5		
George Asshe (£20) [x - K 10s. 6d.][15]		10	
Fraunces Lambert (£100)		50	
Thomas Carmarden (£20)		10	
Thomas Geffrey dier (£100)		50	
Margaret Rider widow (£40)		20	
Richard Carrell (£20)		10	
Straungers			
John Gogebushe (40s.)		2	
Walter Deleane (£20)		20	
Doctor Michell (£20) [a]		20	
James Mr Doctors servaunt (4d.) [a]			4
Summa	129	15	8

52. ALHALLOWES IN THE WALLE			
[English]			
William Stockes (£100)		50	
Henry Wallesse (£50) [ass. 20s. in Bridge ward			
as 'Wales']		25	
Thomas Bromefeld (£30)		15	
Elizabeth Blacklocke (£30)		15	
Thomas Wightbrock (£30)		15	
Richard Logesdonn (£20)		10	
Robert Ederiche (£100)		50	
John Rawe (£20)		10	
John Alcocke (£20)		10	
Straungers in the same parisshe			
Bastarde Fawcunbrige (£20)		20	
Fawcunbrige servaunt (4d.)			4

14. E.359/44, r. 19 gives William as first name.
15. The enrolled accounts mistakenly give £10 as the assessment in Broad Street ward and £10 6d. as the payment in the king's household (E.359/44, r. 19).

	£	s.	d
Nichosmus (£20)		20	
Summa	12		4

SAYNT MARGARETES IN LOTHBURY
[English]

	£	s.	d
Robert Fermor (1000 marks)	16	13	4
Sir Bryan Tuke knight (£2000)			
[x - Process][16]	50		
James Sewen (£20)		10	
William Wilford the elder (£200)	5		
Summa	72	3	4

53. THE CORPORACIONS HALLES AND FELOWSHIPS
HERUNDER WRITTEN BEN ASSESSED AS FOLOWITH

	£	s.	d
First the wardens of the merchaunt taillors in landes (£180 5s. 8d.) [x - Tower ward £9 4d.]	9		4
The wardens of the carpenters (£74 18s. 4d.) [x - Tower ward £3 14s. 10d.]	3	14	10
The wardens of the lethersellers (£93 12s.) [x - Tower ward £4 13s. 8d.]	4	13	8
The wardens of the bachelers of merchaunt taillors (£83 6s.) [x - Tower ward £4 3s. 4d.]	4	3	4
Summa	21	12	2
Totalis huius ward pro parte dominus Regis	567	19	6

54. [r.13] THE WARDE OF BAYNARDES CASTELL
[Petty collectors: Hugh Loste[17] of the parish of St. Benet Paul's Wharf and William Cowyk of the parish of St. Gregory by St. Paul's.]

PAROCHIA SANCTI BENEDICTI
[St. Benet Paul's Wharf]
[English]

	£	s.	d
John Smyth Baron of theschequyer in landes & fees (£333 13s. 4d.)	16	13	8
Wylliam Ibgrave (£600)	15		
Letyce Hyll wydowe (200 marks) [ass. 50s. in Bucks.]		66	8
Robart Cosyne (200 marks)		66	8
Mathewe Coltes Audytor in the Court of Augmentacyon (£200)	5		

16. Sir Brian Tuke claimed that whereas subsidy commissioners living within the limits of their commissions should be assessed there and whereas he was a commissioner for Essex and had a residence there he should not be assessed in London. The barons discharged him in London on payment of an assessment of £16 13s. 4d. in Essex (E.159/321, *communia* Trinity 34 Hen. VIII, r. 25).

17. E.359/44, r. 19 gives surname as Loft.

	£	s.	d
John Thurston (£300)	7	10	
Thomas Vycary in fees (£50)		50	
Gilbert Walter (£80)		40	
Edmund Notte (£66 13s. 4d.)		33	4
Wylliam Revell (£50)		25	
Thomas Gythens (£50)		25	
Wylliam Stapulton (£20)		10	
Wylliam Cowper (£40)		20	
John Newman (£40)		20	
Stephyne Brakenbery (£40) [x - K 21s.]		20	
John Ade (£30) [ass. 10s. in Cordwainer ward]		15	
John Armestrong (£20)		10	
Gooddyth Pett wydowe (£20)		10	
John Agat (£20)		10	
Laurence Heydoc (£20)		10	
Henry Warde (£20)		10	
Robert Porsar (£20)		10	
Thomas Thonson (£20)		10	
Maistres Scote (£40)		20	
Hugh Lost (£300) [ass. £5 in Queenhithe			
ward and 50s. in Mddx.][18]	7	10	
Rychard Jonys (£20)		10	
Jamys Hogle (£20)		10	

55. Straungers

	£	s.	d
Nycholas Rusticus (£20)		20	
Robart Osey (£10)		10	
Lewys Morall (60s.)		3	
John Wyllyams (£20)		20	
Peter [Blank]			4
Deryk [Blank]			4
Van de Vamus			4
Lewes Sympons			4
John Tuckfeld			4
Gyllam Cowssell			4
Mathewe Prelio (£10)		10	
John Alon			4
Nycholas Harrys			4
John Acott (20s.)			12
Mary Wever			4
Katheryn Lambart			4
[Blank] Genyns			4
John Dyaker			4

18. E.359/44, r. 19 gives surname as Loft.

	£	s.	d
56. PAROCHIA BEATAE MARIE MAGDALENE			
[English]			
John Godsalve landes & fees (£100) [x - K £5]	5		
Rychard Basden (£140) [x - P 70s.]		70	
Thomas Genyns (100 marks)		33	4
Peter Pore (100 marks)		33	4
Rychard Grey (£40)		20	
Wylliam Kendall (£40)		20	
Wylliam Stone (£40)		20	
George Hyll (£40) [x - K 20s.]		20	
John Bylersbye (£30)		15	
Crystofer Jane (£26 13s. 4d.)		13	4
Wyllyam Wynkyll (£30)		15	
Wyllyam Walton (£30)		15	
Rychard Pursell (£20)		10	
Ambrose Wharcope (£20)		10	
John Stocher (£20)		10	
Wylliam Danby (£20)		10	
Wylliam Ward (£20)		10	
Wylliam Snowden (£40)		20	
Rauf Johnson (£20)		10	
Laurence Moleners (£20)		10	
Robart Kyng (£40)		20	
Thomas Hale (£20)		10	
Straungers			
Colbard Mathewe (20s.)			12
Jasper Hylbourn (20s.)			12
Marten Detter (£15)		15	
Dereke Baker			4
John Almer			4
John Boden			4
John Pottlen			4
57. PAROCHIA SANCTI ANDREE			
[English]			
Robart Hamon (£400) [ass. £5 in Mddx.][19]	10		
Laurence Goore (£100)		50	
Robert Shyrlok (£100)		50	
Laurence Jockson (£50)		25	
Thomas Ellys (£40)		20	
Wyllyam Foster (£30)		15	
Edward Whytwell (£20)		10	
Robart Furneys (£40)		20	
John Ledys (£20)		10	
John Puddell (£30)		15	
John Venyte (£20)		10	

19. E.359/44, r. 11 gives surname as Hamond.

	£	s.	d
Wylliam Gysnam (£20)		10	
Rychard Stokden (£20)		10	
Thomas Whyte (£20)		10	
Jamys Lorde (£20)		10	
John Hamond (£20)		10	
Mayster Newton (£100)		50	
Phelypp Banbery (£20)		10	
John Bonde (£40)		20	
John Case (£20)		10	
Letyce Harper (£100)		50	

58. Straungers

	£	s.	d
John Bocher (£40) [a]		40	
Anthony Levessen (£30)		30	
John Gydfeld (£10)		10	
Rouland Jurden (£20)		20	
Henry Turpyne (£20)		20	
Alexander Walker (£4)		4	
John Dune (40s.) [a]		2	
Peter Domyas (£10) [a]		10	
Peter Vuderbruer (20s.)			12
Phelyp Gyllett (20s.)			12
John Vendate in wages (40s.)		2	
Jamys Stowte [a]			4
Odam Scarman in wayges (40s.) [a]		2	
Denys Gylbet [a]			4
Maryon Vyllowe [a]			4
Jamys Cobler [a]			4
John Dylleter			4
John de Butter (20s.)			12
John Hanyell (20s.)			12
Gyllam Venere			4
Henry Levy (£10)		10	

59. PAROCHIA SANCTI GREGORII
[English]

	£	s.	d
John Ap Ryce (£300) [ass. £5 in city of Hereford]	7	10	
John Coke (1000 marks) [x - Bassishaw ward £16 13s. 4d.]	16	13	4
Rychard Watkyns (£500)	12	10	
Wylliam Wyld (£140)		70	
Wylliam Cowyke (£200)	5		
Agnes Bell (£100)		50	
John Watson (200 marks)		66	8
Thomas Kelse (100 marks)		33	4
Anthony Cave (£300) [a]	7	10	
Wylliam Beswyke (£100)		50	

	£	s.	d
Robart Laurence (£100)		50	
Robart Broke (200 marks)		66	8
Lucy Knyght wydowe (100 marks)		33	4
John Lambe (£20)		10	
Anne Auncell wydowe (£40)		20	
Hugh Pope (£40)		20	
Robart Davyson (£40)		20	
Rychard Knyght (£40) [ass. 10s. in Bassishaw ward]		20	
Rychard Treveys (£50) [a]		25	
Roger Newyes (£200) [ass. 66s. 8d. in Farringdon ward Within]	5		
Rychard Maister (£40)		20	
Robart Ibgrave (£40)		20	
Thomas Smythson (£40)		20	
Thomas Bolt (£30)		15	
Wylliam Blyghman (£30) [ass. 10s. in Aldersgate ward as 'Blitheman']		15	
John Payne (£30)		15	
Wylliam Thornby (£20)		10	
Reynold Parkyns (£20)		10	
Peter Robynson (£20)		10	
Robert Goslyne (£20)		10	
Elyn Meryngton wydowe (£20)		10	
60. Rychard Wyllyams (£20)		10	
Dorothe Chamley (£20)		10	
Anthony Porter (£46)		23	
Roger Pare (£20)		10	
John Shepard (£300) [ass. 20s. in Northants.]	7	10	
Rychard Lanysdall (£20)		10	
John Elyat (£20)		10	
Davy Clopton (£20)		10	
Wylliam Bowman (£20)		10	
John Barker (£20)		10	
Thomas Jacket (£20)		10	
Edmund Taylefer (£20)		10	
Wylliam Clerkeson (£20)		10	
Wylliam Pultrell (£20)		10	
Cristofer Basse (£20)		10	
Richard Churcheman (£20)		10	
John Robynson (£20)		10	
Roger Cotes (£20)		10	
Wyllyam Myles (£20)		10	
John Redford (100 marks)		33	4
John Graungyer (£20)		10	
Straungers			
Thomas Walker (£10)		10	

	£	s.	d
Phylyp Spanspons (£7)		7	
Thomkyng Flemyng (20s.)			12
Jamys Shorte			4
Bartylmewe [Blank]			4
John Bonsemeth (20s.)			12
Elys Marchayd (40s.)		2	
Summa totales			
huius wardi	253	9	

61. [r.23]   CANDELWEKSTRETE WARDE
[Petty Collectors: James Apott of the parish of St. Clement Eastcheap and William Hewett of the parish of St. Martin Orgar]

[St. Mary] ABCHURCH PARISHE

	s.	d
James Haveley (£25)	12	6
Thomas Skydamore (£20)	10	
John Southe broker (£20)	10	
John Branche the yonger (£25)	12	6
William Walle clothworker (£20)	10	
Richard Burgan clothworker (£20)	10	
Morrys Cassyon smyth (£20)	10	
John Busshe (£20)	10	
Richard Asselden (£20)	10	
Edwarde Pratte (£25)	12	6
Myghell Smythe (£25)	12	6
James Medcoff (£25)	12	6
Humfrey Wagstaff (£25)	12	6
John Stocker (£40)	20	
Richard Lenney (£20)	10	
John Myghell (£20)	10	
John Branche the elder (£100)	50	
Walter Ashelen (£66 13s. 4d.)	33	4
Mystres Pynner (£66 13s. 4d.)	33	4
William Newman (£100)	50	
Richard Coke (£40)	20	
John Myners (£40)	20	
John Swanne (£100)	50	
John Evens (£40)	20	
Robert Wyndover (£30)	15	
Anthonye Fabyan (£100)	50	

62.   Straungers

	s.
John Reconger (£500) [Process-discharged £22 10s.][20]	25

20. John Reconger swore before the barons of the exchequer that the value of his goods and chattels at the time of taxation did not exceed £20. The barons discharged him and the collectors of £22 10s. of the £25 assessed on him (E.159/321, *communia* Easter 34 Hen. VIII, r. 66).

	£	s.	d
Peter Derover (£20)		20	
Anne Stagg, wedowe (£5)		5	
Haunce Beame, servaunt, by yere (£5)		5	
Gyon Ladock servaunt			4
Steven the Grade merchaunt aragos (£40)		40	
Tryson Damyon venysscion (£5)		5	
Barthyam de Lasale & John al[ien] frenchmen			
in wood c [100] baletes (£100)		100	
Nycholas Batelya servaunt			4
John servaunt with Barthyam de Lasale			4
Haunce Ryche (40s.)		2	
In the house of Tryson Damyon Clx baletes			
of wodd which he saithe is Thomas			
Calvacant Florantyne (£100) [x - Bridge			
ward][21]	5		
Summa parochiae	65	4	8

63.   SEYNT MARTYNS PARISHE

	£	s.	d
John Tryckes (£40)		20	
James Hawes (£40)		20	
John Nache (£66 13s. 4d.)		33	4
John Madenhed (£80) [ass. 40s. in			
Cordwainer ward]		40	
Richard Platter (£40)		20	
Thomas Hewett (£40)		20	
Robert Westmore (£40)		20	
Mathewe Water baker (£40)		20	
Thomas Gibson (£20)		10	
Richard Champyon (£60)		30	
Thomas Frank executor to Mrs. Hawkyns			
wydowe (£200) [ass. 66s. 8d. in Essex]	5		
Thomas Cresse (£40)		20	
Sir Humfrey Brown knight (£400)	10		
Hamond Hamcottes (1000 marks)	16	13	4
William Hewett (£800)	20		
Gyles Bridges (£1000)	25		
Straungers			
Barnarde Busshe merchaunt (£66 13s. 4d.)			
[ass. 40s. in Farringdon ward Within]	3	6	8
Giles Busshe servaunt			4
Peter Blanke servaunt			4
Summa parochiae	92	14	

64.   SEYNT CLEMENTES PARISHE

	£	s.	d
James Apott (£800)		20	
Thomas Nycholson (£400)		10	

21. Neither Damyon nor Calvacant was listed in the certificate for Bridge ward.

	£	s.	d
John Care (£30)		15	
Thomas Spensser (£30)		15	
John Carter (£20)		10	
Nycholas Wyatt (£60)		30	
Bennett Jackson (£60)		30	
Thomas Trent (£210) [ass. 33s. 4d. in P]	5	5	
Johane Eggyns wedowe (£20)		10	
John Grene (£20)		10	
John Prince (£20)		10	
Robert Normanton (£20)		10	
Summa parochiae	42	5	

SEYNT LEONARDES PARISHE

	£	s.	d
John Hunter (£20)		10	
John West (£40)		20	
Adam Asheton (£30)		15	
Anthonye Coole (£40) [ass. 10s. in Bridge ward as 'Coley']		20	
William Lette (£20)		10	
Thomas Champney (£40)		20	
William Herde (£30)		15	
John Bradburye (£20)		10	
Margaret Owtered (£30)		15	
Summa parochiae	6	15	

65. SEYNT MYGHELLES PARISHE

	£	s.	d
John Harryson (£20)		10	
William Broke (£300)	7	10	
William Alleyn (£20)		10	
Nycholas Lyverhed (£20)		10	
John Frebrige (£100)		50	
James Staveley (£200)	5		
Thomas Huggans (£20)		10	
John Cloker (£40)		20	
Richarde Wayne (£50)		25	
John Walker (£20)		10	
Thomas Moylle (£20)		10	
John Collard (£30)		15	
John Burdock (£30) [x - Langbourn ward 15s. 6d.]		15	
William Cleare (£20)		10	
William Yeldeam (£20)		10	

Straungers

	£	s.	d
Cornellys Peterson (20s.)			12
James Richardson servaunt with Herry West			4
John Water servaunt with Herry West			4
John Dychman servaunt with Adrean Artham			4

44

	£	s.	d
Summa parochiae	22	17	
Summa totales huis warde	229	15	8

66. [r.18]   CHEPE WARDE
[Petty collectors: George Barons and Thomas Abram.]

SAYNT MARY BOWE PARYSHE
[English]

	£	s.	d
Thomas Edmondes (£40)		20	
John Peke (£20)		10	
William Carkeke (£150)	3	15	
John Rookes (£20)		10	
John Warner (£40) [a]		20	
John Edwardes (£40)		20	
Robert Luce (100 marks)		33	4
Thomas Jennyns (£40)		20	
John Hevans (£40)		20	
John Thomson (£20)		10	
John Slanyell (100 marks)		33	4
William Bigneill (200 marks)	5	marks	
Edward Bankes (£20)		10	
Thomas Bartilmewe (£100)		50	
Walter Porter (£40)		20	
John Hare (£333 6s. 8d.)	8	6	8
Thomas Abraham (£400)	10		
Stephyn Vaghan (1000 marks) [ass. £15 in Mddx.]	16	13	4
Antony Marler (£400) [x - Vintry ward £10][22]	10		
Summa	65	18	4

67.   HONY LANE
                    [English]

	£	s.	d
Nicholas Fuller (£150)	3	15	
John Eglyston (£120)	3		
Henry Phillypis (£33 6s. 8d.)		16	8
Fraunces Edwarded [and] Antony Bosum (100 marks)		33	4
Robert Essynton (£20)		10	
Thomas Woodlocke (£40)		20	
Edmond Sprett (£20)		10	
Henry Marre (100 marks)		33	4
Edward Tailor (£300)	7	10	
John Collyns (£33)		16	8
Thomas Cole (£20)		10	
John Butler (£120)	3		

22. E.359/44, r. 19 records the discharge of the collectors for the £10 assessment in Cheap ward of Anthony Marlowe who is probably the same person as Antony Marler. The enrolled accounts record Marlowe's payment of £10 in Vintry ward, but no Marlowe or Marler was assessed in that ward. One Anthony Marlar was assessed £10 in Cordwainer ward.

	£	s.	d
Nicholas Baynton (£300)	7	10	
Thomas Carre (£20)		10	
John Holdam (£20)		10	
Richard Bushe (£20)		10	
William Coter (£20)		10	
John Marre (£20)		10	
George Barnes (£1500)	37	10	
Thomas Lodge (£800)	20		
Summa	92	5	

68. SAYNT LAURENCE PARYSHE
[English]

	£	s.	d
Robert Longe (£150)	3	15	
John Popham (£20)		10	
Thomas Foster (£40)		20	
Henry Brynckeley (£100)		50	
James Slyght (£40)		20	
Lyonell Ducatt (£20)		10	
Humffrey Lune (300 marks)	5		
John Grey (£20)		10	
Robert Votia (£40)		20	
Berthelmewe Foster (£20)		10	
Robert Laurent (200 marks)	5	marks	
David Appoell (£120)	3		
William Mydleton (£30)		15	
John Fletcher (£30)		15	
Robert Merideth (£300)	7	10	
Thomas Kytley (£20)		10	
William Dankes (£40)		20	
Christofer Lambert (£20)		10	
Elisabeth Malyn (100 marks)		33	4
Edward Byllyng (£40)		20	
Ales Lupsed (£40)		20	
Thomas Underhill (£20)		10	
Robert Wynke (£50)		25	
John Smythe (£40)		20	
Nicholas Lune (£50)		25	
William Rede (£100)		50	
Nicholas Bacon (£40)		20	
John Banen (£20)		10	
Henry Vaghan (£20)		10	
Thomas Michell (£20)		10	
William Holylond (£20)		10	
William Newyngton (£20)		10	
John Crymes (£500)	12	10	
Johane Barkers wedowe (£500)	12	10	
Richard Grymes (1000 marks)	16	13	4
Summa	88	18	4

46

	£	s.	d
69. SAYNT MARTYNS PARYSHE [English]			
William Goodwyn (£20)		10	
Richard Paladyn (£20)		10	
Christofer Meryng (£100)		50	
William Chelsham (£50)		25	
Ambrose Barker (£200)	5		
Nicholas Withers)£150)	3	15	
John Ferre (£20)		10	
Leonard Barker (£150)	3	15	
William Kyng (£20)		10	
David Johns (£100)		50	
Summa	20	15	

[St. Mary] COLCHURCHE PARYSHE
[English]

	£	s.	d
John Broke (£50)		25	
Robert Lewes (£60)		30	
John Blagge (£200)	5		
John Myrffyn (£50)		25	
Edward Sole (£40)		20	
Antony Cottell (£150)	3	15	
Edward Cole (£20)		10	
William Smythe (£20)		10	
Richard Miles (£40)		20	
Amias Sendall (£300)	7	10	
John Fysher (£40)		20	
Roger Metcalff (£20)		10	
Roger Nicholles (£20)		10	
Robert Hobbey (£150)	3	15	
John Wendon (£333 6s. 8d.)	8	6	8
Robert Austen (£300)	7	10	
Faulegarret straungers (£5)		5	
Robert Reyborne (£20)		10	
70. William Attkyns (£20)		10	
Thomas Masten (£40)		20	
William Buckfeld (£40)		20	
George Conyers (£100)		50	
Margaret Throme widowe (£40)		20	
John Holdebeme (£30)		15	
Barthelmewe Husburd (£40) [a][23]		20	
James Lambert [and] John Vanderhedon straungers			8
too straungers dwelling with Mr Osborne			8

23. E.359/44, r. 19 records the discharge of the collectors for assessment in Cheap ward of Bartholomew Osborne, who can probably be identified with Husburd.

	£	s.	d
Robert Downes (£500)	12	10	
John Fene (£400)	10		
John Swetyng (£600)	15		
Rychard Osborne (2000 marks)	33	6	8
Stephyn Cobbe (£500)	12	10	
Summa	136	14	8

SAYNT MYLDREDES PARYSHE
[English]

	£	s.	d
Blase Whyte (£40)		20	
Annes Skynner (£20)		10	
Henry Mylles (£150)	3	15	
Thomas Colte (£20)		10	
William Wyate (£200)	5		
Thomas Sersey (£20)		10	
Johan Brograve (£30)		15	
Julyan Hodsale (£60)		30	
William Mosier (£80)		40	
Edward Saunders (£200)	5		
John Askewe (£100)		50	
David Wilkynson (100 marks)		33	4
William Dormer (£20)		10	
Roger Bettes (£20)		10	
Stephyn Holyngbery (£20)		10	
John Miller (£500)	12	10	
William Hobson (£400)	10		
William Mery (2000 marks)	33	6	8
William Butler (£2000)	50		
William Brothers (£800)	20		
John Blakesley (£400)	10		
Summa	162		

71.   SAYNT STEPHEN & SAYNT BENET PARYSHE

	£	s.	d
Thomas Heyshe (£200)	5		
William Lynke (£20)		10	
Doctor Clement (£300)	7	10	
Nicholas Crecher straunger (£20)		20	
Richard Grove (200 marks)	5 marks		
Roger Thatcher (£40)		20	
William Normanfeld (£100)		50	
John Stemkelley (£26 13s. 4d.)		13	4
Elisabethe Swane (£20)		10	
William Bromley (100 marks)		33	4
John Bodman (£666 13s. 4d.)	16	13	4
Richard Peryson (£40)		20	
Edward Deane [and] Thomas Rydley (£250)	6	5	
Robert Riche (£100)		50	
Henry Barnes (£400)	10		

	£	s.	d
Edward Morton (£400)	10		
John Lyons (£600)	12	10	
Summa	82	11	8

SAYNT PANCRESE PARYSHE

	£	s.	d
William Castelyn (£40)		20	
Elleme Ashe (100 marks)		33	4
Richard Skynner (£40)		20	
William Morrer (£20)		10	
Cornelis Bomer straunger			4
John Luff straunger (£10)		10	
John Elmer straunger (£5)		5	
Robert Hyxe (£20)		10	
Gilbert Styll (£20)		10	
John Sircott (£40)		20	
Thomas Person (£20)		10	
William Wakefeld (100 marks) [ass. 20s. in Mddx.]		33	4
Phillyp Yorke (£400)	10		
Thomas Marbery (400 marks)	6	13	4
The Corporacion of mysterye of Mercers beyng in the warde of Chepe in londes by yere (£150)	7	10	
The Corporacion of the mysterye of Grocers beyng in the said warde of Chepe in londes (£100)		100	
Summa	38	5	4
Summa istius warde	687	8	4

72. [r.10]   COLMANSTRETE WARDE
[Petty collectors: John Garway of the parish of St. Stephen, Coleman Street, mercer, and Robert Nicolles of the parish of St. Olave, Old Jewry, brewer.]

SEINCT STEVINS PARISHE

	£	s.	d
The Armorars hawll with landes ther unto belonging by yere (£20)		20	
Fraunces Morris widow (£50)		25	
Richard Poyntor (£200)	5		
Patysons widowe (£50)		25	
John Wytthers (£200)	5		
Phelip Kewr (£40)		20	
Edwarde Willes (£20)		10	
Mr [William] Barnes Auditor in londes and Fees (£120) [x - Essex £8 13s. 4d.][24]	6		
John Edwardes (£30)		15	
William Heywarde (£40)		20	

24. E.359/44, r. 19 gives William as first name.

49

	£	s.	d
George Baldok (£50)		25	
John Thruche (£200)	5		
John Sherryf (£20)		10	
John Wysdon (£60)		30	
Thomas Tyrry (£20)		10	
William Bradfot (£20)		10	
Richard Hewchyn (£40)		20	
Robarte Jusson (£20)		10	
Richard Askewe (200 marks)		66	8
The company of woll packers (£23)			
[x - Tower ward 23s.]		23	
William Irfote (£20)		10	
William Shepton (£20)		10	
Richard Andelby (£40)		20	
Mistres Fayry wido (£700)	17	10	
And of executors and Childerne of			
Fayry (£1000)	25		
John Garwaye (1000 marks)	16	13	4
Summa huius perrochie	99	3	

73.　　　　　SAINCT OLUS PARISHE

	£	s.	d
Robert Nicholas (£60)		30	
Arthure Denchar (£200)	5		
Richard Chamorlen (£30)		15	
Edward Fowlar (£40)		20	
William Goodhew (£30)		15	
William Asheley (£30)		15	
Clement Cornall (£20)		10	
Mistres Clifford widow in landes (£30)		30	
Robert Smyth (£100)		50	
Richard Jenkynson (£30)		15	
Richard Newcom (£20)[25]		10	
Edmound Baker (£20)		10	
Richard Smyth (£40)		20	
Gabriell Cawdewell (£30)		15	
William Kyrkby (£40)		20	
William Abbott (£20)		10	
Henry James (£20)		10	
Antony Whyte (£20)		10	
Summa huius perrochie	19	15	

74.　　　　　SEINCT MARGARET PARYSHE

	£	s.	d
Mistres Clopton widowe (£40)		20	
Thomas Archar (£40)		20	
John Googe (£100)		50	
Thomas Hylton (£20)		10	

25. This entry is crossed out.

50

	£	s.	d
Jetars wydow (£20)		10	
Edwarde Clapton (£30)		15	
Hawley in landes in Fees (£20)		20	
Morrys Davye (£20)		10	
Mr [John] Sadler Alderman (£1333 6s. 8d.)	33	6	8
Straungers			
John Mymbroker (40s.)		2	
Christofer Mount in Fees (£20)		20	
Thomas Lucas (20s.)			12
James Goldsmyth (4d.)			4
Summa huius perrochie	42	5	
Totalis huius ward pro			
parte dominus Regis	161	3	

75. [r.1]   CORDWENERSTRETE WARDE
[Petty collectors: Edward Burlace, mercer, and Rauff Davenett.]

IN THE PARYSSHE OF SAINT ANTHONYNS
[St. Antholin Budge Row]
[English]

	£	s.	d
William Woodlyff (£500)	12	10	
Myles Perkyns (£500)	12	10	
William Daunse Alderman (£3000)	75		
William Wilkynson (2000 marks)	33	6	8
Barnard Jenyns (2000 marks)	33	6	8
Thomas Adyngton (2000 marks)	33	6	8
Richard Maye (£866 13s. 4d.)	21	13	4
William Clynche (£20)		10	
Martyn Dennam (£30)		15	
Thomas Myddellton (£300)	7	10	
Henry Susshe (£20)		10	
Mylles Pewterar (£20)		10	
Thomas Taillor (£20)		10	
Richard Clyfton (£20)		10	
John Ady (£20) [x - Castle Baynard			
ward 15s.]		10	
Maystres Wollfe (£40)		20	
William Addams (£20)		10	
Wyddowe Cannone (£20)		10	
John Banckes the yongar (£20)		10	
William Layngesdaylle (£40)		20	
John Mayxfellde (£20)		10	
Richard Wylkynson (£40)		20	
Thomas Rede (£20)		10	
John Banckes thelder (£40)		20	
Wydowe Bromelles (£50)		25	
William Layne (£20)		10	
William Parcker (£120)		60	

	£	s.	d
William Allday (£100)		50	
Henry Tompson (£250)	6	5	
George Wellpeley (£20)		10	
Otewell Hyll (£100)		50	
Crystofer Fyssher (£20)		10	
Thomas Blunt (£40)		20	
Summa	257	8	4

76.   [St. Mary] ALLDERMARY PARRYSSHE
[English]

	£	s.	d
Cristofer Fraunces (£80)		40	
Rauf Preston (£80)		40	
Thomas Persy (£300)	7	10	
Philipp Stokkewell (£20)		10	
Robart Bellingame (£20)		10	
Edward Ley (£200)	5		
Reyneborne Baynckes (£100)		50	
Richard Bewe (£80)		40	
James Baynckes (£20)		10	
William Campyone (£100)		50	
Thomas Crakyngthorpe (£20)		10	
Christofer Lording (£20)		10	
William Body (£100)		50	
Humfrey Nallson (£60)		30	
Robart Dofe (£30)		15	
Richard Castell (£40)		20	
Richard Petingayle (£120)		60	
John Wattson (£60)		30	
Thomas Waneles (£100)		50	
William Bennet (£60)		30	
Richard Dyxson (£20)		10	
Robart Gybbes (£20) [x - K 23s. 4d.]		10	
John Apseley (£80)		40	
John Bowth[e]t (£200) [x - Surrey £8 6s. 8d.]	5		
Richard Jermayne (£40)		20	
Robart Dawson (£60)		30	
Gye Wayde (£120)		60	
John Rowe (£200)	5		
Henry Bewford (£40)		20	

	£	s.	d
77. John Maydenhed (£80) [x - Candlewick ward 40s.]		40	
Mistress Champion wydowe (£500)	12	10	
Mistress Banckes wydowe late Bankes wyfe (£400)	10		
Walter Yonge (£500)	12	10	
William Laxton Alderman (2000 marks)	33	6	8

52

	£	s.	d
Thomas Whyte (£2000)	50		
Robart Dawbeney (£1000)	25		
John Coxton sonne and heier of and also			
Executour unto Vynsente Coxton			
(£200)	5		
George Robynson (£1000)	25		
Summa	235	20	

BOWE PARRYSSHE
[English]

	£	s.	d
Richard Jervys (£3000)	75		
William Lock (£1600)	40		
William Gressham (£1000)	25		
John Ellyott (£40) [x - Herts. 20s.]		20	
Robart Bowckas (£20)		10	
George Blanchard (£20) [x - Tower ward 15s.]		10	
Owyn Hawkyns (£80)		40	
Anthony Marlar (£400) [ass. £10 in Cheap ward]	10		
Maystres [Alice] Marlowe (£200) [ass. £5 in Mddx.][26]	5		
George Elyott (£200) [ass. 20s. in Essex]	5		
Andrewe Fowllare (£40)		20	
William Hanson (£50)		25	
Robart Shackerley and Kyng (£200)	5		
Nicholas Chowne (£80)		40	
Christofer Campyon (£100)		50	
William Parson (£40)		20	
John Worlley (£400)	10		
Summa	186	15	

78. SAYNT PANCKRES & SAINT SYTHES [St. Benet Sherehog]
[English]

	£	s.	d
Sir Rauf Waren knight Allderman (£4000)	100		
Rouland Sharkerley (1000 marks)	16	13	4
William Lambard (£200)	5		
Edward Bowlande (200 marks)			
[ass. 50s. in Essex]		66	8
Henry Smyth (£20)		10	
Maystres Hall (£150)		75	
Peter Brystowe (£50)		25	
Richard Rattlyth[e]t (£20)		10	
Thomas Colly (£20)		10	
Richard Wyllson (£60)		30	
Summa	133		

26. E.359/44, r. 11 gives first name as Alicia.

	£	s.	d
TRYNYTE AND SAYNTE THOMAS APOSTELL			
[English]			
Hugh Apoell (£40) [x - K 20s.]		20	
Wydowe Heyford (£20)		10	
Robart Williams (£20)		10	
Humfrey Hyckhcok (£20)		10	
John Beneles (£60) [x - Vintry ward			
30s. 6d, as 'Bendles']		30	
Nicholas Spenssar (£20)		10	
William Pettinggall (£60) [x - Vintry			
ward 30s. 6d.]		30	
Summa	6		

	£	s.	d
ALLHALLOWE PARYSHE			
[English]			
Henry Sukley (2000 marks)	33	6	8
Raulf Davenet (£600)	15		
John Jenkyn (£700)	17	10	
Summa	65	16	8
Totalis huius ward			
pro parte dominus Regis	884		20

79. [r.15]   CORNEHYLL WARD

[Petty collectors: George Brygges and Rauf Hammersley.]

	£	s.	d
John Jakes (£500)	12	10	
John Tolowes (£2000)	50		
George Crowche (£400)	10		
George Forman (£200)	5		
Wyllyam Ramesey (£20)		10	
John Dockett (£200)	5		
John Thorogood (£20)		10	
Wyllyam Lawne (£20)		10	
Wyllyam Beede (£20)		10	
John Horsepole (£20)		10	
Robart Jennyns (£20)		10	
Wyllyam Chambers (£100)		50	
Edward Folyett (£40)		20	
The Wyffe of the late Wylliam			
Macham Clotheworker (£30)		15	
Maystres Parson wydowe (200 marks)		66	8
Fraunceys Bustard (£40)		20	
Maistres Wynge wydowe (£40)		20	
George Brygges (£500) [ass. £10			
in Bridge ward]	12	10	
Robart Donkyns (£100)		50	
Thomas Hardwycke (£30)		15	
Edmound Perry (£120)		60	
Wyllyam Beare (£20)		10	

	£	s.	d
Thomas Wheaton (£40)		20	
George Hynde (£20)		10	
Maystres Taylor wydowe (£200)	5		
Thomas Bayles (£20)		10	
John Dudley (£60)		30	
John Lute (£60)		30	
Stephyn Roulynson (£20)		10	
Wylliam Fetzharry (£40)		20	
80. Thomas Stowe (£20)		10	
John Bulley (£20)		10	
William Crofton (£100)		50	
John At Wood (£20)		10	
Maystres Smyth wydowe (100 marks)		33	4
George Edyson (£20)		10	
Robart Saunders (£20)		10	
Randall Atkynson (£20)		10	
John Brewer (£20)		10	
Robert Chapman (£60)		30	
John Halywell (£40)		20	
John Leyland (£100) [x - Process][27]		50	
John Jaques (£20)		10	
Harry Typper (£20)		10	
Wylliam Hynton (£200)	5		
Wylliam Clark (£100)		50	
Cristofer Payne (200 marks)		66	8
Peter Bland (£20)		10	
Roger Wardner (£100)		50	
John Skampyan (£40)		20	
Wyllyam Assheley (£20)		10	
Peter Hunyngborne (£100)		50	
Wyllyam Austyn (£40)		20	
Robart Hardy (100 marks)		33	4
Thomas Dudley (£100)		50	
Rychard Poule (100 marks)		33	4
John Heard (100 marks)		33	4
Raffe Hammersley (£200)	5		
81. Thomas Ducke (£20)		10	
Rychard Downes (£100)		50	
Thomas Carter (£40)		20	
Nycholas Crystyen (£20)		10	
Wylliam Ryckysman (£40)		20	
Thomas Spencer (£100)		50	

27. Leyland was discharged by the barons and royal writ directed to the collectors in Cornhill ward on the ground that he was liable to the clerical disme and the clerical subsidy and that he had no lands or hereditaments whereby he could be taxed for the lay subsidy (E.359/44, r. 19; E.159/321, *communia* Easter 34 Hen. VIII, r. 59).

	£	s.	d
Wyllyam Rysse (£20)		10	
Wyllyam Mathewe (£20)		10	
Nycholas Marsshe (£40)		20	
Thomas Chapell (£80)		40	
Wyllyam Macham (£60)		30	
Rychard Stanfeld (£400)	10		
Phylyp Gunter (£200)	5		
Thomas Chapman (£30)		15	
Rychard Forrand (£30)		15	
Nycolas Maston (£20)		10	
Thomas Bakar (£20)		10	
Maistres Emery wydowe (£80)		40	
Edmound Barton (100 marks)		33	4
George Okeley (£20)		10	
Hary Clytherowe (200 marks)		66	8
Thomas Smyth (£20)		10	
Stephyn Tego (100 marks)		33	4
John Kebull (£30)		15	
Summa totales huius wardi	212	5	

82. [r.21]   CREPULGATE WARD
[Petty collectors: Vyncent Randell of the parish of St. Mary Aldermanbury and Richard Pykryng of the parish of St. Giles Cripplegate.]

THE PARTE OF THE PARISH OF SEYNT MARYE
MAGDALEYN IN MYLKSTRETE
[English]

	£	s.	d
Margarete Ladye Kytson (2000 marks)	33	6	8
Elezabeth Statham (£2000)	50		
John Wiseman (£400)	10		
Anthonye Ellyott (400 marks)	6	13	4
William Harding (£266 13s. 4d.)	6	13	4
Mathewe Dale (200 marks)	3	6	8
James Page [?] (100 marks)		33	4
Thomas Bradley (£80)		40	
John Ilard (£20)		10	
Nycholas Byngham (£26 13s. 4d.)		13	4
Nycholas Kyng (£100) [ass. 50s. in Cordwainer ward][28]		50	
John Wethye (£20)		10	
William Knyght (£20)		10	
Thomas Boune (£100)		50	
Humfrey Johns (£40)		20	
Nycholas Roofe (£80)		40	
Edwarde Bradley (£20)		10	

28. So according to E. 359/44, r. 19, but his name does not appear in the certificate for Cordwainer ward.

	£	s.	d
Thomas Gonnell (£20)		10	
Summa parochiae	124	16	8

83. SEYNT MARYE IN ALDERMANBURYE
[English]

	£	s.	d
Thomas Ryshton, serjeant (£1000)	25		
John Preist (1000 marks)	16	13	4
Vyncent Randell (£1000)	25		
Sir John Gressam, knyght (£5000)	125		
Straungers			
Sir John Gresham for Anthony Fenendoo			
(£200) [ass. £10 in Langbourn ward			
as Doctor Antony]	10		
Itm for Symond Fernando (£500)	27	10	(sic)
It for Albert Aldorigus (£80)	4		
[English]			
William Pagett in landes & fees (£100)			
[x - K £5 4s.]	5		
Thomas Atkyns (£40)		20	
Thomas Parrys (£20)		10	
Robert Maddye (£30)		15	
John Durraunt (40 marks)		13	4
Stocker Jeckett (100 marks)		33	4
William Boroughe (£20)		10	
William Swane (£20)		10	
Gregorye Richardson (£30)		15	
Thomas Westoo (£60)		30	
Fraunces Stelcragg (£80)		40	
Robert Woodland (£60)		30	
John Reames (£66 13s. 4d.)		33	4
Robert Shepperd (£20)		10	
84. William Mundye (£20) [x - Aldersgate			
ward 33s. 4d.]		10	
[Blank] Festone (£20)		10	
Christofre Washwood (£20)		10	
John Alexsaunder (£40)		20	
John Forrest (£40)		20	
Thomas Gwynne (100 marks)		33	4
Nycholas Gascoyne (£20)		10	
Straungers			
Peter Reynoldson, servaunt with Richard			
Prevall, in wages (40s.)		2	
John de Pole, servaunt with the saide			
Prevall, in wages (£3)		3	
Summa parochiae	257	11	8

	£	s.	d
SEYNT MYGHELLES IN WOODSTRETE			
[English]			
Christofre Bellamye (£20)		10	
George Medley (300 marks)	5		
Robert Danyell (£20)		10	
Robert Wrythock (£20)		10	
William Rawlyns (400 marks)	6	13	4
John Vernam (40 marks)		13	4
Robert Johnson (£26 13s. 4d.)		13	4
Robert Andrews (£50)		25	
Thomas Bande (£50)		25	
John Pylkyngton (£140)	3	10	
85. Elizabethe Brown (200 marks)	3	6	8
John Loune (400 marks)	6	13	4
Adam Gardyner (£40)		20	
William Pyckring (£20)		10	
Anne Wood (£100)		50	
John Leye (£50)		25	
John Banckes (£40)		20	
Thomas Raynton (£20)		10	
Richard Oxley and William Gotheryk (£40)		20	
Walter Sawkyns (£50)		25	
George Kyng (£20)		10	
Thomas Huntwade (40 marks)		13	4
John Tryll (£30)		15	
Thomas Walker (£30)		15	
Richard Wright (£20)		10	
Raff Hill (£20)		10	
John Estott (£20)		10	
John Medley (£20)		10	
Philip Jackson (£20)		10	
Wardens of ye scryveners (£22)			
[ass. 22s. in Tower ward]		22	
Straungers			
John Williamson (£6 13s. 4d.)		6	8
John Joneson, his servaunt			4
William Harmanson, his servaunt			4
Nycholas Clayse (£20)		20	
Lambert Joneson			4
Summa parochiae	47	3	
86. SEYNT ALBONS IN WOODSTRETE			
[English]			
Edward Northam (£1000)		25	
John Browne (£1000)		25	
Richarde Buttell (£600)		15	
John Olyff, surgeon (300 marks)		5	

	£	s.	d
Margerye Paynter (100 marks)		33	4
Richarde Maynard (£20)		10	
John Aspelyn (£20)		10	
Dorathee Lake (£50)		25	
Thomas Alexsaunder (£30)		15	
Mr Wotton, Doctor of Physyke (£150)	3	15	
Thomas Cottington (40 marks)		13	4
Walter Coper (£26 13s. 4d.)		13	4
John Bullock (£20)		10	
William Parker (£20)		10	
Richard Henman (£20)		10	
Richard Powrye (£100)		50	
Richard Myrthe (£20)		10	
William Raynton (£20)		10	
John Reve (100 marks)		33	4
John Norkowe (40 marks) [x - K 23s. 4d.][29]		13	4
Doctor Owen (£320 [x - P £8 4s.]	8		
Robert Hutton (£20)		10	
William Walker (£40)		20	
William Wilson (£40)		20	
John Revell (£20)		10	
Straunger			
Doctor Cromer (£100)		100	
Summa parochiae	103		20

87.   PARTE OF SEYNT OLAVE PARISH IN SILVERSTRETE
[English]

	£	s.	d
Richard Thomewe (£100)		50	
John Darnall (100 marks)		33	4
John Burges (£30)		15	
Elizabeth Typlarye (£40)		20	
Thomas Mundes (£20)		10	
Straungers			
Jerom Lambrase (£3 6s. 8d.)		3	4
Herrye Andrewe, his servaunt (26s. 8d.)			16
Asten Harnok, his servaunt			4
John Pennok, servaunt with Churchman (40s.)		2	
Summa parochiae	6	15	4

SEYNT ALPHEY BESYDE CREPULGATE
[English]

	£	s.	d
Thomas Audley (100 marks)		33	4
John Chandler (£66 13s. 4d.)		33	4
Nycholas Bromefeld (£30)		15	
John Rowe (£100)		50	
George Foster (£100)		50	

29. E.359/44, r. 19 gives surname as Northcote.

	£	s.	d
John Shyrryf (£40)		20	
John Webbe (£30) [ass. 10s. in			
Dowgate ward]		15	
Richard Cockes (£20)		10	
Straungers			
Peter Damyan (£5)		5	
John Morrewe, his servaunt (26s. 8d.)			16
George Rock, his servaunt			4
Summa parochiae	11	13	4

88. SEYNT GILES WITHOUT CREPULGATE
[English]

	£	s.	d
Philice Wright, in landes (£40)		40	
Roger Horne, in landes (200 marks)			
[ass. £5 in Aldgate ward]	6	13	4
William Stampford, in landes (40 marks)		26	8
George Kevell, in landes (£80)	4		
Robert Langley (200 marks)	3	6	8
Herry Woodland (£20)		10	
Richard Pykryng (400 marks)	6	13	4
Mr. York Harrold (£50)		25	
Clarencious Kinge of Armys (£100)		50	
John Parkyns (£40)		20	
John Genyse (£40)		20	
John Hall (200 marks)	3	6	8
John Whethed (£20)		10	
Thomas Stafford (£20)		10	
Robert Strachye (£20)		10	
John Frend thelder (£40)		20	
John Creke (£20)		10	
John Seffold (200 marks)	3	6	8
John Garrett (200 marks)		66	8
John Collens (£80)		40	
Reynolde Moore (£20)		10	
William Asheton (£20)		10	
Thomas Grenald (£20)		10	
Anne Fox (200 marks)	3	6	8
Edward Gregorye (£40)		20	
Roger Turner (£30)		15	
Richard Culle (£40)		20	
George Myddleton (£20)		10	
Arthur Lurkyn (£30)		15	
Edmonde Goodwyne (£80) [x - Mddx. 40s.]		40	
Robert Byrcham (£20) [x - Aldersgate			
ward 15s.]		10	
John Humfrey (£20)		10	
Thomas Sherys (£20)		10	
John Kenedeye (£40)		20	

	£	s.	d
John Watson (£20)		10	
Robert Goodby (£20)		10	
John Smythe (£400) [x - Q £10 13s. 4d.]	10		

89. Straungers

Deryk Joneson (£4)		4	
Arnolde Gardes (40s.)		2	
Thomas Parchmentt			4
Barthelmewe Shamelman (20s.)			12
Peter Goodfrey (20s.)			12
Garrett Splenderson			4
Edward Richardes (20s.)			12
Larence Bull (20s.)			12
Thomas Boge (20s.)			12
Walter Camble (40s.)		2	
Austen Joneson (40s.)		2	
Summa parochiae	70	7	4

PARTE OF SEYNT LAURENCE PARISHE IN THE JURYE
[English]

Robert Chersey (£1000)	25		
Roger Sterkey (£500)	12	10	
Myghell Dormer, alderman (4000 marks)	66	13	4
Sir Richard Gressam, knyght (4000 marks)	66	13	4
Mistress Parke, in landes (£230) [x - Kent £10; owes £1 10s. in Cripplegate ward]	11	10	
Olyver Okes (40 marks)		13	4
John Laurence (£20)		10	
John Waterhouse (£20)		10	
Thomas Wylkes (£220)	5	10	
James Brown (100 marks)		33	4
William Southwood (£120)	3		
John Marshe thelder (£30)		15	
John Marshe the yonger (£100)		50	
Agnes Hochens (500 marks)	8	6	8
John Blunden (200 marks)	3	6	8
Thomas Fuller (200 marks)		66	8

90. Straungers

John Malyerd (£10)		10	
James Buckett (100s.)		5	
Cornelys Gregorye, his servaunt			4
Thomas Fulkerston (£20)		20	
Jacob Warner, his servaunt (26s. 8d.)			16
Stephan Stephanson, his servaunt (40s.)		2	
Arthur Andwarp (20s.)			12
Robert Danker, his servaunt			4

	£	s.	d
Richard Gatson, servaunt with James			
Buttes (26s. 8d.)			16
James Harryson, his servaunt (40s.)		2	
Summa parochiae	214	11	8

PARTE OF SEYNT PETERS PARISH IN CHEPE
[English]

	£	s.	d
Vyncent Mundye, in landes (£125)	6	5	
Austen Hynd (£2000)	50		
John Machell, for William Machell (£600)	15		
William Moreton (£40)		20	
John Wythorne (£20)		10	
Richard Fox (£50)		25	
John Dane (£40)		20	
Robert Gage (£200)		100	
Herrye Bryan (£20)		10	
William Chamber (£20)		10	
Ales Meltham (£50)		25	
Summa parochiae	82	5	

91. PARTE OF THE PARISH OF SEYNT JOHN ZACHARYS
[English]

	£	s.	d
George Stalker (£20)		10	
Thomas Sessyngdale (£20)		10	
James Collens (£20)		10	
John Crowcock (40 marks)		13	4
John Wynd (£26 13s. 4d.)		13	4
John Raynoldes (£30) [ass. 10s. in Langbourn ward]		15	
Summa parochiae	3	11	8

CORPORACIONS & HALLES

	£	s.	d
The wardens of the brewers for theyr			
hall (£171 4s. 3¹/₂d.)	8	11	2¹/₂
The wardens of the haberdasshers for			
their hall, in landes (£54 3s. 1d.)		54	2
Summa de le corporacions	11	5	4¹/₂
Summa totales huis warde	933	2	8¹/₂

92. [r.22] DOWGATE WARDE
[Petty collectors: Herry Posyer and Herry Pott of the parish of Alhallows the Great]

ALHALLOWS THE MORE
[English]

	£	s.	d
Herry Posyer (£400)	10		
John Lambert (£133 6s. 8d.)	3	6	8
William Parnes (£40)		20	
Thomas Spenser (£80)		40	

	£	s.	d
William Mento (£60)		30	
William Baynarde (£40)		20	
Henry Pygnell (£40)		20	
Nycholas Smale (£40)		20	
John Hanyett (£40)		20	
Peter Dayesman (£40)		20	
William Hawkes (£30)		15	
George Hyde (£20)		10	
John Stone (£25)		12	6
Robert Mekylfeld (£20)		10	
John Hall (£20)		10	
Richard Bowle (£50)		25	
John Dawson (£60) [x - K 25s.]		30	
Robert Hunt (£30)		15	
Robert Waterford (£20)		10	
Evan Flod (£30)		15	
John Everyngham (£30)		15	
Richard Erley (£30)		15	
Nycholas Bell (£30)		15	
Edmonde Keye (£40)		20	
Thomas Felsted (£20)		10	
Robert Molson (£60)		30	
Christofre Bolton (£20)		10	
Richard Thomewood (£20)		10	

93. Straungers

	£	s.	d
Cornellys Hayes denysen (£400)	20		
Herry Pott (£220)	11		
Christofre Marche (40s.)		2	
Hance Mynstre (£3)		3	
Thomas van Osperey (£3)		3	
Herry Pottes servauntes			
Godfrey Derykson (£4)		4	
Herry Underbrewer (£3)		3	
John Ducheman drayman (£4)		4	
William Drayman (£3)		3	
Peter Franke (£3 6s. 8d.)		3	4
Nycholas Gonport bocher (£6 13s. 4d.)		6	8
Raynold Cornelynson his servaunt (40s.)		2	
Henry servaunt with the same Gonport			4
Mathewe Senson (£10)		10	
Nycholas Jelowse servaunt with Senson			4
William Cresse servaunt with Senson			4
John Rayne (40s.)		2	
Harman Joneson servaunt with Rayne (16s. 8d.)			10
Cornelys Derykson servaunt with Rayne			4
Edwarde Peterson in Heywarselane (£4)		4	
Lewys Williamson (20s.)			12

63

	£	s.	d
94. Phillip Parentyne			4
Angell Mathewe (£4)		4	
servaunt with Robert Molson			
Mathewe Nonesuche (£3)		3	
servauntes with Evan Flodd			
Crane Tonman (40s.)		2	
Bastean Tonman (30s.)			18
Myghell Drayman (40s.)		2	
William Drayman (40s.)		2	
servauntes with Cornellys Hayes			
Lambert Wolf (£4)		4	
John Pynne			4
John Barnett			4
Sympson Gladbeck			4
servauntes with Mondye Coper			
Cornelis Johnson (£3)		3	
Leonarde Hester (£3)		3	
Barnarde John			4
Summa parochiae	71	13	6

		£	s.	d
95.	ALHALLOWES THE LESSE			
	[English]			
uxor Wannesworthe (£60)			30	
Robert Rose (£30)			15	
Thomas Anderson (£20)			10	
John Baker (£50)			25	
John Thorneton (£20)			10	
Edmonde Eyton (£20)			10	
John Balden (£30)			15	
Thomas Butler (£20)			10	
Thomas Rutte (£40)			20	
uxor Newman (£20)			10	
William Heblethwayte (£20)			10	
Anthony Brigham (£100) [x - K 50s.]			50	
William Felips (£20)			10	
Richard Byndynge (£20)			10	
William Colmere (£20)			10	
Robert Dykynson (£20)			10	
William Gryffithe (£20)			10	
uxor Rankyn (£20)			10	
Richarde Rome (£20)			10	
John Belson (£20) [x - K 10s.]			10	
John Webbe (£20) [x - Cripplegate ward 15s.]			10	
Straungers				
Deryk Burbusshe (£20)			20	
George Sadler his servaunt (20s.)				12
Summa parochiae		16	6	

64

		£	s.	d
96.	SEYNT LAURENCE POUNTNEY			
	[English]			
Sir George Monnox knight (£1,000)				
[ass. £15 in Essex]		25		
Paule Wethypole (2000 marks)		33	6	8
James Wylkynson (£60)			30	
John Page (£20)			10	
Robert Coper (£60)			30	
William Chayrde (£60)			30	
Richard Beffyn (£20)			10	
John Guye (£20)			10	
uxor Norwoode (£20)			10	
William Boyse (£20)			10	
George Sklater (£20)			10	
Roger Wynder (£20)			10	
John Yeldam (£40) [ass. 20s. in				
Farringdon ward Without]			20	
Thomas Baylye (£20)			10	
William Halle (£20)			10	
	Summa parochiae	68	6	8

	£	s.	d
SEYNT JOHNS IN WALBROKE			
[English]			
John Vawdye (£100)		50	
Robert Lylborne (£20)		10	
William Harberye (£30)		15	
William Rogers (£20)		10	
Thomas Gybson (£20)		10	
William Kendalle (£20)		10	
John Over (£40)		20	
Anthony Crede (£30)		15	
Thomas Smythe (£20) [x - Q 20s.]		10	

		£	s.	d
97.	Straungers			
William Systres servaunt with				
William Rogers (£3 6s. 8d.)			3	4
Herry Hode servaunt with William				
Harberye (50s.)			2	6
William Calles				4
William Skynner				4
	Summa parochiae	7	16	6

	£	s.	d
CORPORACIONS AND HALLES WITHIN THE FORESAIDE WARDE			
First the Wardens of the Skynners			
(£264 8s. 4d.)	13	4	6
The Wardens of the Inholders (£42)		42	
The Wardens of the Tallowchandlers			
in landes (£25 7s. 1/2d.)		25	6

65

	£	s.	d
The Wardens of the Dyers (£40)		40	
Summa de le corporacions	18	12	
Summa totalis huius warde	182	14	8

98. [r.25]   THE WARD OF FARRYNGTON WITH IN
[Petty collectors: Nicholas Allwyn and Robert Spendeley of the parish of St. Vedast Foster Lane.]

THE HALFF PARISH OF SEYNT PETERS IN CHEPE
[English]

Robert Wygges (£20)		10	
Thomas Pyggon (£20		10	
Richarde Mallerye (£66 13s. 4d.)		33	4
Alexsandre Evelande (£60)		30	
Anthonye Nevell (£60)		30	
William Calton (£100)		50	
George Sympson (£30)		15	
John Germyn (£66 13s. 4d.)		33	4
Straungers			
John van Kyrkham (£30)		30	
Herrye Comforthe (40s.)		2	
Fraunces Bellyng, his servaunt			4
Rycharde Clowte (40s.)		2	
Richarde Beward, watterberer			4
Summa parochiae	12	6	4

99.   THE HALF PARISH OF SEYNT MATHEWE IN FRYDAY STRETE
[English]

William Etys (£500)	12	10	
Raff Rowllett (£3,000)			
[ass. £16 13s. 4d. in Herts.]	75		
William Sadler (£30)		15	
Nycholas Dykson (£30)		15	
William Averey (£20)		10	
Richard Doo (£30)		15	
John Dormer (£20)		10	
Nycholas Russell (£40)		20	
Christofre Hynkstell (£20)		10	
Edwarde Gylbert (£30)		15	
John Reed (100 marks)		33	4
Barthelmewe Cleving (£40)		20	
John Bolter (£30)		15	
Herry Coldwell (£40)		20	
John Wykes (£40)		20	
John Gardyner (40 marks)		13	4
William Kyrkham (£20)		10	
Richard Joneson (£20)		10	
Summa parochiae	100		20

66

		£	s.	d
100.	THE PARISH OF SEYNT FOSTERS [St. Vedast Foster Lane] [English]			
William Fermer (£400)		10		
Richard Callard (£2,000 [ass. £50 in Mddx.]		50		
Morgan Wolf (£1,000)		25		
Thomas Calton (£1,000)		25		
Raff Lathom (£1,000)		25		
Robert Baxster (£800)		20		
Robert Spendley (£500)		12	10	
Nychoas Alwyn (1,000) marks)		16	13	4
John Averell, executor to Herry Averell, his Father (2,000 marks)		33	6	8
Robert Hartop (400 marks)		6	13	4
William Sympson (£20)			10	
James Aldersley (40 marks)			13	4
John Coke (£110)			55	
John Wast (£40)			20	
Nycholas Joneson (£110)			55	
Laurence Warren (£20)			10	
Robert Ashehurst (400 marks)		6	13	4
Thomas Rede (100 marks)			33	4
John Chaundler (£40)			20	
John Langley (100 marks)			33	4
Robert Maddox (40 marks) [x - P 20s.]			13	4
Nycholas Molde (£30)			15	
John Harryson (£80)			40	
John Clerk (£30)			15	
Nycholas Bull (540 marks)		9		
Oswolde See (£30)			15	
Richard Grace (£40)			20	
John Byston (200 marks)		3	6	8
Thomas Hargrave (£50)			25	
101. Thomas Hollande (£100)			50	
Richard Yonge (£30)			15	
John Smale (£20)			10	
George Osborn (£20)			10	
James Jennyns (£20)			10	
Thomas Ellyott (£20)			10	
John Sharp (£40)			20	
Melcher Ingleberd (£20)			10	
Thomas Browne (£100)			50	
Herry Glover (40 marks)			13	4
Sylvester Todd (£80)			40	
George Wrightte's wyddowe (£20)			10	
Alexsandre Mason (£20)			10	

	£	s.	d
Martyn Goose (£20)		10	
Gyles Evenett (£40)		20	
Rychard Jones (£20)		10	
Rychard Clement (100 marks)		33	4
Thomas Dean (£30)		15	
Robert Suttrington (£20)		10	
William Williamson (£20)		10	
Andrewe Wright (£300)	7	10	
John Warren (£20)		10	
Summa parochiae	289	3	4

Mugwell Strete of the same warde
[English]

	£	s.	d
Roger Upholl, wever (£20)			10
William Cranewaye, tayleor (100 marks)		33	4
William Lambe of the chappell (£100) [x - K £5]			50

102. Straungers

	£	s.	d
Mr. John, Phisicion (100 marks)	3	6	8
Hans Evell, Jeryck Docheman, servauntes with Morgan			8
Godfrey Vanhowden, Albert Vanmynster, servauntes with Gyles Evenet			8
Barnard Cope, broderer			4
Garrett Cock, poche maker			4
Summa	8	2	

THE HALF PARISH OF SEYNT AUGUSTYN
[English]

	£	s.	d
Robert Ravyn (£500)	12	10	
James Jacob, ussher of Pooles Scole (100 marks)		33	4
Thomas Lowe (£60)		30	
Robert Raylton (£60)		30	
John Pecock (100 marks)		33	4
Robert Fust (£30)		15	
Thomas Preston (£20)		10	
William Styper (£20)		10	
Richard Hylton (£20)		10	
Thomas Gardyner (£20)		10	
William Weyfolde (£20)		10	
William Holte (£100) [x - K £5]		50	
Summa parochiae	24	11	8

103. THE HALF PARISH OF SEYNT MYGHELL AT THE QUERNE
[English]

	£	s.	d
John Chaunterell (£400)	10		
William Smythe (£30)		15	

	£	s.	d
Stephan Mason (200 marks)	3	6	8
John Bull (£20)		10	
Austyn Kytson (£20)		10	
Richard Buckland (£40)		20	
John Wethersbye (£20)		10	
John Leylonde (£50)		25	
Myles Partriche (£40)		20	
Bawdwyn Smythe (£20)		10	
Roger Newys (200 marks)			
[x - Castle Baynard ward £5]	3	6	8
William Mathewe (200 marks)	3	6	8
John Peterson (£20)		10	
Robert Steward (£30)		15	
Richarde Hardye (£20)		10	
Thomas Butler (100 marks)		33	4
Thomas Laurence (£30)		15	
John Ledyatt (400 marks)	6	13	4
Raff Cressye (£20)		10	
John Curtesse (£100)		50	
Henry Abell (£30)		15	
William Dunne (£20)		10	
Raff Hychecockes (£60)		30	
Thomas Kynge (£50)		25	
Thomas Joneson (£50)		25	
Henry Lyard (£20)		10	
Alice Baylye, wydowe (100 marks)		33	4
Elizabeth Osborn, wedowe (£20)		10	
Johan Westmere, wedowe (£20)		10	
Thomas Walker (£100)		50	
Edward Bover (£80)		40	
George Warren (£40)		20	
Margaret Phillips, wedowe (£20)		10	

104.   Straungers

	£	s.	d
Nycholas Deryk (£6 13s. 4d.)		6	8
Hughe Franchampyon, his servaunt			4
Jerome Nooke (£40)		40	
Erasymis, his servaunt			4
Cornellys Gregorye, capper			4
Walter Connye, joyne [sic] (20s.)			12
Garrett Clerk, Mathewe Skrame, John			
Harryson, servauntes with John Peterson			12
John Dylperye, William James, servauntes			
with Rycharde Peterson			8
Summa parochiae	56	15	4

69

	£	s.	d
THE PARISH OF SEYNT NYCHOLAS [English]			
Agnes Ladye Clerk (1000 marks)	16	13	4
John Baynton (£400)	10		
Robert Barker (1,000 marks)	16	13	4
Nycholas Sullyntan (100 marks)		33	4
Edwarde Castell (300 marks)	5		
Edmond Randehurst (£200)		100	
William Egleston (£100)		50	
William Smalewood (100 marks)		33	4
William Otterborn (£20)		10	
William Hethe (100 marks)		33	4
John Ilcockes (200 marks)	3	6	8
William Lychefelde (£20)		10	
William Dalyson (£20)		10	
Richarde Maskrye (£40)		20	
Davyd Sandbrok, the kinge's servaunt (100 marks) [x - K 33s. 6d.]		33	4
105. William Peter (100 marks)		33	4
Andrewe Castell (£40)		20	
Thomas Bracye (£40)		20	
Robert Redemer (£60)		30	
John Tayleor (£40)		20	
Thomas Playsot (200 marks) [x - K 67s. 6d.][30]	3	6	8
George Wheler (£30)		15	
John Gyles (£20)		10	
Robert Smere (£20)		10	
Thomas Underwood (£30)		15	
Roger Leversege (£40)		20	
William Woodshawe (£60)		30	
John Dodges (£40) [x - K 10s.][31]		20	
James Woodland (£50)		25	
Julyan Woodshawe, wedowe (£20)		10	
John Martyn (£40)		20	
William Yoxsall (£40)		20	
John Rychardson (£40)		20	
Thomas Ebeden (£20)		10	
Richard Born (£20)		10	
Robert Chamber (£20)		10	
John Kyngton (£20)		10	
John Lawnde (£40)		20	
Elyn Castell, wedowe (£20)		10	
Martyn Eddes (£20)		10	

30. E.359/44, r. 19 gives surname as Playfote.
31. E.359/44, r. 19 gives surname as Dodge.

	£	s.	d
Straungers			
Roger Freyse (20s.)			12
John Deryk, his servaunt			4
Summa parochiae	92	13	

106. THE PARISH OF SEYNT EWEN
[or St. Audoen]
[English]

	£	s.	d
Henrye Horne (£200)	5		
William Coke, Doctor of Lawe			
(100 marks)		33	4
Hugh Egglebye, gent. (£20)		10	
Thomas Bughe (40 marks)		13	4
Edward Metcalf (£40) [x - K 26s.]		20	
Richard Ferror (£100)		50	
Symond Rychardson (£40)		20	
William Wytt (40 marks)		13	4
Thomas Walden (40 marks)		13	4
William Hyllyard (£20)		10	
John Holte, coke (£20)		10	
Thomas Martyn (£30)		15	
Henrye Hamond (£20)		10	
Mr. Wylloughbye, serjeant at armys, in			
landes & Fees (£40)		40	
Richard Bradborrye (£20)		10	
John Derdrewe (£20) [x - K 21s. 4d.]		10	
Straungers			
Jerom Bennell of Veromis in Fee (£10)		20	
Fraunces Bennell & Isack Mountanye, his			
servauntes			8
John Marya (£20) [x - K 37s.]		20	
who hath iii straungers to his servauntes			12
Summa parochiae	21		

107. THE PARTE OF SEYNT FAYTHES PARISHE
[English]

	£	s.	d
John Talkerne (£1,000)	25		
John Hughes (1,000 marks)	16	13	4
Anthonye Hussye (£400)	10		
Christofre Barker, Kinge of harroldes			
(£200) [ass. £4 in Essex]	5		
Robert Bannaster (£200) [x - K £5]	5		
Doctor Tregonnell (£300)			
[x - Herts. £8]	7	10	
John Storye, Doctor of tharches			
(100 marks)		33	4
Thomas Argall, Regestry of the Prerogatyve			
(400 marks)	6	13	4

	£	s.	d
Robert Joneson, proctor of tharches (£200)	5		
Robert Goode (200 marks)	3	6	8
John Heryng (100 marks)		33	4
Thomas Dockrey (100 marks)			
[ass. 10s. in Berks.][32]		33	4
Herry Bonsfell (100 marks)		33	4
Thomas Stacye (£30)		15	
John Kydde (40 marks)		13	4
Roger Huntstribe of thadmyraltye (100 marks)		33	4
George Selye, gentilman, in landes and			
Fees (£30) [x - Essex 40s.]		30	
Jone Ashley, wedowe (200 marks)		66	8
William Wylbert (£200)	5		
John Turner (100 marks)		33	4
Thomas Pettytt (£100)		50	
William Bonham (200 marks)		66	8
Peter Turner (£100)		50	
Richard Jones, Scolmaister of Poolles			
(100 marks)		33	4
John Clampert (£20)		10	
Herry Dabbys (£40)		20	
George Thomeson (40 marks)		13	4
Edmond Campyon (£40)		20	
Symond Coston (£30)		15	
William Bull, verger of Poolles (£40)		20	
Robert Toye (£20)		10	
Robert Bull (£20)		10	
John Fyssher (£20)		10	

108.   Straungers

	£	s.	d
John Reynes, fredenysen (£100)	5		
Ranulphe Docheman, fredenysen			
(100 marks)	3	6	8
Arnolde Brightman, keping shopp & stock			
in Paule's Churchyard, by Herry			
Harman, his Factor (100 marks)		66	8
John Cockes, fredenysen (100 marks)	3	6	8
Johan Andrewe, wedowe (£6 13s. 4d.)		6	8
James Fox, servaunt to John Raynes			4
John Gybkyn, servaunt to John Cockes			4
Thomas Grey, servaunt to Thomas Pettytt			4
John Rowe, servaunt to Harry Harman			4
John Brightman, kepyng shopp in Paule's			
Churche yarde with one John Calwood			
(100 marks)		66	8
Summa parochiae	140	11	4

32. E.359/44, r. 14 gives surname as Dockrell.

	£	s.	d
THE PARISH OF SEYNT SEPULCRE FOR THE PARTE WITHIN NEWGATE [English]			
John Bargayn, brewer (100 marks)		33	4
Gilbert Pennyngton (£40)		20	
Thomas Clayton (£20)		10	
Robert Jewet, letherseller (£20)		10	
Thomas [Wyer?] (200 marks)	3	6	8
Humfrey Gaudy (£20)		10	
George Wynyard (£20)		10	
Robert Moldyng (£20)		10	
Edmonde Wheler (£20)		10	
Edward Steward (200 marks) [x - Q 66s. 8d.]		66	8
Richarde Parkyns (£20)		10	
Summa parochiae	12	16	8

109.   THE PARTE OF SEYNT MARTYNS PARISH AT LUDGATE
[English]

	£	s.	d
Dame Margarete Pecok, wedowe (2,000 marks)[33]	16	13	4
Andrewe Fraunces (£600) [ass. £5 in Kent]	15		
William Tayleor (£600)	15		
John Wilford (£400)	10		
Charles White (£40)		20	
William Braban (100 marks)		33	4
Rychard Alen (£20)		10	
Agnes Codnam, wydowe (£50)		25	
Richard Cade (200 marks)	3	6	8
Mr. John Wellesborne, in landes and Fees (500 marks) [Process][34]	16	13	4
Margerye Thomeson, wedowe (100 marks)		33	4
John Erley (100 marks)		33	4
William Chertsey (£100)		50	
William Cottingham (£100)		50	
Christofre Hatche (£20)		10	
Thomas Orwell (£20)		10	
John Fyssher (£20)		10	
Robert Gower (£20)		10	
Elizabeth Turke, wedowe (40 marks)		13	4
Robert Thrower, keper of Ludgate (£40)		20	
Thomas Foster (40 marks)		13	4
Thomas Blagg (£50)		25	

33. There is an error either in the valuation or in the assessment.
34. John Wellesborne, esq. claimed before the barons that he was a Gentleman of the Privy Chamber in the King's household and attended there daily, that he had been assessed £7 10s. by the subsidy commissioners of the King's household, and that he had no residence in the city of London. He was discharged in London (E.359/44, r. 19; E.159/321, *communia* Trinity 34 Hen. VIII, r. 24).

	£	s.	d
Stephan Walden (£40)		20	
Gregorye Conyers (£50)		25	
Rychard Bramfeld and John Lacye,			
partners (£20)		10	
Straungers			
James Terhoven, keper of Burgayne			
place (40s.)		2	
Richard Wayer (£4)		4	
John William & Myghell George			
his servauntes			8
Henry Thomas servaunt to Tors			4
Summa parochiae	98	2	

110. THE PARISH OF SEYNT ANNE AT LUDGATE

	£	s.	d
Marye Ladye Kyngeston in landes (£200)	10		
Anne Ladye Greye in landes and Fee			
(£123 6s. 8d.)	6	3	4
Anne Partriche wedowe in Fee (£20)		20	
Sir Christofre Moore Knyght in landes			
and Fee (200 marks) [Process][35]	6	13	4
Mr. [John] Lucas in landes (£100)			
[Process][36]	5		
Alexsaundre Fundant (£30)		15	
John James (£30) [x - Farringdon ward			
Without 50s.]		15	
Mr. Kyllygrave (40 marks)		13	4
William Curson (40 marks)		13	4
Straungers			
John Partynarye pencioner in Fee			
(£48) [x - K £5 11s. 4d.]	4	16	
Peter Greke broderer (£100)		100	
whoo hathe fyve servauntes			20
John Growte, bokebynder (£20)		20	
John Tyrrart hosyer (£6 13s. 4d.)		6	8
Barnard Busshe merchaunt (£40)			
[x - Candlewick ward 66s. 8d.]		40	
Summa parochiae	44	17	8

Corporacions or halles

	£	s.	d
The Sadlers hall in landes (£82 6s. 8d.)	4	2	4

35. Sir Christopher Moore claimed that whereas subsidy commissioners living within the limits of their commissions should be assessed there and whereas he was a commissioner in Surrey and had a residence there he should not be assessed in London. The barons of the exchequer discharged him in London on payment of an assessment of £5 in Surrey (E.359/44, r. 19; E.159/321, *communia* Easter 34 Hen. VIII, r. 48).

36. John Lucas, esq., subsidy commissioner in Kent, was discharged in London on payment of assessment of 50s. in Kent (E.359/44, r. 19; E.159/321, *communia* Trinity 34 Hen. VIII, r. 69). See preceding note.

	£	s.	d
The Broderers hall in goodes (£26 18s. 7d.)		26	11
The Barbors hall in goodes (£108 2s. 8d.)	5	8	1
Summa corporac'	10	17	4
Summa totalis huis warde	911	18	4

111. [r.12] THE WARDE OF FARYNGTON WYTHOUT

[Petty collectors: Thomas Rychardes of the parish of St. Dunstan in the West and John Goodlad of the parish of St. Sepulchre, Holborn.]

	£	s.	d
SAYNT DUNSTONES PARYSSHE			
John Pakyngton gent (500 marks)	8	6	8
John Crooke gent (£200)	5		
Thomas Broke (1000 marks)	16	13	4
Thomas Whyte executour to			
Robart Walworth (£400)	10		
Margaret Kyrkeby Wydowe (£400)	10		
Robert Southwell Mr of the Rolles in			
landes & Fees (500 marks)			
[ass. 56s. 8d. in Surrey][37]	16	13	4
John Baker knyght under tresorer in			
landes & Fees (500 marks)	16	13	4
Rychard Pollard Esquyar generall			
surveyour in landes & Fees (£230)	11	10	
Symon Estoffe (£20)		10	
Robart Brown (40 marks)		13	4
Thomas Packer (200 marks)		66	8
Alyce Flaxton (£200)	5		
Robert Thomas (£40)		20	
George Spencer (40 marks)		13	4
Robert Bucke (£40)		20	
John Wytsyndell (£40)		20	
Henry Lygh (£200)	5		
Wylliam Thomas (£20)		10	
Wylliam James (£200)	5		
Thomas Clayton (£20)		10	
Reynold Conygrave (200 marks)		66	8
Dyonyse Wylson (£30)		15	
John Penson (£40)		20	
Robert Shawe (£30)		15	
Wylliam Rose (£20)[38]		10	
Alyce Dakers Wydowe (400 marks)	6	13	4
John Whytepayne (200 marks)		66	8
John Jamys (£100) [ass. 15s. in Farringdon			
ward Within]		50	

37. Southwell is styled knight in E.359/44, r. 5.
38. Either this person or another of the same name assessed for the same amount in this ward (William Rose, below, **122**) defaulted (E.359/44, r. 19).

	£	s.	d
112. Thomas Sewell (£30)		15	
Robert Pascall (£30)		15	
John Armyne (£100)		50	
John Fysshar (£200) [x - ?][39]	5		
John Olestre (£30)		15	
John Scott grocer (£40)		20	
Roland Shakelady (£100)		50	
Robert Fletewood (£80)		40	
Thomas Humfrey (£20)		10	
Eustace Kyteley (40 marks)		13	4
Elyzabeth Mychell Wydowe (£20)		10	
Thomas Haryson (£40)		20	
Rafe Rathebone (£20)		10	
Rychard Studley (£30)		15	
Mychaell Bryseworth (100 marks)		33	4
Roger Gaton (£20)		10	
Wylliam Garrard (£300)	7	10	
Gyles Atkynson (£20)		10	
Rychard Whealer (£20)		10	
John Machyn (£20)		10	
Bertholomewe Brokesby (£20)		10	
John Hogane (£20)		10	
Thomas Holbecke (£200)	5		
John Wayland (£40)		20	
Nycholas Mellowe (£30)		15	
113. Nycholas Gybson (£20)		10	
John Styckeman (£20)		10	
John Horneby (£100)		50	
Wyllyam Langham (£20)		10	
John Leycetour (£40)		20	
Bertholomewe Cane (£20)		10	
John Colyns (£20)		10	
John Parker (£20) [a]		10	
Symon Pondar (£30)		15	
Edward Morley (£40)		20	
Thomas Rychardes (£300)	7	10	
Wyllyam Peghenne (400 marks)	6	13	4
Wyllyam Anderson (£20)		10	
Thomas Hall (£20)		10	
Wylliam Cholmeley (£400)	10		
John A Deane (£20)		10	
John Tholmewood (£20)		10	
Syr Wylliam Pounder knyght in land (£20)		20	
James Harward (£200)	5		

39. E.359/44, r. 19 records Fisher's and the collectors' discharge on the basis of an assessment paid in another place, but the other place is omitted from the enrolled accounts.

	£	s.	d
Wylliam Rydgeley (£200)	5		
Rychard Aleyn (£30)		15	
Rychard Danson (£20)		10	
[Blank] Barthelett (£20)		10	
Rychard Hoppar (£40)		20	
Thomas Shyngeleton (£20)		10	
Henry Eve (£40)		20	
Wylliam Lordyng (£20)		10	
Wylliam Jonys (£20)		10	
Robert Longe (£40)		20	
Willyam Spaynyard (£20)		10	
Thomas Spownar (200 marks)		66	8
Barnard Foxe (£20)		10	
Rychard Tonge (£200)	5		
Wylliam Tonge (£20)		10	
Gyles Polynere (£100)		50	
Edward Peche (£100)		50	
Wyllyam Wendon in lande (£20)		20	
Rychard Tavernar (£200)	5		

114.　　　　　CHAUNCERY LANE

	£	s.	d
Edward Garthe (£40)		20	
Symon Dygby (£30)		15	
Edmond Walter (100 marks)		33	4

THE WHYTE FREARS

	£	s.	d
Dame [Katherine] Edgecombe in land (500 marks) [x - Cornwall £6; owed £10 13s. 4d. in Farringdon ward Without; Process][40]	16	13	4
George Rolles (400 marks)	6	13	4
Andrewe Barnard (£100)		50	
Agnes Tycle Wydowe (£20)		10	
John Gerrard (£200) [a]	5		
Rychard Morysyne (£200)	5		
John Yeldam (£50) [x - Dowgate ward 20s. owes 5s. in Farringdon ward Without]		25	
Saynt Dunstones Brotherhed (100 marks)		66	8

Alyens

	£	s.	d
Cornelius Feyth			4
Denyse Roe			4
John Burrett			4
John Roe			4
Wyllyam Vyncent (£5)	5		

40. Dame Katherine Edgecombe apparently paid an assessment of £6 in Cornwall. Of the £10 13s. 4d. remaining to be paid in London she and the collectors received exoneration of £4 13. 4d. (E.359/44, r. 19, dorse). The grounds for this action are unclear. The record of the proceedings in the K. R. Memoranda Rolls has not been located.

	£	s.	d
WHYTE FREARS			
James Mercady (60s.)		3	
John Swerebourn			4
Hannet Fugelder			4
Andrewe Janson, with Longe			4
Henry Lowman, with Longe			4
115.　　　　SAYNT BRYDES PARYSSHE			
Thomas Barthelett (500 marks)	8	6	8
Symon Webbe (£400)	10		
John Joynour (£400)	10		
Edward Hasylwood (£300)	7	10	
John Coke (£25)		12	6
John Studde (£200)	5		
Edmonde Adams (£40)		20	
Edward Rydge (200 marks)		66	8
Johane Pegge Wydowe (£200)	5		
John Guylmyn (£300) [x - K £7 10s. 6d.]	7	10	
James Ganer Alyen (£50)		50	
John Beddyll (£50)		25	
John Wardroper (£20)		10	
Wylliam Southwell (£20)		10	
Anthony Skynnar (£200)	5		
George Broodes (£30)		15	
John Pursell (£30)		15	
Crystofer Alygh (£40)		20	
John Hulson (100 marks)		33	4
Wyllyam Stockeley (100 marks)		33	4
Thomas Warnar (£20)		10	
Wylliam Fostar (£20)		10	
Robart Buckett (£20)		10	
Wyllyam Stoddard (£30)		15	
John Sandy (£40)		20	
John Heyward (£20)		10	
John Spurnestone (£20)		10	
John Louthe (£20)		10	
John Barton (£40)		20	
Wylliam Hynyon (£20)		10	
Water Chylderhouse (£30)		15	
Lawrence Taylour (£40)		20	
John Smyth (£30)		15	
Rychard Cartar (£30)		15	
John Ayland (100 marks)		33	4
John Craythorne (100 marks)		33	4
116. Wyllyam Page (£20)		10	
Thomas Cousyn (200 marks)		66	8
George Davyson (£200)		100	

	£	s.	d
Crystofer Drey (£60)		30	
Frauncys Waferer (£40)		20	
Roger Carelyle (£30)		15	
Thomas Clyffe (£40)		20	
Henry Naylar (200 marks)		66	8
John Robynson (200 marks)		66	8
Rychard Sellar (£50)		25	
Antony Hylle (£40)		20	
Thomas Furneys (£20)		10	
Stephan Cocke (£100)		50	
Thomas Jackeson (£80)		40	
Edmond Brygges (£20)		10	
Thomas Pyers (£40)		20	
John Connyngham (£20)		10	
Wylliam Watkynson (£50)		25	
Henry Byrd (100 marks)		33	4
Robart Huyc (£100)		50	
Anthony Tote Alyen (£100)	5		
Edmond Powell (500 marks) [a]	8	6	8
Wylliam Beton (£30)		15	
Thomas Gains (£20)		10	
Alexander Hudson (£100)		50	
John Deane (£50)		25	
Thomas Stephanson (£20)		10	
Thomas Geffrey (200 marks) [ass. 40s. in K]		66	8
Robart Warter (100 marks)		33	4
Rychard Mody (200 marks)		66	8
Robert Mathewe in land (£55)		55	
John Fyttys (£30)		15	
Francys Archan Alien (£50)		50	
Rychard Heywood (£100)		50	
Wylliam Mortymer (£30)		15	
Henry Maxwell (£200)		100	
117. Peter Sampford (£20)		10	
Peter Newes (£20)		10	
John Grey (£30)		15	
John Poope (£20)		10	
Prudens Davyds Wydowe (£20)		10	
Robert Postell (£20)		10	
Rychard Wynkyn (200 marks)		66	8
John Bearde (£40)		20	
The Brothered of Saynt Brydes (£40)		40	

Alyens

	£	s.	d
Nycodemus, with John Beddyll		4	

SALYSBURY COURT

	£	s.	d
Robert Turen			4

79

	£	s.	d
Robart Lambart			4
Frauncys Jeram			4
Symon de Bruges			4

THE CATHERYNE WHELE ALEY

	£	s.	d
Barnard Bartolmewe			4
Gerveis Soyer (20s.)			12
Denyse Nycols			4
Thomas Rycus			4
Hamon Rygolly			4
Denyse Campe			4
Antony Gylbart			4
Vyncent Janson (20s.)			12
John Turnar (20s.)			12

ALYENS IN SHOWE LANE

	£	s.	d
William Danna (20s.)			12
John Courteyn (20s.)			12
John Ansell			4
Robart Damaney			4
John Dunne (£4)		4	
Laurence Marchaunt			4
Anthony Barbor			4
John Nycols Scott			4
Wylliam Honsher			4
Nowell Havy			4
John Pollard			4
John Rouse (£4)		4	
Maryone Rowse			4
Gyles Lorret (£4)		4	

	£	s.	d
118. with John Elyot			
Nycolas Hubert (20s.)			12
James Bukere (20s.)			12
John Perer			4
John Lumbard			4
Peter Hubert			4
George Barkeman			4
Wyllyam Tulene (40s.)		2	
John Colt			4

POPYNIAY ALEY

	£	s.	d
Clement Mauryce (20s.)			12
Nycolas Pelleryn			4
Wylliam Janson			4
Bastyan Pelleryn			4

	£	s.	d
OUR LADYES WHARF			
Nycolas Hyles (20s.)		12	
Nycolas Franker (20s.)		12	
BRYDE LANE			
Antony Peterson (20s.)		12	
Mychaell Faunoures		4	
Roland Hartone		4	
BLACKE HORSE ALEY			
Gyles de Barre (20s.)		12	

119. SAYNT MARTYNS PARYSSHE

	£	s.	d
Richard Aleyn (£500)	12	10	
Nycholas Spakeman (£1000)	25		
John Usshe alias Wysse (£666 13s. 4d.)	16	13	4
Sir Roger Cholmely knyght (£1000)	25		
George Alen (£300)	7	10	
Crystofer Harbottell (£300)	7	10	
Henry Settaby (£20)		10	
Laurence Elyotte (£40)		20	
Agnes Nansan Wydowe (£40)		20	
John Dale (£300) [x - K £7 10s. 6d.]	7	10	
Robart Shankes (£30)		15	
Nycolas Gore (£20)		10	
Robert Phylyppys (£200)		100	
Rychard Cawood (100 marks)		33	4
Rychard Holand (100 marks)		33	4
Wylliam Shortred (£30)		15	
Willyam Wodland (£20)		10	
Benet Burton (£300)	7	10	
Thomas Atkynson (100 marks)		33	4
Laurence Robiant (£300)	7	10	
John Elyce (£20)		10	
John Ayland (£20)		10	
Hugh Holmes (£40)		20	
Antony Tuckehyll (£30)		15	
Thomas Fountayne (£50)		25	
John Tomson (£20)		10	
Thomas Patryke (£20)		10	
John Hawood (£30)		15	
Margaret Southworth Wydoo (£50)		25	
Rychard Hanysworth (£20)		10	
Robart Bracy (£20)		10	
John Lyne (£30)		15	
Margery Robynson Wydoo (£20)		10	
Rafe Alyson (£30)		15	
Wylliam Draper (£40)		20	

	£	s.	d
Alyens			
Peter Fortune			4

120.   SAYNT SEPULCRES PARYSSH

	£	s.	d
Wylliam Squyar (£400)	10		
Mary Taylor Wydowe (£400)	10		
Thomas Acon (£400)	10		
Andrewe Carr (£20)		10	
Wylliam Holand (100 marks)		33	4
John Soule (£20)		10	
Edmund Spencer (£20)		10	
Nycolas Cooke (£40)		20	
Wylliam Bodyley (£60)		30	
Henry Ward (200 marks)		66	8
Thomas Spence (£40)		20	
Wylliam Shawe (300 marks)	5		
Thomas Hodgeson (£20)		10	
Rychard Pygotte (£20)		10	
Thomas Elyce (£20)		10	
Humfrey Aleyn (£30)		15	
Thomas Parker (£30)		15	
Roland Tweddyll (£20)		10	
Robert Clerk Woodmonger (£40)		20	
John Edlyn (200 marks) [x - K 50s.; owes 16s. 8d. in Farringdom ward Without]		66	8
Robert Clerk haberdassher (£200)		100	
Elyzabeth Brycker Wydowe (£200)		100	
John Neveyll (100 marks)		33	4
John Grymeshaue (200 marks)		66	8
John Ward (£40)		20	
Thomas Hodges gent (100 marks)		33	4
Thomas Thredder (£40)		20	
Thomas Oldnall (£100) [x - K 40s.; owes 10s. in Farringdon ward Without]			50
John Chapman (£20)		10	
Rychard Martyn (£400)	10		
John Goodladde (£400) [ass. 50s. in Westminster]	10		
John Ramsey (£20)		10	
Elyzabeth Conway (£40)		20	
Crystofer Jackeson (£100)		50	
John Kenyam (£40)		20	
Thomas Jordeyn (£40)		20	
John Grey (100 marks)		33	4
Henry Garrett (£20)		10	
Thomas Lyney (£40)		20	
121. John Downynge (£20)		10	

82

	£	s.	d
Wylliam Wytham (£20)		10	
Wylliam Mauryce (£20)		10	
Thomas Nasshe (£30)		15	
Rychard Mauryce (£30)		15	
Rychard Hudson (£150)		75	
John Laurence (£20)		10	
Hugh Walsshe (£20)		10	
George Depynge (£30)		15	
Wylliam Smyth (£20)		10	
Wylliam Grene (£20)		10	
Wylliam Twynam (£20)		10	
John Jeram (£20)		10	
Wylliam Rawlyns (100 marks) [x - K 33s. 6d.]		33	4
Wyllyam Bulle (£20)		10	
Robert Reason (£40)		20	
John Pope (£20)		10	
Wyllyam Hardewood (£30)		15	
Thomas Blackewell (£20)		10	
John Duffeld (£20)		10	
John Angell (£20)		10	
Geffrey Chambre (£200)		100	
Thomas Bryght (£40) [ass. 15s. in Herts.]		20	
Anne Touny Wydowe (£20)		10	
John Twyford (£150)		75	
Thomas Hodges (£40)		20	
Henry Mallery (£30)		15	
Wylliam Janson (£20)		10	
Laurence Wylson (£20)		10	
Gregory Newman (£100)		50	
Thomas Myrryall (£40)		20	
Wylliam Storyar (£30)		15	
Wylliam Hasyll (£50)		25	
Wylliam Yonge (£40)		20	
Robert Bolmer (£20)		10	
William Robynson (£40)		20	
122. Johanne Ryce Wydowe (£60)		30	
Thomas Worme (£20)		10	
Robart Hylton (£20)		10	
William Moore (£100) [x - Hants. 51s.]		50	
Robart Northfolke (£20)		10	
John Lause (£30)		15	
Robart Clerk yoinor (£20)		10	
Edmund Wythars (£30)		15	
Wylliam Candy (£20)		10	
Thomas Ratclyff (£50)		25	
Wylliam Chamberlayne (£20)		10	

	£	s.	d
Robert Straker (£20)		10	
Ambrose Beckewyth (£30)		15	
Robert Mount (£20)		10	
Wylliam Hasylwood (£20)		10	
Roger Gryswytte (£20)		10	
Thomas Butlar (£20)		10	
John Fullar (£20)		10	
Wylliam Rose (£20)[41]		10	
Wylliam Tompson (£40)		20	
Nycolas Cryspyn (£20)		10	
Margaret Yoinour Wydowe (100 marks)		33	4
Edmund Lone (100 marks)		33	4
Geffry Robjohn (£40)		20	
Hugh Woodhouse (£30)		15	
Wyllyam Bodyan (£20)		10	
Wylliam Colyns (300 marks)	5		
Wylliam Northew (£20)		10	
John Samson (£40)		20	
Simon Goldsmyth (£40)		20	
Alyce Percyvall Wydowe (£20)		10	
Thomas Whyte gent (£300)	7	10	
John Montacue (£20)		10	
John Talam (£20)		10	
Wylliam Laurence (£20)		10	
123. Wylliam Ottee (£40)		20	
George Holand (100 marks)		33	4
Wylliam Bolton (£20)		10	
Thomas Doughty (£20)		10	
Wyllyam Elyff (£20)		10	
Rychard Phylpott (£50)		25	
George Aylesbury (£50)		25	
John Mychell (£50)		25	
Wyllyam Proutyng (£40)		20	
Wylliam Rynge (£20)		10	
Robart Graunt (100 marks)		33	4
Wyllyam Dunkyns (£40)		20	
John Goose (£50)		25	
Thomas Sneppe (£40)		20	
Robart Chydeley (£400)	10		

Alyens in Saynt Sepulcres parysshe

	£	s.	d
Rychard Haryson			4
Robert Frese			4
Savery Goodson (40s.)		2	
Henry Mangam			4

41. Either this person or another of the same name assessed for the same amount in this ward (William Rose, above, **111**) defaulted (E.359/44, r. 19).

	£	s.	d
Garrett Cole (£10)		10	
Symon Fyngartret			4
Arnold dwellyng with Banester			4
Andrewe Walker Scot (20s.)			12
Antony Sherbord			4
Alexaunder Min[?]ey			4
John Rocke (20s.)			12
Robert Aragon (20s.)			12
Henry Hercules			4
Richard Johnson (20s.)			12
Reynold Worley			4
Robert Frencheman			4
Arnold Pycke (£6)		6	
John Holand [x - Mddx. 12d.]			4
Matthy Tyce			4
Antony Feuer (£10)		10	
Clode Peynter			4
Antonina Broke (£6)		6	
Sebastiana Augustina (£6)		6	
Bertholmewe Penne (£30)		30	
Francys Mandes (20s.)			12
Nycholas Stoke			4
Antony Tonar (£10)		10	

124. GREATE SAYNT BERTHOLMEUS

	£	s.	d
Doctor Bartelett (£800)	20		
Sir Rychard Ryche knyght in landes & Fees (£800)	40		
And in goodes for Elys Baldery in his kepyng (£200)	5		
Thomas Burgayne (£300)	7	10	
Robert Burgayne (£300)	7	10	
George Gylle (100 marks) [ass. 20s. in Herts.]		33	4
John Dodyngton (100 marks) [x - Herts. 20s.; owes 13s. 4d. in Farringdon ward Without]		33	4
Thomas Androse (100 marks)		33	4
John Plumstede (200 marks)		66	8
Wyllyam Bellamye (100 marks) [a]		33	4
Rychard Aleyn (£40)		20	
Rychard Mody (100 marks)		33	4
John Hygham (200 marks) [a]		66	8
Mathewe Whyte (£30)		15	
John Mantyll (£40)		20	
Rychard Duke (£400) [ass. £7 10s. in Aldgate ward]	10		
Dorathye Pavyer (40 marks)		13	4

	£	s.	d
Doctor [Thomas] Bylle (£200) [x - Q			
66s. 8d.; owes 33s. 4d. in			
Farringdon ward Without][42]		100	
Wylliam Wadley (£50)		25	
Hugh Apparree (£50)		25	
John Stele Alyen (40s.)		2	
Rychard Garrett Alyen (40s.)		2	

125.   LYTTELL SAYNT BARTHOLMEWES

	£	s.	d
Thomas Golde (£40)		20	
William Poppeley (£200) [a]		100	
John Taylor grocer (£40)		20	
Nycholas Webstar (£20)		10	
Johane Petyte Wydowe in lande (£20)		20	
Phylyp Day (£20) [a]		10	
Thomas Woodward (£40)		20	

Alyens

	£	s.	d
Rychard Strode (20s.)			12
Roger de Laune (20s.)			12
Nicolas Grote			4
Rychard Forture			4
John Bertholmewe (20s.)			12
Garrett Hubart			4
Godfray Emons			4
Arnold Wylson			4
Clode Parno			4
Robert Caunerley (20s.)			12
Geffrey de la Pynne (£10)		10	
Wylliam Bryght			4
Rychard Colles			4
Hugh Aldren			4
Goson Garrett		.	4
Fren Gyson			4
Arnold Ryner			4
Dyryke Bonemay			4

126.   SAYNT ANDREWES PARYSSHE

	£	s.	d
John Whyttryge (200 marks)		66	8
John Romayne (100 marks) [x - Mddx. 30s.;			
owes 3s. 4d. in Farringdon ward Without]		33	4
Robert Gryffyn (£20)		10	
Thomas Hasylwall (£20)		10	
Rychard Hone (£100)		50	
Rychard Wylkes (100 marks)		33	4

42. This follows the enrolled account for London (E.359/44, r. 19), but one would infer from the enrolled account for the queen's household that he paid the £5 assessed in Farringdon ward Without and was discharged from the 66s. 8d. (E.359/44, r. 15).

	£	s.	d
Robert Hunton (£30)		15	
Thomas Dalton (£20)		10	
John Mylles (£20)		10	
Thomas Belson (100 marks) [x - Mddx. 10s.;			
owes 23s. 4d. in Farringdon ward Without]		33	4
Roland Atkynson (£50)		25	
Rychard Hunt (100 marks)		33	4
John Danlyns (£30)		15	
Crystofer Ward (£20)		10	

Alyens

	£	s.	d
Henry Cockes			4
Henry Harte (£20)		20	
Henry Stylt			4
Harman Rycke			4
Wylliam Garrett (20s.)			12
John Tetys			4
Peter Sanderson			4
Guyllam Gybotte (60s.)		3	
Charles Curdo			4
Matthewe [blank]			4
Summa totales huius wardi	962	6	2

127. [r.6a] LANGBORNE WARDE

[Petty collectors: Thomas Curtes of the parish of St. Edmund the King and Martyr, pewterer, and William Chester of the same parish, merchant taylor.]

SEYNT MARY WOLNETH PERRYSHE
[English]

	£	s.	d
John Bardolf (£50)		25	
Thomas Wetherhill (£20)		10	
Richard Pawsyn (100 marks)		33	4
Fabyan Wether (£50)		25	
Thomas Hancock (£20)		10	
John Raynoldes (£20) [x - Cripplegate			
ward 15s.]		10	
Thomas Stephins (£60)		30	
Stephin Hawkyns (£30)		15	
Henry Boshall (£20)		10	
Thomas Boughton (£20)		10	
John Rok (£30)		15	
George Webbe (£50)		25	
Jamys Stephins (£30)		15	
Thomas Marshall (£20)		10	
John Robson (£20)		10	
Christofer Salmon (£20)		10	
Edward Barbor (£30)		15	
Thomas Atkynson (£20)		10	
George Tadlow (£40)		20	

	£	s.	d
Thomas Fowle (£30)		15	
Jamys Mighell (£20)		10	
Thomas Taylor (£20)		10	
John Oteringham (£30)		15	
Marten Bowes alderman (5000 marks)	83	6	8
Thomas Bowyar (£1000)	25		
William Rest (1000 marks)	16	13	4

128. Straungers

	£	s.	d
Dyego de Isonsa (£20) [a]		20	
Charles Varlendo his Apprentyse [and]			
Nowell Gorryxson his Apprentyse [a]		8	
Stephin Blanchard and Mary Dornelles			
his servauntes [a]		8	
Balthezar Crowson servaunt with			
Thomas Marshall (40s.)		2	
Nicholas [Blank] servaunt with			
Thomas Boughton (40s.)		2	
Guylham Marten servaunt with			
Thomas Stephins (40s.)		2	
Mathew Rony servaunt with the same			
Stephins (20s.)			12
Zachary Scult denyzen (£4) [a][43]		4	
Hans Comber his servaunt (40s.) [a]		2	
Hermand Newman his servaunt (30s.) [a]			18
Charles Combergher servaunt with			
John Raynoldes (40s.)		2	
Dyego Negro servaunt with Thomas Bowyer			4
John Sure of Turney haveing in his			
possession hattes pynnes and other			
small Tryfulles of John & Anthony			
Croyen of Turney to the value of			
(40s.)		2	
The same John Sure & Gertrude his wyf for			
ther polles			8
Agnes ther servaunt and Lawrencia a Dane			
servaunt with Davy Rogers			8
Summa Totalis huius perrochie 144		19	10

129. SEYNT NYCHOLAS ACON PERRYSHE
[English]

	£	s.	d
Raulf Johnson (£60)		30	
Robert Kyng (£20)		10	
Nicholas Allcok (£30)		15	
Lawrence Johnson (£20)		10	

---

43. E.359/44, r. 19 gives surname as Stowlt.

	£	s.	d
George Brugg (£60)		30	
Raulf Bernard (£20)		10	
George Brugge for Orphanage of the			
Chyldren of Humfray Munmouth (£20 6s.)		Charged in the	
		orphanage boke	
Straungers			
Benedyk Gundolo straunger (£200)	10		
John Vandergow alias van Andwerep (£30)		30	
Nicholas de Nale (£200)	10		
Fraunceis Gebon servaunt to			
Benedyk Gondola (60s.)		3	
John Cadalor servaunt also with			
Nicholas de Nale (£5) [a]		5	
Antony Pons butler to the same (60s.)		3	
Bernard Assefat (£40)		40	
Antony Crosse his servaunt			4
Christofer de Carcano and Baptyst his			
factor and Baptyst Mosato[44] factor			
also to the same Christofer de			
Carcano (£100) [x - K £6]		100	
John Meltor (60s.)		3	
Jamys his servaunt (20s.)			12
Donam Moris servaunt to the			
said Meltor (20s.)			12
Vyncent Clothe (40s.) [a]		2	
Elyzabeth Annes (£6)		6	
George [Blank] in Roydens house (40s.) [a]		2	
Nicholas Pellen servaunt to Boron Millen			
(40s.)		2	
John Baptyst (1000 marks)	33	6	8
Summa huius parrochie	68	10	

130.   SEYNT EDMUND IN LUMBERDSTRETE
[English]

	£	s.	d
Robert Clerke (£40)		20	
William Buknenan [?] (£40)		20	
Thomas Bowar for Orphanage of the			
Chyldren of Thomas Grafton (100 marks)		charged in the	
		orphanage boke	
Thomas Bower (£40)		20	
John Roys (100 marks)		33	4
Robert de Crow (£20)		10	
uxor Sest (100 marks)		33	4
Roger Andrewes (£30)		15	
William Gurnard (£20)		10	
Robert Harris (£20)		10	

44. E.359/44, r. 19 gives surname as Mouchate.

	£	s.	d
William Benyfold (£20)		10	
Nicholas Sympson in landes and Fees (£54)			
[ass. 52s. in Essex]		54	
William Baynbridge (£50)		25	
Jamys West (£20)		10	
Richard Mariet (£30)		15	
Richard Hunt (£30)		15	
John Lowen (£50)		25	
The same John Lowen for Orphanage of			
the Children of [Blank] (£88)		Charged in the	
		orphanage boke	
George Richardson (£30)		15	
Thomas Curtes (£600)	15		
Lady Milborne (1000 marks)	16	13	4
William Chester (£400)	10		

131.   Straungers

	£	s.	d
Peter Bryart within Pantelyn			
Spynnell (£10)		10	
John Maria Janney			4
Raynold Deryk (40s.)		2	
Gertrude his mayde			4
Everard [Blank] (20s.)			12
John Pakot (20s.)			12
Albert Deryk (£4)		4	
Jacob van Tright			4
Cornelis the post (40s.)		2	
Lawrience Burgon within Richard			
Mariet (£20)		20	
John Matyse at the iii kinges (£100)		100	
John Lumbert within Turpin			4
Antony Ponche within Pantalyn Spynell			4
Paintellyn Spynnell (£1000)	50		
Summa huius perrochie	115	13[?]	8

ALHALLOWES IN LUMBERDSTRETE
[English]

	£	s.	d
Robert Crowle (£300)	7	10	
Raulf Garland (£40)		20	
Robert Shosmyth (£25)		12	6
Robert Watles (£30)		15	
Antony Sylver (£30)		15	
William Pellen (£40)		20	
William Chamber (£20)		10	
Henry With (£20)		10	
Thomas Bowrne (£20)		10	
Bernard Kyngeston (£20)		10	
John Raulf alias Davy (£50)		25	

90

	£	s.	d
Robert Stretton (£20)		10	
Straungers			
Austyn Alencort (40s.)		2	
Hercules de Lagard (40s.)		2	
Garrard Ducheman servaunt with			
Bernard Kyngeston (20s.)			12
Summa huius perrochie	15	12	6

132.   SEYNT DENYS BACKCHURCHE
[English]

The Mystery of the pewterers (£20)		20	
Robert Barefote for the Orphanage of			
Jamys Hayden (£87 15s.)	Charged in the		
	orphanage boke		
Philip Cowsyn (£20)		10	
John Cowsyn (£20)		10	
Henry Dolphin (£20)		10	
Philip Benet (£20)		10	
William Robynson (£20)		10	
Lady [Eleanor] Lee in landes (£60)			
[x - Rochester 40s.; owes 20s. in			
Langbourn ward][45]		60	
Thomas Smyth (£30)		15	
Thomas Ursewyke (£30)		15	
John Franke (£25)		12	6
Bryan Chafer (£20)		10	
Robert Isotson (£20)		10	
John Raven (£20)		10	
John Mokes (£26 13s. 4d.)		13	4
John Medringham (£20)		10	
John Hall (£20)		10	
Barthillmew Tycheborne (£40)		20	
Edmund Mede (£20)		10	
George Eton (£60)		30	
The same George for the Orphanage of			
Hazilfyld (£175 10s.)	Charged in the		
	orphanage boke		
Antony Cave (£200) [x - Bucks. 100s.]		100	
Robert Barfort (£1000)	25		
Mr Paget Alderman (2000 marks)	33	6	8
Humfray Style for the goodes of			
the Lady Baldry (£400)	10		
John Hethe (£50)		25	
Walter Hykman (£40)		20	

45. E.359/44, r. 19 gives Eleanor as first name.

		£	s.	d
133. Straungers				
Doctor Augustyne in landes and Fees				
by the kyng (£70)		7		
John Dymmok (£30)			30	
John Bawdwyn (£10)			10	
Guylham Basson (40s.)			2	
John Bewers in his house (£4)			4	
Adryan in the same house [a]				4
Nicholas Monday (£10)			10	
Peter Halowen his servaunt wages by				
the yere (26s. 8d.) [a]				16
Nicholas Pessan broker (20s.) [a]				12
Guylbert Cusson (£4)			4	
Jacob Derykson and William Sawderson his				
servauntes ther wages by the yere				
apece xxs. (40s.)			2	
Peter Cornelis (40s.)			2	
Edward Strete his servaunt in wages				
by yere (20s.)				12
Herman Skynnar [a]				4
Marten Strong (40s.)			2	
Fraunceis Hoverling his servaunt				
in wages by yere (20s.)				12
Saunders Marvell his boy				4
John with Edmund Mede, Jerom with				
Chamberleyn, Jacomy Kyldersmas				
with Dymmok & Katheryn Johnson				16
Christofer Storing servaunt with				
Thomas Pacy in wages (26s. 8d.) [a]				16
Guylbert Tyson with the same Pacy in				
wages by yere (20s.) [a]				12
Agnes Haslym wyf to Robert Haslym				
Inglysheman [a]				4
Summa huius perrochie	101	2	10	

134. SEYNT GABRYELL FANCHURCHE [English]		£	s.	d
John Worrall (£25) [x - K 13s. 4d.]			12	6
Lewes Davy (£20)			10	
uxor Belle vidua (£40)			20	
Thomas Spert (£30)			15	
Oswald Docwra (£20)			10	
Thomas Williamson (£20)			10	
Thomas Darland (£20)			10	
Henry Salvage (£500)		12	10	
Straungers				
Hans van Buttseller (£10)			10	
Mighell Bond (20s.) [a]				12

	£	s.	d
Guylham Cornyp (£40)		40	
Guylham Nowell			4
Lewes Suffingham (£50)		50	
Peter Bawde (20s.) [a]			12
Gylys Vyolet			4
Nicholas Lambert (20s.)			12
Massy Bysmer (40s.)		2	
John de Labord (20s.)			12
John Barrowes (20s.) [a]			12
Antony Brusket (£20)		20	
John Water Scot (30s.)			18
Asselyn Salvage (£10)		10	
Nicholas de Furnariis (100s.)		5	
Morysyne de Marinis (£50)		50	
Lewes Hedge (20s.)			12
Jakeman a woman coke (20s.)			12
Fraunceis the post (100s.)		5	
Jenyn Wyat (40s.)		2	
George Bernard (100s.)		5	
Nicholas Rassylyen (100s.)		5	
Coppyn Mafame (£10) [a]		10	

	£	s.	d
135. John Harmand in thouse of Thomas			
Darland and John Rogers alias			
John of Calis servaunt to			
William Byrche			8
Alyxaunder Theymor (£10) [ass. 10s. in			
Broad Street ward as 'Tonis']⁴⁶		10	
Horwart Adrat (100s.) [a]		5	
Arnold Fyllene (100s.) [a]		5	
Doctor Antony & his ii sonnes (£200)			
[x - Cripplegate ward £10 as			
'Anthony Fenendoo']	10		
Summa huius parrochie	39		16

ALLHALLOWES STAYNEING
[English]

	£	s.	d
John Bewyk (£20)		10	
John Flode (£20)		10	
Rychard Newport (£25)		12	6
Margaret Braunche wydow (£20)		10	
John Meryfyld (£20)		10	
Edmund Bryklyng (£20)		10	
Richard Megre (£30)		15	
Andrew Cutler (£20)		10	
Antony Maryne (£20)		10	

46. E.359/44, r. 19 gives surname as Tonys and Tomer.

	£	s.	d
Nicholas Maryne (£25) [ass. - 10s. in			
Southampton]		12	6
Straungers			
Nowell Crowon (£10)		10	
William Savelar his servaunte in wages			
(20s.)			12
Marten his servaunt			4
John de Wayne his servaunt (20s.) [a]			12
Richard Carre Scot (40s.)		2	
John de Mayne (£10)		10	
his ii servauntes & Paule Frelyng			12
Mighell Jonys (20s.) [a]			12
his servaunt Frencheman [a]			4
Guylham one of the kinges servauntes			
(£15) [x - K 76s. as William Thrush]			15
136. John Fesaunt [a]			4
Guylham Ballet (20s.)			12
Paule Cleveing, Guilham Cavylley, &			
Peter Viller, & Guilham Corwalis			16
Cristofer Nowell Coke in wages (£4)		4	
Alyce Corde Frencheman in wages (20s.)[a]			12
Fraunceis de Behante of Antwerp dwelling			
in the house of John Baptyst Borono			
in the paryshe of Seint Nicholas Acon			
(£40) [a]		40	
Summa huius Parrochie	9	19	4

SEINT GABRYELL FANCHURCHE

	£	s.	d
Strangers			
John Baptest and Alexander in thouse of			
Violet, strangers (£11) [a]		11	
Piers Vyvy servaunt to John de Bons in			
wages by yere (20s.) [a]			12
John A Lee servaunt to Mistress			
Violet in wages (40s.) [a]		2	
Bastian Bony post master (£15) [x - K			
40s.; ass. 10s. in Billingsgate ward]		15	
Benedict Spynell his Clarke in wages			
by yere (40s.)		2	
Clement Robery clarke in wages (£5)		5	
Jerram de Doreo merchaunt (£20)		20	
Leonard St. Avrea (£5)		5	
Nicholas de Neapolye his servaunt in			
wages (20s.)			12
George Franke in wages (20s.)			12
Summa		63	

94

	£	s.	d
137. SEYNT EDMOUND IN LUMBARDSTRETE			
Strangers			
Meladus Spynell merchaunt, servant in			
thouse of Pantlyn Spynnell (£20)		20	
Philip Spynell (£20)		20	
Denes his servaunt in wages by the			
yere (20s.)			12
Thomas Hartall Frencheman in wages (40s.)		2	
John de Sale servaunt to William			
Sympson in wages by yere (40s.)		2	
Inglishmen			
Thomas Burdok (£31)		15	6
Robert Whelar (£100) [ass. [blank] in			
Mddx.]		50	
Summa	5	10	6
SEINT NICHOLAS ACON PARRYSHE			
Strangers			
Antony Crosse servaunt to Nicholas Donaire			
at the value in goodes of (£10)		10	
Adrian Goldsmyth servaunt to John			
Baptest in wages by yere (40s.)		2	
George Francisco and Antony Penne			
servauntes to Thomas Royden at			
v li wages a pece by the yere (£10)		10	
Summa		22	
Totalis huius wardi pro			
parte dominus Regis	504	17	
138. [r.24] LYMESTRETE WARDE			
[Petty collectors: John Jerrard and John Bennett.]			
William Boyer (£2666 13s. 4d.)	66	13	4
Stephyn Kyrvin (£1000)	25		
William Browne (£2500)	62	10	
Andrewe Jude (£2666 13s. 4d.)	66	13	4
Dennys Lewson wydowe (£1000)	25		
Edwarde Elderton in landes (500 marks)	16	13	4
Davithe Wooderoff (£300)	7	10	
Thomas Grove (£66 13s. 4d.)		33	4
Thomas Hosse (£20)		10	
Richarde Blake (£40)		20	
John Barnard (£50)		25	
Roland Staper (£50)		25	
Richarde Maddok (£24)		12	
Thomas Symondes (£60) [ass. 24s. in Mddx.]		30	
Kathryn Dygbye wydowe (£40)		20	
Thomas Stokes (£20)		10	
William Stryte (£60)		30	

	£	s.	d
William Dolphyn (£66 13s. 4d.)		33	4
John Batt (£22)		11	
Herry Spede (£60)		30	
John Dalton (£60)		30	
George Colley (£40)		20	
Robert Nysam (£200)	5		
John Gerard (£266 13s. 4d.)	6	13	4
John Bennett (£266 13s. 4d.)	6	13	4
Edwarde Gonne (£20)		10	
Thomas Gybyns (£30)		15	
Thomas Tempernelle (£25) [x - K 10s. as			
'Tymperley'; owes 2s. 6d. in			
Lime Street ward]		12	6
Davythe Playne (£20)		10	
Henry Bennett (£20)		10	
John Brograve (£20)		10	
William Heybourne (£20)		10	
Herrye Jude in landes Fees and Offices			
(£50) [ass. 40s. in Essex]		50	
Straungers			
John Marten (£30)		30	
Aungell Tacke (20s.)			12
William Cheven his servaunt			4
Myghell Gourdenye			4
[Blank] Castell his servaunt			4
Summa totales huius Warde	313	5	10

139. [r.5]   PORTESOKEN WARDE
[Petty collectors: William Grene of the parish of St. Botolph without Aldgate, merchant taylor, and Richard Strette of the same parish, woolpacker.]

THE PARISSHE OF SAINT BOTULPHES WITHOUTE ALGATE

	£	s.	d
Antony Antony Englisshman (£400)	10		
Straungers there			
John Franke straunger (£1000)	50		
Giles Harryson straunger (£400)	20		
Englisshmen			
Andrew Morrys (200 marks)		66	8
John Margettson (£30)		15	
William Grene (£60)		30	
John Awstyn (£40)		20	
Elynor Lang widowe (£20)		10	
Thomas Castyll (£20)		10	
William Morrys bocher (£20)		10	
John Fyrmynger (£20)		10	
Richard Strett (£20)		10	
Thomas Cawse (£20)		10	

	£	s.	d
John Ewyn (£20)		10	
Robert Ewyn (£20)		10	
Edwarde Rowseley (£20)		10	
Roger Hyam (£40)		20	
John Randall (£20)		10	
Cristofer Chamber (£20)		10	
Sir Arthur Darcy knight in landes			
(500 marks)	16	13	4

140. Straungers

	£	s.	d
Luke de Larde in fees by yere (£18)		36	
Peter Bawde in fees by yere (£20)		40	
Cornelys Brystowe (£20)		20	
Henry Clarke (£4)		4	
John Barroy (£4)		4	
John Sclave (20s.)			12
Edward Wyllyams (4d.)			4
Harman Pyper (4d.)			4
John Mevars (4d.)			4
Henry Johnson servaunt (4d.)			4

Englisshmen

	£	s.	d
William Nevell (£30)		15	
Henry Chamberleyn (£30)		15	
Richard Wrowton (£30)		15	
William Haddok (£40)		20	
Antony Johnson (£100)		50	
William Wylde (£20)		10	
John Doffelde (£40)		20	

Straungers

	£	s.	d
John Ruston phisician (£20)		20	
James Williamson (£30)		30	
Mighell Johnson (£50)		50	
Henry Neskyn (£40)		40	
Rowland Bogard (£40)		40	
Giles Johnson (£5)		5	
Walter Johnson (£7)		7	
John Rogers (£10)		10	
Richard Williamson (£7)		7	
George Harrison (£13 6s. 8d.)		13	4
John Bartilmewe (£10)		10	
John Antony (£13 6s. 8d.)		13	4
John Vangolyk (£5)		5	
Lawrence Tyllman (£60)		60	
William Screvar (£10)		10	
James Myller (£10)		10	
Cornelys Johnson (£30)		30	

	£	s.	d
141. John Corrant (£30)		30	

	£	s.	d
Henry Johnson (40s.)		2	
James Dennys (£23)		23	
Cristofer Hande in goodes, xiii li			
vi s. viii d., and in fees, ix li (£9)		18	
Polle Nicholson (£5)		5	
Martyn Johnson (40s.)		2	
Harman Harryson (40s.)		2	
Dyrryk Johnson (40s.)		2	
Stayfe Joyner (£10)		10	
John Sexton (40s.)		2	
John Cremer (40s.)		2	
John Sewer (40s.)		2	
Chryste Polle (40s.)		2	
John Vanlayre (40s.)		2	
Richard Wyllyams (£4)		4	
Peter Johnson (40s.)		2	
John Piper (£3)		3	
Harman Coper (40s.)		2	
William Gillabran (40s.)		2	
John Wystyll (40s.)		2	
Cornelys Habardson (40s.)		2	
Henry Harmanson (40s.)		2	
Antony Wesell (40s.)		2	
Henry Coper (£4)		4	
James Gylson (£4)		4	
Rankyn Johnson (£5)		5	
Garrardes widowe (40s.)		2	
John Sewyn (£5)		5	
Markes Adam (£5)		5	
Adrian Boyve wyfe to Mathew Boyve (£20)		20	
John Harryson (40s.)		2	
John Carwyn in fee xviii d. a day			
(£27 7s. 6d.)		55	4
William Lovers (£20)		20	
Marian Ivans servaunt no goodes (4d.)			4
Henry Stone servaunt (4d.)			4
Andrew Johnson no goodes (4d.)			4
Frybryte servaunte (4d.)			4
John Carren servaunt (4d.)			4
John Gyllam servaunt (4d.)			4
John Laurenson servaunt (4d.)			4
142. Angell Antony servaunt (4d.)			4
Jenkyn servaunt to Cornelis Hubberdson (4d.)			4
Thomas Reymond servaunt (4d.)			4
Pondrell Pollys servaunt (4d.)			4
Martyn Harnoldson servaunt (4d.)			4
Peter Coke servaunt (4d.)			4

	£	s.	d
John servaunt to Harman Harryson (4d.)			4
Martyn Coper servaunt (4d.)			4
John Martyn servaunt (4d.)			4
Peter Blake no goodes (4d.)			4
John Johnson no goodes (4d.)			4
Harman Adrian servaunt to Stafe Joyner (4d.)			4
Johan servaunt to John Sexton (4d.)			4
Howrbirke Ostyn (4d.)			4
Derryk Vanhelthon servaunt (4d.)			4
Fraunces servaunt to Walter Johnson (4d.)			4
Rambold servaunt to John Rogers (4d.)			4
Harman servaunt to Richard Williams (4d.)			4
John Peterson servaunt (4d.)			4
James Martyn servaunt (4d.)			4
Alard servaunt no goodes (4d.)			4
Lennardes servaunt to James Royt (4d.)			4
Godfrey Lynkys servaunt (4d.)			4
Peter Rolys servaunt (4d.)			4
John Elton servaunt to John Antony (4d.)			4
143. Arnold Tryck servaunt to John Bartilmew (4d.)			4
Pollys his servaunt (4d.)			4
John Louer servaunt to James Gylson (4d.)			4
Grete and Elyn servauntes to Laurence Tyllman (8d.)			8
Godfry Harrison servaunt to Reynold Johnson (4d.)			4
Henry Williamson servaunt to the same Reynold (4d.)			4
Nicholas Loyrys servaunt to the same Reynold (4d.)			4
Harman & Henry servauntes to George Harryson (8d.)			8
Henry Grymkyn & John Hollonder servauntes to Antony Johnson (8d.)			8
Lyskyn maide servaunt to John Ruston (4d.)			4
John Laurence, Harman Brown, Dennys Frank & Robert Hart servauntes to Antony Antony (16d.)			16
Giles Harrisons servauntes			
Peter Vantongren (4d.)			4
William Verlake (4d.)			4
Cornelis Adrianson (4d.)			4
Helynger Almayns (4d.)			4
Fraunces Henwyer (4d.)			4
Dennys Myller (4d.)			4
Harman Boteman (4d.)			4
John Gysbreth (4d.)			4

	£	s.	d
Mighell Drayman (4d.)			4
John Myllar (4d.)			4
Lambert Gybland (4d.)			4
Henry Underbruer (4d.)			4

144. John Frankes servauntes

	£	s.	d
John Vancollen (4d.)			4
Poll Johnson (4d.)			4
Mighell Johnson (4d.)			4
John Custar (4d.)			4
John Collyn (4d.)			4
John Danffyll servaunt to Markes			
Adam (4d.)			4
John Chesters servauntes			
John Gover (4d.)			4
John Voklond (4d.)			4
Stevyn [?]xendbarwik (4d.)[47]			4
Totalis huius ward pro			
parte dominus Regis	153	17	8

145. [r.14]   QUENEHYTH WARD
[Petty collectors: Olyver Dawbeney and Wylliam Blackwall.]

SAYNT MYGHELLES AT QUENEHYTH PARYSSHE

	£	s.	d
Mr [John] Mason (£40) [x - Hampshire 26s. 8d.][48]		20	
Elynor Stadley (£50)		25	
Rychard Broke (£40)		20	
Robert Parker (£100) [x - K 50s.]		50	
John Cokes (£50)		25	
Robart Platt (£40)		20	
Olyver Dawbeney (£140)		70	
John Alborough (£50)		25	
John Hyll (£40)		20	
Rychard Denbold (£40)		20	
Rychard Dyconson (£20)		10	
Robart Malmer (£20)		10	
Rychard Nyckson (£20)		10	
Thomas Aleygh (£20)		10	
Robert Smyth (£25)		12	6
John Porter (£20)		10	
John Brown (£20)		10	
Robert Rede (£20)		10	

47. An ink blot renders the initial letter illegible. The Kirks give the reading '[W?]endbarwik' (R. E. G. Kirk and Ernest F. Kirk, eds. *Returns of Aliens...*, Publications of the Huguenot *Society of London*, Volume X, Part I (1900), p. 45.
48. E.359/44, r. 19 gives John as first name.

	£	s.	d
SAYNT MARY SOMERSETTES PARYSSHE			
Henry Sonday (£40)		20	
John Robynson (£40)		20	
Roger Thacker (£20)		10	
Davyd Garrett (£30)		15	
Raulf Davy (£20)		10	
Thomas Cerrey (£100)		50	
John Harrys (£50)		25	
Agnes Cantwell (£30)		15	
Katheryn Cryan (£40)		20	

146.   SAYNT PETERS AT POULES WHARF

	£	s.	d
John Good (£40)		20	
Rychard Haddon (£20)		10	
John Weller (£40)		20	
Margarete Archer (£20)		10	
Nycholas Pykkett (£40)		20	
Smalege Stanley (£25)		12	6
Hugh Loost (£200) [x - Castle Baynard ward £7 10s.; ass. 50s. in Mddx.]	5		

SAYNT NYCHOLAS COLDABBAY PARYSSHE

	£	s.	d
Wylliam Hounyng (£200)	5		
Nycholas Woodward (£40)		20	
George Broun (£20)		10	
John Saunderson (£80)		40	

THE NAMES OF THE PRESENTERS

	£	s.	d
Rychard Townesend (£100)		50	
Henry Nortryg (£40)		20	
Nycholas Harrys (£85)		42	6
Thomas Cheyny (£45)		22	6
Percyvall Skern (£40)		20	
Wylliam Bard (£500)	12	10	

147.   SAYNT NYCHOLAS OLYFF PARYSSHE

	£	s.	d
Thomas Lewyn Alderman (£800)	20		
Robert Fermer (£50)		25	
Thomas Barbor (£60)		30	
Edward Warnar (£40)		20	
Thomas Lytton (£50)		25	
Roger Norreys (£20)		10	
Wylliam Draper (£30)		15	
John Savage (£20)		10	
Wylliam Clerk (£20)		10	
Wylliam Blackwall (£160)	4		

	£	s.	d
SAYNT MYLDREDES PARYSSHE			
Robert Pecok (£120)		60	
[HOLY] TRYNYTYE PARYSSHE			
John Saundres (£100)		50	
Jerves Walter (£20)		10	
STRAUNGERS IN QUENEHYTH PARYSSHE			
John Cockes master			
John Wyler wages by the yere (53s. 4d.)		2	6
Reynold Burneck servaunt wyth Rychard			
Denbold by here (£4 13s. 4d.)		4	8
Fitzwan by yere (£5)		5	
John Johnson by yere (60s.)		3	
Ingle van le Byck by yere (66s. 8d.)		3	4
John Cockes (40s.)		2	
An apprentyce			4

148. STRAUNGERS IN SAYNT MARY SOMERSETTES PARISHE

Wylliam Jenyns master	£	s.	d
Item iii Apprentyces			12
Henry Fysshe Denyzeon (£16)	16		
Item ii servauntes At xxs. le yere a pece		2	
John Fallyng mayster (£14)	14		
Item ii Apprentyces			8
Jenyns Mager master (60s.)		3	
Frauncys Deny by yere (40s.)		2	
Gyles Close by yere (20s.)			12
Item goodwyfe Cryandes twoo servauntes			
wages by yere (£8)		8	
Thomas Lambard (40s.)		2	

STRAUNGERS IN SAYNT MARY MONTHAWE PARYSSHE	£	s.	d
Robart Ewyn (£6)	6		
George Hayes servaunt wyth Dent			12
John Berman (40s.)		2	

STRAUNGERS IN SAYNT PETERS PARYSSHE	£	s.	d
Gyllam Browderer (£250)	12	10	
Item A prentyce			4
Summa totales huius Wardi	120	4	10

149. [r.8]   TOWER WARDE

[Petty collectors: Thomas Blower of the parish of St. Dunstan in the East, draper, and Robert Newton of the parish of St. Olave Hart Street, upholder.]

Master Asheton in landes and fees (£160)	£	s.	d
Master Asheton in landes and fees (£160)	8		
Master Vyllers (£100)		50	

	£	s.	d
Henry Browne (£20)		10	
Thomas Hugyn (£60)		30	
Andrew Wodcok (£60)		30	
John Prat (£20)		10	
Richard Eton (£100)		50	
William Barry (£200)		100	
Alyxaunder Haynes (£20)		10	
Richard Ambrose (£20)		10	
George Blanchard (£30) [ass. 10s. in			
Cordwainer ward]		15	
Robert Newton (£100)		50	
Richard Tatt (£200)		100	
Thomas Burnell (£250)	6	5	
George Borall (£20)		10	
Mr Stepney lorde Chauncelor			
servaunt (£20)		10	
John Burnell (£40)		20	
Thomas Wattes (£200)		100	

150. Straungers

	£	s.	d
Fraunceys Nonys (100s.)		5	
John Decon (20s.)			12
Robert Cenarde (40s.)		2	
John servaunt with John Decon			4
Antony Donoroyne (£20)		20	
Peter Lopis (20s.)			12
ii Children over age			8
Nicholas Bywhot (20s.)			12
Clawde & Cornelis Peterson			8
Garret Screvener (40s.)		2	
John Affoo his servaunt and			
Raynold Harryson			8
John Howlard (40s.)		2	
Garren Mighell (20s.)			12
his brother (20s.)			12
Baltezar Broker (100s.)		5	
Nicholas Byet (20s.)			12
his ii servauntes			8
John Foke			4

[English]

	£	s.	d
Rychard Ive, Constable (£30)		15	
John Johnson coper (£20)		10	
John Yelde (£100)		50	
Richard Torner (£66)		33	
William Dobson (£20)		10	
Rowland Dee (£100)		50	
Henry Holland (£200)		100	
Thomas Hunt (£20)		10	

	£	s.	d
William Bulley (£60)		30	
Jesper Sabe in landes (£20)		20	
John Grymbery (£20)		10	
Straungers			
Peter Bulman (60s.)		3	
Henry Bylman & Henry Garret his			
servaunt, John Robertes Grymberis			
servaunt, & Fraunceis Newland			
John Yelde servaunt			16

151. [English]

	£	s.	d
Cristofer Wolley (£20)		10	
William A Woodde (£100)		50	
John Younge (£20)		10	
Christofer Draper (£20)		10	
Raulf Hulson (£50)		25	
Water Jobson (£200)		100	
Thomas Cottell (100 marks)		33	4
Nicholas Ive (£30)		15	
Olyver Whithed (£20)		10	
Henry Annarson (£40)		20	
Thomas Constable his goodes (£100)		50	
Mistres Nell wydow (£40)		20	
Edward Water (£300)	7	10	
Thomas Bacon (£200)		100	
John Sharwod (£100)		50	
Thomas Langton (£100)		50	
Richard Harris (£40)		20	
William Anstede (£20)		10	
Jamys Harryson (£30)		15	
Richard Halley (£20)		10	
William Gryslyng (£20)		10	
John Daye (£40)		20	
William Devell (£20)		10	
William Andrew (£20)		10	
George Lording (£20)		10	
Straungers			
John Tollarge (200 marks)	6	13	4
John Dyas (£90)	4	10	
Antony Naples (£30)		30	
Messor Nownys Thomas Frencheman			
Symond Grego & John Dayes servaunt			16

152. [English]

	£	s.	d
Thomas Blower (£300)	7	10	
Thomas Raynoldes (£20)		10	
Thomas Warnar (£66)		33	
George Gyn (£20)		10	

	£	s.	d
Adam Owtlaw (£30)		15	
Symond Couper (£20)		10	
Clement Townes wydow (200 marks)		66	8
John Nidigat (£20)		10	

Straungers

	£	s.	d
Marriat Neryat (100 marks)		66	8
Damyan Doffe (£20)		20	
Jamys Bechet (20s.)			12
Andrew Ghedat Nicholas Whithed			
Thomas Doffe			12
Fraunceis Dowtna (20s.)			12
Domynyk John (40s.)		2	
Marke Morano (20s.)			12
John Demetre (20s.)			12
Antony Devenis (£20)		20	
Fraunceis Frederik (£20)		20	
Lucas Spetsa (20s.)			12
Edward Coste bowcher (20s.)		12	
Cornelis Johnson Peter Andrean & iii			
Straungers in Frederykes house			20

153. [English]

	£	s.	d
Rychard Forde (£40)		20	
Robert Forde (£90) [x - K 45s.][49]		45	
Henry Holland (£40)		20	
Richard Wheler (£20)		10	
Thomas Showell (£20)		10	
Cristofer Wotton (£20)		10	
Frankes Wordow (£20)		10	

Straungers

	£	s.	d
Domyng Cretsa (£100)		100	
Antony Cassadonny (£100)		100	
Fraunceis Cassadony (60s.)		3	
Angell Melonys (100s.)		5	
George Skatt, Hans Andwarpe, Fraunceis			
Dowche, & George Dowche			16
John Sodall (£50)		50	

[English]

	£	s.	d
Robert Lord (£300)	7	10	
Nicholas Michell (£100)		50	
Leonard Mannyng (£30)		15	
Thomas Peyk (£250)	6	5	

154. Straungers

	£	s.	d
Jasper Brewkhewson (£100)		100	
Henry Wolf (20s.)			12

49. E.359/44, r. 19 gives surname as Forth.

	£	s.	d
Leonard Loke (20s.)			12
John van Gallyk (20s.)			12
Henry van Wossyk, Henry Levorson,			
Markes Vannys, Gossyn Foxe,			
Tyllman Vanhoffe, Henry Johnson,			
Tyse Johnson and John Vanbon		2	8
William Johnson Aqua vite maker (100s.)			5
John Johnson Master brewer (40s.)		2	
Henry Johnson bowcher (60s.)		3	
his ii men			8
Face Mewlos at the Rammes hedde (£100)		100	
Dyrik Pott, William Tylman, John Harris,			
Corren Botman, Henry Mynster, Tysse			
van Tor, Antony Hans, Tysse Vansester,			
& John Vanwart		3	
[English]			
Sir Thomas Palmer knight (£200)		100	
Edmund Redeing (£20)		10	
Mastres Everingham (£40)		20	
John Brykshawe (£30)		15	
Pattis Wydow (£30)		15	
Willyam Armerar (£100)		50	
Mastres Bonde wydow (100 marks)		33	4
Sir John Dudley knight in landes			
(1000 marks) [x - Q £33 6s. 8d.][50]	33	6	8
Straungers			
Cornelys Crowell (£20)		20	
Hans Fyrmort (£30)		30	
Jerom Brown (£30)		30	
William Hewson John Vanbraghen and			
Elysabeth a mayde			12
John Vanstroke (£10)		10	
his man			4
Gervis Salvage (100s.)		5	
John Baptyst (100s.)		5	
155. [English]			
John Samson (£100)		50	
Henry Clerke (£100)		50	
Antony Douryge (£100)		50	
Guybsons wydow (£40)		20	
John Philipis (£20)		10	
William Tomson (£20)		10	
William Philippes (£40)		20	
John Gyll (£40)		20	

50. E.359/44, r. 19 identifies this taxpayer as Sir John Dudley, viscount Lysley. Dudley was created viscount Lisle by patent 12 March 1542.

	£	s.	d
Straungers			
Rossell Clardos, Rossell John			
Hollet & Jasper Herry Peterson			12
[English]			
Mr Philip Dennys (£100)		50	
William Horray (£60)		30	
Sir Thomas Wyat knight in landes			
& fees (£600)	30		
Straungers			
Arnold Harryson (20s.)			12
John Mast (40s.)		2	
Arnold Harrysons ii servauntes			8
[English]			
Wardens of the bakers (£32 11s. 2½d.)		32	4
Edmund Mody (£100)		50	
Thomas Sawyer (£100)		50	
John Vacas (£20)		10	
Robert Smyth (£50)		25	
John Braynkyn (£20)		10	
Thomas Gygges (£20)		10	
Wardens of the Clothworkers in			
landes (£51 7s. 8d.)		51	4
156. **Straungers**			
John Jonson (40s.)		2	
Peter Frebard (20s.)			12
Garret Slevytas bocher (20s.)			12
Henry Weshange and William			
Deryk his servaunt			8
George Williamson (20s.)			12
Mighell Martenson (20s.)			12
Garret Johnson (20s.)			12
Peter Sonder			4
[English]			
Sir John Alen knight (£3000)	75		
Ambrose Wolley (2000 marks)	33	6	8
William Robyns (£1000)	25		
John Pope, Alyen (£1000)	50		
Jamys Nedeham (£500)[x - K £5;			
owes £7 10s. in Tower ward]	12	10	
Sir John Champnes knight (2000 marks)	33	6	8
Sir William Denham (£2000)	50		
William Gunston (£1000)	25		
Thomas A Wodde (£400)	10		
Richard Breme esquier (1000 marks)			
[x - K £6 13s. 4d.; owes £10			
in Tower ward]	16	13	4
Bartyllmew Campayngne [alien] & his wyf			

	£	s.	d
late Capons wyf (£1000) [x - Broad Street ward £50; ass. £50 in Southwark]	50		
Guybsons wydow now maryed to Sir Antony Knevet knight (£800)	20		
[Roland] Lathams wydow [Dorothy] now wyf to John Smyth (£400) [x - Q £10 13s. 4d.][51]	10		
Summa	706	5	8

157. Corporacions & felyshippes whiche were not presentyd this yere ne assessyd at the Ingrossing of the bookes, and therefor writen heere in this warde bycause of most Rome for the wryten of them,

	£	s.	d
Iremoungers hall (£20 14s. 10d.)[52]		20	10
Taylors hall (£180 5s.8d.) [ass. £9 4d. in Broad Street ward]	9		7
Felyship of Scryveners (£22) [x - Cripplegate ward 22s.]		22	
Felyship of Wollpakkers (£23 1d.) [ass. 23s. in Coleman Street ward]		23	
Carpynters Hall (£74 18s. 4d.) [ass. 74s. 10d. in Broad Street ward]		74	10
Marchauntaylors bachelers hall (£83 6s.) [ass. £4 3s. 4d. in Broad Street ward	4	3	4
Felyship of bochers (£57 15s.)		57	9
Lethersellers hall (£93 12s.) [ass. £4 13s. 8d. in Broad Street ward]	4	13	8
Summa	26	15	2
Totalis huius ward pro parte dominus Regis	733		10

158. [r.20]   VYNTRE WARDE
[Petty collectors: William Maynerd and Thomas Gyttons.]

THE PARYSHE OF SAYNT MARTYNS
[English]

	£	s.	d
Roger Tyrry (£66 13s. 4d.)		33	4
Robert Hylton (£100)		50	
Edmond Alexander (£66 13s. 4d.)		33	4
William Maynard (£200)	5		
Richardes Byrde (£66 13s. 4d.)		33	4
William Baker (£40)		20	

51. E.359/44, r. 19 gives Latham's first name as Roland and his widow's first name as Dorothy.
52. This entry is crossed out.

	£	s.	d
Robert Deye (£40)		20	
Robert Swayn (£30)		15	
Thomas Turner (£20)		10	
John Campyon (£20)		10	
John Hyxson (£20)		10	
John Arnolde (£20)		10	
George Symondes (£20)		10	
Johan Delamore (£20)		10	
Edward Burlace (£1000)	25		
Thomas Gyttons (£400)	10		
Straungers			
Shawe Johnson (40s.)		2	
Ranken Justynian (100s.)		5	
Arnold Collett (40s.)		2	
Courte Nicholas (40s.)		2	
Mathewe Wynkell (20s.)			12
John Robertes servaunt to Shawe Jhohnson (20s.)			12
John Garrett (20s.)			12
John Cremer (20s.)			12
Summa	54		

159.　　　SAYNT JAMES PARYSHE
[English]

	£	s.	d
Hughe Mynors (£100)		50	
Robert Smythe (£100)		50	
Richard Hall (£133 6s. 8d.)		66	8
Thomas Walker (£100)		50	
Henry Moppye (£80)		40	
Henry Knyghtbrydge (£60)		30	
John Nyxson (£40)		20	
William Churche (£60)		30	
Stephyn Coldwell (£40)		20	
Henry Wyncott (£200)	5		
Cristofer Machyn (£20)		10	
Robert Merydall (£20)		10	
William Borne (£40)		20	
George Wymarke (£20)		10	
Thomas Chapman (£30)		15	
John Gibbes (£20)		10	
Christofer Towneshend (£20)		10	
Thomas Swynborne (£20)		10	
Richard Floyde (£20)		10	
John Drakes (£20)		10	
John Brue (£40)		20	
Sir James Spencer knyght (£2000)	50		
Straungers			
Garrett Peter (£5)		5	

	£	s.	d
Nicholas Britten (20s.)			12
Saunder Vanhayn (20s.)			12
Laurence Crane (40s.)		2	
Henrike Vannesson (20s.)			12
Peter Giles (20s.)			12
Henryke Wynkyn (20s.)			12
Henryke Yellard (20s.)			12
[Blank] Johnson (20s.)			12
John Williams (20s.)			12
John Wan Collon (20s.)			12
Dirryke Jonson (20s.)			12
Tysse Peterson (20s.)			12
Summa	80	9	8

160. SAYNT MICHELL PATER NOSTER
CALLYD WHYTTYNGTON COLLADGE
[English]

	£	s.	d
Master Whyttofte (£100)		50	
Nicholas Waryng (£100)		50	
William Perry (£100)		50	
Edmond Cokkerell (£200) [a][53]	5		
William Jenkyns (£50)		25	
Roger Redman and John Wades (£200)	5		
Robert Ratclyff (£20)		10	
John Appowell (£20)		10	
Thomas Crosbye (£140)	3	10	
Alyen Kyng (£500)	12	10	
Henry Coke (£500)	12	10	
Straungers			
A cobler and his servaunt (40s.)		2	
Robert Gregges havyng three servauntes straungers dwelling with hym videlicet			
Weldroysse (20s.)			12
John Docheman (20s.)			12
Reynold (20s.)			12
Summa	48	10	

161. SAYNT THOMAS APPOSTELES PARISHE
[English]

	£	s.	d
Randall Barboure (£100)		50	
John Marchaunt (£50)		25	
Arthur Holmes (£20)		10	
William Petyngall (£61)			
[ass. 30s. in Cordwainer ward]		30	6
Thomas Whytwood (£20)		10	

53. Edmund Cokkerell defaulted. London commissioners certified that the collectors declared on oath that at the time of assessment Cokkerell had no goods or chattels on which the collectors could levy the sum he owed (E.359/44, r. 19).

	£	s.	d
Edward Preston (£30)		15	
William Maltby (£20)		10	
John Abbott (£40)		20	
John Harvye (£40)		20	
John Harryson (£20)		10	
John Bendles (£61) [ass. 30s. in Cordwainer ward as 'Beneles']		30	6
Thomas Basford (£40)		20	
Nicholas Brayredge (£20)		10	
Henry Foster (£20)		10	
James Amore (£20)		10	
Nicholas Bristowe (£100)		50	
Thomas Mildmay (£400) [ass. £6 13s. 4d. in Essex]	10		
Olyver Leder (£200)	5		
[Blank] Bromewelles wedowe (£400)	10		

Straungers

	£	s.	d
Robert Dyrryke (20s.)			12
John Swynell in Abbottes rentes (£10)		10	
Summa	42	2	

CORPORATIONS

	£	s.	d
The Wardens of the Vynteners (£200)	10		
The Wardens of the Cuttelers Hall (£55)		55	
Summa	12	15	
Summa istius warde	237	16	8

162. [r.19]   WALBROKE WARDE
[Petty collectors: Roger Pynchester and Richard Harte.]

SAYNT SWYTHYNS PARYSHE
[English]

	£	s.	d
Richard Creswayt (£50)		25	
James Hall (£40)		20	
John Perpoynt (£30)		15	
Robert Alfford (£60)		30	
William Spynke (£20)		10	
Edward Dee (£40)		20	
William Harvey (£20)		10	
Nicholas Dalton (£20)		10	
Phillip Meredith (£120)	3		
Barthelmewe Averell (£40)		20	
Robert Alyen (£20)		10	
Henry Grover (£50)		25	
Henry Becher (£66)		33	
Robert Whytt (£120)	3		
Mastres Maydnall (£20)		10	
Thomas Perpoynt (£500)	12	10	

	£	s.	d
Straungers			
Rombold Johnson (£10)		10	
Nicholas Close			4
Peter Vodstawnt			4
The Wardens of Drapers for there			
hall (£320 15s.)	16		9
Summa	46	19	5

163.   [St. Mary] WOLCHURCHE PARISHE

	£	s.	d
George Holand (£30)		15	
Thomas Stryklond (£20)		10	
Master Alsope in londes and fee (£60)	3		
Thomas Polle (£20)		10	
John Desyll (£20)		10	
Alexander Beste (£20)		10	
Amys Renwyke wedowe (£20)		10	
Robert Hanfford (£40)		20	
Thomas Wanton (£20)		10	
William Spencer (£20)		10	
Roger Pynchester (£1000)	25		
John Clerke (£1000)	25		
Johanne Hanfford wedowe (£400)	10		
Nicholas Nevell straunger (£20)		20	
James Lame stranger (4d.)			4
Summa	69	5	4

SAYNT STEPHYNS PARYSHE
[English]

	£	s.	d
William Brownsmythe (£20)		10	
William Chamberleyn (£20)		10	
John Frear (£40)		20	
William Cheyke (£20)		10	
Richard Harte (£85)		42	6
Robert Kyndersley (£20)		10	
John Nicholles (£20)		10	
Thomas Lee (£200)	5		
Thomas Mawgham (£25)		12	6
John Howe (£60)		30	
William Adams in londes (£20)		20	
Robert Colte (£100)		50	
John Martyn and Hughe Marse (£40)		20	
Richard Turnor (£20)		10	
John Cottes Alderman (£1333 6s. 8d.)	33	6	8
Rowland Hill (5000 marks)	83	6	8
Sir Thomas Pope knyght in londes			
& fees (1000 marks)	33	6	8
Summa	167	15	

		£	s.	d
164.	SAYNT JOHNS PARYSHE [English]			
John Tratt (£35)			17	6
William Ebbes (£25)			12	6
Edward Bartylmewe (£20)			10	
Margery Blondell wedowe (£30)			15	
John More (£20)			10	
Thomas Davey (£60)			30	
John Davey (£120)		3		
Sabastion Hillary in fees (£20)			20	
Master Richemond Harrord [sic] (£20)			10	
John Walter (£20)			10	
	Summa		9	15

		£	s.	d
	SAYNT MARY BOTTOLFF PARISHE [English]			
Thomas Spencer (£20)			10	
Mastres Lee (£40)			20	
Clement Redley wedowe (£20)			10	
Thomas More (£20)			10	
Henry Whythorne (£60)			30	
Thomas Ginere (£240)		6		
William Twyll (£40)			20	
William Freman fysyssion (£100)			50	
Thomas Huntlowe (£1333 6s. 8d.)		33	6	8
Robert Whytston (£40)			20	
	Summa	47	16	8

		£	s.	d
165.	[St. Mary] ABCHURCHE PARISHE WITH PARTE OF SAYNT LAURENCE POUNTENEY [English]			
William Prowde (£100)			50	
Henry Richardes (£40)			20	
Phillyp Warton (£40)			20	
William Cleyffton (£40)			20	
Marget Rogers wedowe (£100)			50	
John Rogers (£100)			50	
Robert Sonnyng (£30)			15	
James Tomson (£30)			15	
	Straungers			
Roger de Prate (£400) [Process - discharged £15][54]		20		
Roger Puyne				4
	Summa	32		4
	Summa istius warde	373	11	9[55]

54. Robert de Prate swore before the barons that the value of his goods and chattels at the time of taxation did not exceed £100. The barons discharged him and the collectors of £15 of the £20 assessed on him (E.359/44, r. 19; E.159/321, *communia* Easter 34 Hen. VIII, r. 66).

55. This figure replaces a previous summa of £389 21d., which is crossed out.

THE 1582 SUBSIDY ROLL FOR LONDON
E.179/251/16

166. [r.1] This Indenture made the first day of August in the xxiiii[th] yeere of the raigne of our sovereigne Lady Elizabeth by the grace of God of England, Fraunce & Ireland, defendor of the faithe etc. Witnesseth that the right honorable Sir James Harvye, knight, Lord Maior of the Citty of London, Sir Rowland Hayward, Sir Lyonell Duckett, Sir John Ryvers, Sir Thomas Ramsey & Sir Nicholas Woodroff, knightes and aldermen of the said Citty, And William Fletewood, Sergeaunt at the law and Recorder of the same Cittye, Commissioners with others deputed appointed and assigned by our said sovereigne Lady the queenes majesty by her highnes Commission under the great seale of England for the taxacion, leveyinge & gathering of the second payment of the subsidye lately graunted to her majestie by her highnes high Court of parliament holden at Westminster by divers prorogacions the xvi[th] day of January in the xxiii[th] yeere of the raigne of our said sovereigne Lady the queenes majesty that now is, have appointed, nominated & assigned William Sebright and Richard Yonge, grocers, Cittizens of the said Cittie, high Collectors for the receyvinge of the said second payment of the said subsidye within the said Cittye to levey, take & receyve to the use of our said sovereigne Lady the queenes, of the severall persons heereunder written whom the said Commissioners by their Indentures to theis Indentures annexed have before this time named and appointed to be petty Collectors of the same subsidye in the severall wardes heereunder expressed, all suche sommes of money as in theis Indentures are Conteyned, viz of

		£	s.	d.
Hugh Heandley & William Bower	petty Collectors of the ward of Breadstreete	341	13	8
Richard Bowdler & Gyles Howland	pettie collectors of the warde of Brodstreete	367	6	8
Thomas Giles & William Cowper	pettie collectors of the ward of Cheape	407	3	4
Richard Cotton & Fraunces Quarles	pettie collectors of the ward of Creplegate	506	7	8
Henry Mathew & John Ballett	pettie collectors of the ward of Farringdon within	448	17	0
Thomas Allen &	pettie Collectors of the			

		£	s.	d
Richard Arnold	ward of Faringdon without	558	18	8
Pawle Banninge John Highlord	pettie Collectors of the ward of Tower	484	4	0

All which said severall sommes of money so by them the said William Sebright and Richard Yonge, high Collectors as aforeseid, receyved and had, They the same William Sebright & Richard Yonge for them, their heires, executors & administrators do covenaunt, promise & graunt by theis presentes to content & pay to the use of our said sovereigne Lady the queenes majestie with all diligence in her exchequer at Westminster according to theffect, purporte & true meaninge of the said act deliveringe, allowinge & payinge to thandes of William Sebright, Comon Clerke of the said Cittie to the use & behoofe of the said Commissioners and of suche others as have taken paines in and about the wrightinge, makinge preceptes, engrossinge of thextractes and bookes of subsidie and other the busines and affaires concerninge the said subsidie the some of iid of every pound so to be Collected receyved or gathered by the said William Sebright and Richard Yonge or either of them, And also makinge & allowinge accordingly all suche other deduccions and allowaunces as in the said act of subsidie is Conteyned, In Wittnes whereof to thone parte of theis Indentures remayninge with the said high Collectors the foreseid Commissioners have putt there seales, And to thother parte of theis Indentures remayninge with the said Commissioners the said highcollectors have putt there seales, yeoven the day and yeare abovewritten. [signed by Sebright and Young, the high collectors].

167. [On rotulets 2, 3, and 4 there are three more indentures between the commissioners and high collectors. They are identical in form; only the names of the high collectors, the petty collectors, the wards, and the sums to be collected vary.]

[r.2]		£	s.	d.
High Collectors:	Nicholas Spencer, merchant taylor Edward Rowley, draper			
Rycharde Atkynson & John Rogers	Pettyecollectors of the warde of Brydge within	224	2	8
John Taylor & Edward Turfutt	Pettycollectors of the ward of Coalemanstreete	173	3	0
John Stubbes and John Wylde	Pettyecollectors of the warde of Byllyngesgate	271	12	4
Wyllyam Shawcrofte & Arnolde Rutton	Pettyecollectors of the warde of Dowgate	128	10	8

		£	s.	d
William Kerwyn and John Edwardes	Pettyecollectors of the warde of Bysshoppesgate	278	18	4
Nycholas Poare & Raphe Rydley	Pettyecollectors of the warde of Vyntrye	131	11	8

[r.3]
High Collectors: Henrye Palmer, merchant taylor
Wyllyam Abraham, vintner

		£	s.	d
Humfrey Huntley & Robert Harryson	Pettyecollectors of the warde of Quenehythe	90	13	4
John Barnarde Frauncys Shingewell	Pettyecollectors of the warde of Portesoken	57	9	8
Thomas Grey & Thomas Thompson	Pettyecollectors of the warde of Langborne	362	14	8
Henrye Faux & Walter Plumber	Pettyecollectors of the warde of Walbrooke	218	14	8
Gregorye Yonge Mathewe Dolman	Pettyecollectors of the warde of Lymestreete	83	9	4
George Cullymore Roberte Cobbe	Pettyecollectors of the ward of Cordwaynerstreete	289	5	4

[r.4]
High Collectors: Raphe Ayloffe, grocer
Henrye Allyngeton, skinner

		£	s.	d
Wyllyam Barnard & Wyllyam Evans	Pettyecollectors of the warde of Candlewyckestreete	198	12	4
James Deane & Edwarde Leaninge	Pettyecollectors of the warde of Allgate	208	2	0
Wyllyam Ryder & Morgan Rychardes	Pettyecollectors of the warde of Cornehyll	115	7	8
Wyllyam Kelsycke & Rycharde Smythe	Pettyecollectors of the ward of Castlebaynerde	202	18	4
John Storer & Robert Crosse	Pettyecollectors of the ward of Bassingeshall	84	16	8
John Stephens Marmaduke Franke	Pettycollectors of the ward of Aldersgate	296	16	0

168. [r.19]   ALDRICHGATE WARDE

This Indenture made the fyrst daye of August in the foure and twenteth yeare of the Reigne of our soveraigne ladye Elizabeth by the grace of god, Queene of Englande Fraunce and Irelande, defendor of the fayth, etc. Betwene the right honourable Sir James Harvy, knight, Lorde Maior of the Cytye of London, Sir Rowlande Haywarde, Sir Lyonell Duckett, Sir John Ryvers, Sir Thomas Ramsey and Sir Nicholas Woodroffe, knightes and Aldermen of the Cytye afforesaide, And William Fleetwood, Serjaunt at the lawe, Recordor of the same Cytye, the Queenes Majesties Commissioners with others, aucthorized by her highnes letters patentes under the great seale of Englande, for the taxacion and levyenge of the seconde payment of the subsydye latelye graunted to her Majestye by her highnes high Court of parlyament holden at Westminster by divers prorogacions the syxtenth day of Januarye, in the three and twenteth yeare of the Reigne of our saide soveraigne ladye, with in the saide Cytye of London on thone partye, And Marmaduke Franck, Cordwayner, and John Stevens, Brewer, Cytizens of London, whom the saide Commissioners have named, deputed and chosen, and by theise presentes do name, depute and chose to be Pettycollectors of the same seconde payment of the saide subsidye within the warde of Aldrichgate, within the saide Cytye on thother partye. Wytnesseth that the same Marmaduke Franck and John Stevens so named, deputed and chosen by the saide Commyssioners to be Petycollectors within the saide warde, and auchthorised by theise presentes therunto, shall receyve, Collect, leavye and gather, of all and everye the severall persones herunder named to the Queenes Majesties use, all suche severall sommes of monye as in this present extract bene taxed and assessed uppon them, and everye of them, for their severall values and substances, rated specyfyed and conteyned as hereafter followeth. That is to say. Of

169.   SAINT LEONARDES PARISH AND ST MARTYNS
[English]

	£	s.	d.
Thomas Atkynson in landes (£50)			
[x - Surrey 40s.]	3	6	8
John Weaver (£80)	4		
John Hylles (£80)	4		
Wydowe Phippes (£60) [x - Westminster 20s.			
by name of David deLaye]	3		
John Nelson (£50)		50	
Thomas Pope (£80)	4		
James Challecome goldsmyth (£3)		3	
Henrye Rylye taylor (£6)		6	
William Benedick scryvener (£4)		4	
John Goodridge goldsmyth (£3)		3	
William Stackforde scryvener (£6)		6	
Symon Hudson (£4)		4	
Thomas Fowler (£3)		3	
Jervace Wordesworth (£4)		4	
Henrye Spylman (£3)		3	

	£	s.	d
Andrewe Quyney (£3)		3	
William Hobson (£3)		3	
Jeromy Monck (£3)		3	
Garret Heath (£6)		6	
Christofer Dirrick gent in wydowe Browkers			
house (£25) [a]		25	
Constantyne Pillicock (£3)		3	
William Aldersey (£3)		3	
Strangers			
Lodovick Tyce (£15)		30	
Anthonye Emerick (£20)		40	
John Pookes (£30)	3		
Christofer Bohere alias Bowyer (£40)	4		
Nicholas de Homy (£10)		20	
Haymon Tyon (£30)	3		
Frauncys Bartye (£40)	4		
John Brand (£30)	3		
Dyonys Restingham (£10)		20	
Martyn Druet (£10)		20	
Michaell Art (£10)		20	
John James (£10)		20	
Derick Harmanson (£10)		20	
Garet Vanbedberete (£15)		30	
Robert Yonge (£10)		20	
Dyonise Restingham sonne to Dyonys			
Restingham per pol			4
Vyncent Kynge goldsmyth (£6)		12	
Christian Depuse wydowe (£3)		6	
Henrye Angence her servant pol			4
John Derub her servant pol			4
Quyntence Coplow her servant pol			4
William Cooke her servant pol			4
Nicholas Shamar her servant pol			4

170. Englishmen within St Martyns and St Leonardes parish

	£	s.	d
Peter Peterson (£8)		8	
William Wilforde (£3)		3	
[r.20]			
Robert Risley (£6)		6	
Wydowe Wicklyff (£3)		3	
John Stonehouse (£3)		3	
Edwarde Woode (£6)		6	
Anthonye Kempe (£3)		3	
Frauncys Gyll (£6)		6	
Symon Floyde (£3)		3	
Harman Johnson (£5)		5	
Morgan Price (£4)		4	
Gryffen Floyde (£3)		3	

	£	s.	d
John Martyn (£3)		3	
John Vailes (£3) [a]		3	
Thomas Fardell (£3)		3	
Edwarde Tedder (£3)		3	
James Vaughan (£3)		3	
Walter Snellinge (£5)		5	
William Kendall (£5)		5	
Nicholas Murryn (£3)		3	
Wydowe Anton (£3)		3	
Nicholas Kytchen (£3)		3	
Robert Lewes (£3)		3	
John Lever (£3)		3	
Edwarde Smyth (£6)		6	
John Wyllforde (£8)		8	
John Sutton (£12)		12	
John Bowrye (£8)		8	
Peter Bowrye (£8)		8	
Raph Busby (£5)		5	
Robert Coller (£3)		3	
James Anton (£12)		12	
Thomas Staples (£12)		12	
Robert Damport (£5)		5	
Thomas Postelet (£5)		5	
Thomas Walker (£6)		6	
William Bray (£3)		3	
Thomas Townsende (£3)		3	
Thomas Gyttens (£16)		16	
Robert Woodborne (£3)		3	
Cutbert Wallet (£3) [a]		3	
John Cane (£3)		3	
Richerd Turnor (£3)		3	
Edwarde Jones (£3)		3	
William Faune (£10)		10	

171. Straungers

Harman Edyn servant to Christian Bowen			4
Jocas Johnson servant to Christian Bowen			4
Henrye Johnson servant to Christian Bowen			4
Roger Swarston taylor (20s.)		2	
Elizabeth wyfe of John James sylkman			4
Jane James his daughter			4
The wyfe of Michaell Art shomaker			4
Johan Morysyn wydowe			4
Andrew Vansutefinde her servant			4
John Cornelish			4
John Manningam (20s.)		2	
his wyfe per pol			4
Mary More his servant			4

	£	s.	d
Peter Focall silkweaver (£3)		6	
The wyfe of Edwarde Tedder			4
Gregory Princell (£3)		6	
George Peterson servant to James Vaughan			4
The wyfe of Gregorye Princell per pol			4
Garret Vandenbusse (40s.)		4	
Annys his wyfe			4
John Seelye taylor (£3)		6	
Julye his wyfe			4
John Deron hosyer			4
Gabryell Harrys buglemaker (£3)		6	
Peter Cortoyd his servant			4
John de Sharfe goldsmyth (20s.)		2	
Abraham Blandsy bugleseller (£5)		10	
his wyfe			4
Wydowe Durant			4
[r.21]			
Jasper Frederick goldsmyth (£4)		8	
The wyfe of John Tewer			4
Nicholas Bomersey bottonmaker (£3)		6	
Bonaventure Lebee goldsmyth			4
Alexander Williamson cobler			4
his wyfe			4
172. John Garsney his servant			4
Gyles Vangale clockmaker (£3)		6	
his wyfe			4
James Lyst goldsmyth (£3)		6	
his wyfe			4
Leonarde Goinge his servant			4
Guillome Pullyn goldsmyth			4
James Billet schoolmaster			4
John Mercer servant to Mr Smyth			4
John Houghman goldsmyth (20s.)		2	
Wydowe Sadler in the same house (40s.)		4	
Adryan Princell sylkman (£6)		12	
his wyfe			4
Sara Tuvye wydowe [a]			4
Poll Richerd			4
Garret Rosey lynnen draper (£10)		20	
his wyfe			4
Adryn de Watch his servant			4
James Detewe bugler (£3)		6	
his wyfe			4
Roberte Fountayne schoolmaster (£3)		6	
Frauncis Derickson pursmaker			4
his wyfe			4
Robert Lyngham servant to John Brand			4

	£	s.	d
Davy Smyth servant to John Brand			4
Humfrey Crewood servant to John Brand			4
The wyfe of John Pookes taylor			4
Paules Vanelsbower his servant			4
Therick Barnes his servant			4
Lodowick Futerer his servant			4
Mark de Campener his servant			4
Stephen Rauthmaker			4
Ellyn Pookes his servant			4
Adryan Vandermere pincker (20s.)			
[ass. 2s. 8d. in Surrey]		2	
Mathias Guilbert taylor (£10)		20	
his wyfe			4
Leonarde Gosinges his servant			4
Marthelington Gilbert his servant			4
The wyfe of Garret Vanbedburye			4
Sara Rook his servant			4
John Cultrye mouldmaker and his wyfe			8
Nicholas Bloome bookbynder (£3)		6	
his wyfe			4
173. Janykyn Swanston			4
Martyn Devysser pynner (£3)		6	
his wyfe			4
John Derickson his servant			4
Arthure Johnson his servant			4
Cornelis Williamson his servant			4
The wyfe of Lodowyke Tuse			4
Katheryne Tuse his daughter			4
Lowicke Tuse his sonne			4
[Blank] Tuse their graundfather [a]			4
Anthonye Rasse servant to Lodowick Tuse			4
Martyn Sewthance his servant allso			4
Ellyn Gossence his servant allso			4
The wyfe of Anthonye Emerick lynnendraper			4
Hale a Colyn wydowe			4
Jacob Poyster lynnen draper (£10)		20	
Guillam Tyon silkweaver (£3)		6	
John Cremer pursmaker			4
Alexander Wilson taylor			4
George Wylson his servant			4
John Wylson his servant			4
Peter Arnall servant to Mr Vaughan			4
James Cornelius servant to Mr Fan			4
Joakyn servant to Mr Connam			4
James Michell shomaker (£3)		6	
John Nickelson servant to Mistress Peacock			4
The wyfe of Martyn Drewet shomaker			4

	£	s.	d
Laurence Demote his servant			4
John Tirsetega his servant			4
[r.22]			
Hugh Cornelis his servant			4
John Myller jerkynmaker (£3)		6	
Michael Fuller shoomaker and his wyfe		8	
Garrat Nobleman sexton			4
Richerd Jacob jerkynmaker			4
Arnold Murren taylor (£3)		6	
his wyfe			4
Grassinge Henrick his servant			4
Wynkyn Puster pursemaker (20s.)		2	
his wyfe			4
Albert Lowse servant to Thomas Brewer			4
Nicholas Harryson servant to John Butt			
shoomaker			4
Summa	[Blank]		

174. ST JOHN ZACHARYES PARISH
[English]

	£	s.	d
Wydowe Harryson and her sonne			
Thomas Harrison (£200)	10		
Humfrey Blount gen in landes and fees			
(£10) [x - Farringdon ward Without 10s.]	13		4
Evans Thomas (£3)		3	
John Kelbeck (£3)		3	
John Beamer (£3)		3	
John Symons (£6)		6	
William Leech (£3)		3	
Thomas Keelinge (£10)		10	
Richerd Reade (£3)		3	
Rice Clarke (£4)		4	
Robert Newton (£3)		3	
Roger Flynt (£4)		4	
William Beale (£3)		3	
George Gybson (£3)		3	
John Collyns (£4)		4	
Raph Whyttle (£9)		9	
Richerde Whytehed (£3)		3	
Robert Greenwood (£15)		15	
Reynolde Strange (£8)		8	
John Byrde (£3)		3	
Michaell Collet (£4)		4	
Henrye Court (£6)		6	
Howell Podmore (£3)		3	
John Milles (£6)		6	
Robert Bee (£5)		5	
William Blackwell (£3)		3	

	£	s.	d
Thomas Binckes (£3)		3	
Edwarde Thomas (£4)		4	
Richerde Symes (£4)		4	
Richerde Harrys (£3)		3	
Thomas Ratcliffe (£4)		4	
Richerd Hollande (£3)		3	
Raph Martyn (£3)		3	
Edmonde Stanley (£3)		3	
Richerd Gybson (£4)		4	
Anthonye Tyffen (£4)		4	
Richerde Trewchilde (£3)		3	
Edmonde Saxton (£5)		5	
John Clarke (£3)		3	
Richerde Maynarde (£3) [a]		3	

Strangers

	£	s.	d
Arnolde Tant botcher (£3)		6	
Nicholas Crenne his servant			4
John Aske botcher			4
Jane Leach Frenchwoman wyfe to			
[Blank] Leache stonecutter			4

Summa   [Blank]

175.   ST ANNE AND AGNES PARISH
[English]

	£	s.	d
John Daye (£50)		50	
William Squyre in landes and fees (£15)		20	
Edmunde Knight alias Chester Harrold in fees (£10)[56]		13	4
John Warner gen in landes and fees (£10)		13	4
The right honorable therle of Northumberlande [Blank]			
John Nelson [Blank]			
Enego Johnes (£5)		5	
[r.23]			
John Greene (£4)		4	
Edmonde Hull (£4)		4	
John Johnson (£4)		4	
Mathewe Bolton (£3)		3	
John Nicholles (£3)		3	
Andrewe Morgan (£3)		3	
John Colley (£4)		4	
Marmaduke Francklande (£8)		8	
Henrye Gybson (£3)		3	
John Stephen (£10)		10	
John Hart (£4)		4	
Morgan Fludde (£3)		3	
Richerd Hill (£4)		4	

56. Knight was exonerated by virtue of letters patent to the heralds of 4 June 1549 and the queen's writ to the treasurer and barons dated 1 July 1581.

	£	s.	d
Edwarde Poole (£3)		3	
Robert Greene (£10)		10	
Myles Okeley (£4)		4	
John Hytchenson (£3)		3	
Thomas Coney (£4)		4	
Maryan Smyth wydowe (£3)		3	
Richerde Chambers (£4)		4	
Stephen Wright (£3)		3	
Richerde Gee (£3)		3	
John Blackman (£3)		3	
Barnarde Chazley (£4)		4	
Thomas Redforde (£8)		8	
Christofer Bell (£3)		3	
William Harvy (£8)		8	
Phillippe Woodhouse (£10)		10	
John Smyth (£3)		3	
Oliver Sherland resydent in the same house (£3)		3	
Andrewe Goodyeare (£10)		10	
Hugh Whittingham (£3)		3	
Thomas Woodhouse (£5)		5	
Nicholas Cadye (£3)		3	
John Tree (£4)		4	
Thomas Ashley (£3)		3	
Bartholomew Isburde (£15)		15	
William Gale (£8)		8	
Edwarde Jarvys (£8)		8	
Abraham Elston (£3)		3	
Thomas Reddock (£3)		3	

176. Straungers

	£	s.	d
Peter de Drossat chaundeler (£3)		6	
Katheryne his wyfe			4
Katheryne his servant			4
John Curle botcher in wydowe Garrettes house			4
James Boweman botcher ibidem [a]			4
Wydowe Hood [a]			4
William Peterson Vitteller (£12)		24	
Alexander Denison Hosyer			4
Arnolde Lawe shoomaker			4
John Peat taylor			4
Margaret Evdinge wydowe [a]			4
Johan Sebrance [a]			4
James Blenkester shomaker			4
James Smyth botcher			4
Gyles Seras bookebynder			4
Nicholas Deport letherdresser			4
John Bowman cobler			4
Harman Dewman taylor			4

	£	s.	d
Elizabeth Viat wydowe			4
Katheryne Stone wyfe to Thomas Stone			4
John Abraham servant to John Rutt			4
Frauncys Derickson hosyer (£3)		6	
his wyfe			4
Derick Womst his servant			4
John Lambert botcher and his wyfe			8
John Dewman taylor (40s.)		4	
his wyfe			4
Nicholas Armesford his servant			4
Clause Valore his servant			4
[r.24]			
Anthonye Dewman his servant [a]			4
Christofer Mongey his servant [a]			4
[Blank] Mongey his wyfe [a]			4
Esia Glassor taylor (20s.) [a]		2	
Glothin de Pere his servant [a]			4
Summa	[Blank]		

177. ST MARYE STAYNINGES PARISH
[English]

	£	s.	d
Mr William Fleetwood, Serjant at lawe, Commissioner (£40)		40	
Richerd Lyttler in landes and fees (£10)		13	4
Christofer Barker (£50)		50	
Davyd Gyttyns (£3)		3	
William Eyre (£6)		6	
Ellis Murryn (£3)		3	
Thomas Whitlock (£6)		6	
George Barker (£3)		3	
Straungers			
James Whyte (£40)	4		
Gilbert Hynde his servaunt			4
Summa	[Blank]		

178. ST BOTULPHES PARISH WITHOUT ALDRICHGATE
[English]

	£	s.	d
Sir Christofer Wray knight Lorde Chiefe Justice of Englande Commyssioner [Blank]	[Blank]		
Sir Edmond Anderson knight Lorde Chyefe Justice of the Commen plees, in landes (£40)		53	4
Sir John Peter knight in landes (£200) [x - Essex £9 6s. 8d.]	13	6	8
Mr William Doddington gen in landes and fees (£60)[57]	4		

57. Designated 'official turr' London' in margin, and, as such, he received exoneration by writ of privy seal dated 23 June 23 Eliz. directed to the Lord Treasurer and barons (E.359/52, r. 14).

	£	s.	d
Mr Thomas Morryson in landes and fees			
(£40) [x - Lincs. 53s. 4d.]		53	4
Doctor Fryer in Fees (£10)			
[x - Surrey 8s.]		13	4
Robert Wythe (£50) [x - Worcs.?]		50	
Mr Edwarde Carewe in landes (£100) [a]	6	13	4
Robert Hayes in fees (£10) [x - Mddx. 20s.]		13	4
Christofer Paighton in fees (£10)			
[x - Suff. 6s. 8d.]		13	4
John Conyers gen in landes & fees (£60)			
[x - Notts. 26s. 8d.]	4		
Richerd Gadburye in fees (£20)			
[x - Herts.?]		26	8
Robert Kentysh (£50)		50	
William Tuck gen in landes (£80)			
[x - Herts. £2]	5	6	8
Henrye Perpoynt gen in landes (£100) [a]	6	13	4
Thomas Fowler (£50)		50	
Thomas Taylor (£50) [x - Mddx. 21s. 4d.]		50	
Elizabeth Wilcockes in landes (£20) [a]		26	8
Margerye Lambert wydowe (£50)			
[x - Somerset 15s.]		50	
Cycely Fetiplace in landes (£30)			
[x - Gloucs. 26s. 8d.]		40	
Humfry Smyth gen in landes and fees (£80)			
[x - Mddx. £1 12s.]	5	6	8
William Necton in landes and fees (£10)		13	4
Mr Baron Sotherton in landes and fees (£20)		26	8
John Trye in landes and fees (£50) [a]	3	6	8
John Morley in fees (£20)		26	8
William Udall in landes (£10)			
[x - Essex 13s. 4d.]		13	4
Richerd Stoneley gen in landes (£100)			
[x - Essex?]	6	13	4
179. Sir Drewe Druery knight in landes (£40)			
[x - Norf. 40s.]		53	4
William Fuller audytor in			
landes and fees (£60)	4		
John Thompson audytor (£150)			
[x - Beds. £2]	7	10	
William Butler in fees (£10) [x - Sussex?]		13	4
Richerde Drake gen in landes (£20) [a]		26	8
Nowell Sotherton in fees (£10)		13	4
Edwarde Woode esquyre in landes (£100)			
[x - Cambs. £6 13s. 4d.]	6	13	4
Anthonye Roper gen in landes and fees			
(£40) [ass. 80s. in Kent]		53	4

	£	s.	d
Pierce Pennon gen in landes and fees			
(£50) [x - Q £1 6s. 8d.]	3	6	8
Henrye Jaslyn in landes (£20) [x - Essex?]		26	8
James Skevington gen (£50) [x - Mddx. 16s.]		50	
William Spencer auditor in landes and fees			
(£30) [x - Oxon. 16s.]		40	
John Morley marchanttaylor (£3)		3	
[r.25]			
Davyd Thomas (£3)		3	
John Bond thelder (£4)		4	
Edwarde Dorret (£3)		3	
John Boulstred (£3)		3	
Thomas Woodwarde (£3)		3	
James Appowell (£3)		3	
Laurence Byllington (£4)		4	
Thomas Denby (£3)		3	
Henrye Sharpe (£3)		3	
Richerd Robertes (£3)		3	
John Allyson (£3)		3	
Roger Jarman (£5)		5	
Richerde Dumbleton (£3)		3	
Roger Cope glasyer (£3)		3	
Edmonde Essex (£6)		6	
William Browne (£3)		3	
Thomas Daye (£6)		6	
180. John Fysher (£4)		4	
Davyd Faldoe (£3)		3	
James Cole (£4)		4	
Edwarde Cordall (£4)		4	
John Walker (£3)		3	
Raph Gryffen (£3)		3	
John Clarke (£3)		3	
Richerd Storye (£4)		4	
Andrewe Huntington (£5)		5	
Elias Jarman (£3)		3	
William Fysher (£3)		3	
Robert Hawkyns (£4)		4	
Arnolde Apprice (£3)		3	
Raph Treswell (£5)		5	
[Blank] Gryffen (£3) [a]		3	
Thomas Lambert (£8)		8	
William Edmondes (£3)		3	
Lewis Fuellen yoman (£3)		3	
William Stephens (£3)		3	
Edward Terry (£3)		3	
Thomas Golde (£5)		5	
Anthonye Cave (£10)		10	

	£	s.	d
William Ducket (£3) [a]		3	
William Goble auditors clerke (£4)		4	
Robert Right (£5)		5	
John Kettle (£6) [x - Herts. 10s. 8d.]		6	
Richerde Scarlet (£6)		6	
John Spurlinge (£3)		3	
Thomas Garret (£5)		5	
John Booth (£6)		6	
Thomas Bostock (£3)		3	
181. Charles Hytchcock (£4)		4	
William Goodrich (£5)		5	
William Hopton (£3)		3	
John Springe (£3)		3	
John Butterick lyenge at John Springes house (£4)		4	
Robert Johnson (£10) [a]		10	
Thomas Woddall (£3)		3	
Humfrye Woodall (£3)		3	
Richerde Barker (£3)		3	
Morrice Apprice (£6)		6	
Randall Tilston (£4)		4	
John Hytchen (£8)		8	
John Taverner (£10) [a]		10	
William Hall (£3)		3	
Henrye Bornforde (£12)		12	
Richerd Barefelde (£4)		4	
William Freeman (£12)		12	
John Johnson (£4) [x - Q 26s. 8d.]		4	
Henrye Mathewe gen (£8)		8	
Walter Ryvers (£3)		3	
Thomas Kettle (£4)		4	
John Love (£3)		3	
[r.26]			
John Williamson (£5)		5	
Henry Bracy (£3)		3	
Thomas Dalton (£3)		3	
John Samont (£3)		3	
John Roccadyne (£3)		3	
Edwarde Graves (£3)		3	
James Platt gen (£12) [x - Essex 8s.]		12	
Hugh Cuffe gen (£10)		10	
John Lees (£5)		5	
182. Peter Toppinge lyenge within John Lees (£3) [a]		3	
William Gilson dwellinge in Mr Taylors rentes (£6) [a]		6	

	£	s.	d
Robert Pryor (£3)		3	
Richerde Gryffyn gen within Robert Priors			
house (£3) [a]		3	
William Hagon clerk (£3)		3	
William Votyer budgetmaker (£3)		3	
Edmonde Frost gen (£4)		4	
Maurice Wade (£4)		4	
Richerde Lambe (£3)		3	
Robert Johnes (£3)		3	
John Byrd (£5)		5	
William Maior (£3)		3	
Frauncys Myll (£4)		4	
Richerd Selby (£8)		8	
Robert Bell (£3)		3	
Edwarde Scott (£4)		4	
Margarett Edwardes (£3)		3	
Thomas Man (£3)		3	
John Knolles (£3)		3	
Roger Tanner (£5) [a]		5	
Peter Dyaper (£3)		3	
Richard Bettes (£3)		3	
John Curtesse (£3)		3	
Robert Gurnarde (£3)		3	
Henrye Peakyns (£3)		3	
Thomas Copcot (£3)		3	
Richerde Rayment (£3)		3	
John Morrys (£3)		3	
Thomas Jugges (£3)		3	
Henrye Fysher (£3)		3	
John Whaplot (£3)		3	
183. John Smyth (£3)		3	
Anthonye Wilmot gen (£6) [a]		6	
John Marrowe gen (£6)		6	
John Smyth within Mr Edwarde Woodes			
house (£5) [a]		5	
William Maior pewterer (£5)		5	
Richerde Algood (£5)		5	
Henrye Estcroft (£3)		3	
Robert Cryppes (£5)		5	
Henrye Beech (£8)		8	
Robert Stephens (£12)		12	
Richerd Baker (£3)		3	
William Taylor (£8)		8	
Johan Lawe wydowe (£3)		3	
Robert Hudson (£3)		3	
Nicholas Smythson (£3)		3	
Thomas Wylkes (£3)		3	

	£	s.	d
Mr Thomas Eve gen (£4) [ass. 11s.			
in Essex]		4	
Straungers			
Wynne Johnson botcher			4
Cecilye Johnson his wyfe			4
Gyles Wall [a]			4
Gosen Hall			4
Bennet Richerd bookbynder (£3)		6	
James Nepper [a]			4
Nicholas Nokes (£6)		12	
Marye his wyfe			4
James Deneple marchant (£6)		12	
[r.27]			
Isabell Deneple wyfe of James Deneple			4
Suzan Deneple his daughter			4
Johan Deneple his daughter			4
William Baylye silkeweaver (£3)		6	
Tennet Bartram wydowe			4
Suzan her servant			4
Robert Allen Scott (£3)		6	
Christian his wyfe			4
Powrish Pencon (£3)		6	
Magdalen his wyfe			4
Frauncys Delbocall his servant			4
Peter Bowen his servant			4
Marye Browne wydowe			4
Elizabeth Payne wydowe			4
Derick Vannasson servant to Allynson			4
COMPANYES			
The Company of Goldsmythes in landes (£150)	10		
The Cookes in landes (£4)		5	4
[Endorsed] Summa	285	2	

184. All which sommes of monye before expressed, so by the saide Marmaduke Franck and John Stevens, Petycollectors, to be collected and receyved, they the same Petycollectors shall trulye content and pay unto Raphe Ayloffe grocer and Henrye Allyngeton skynner, high Collectors of the sayde seconde payment of the saide subsydye wythin the saide warde of Aldrichgate, at such dayes, tymes, and places, as the saide high Collectors shall herafter to them the saide Petycollectors name and appoynt, they the saide Petycollectors retayninge in their owne handes to and for their owne proper use, of everye pounde of the saide sommes of monye so by them to be receyved for their owne laboures ii d. And makinge suche other Deductions and allowaunces as in the saide act of subsidye ys conteyned in that behalfe, accordinge to the tenor of the same act. In Wytnes whereof to thone part of theis Indentures remayninge with the saide Petycollectors, the saide Commyssioners have put their handes and seales. And to thother part of the

130

same Indentures remayninge with the saide Comissioners, the saide Petycollectors have put their handes and seales. Yeouen the daye and yeare abovewrytten.

185. [r.5]   ALGATE WARD
[Petty collectors: Edward Leanynge, draper, and James Deane, draper.]

	£	s	d
ST KATHERINE CHRECHURCH PARISHE			
Sir Fraunces Carowe in landes (£150) [a]	10		
Sir William Fitzewilliams in landes (£100) [a]	6	13	4
Sir Fraunces Hinde in landes (£60) [a]	4		
Sir Henry Darcey in landes (£60) [a]	4		
Mistress Gomblet alias Barbor in landes (£20)		26	8
George Dodde in landes (£10)		13	4
Edward Darcie in landes (£20) [a]		26	8
William Heard (£50) [x - Essex 50s.]		50	
William Atkines (£50)		50	
William Gilborne (£300)	15		
Edward Herdson (£200) [a]	10		
John Jefford (£70)	3	10	
John Smyth in Fees (£20)		26	8
Adrian Stokes in landes (£100) [x - Leics. £6 13s. 4d.]	6	13	4
Margaret Mullines widow in landes (£10)		13	4
Thomas Fulkes (£50) [x - Staffs. 50s.]		50	
Richard Johnson in landes (£20)		26	8
Strangers			
Fraunces Boules (£40) [b - Antwerp mer.]	4		
Jacob Johnson (£50) [b - Antwerp mer.]	5		
Englishmen			
John Nortrige (£3)		3	
Robert Chaundler (£30)		30	
Thomas Alline chaundler (£5)		5	
Augustine Willis inholder (£4)		4	
Nicholas Buck brownebaker (£12)		12	
Thomas Wetherall horner (£3)		3	
James Pilkington plumer (£3)		3	
Richard Rodes chaundler (£3) [a]		3	
Robert Dodd fishemonger (£5)		5	
John Manby inholder (£3)		3	
Thomas Shepard hosier (£3)		3	
186. Richard Saloman joyner (£3)		3	
Richard Clarke glasier (£6)		6	
William Fresingefeild painter (£3)		3	
Raphe Mullines pewterer (£4)		4	
Raphe Turnor grocer (£4)		4	

	£	s.	d
Edmond Ellis cutler (£4)		4	
Hugh Roberdes joyner (£3)		3	
George Lee sadler (£6)		6	
Alice Ferrymont widowe (£10)		10	
Richiard Harrison bowyer (£3)		3	
William Elam horner (£3)		3	
Peter Kinge chaundler (£3)		3	
Christofer Thornefeild taylor (£3)		3	
Fraunces Bradshawe salter (£5)		5	
John Bigeby pewterer (£3)		3	
Thomas Gorner, turnor (£3)		3	
George Bassat joyner (£3)		3	
William Rippingeton painter (£3)		3	
Edward Humfrey letherseller (£10)		10	
Thomas Hunt taylor (£3)		3	
John Jane habberdasher (£5)		5	
John Griffine carpenter (£3)		3	
Thomas Wood silkeweaver (£3)		3	
John Turpine habberdasher (£3)		3	
Henrye Eversham tayllor (£3)		3	
Silvester Glassopp joyner (£5)		5	
John Jackson chaundler (£3)		3	
Robert Alistoine coke (£3)		3	
Elizabeth Ingrame widowe in landes (£5)		6	8
Richard Cotman bricklaier (£3)		3	
James Oliver fremason (£3)		3	
187. George Bestbrowne cordwainer (£3)		3	
Henry Lee gerdler (£3)		3	
Jerome Feast pewterer (£3)		3	
Morris ap Robertes smythe (£3)		3	
Nicholas Hewett draper (£3)		3	
Percivall Gaskarre pewterer (£3)		3	
Thomas Whitefeild plaister (£3)		3	
John Prestwood stacioner (£3) [a]		3	
George Anderson purser (£3)		3	
Mathewe Cheston purser (£6)		6	
Thomas Bisley victuler (£3)		3	
Davie Walters silkeweaver (£3)		3	
John Steward pewterer (£3)		3	
Raphe Batman cowper (£3)		3	
John Prestwick lynnen draper (£8)		8	
John Vincent one of Lord Maiors officers (£3)		3	
Cutbert Lunte purser (£3)		3	
Gedeon Nott chesmonger (£4)		4	
Richard Alline mercer (£3)		3	
Nicholas Milles joyner (£3)		3	

	£	s.	d
Nicholas Haynes painter (£3)		3	
Laurence Overton merchaunt (£4)		4	
Thomas Newman skrivener (£6)		6	
Thomas Langhorne salter (£4)		4	
William Batman bricklaier (£20)		20	
Henrye Allen porter (£3)		3	
Peter Hewes grocer (£3)		3	
Richard Rowe whitbaker (£6)		6	
William Oliver (£3)		3	
John Barbor pewterer (£3)		3	
John Pennyfather cordwainer (£5)		5	
Leynard Larkine officer (£3)		3	

188.   Strangers

	£	s.	d
Lawrence Shrife cobler (40s.)		4	
George Ford perfumer (20s.)		2	
Peter Barton his servant per poll (4d.)			4
William de Rye silketwister (20s.)		2	
John de Vicque poste rider (20s.)		2	
Romano Cavalliero per poll (4d.)			4
Henrick Van Semer (20s.)		2	
Mawdline Bentley his servant (4d.)			4
Bartholmew Van Lowsett taylor (20s.)		2	
Cornelius Johnson cobler (4d.)			4
John Englishe post per poll (4d.)			4
Katherine Brunckey widow per poll (4d.)			4
Maria de Leckes per poll (4d.)			4
Peter Martine per poll (4d.) [a]			4
Michell van Father per poll (4d.)			4
Nicholas Lambertson per poll (4d.)			4

189.   SAINT KATHERINE COLMANES PARISHES
Englishmen

	£	s.	d
James Deane (£50)		50	
Edward Leaninge (£50)		50	
Michaell Hinage in Fees (£10) [ass. 8s. in Cambs.] [r.7]		13	4
Henry Billingesley (£120)	6		
Mistress [Dorothy] Eldrington widowe in landes (£40) [x - Essex 21s. 4d.][58]		53	4
Mr [Richard] Cuttes gentleman in landes (£40) [x - Essex 26s. 8d.][59]		53	4
Thomas Margetson (£60)	3		
Henry Brooke in Fees (£20) [x - Kent 26s. 8d.]		26	8

58. E.359/52, r. 14 gives Dorothy as first name.
59. E.359/52, r. 14 gives Richard as first name.

	£	s.	d
Strangers			
Jasper Graphine (£20) [x - Q 64s.][60]		40	
Sir John Portunado (£20)		40	
Dominico Busher (£50)	5		

190. Englishmen

	£	s.	d
William Buttermore carpenter (£8)	8		
William Gresham joyner (£3)	3		
Robert Taylfare carpenter (£3)	3		
John Mathewe joyner (£3)	3		
Henry Sanderson merchaunt (£10)	10		
Edward Kirkby glasier (£3)	3		
Thomas Gardiner merchaunt (£5)	5		
John Fraunces fishemonger (£3)	3		
Richard Langham painter (£3)	3		
Thomas Spencer bricklaier (£5)	5		
Edward Banckes goldsmith (£3)	3		
Richiard Aliston (£3)	3		
Robert Alistone (£3)	3		
Laurence Ripley joyner (£6)	6		
Robert Wilson brewer (£3)	3		
William Harison woodmonger (£5)	5		
Humfrey Baker pewterer (£3)	3		
Mathewe Hadwine victualler (£3)	3		
Trustram Upchurche cowper (£3)	3		
Thomas Paradice broker (£3)	3		
John Peacock carpenter (£3)	3		
Richard Isackson painter (£4)	4		
Roger Nore chaundler (£3)	3		
George Starre merchaunt (£3) [a]	3		
Hughe Davies cowper (£3)	3		
Strangers in ye same parishe			
Oratio Vellutelli merchaunt (40s.)	4		
Peter Brasier per poll (4d.) [a]			4
Marie Petros per poll (4d.) [a]			4
John Mountenamt per poll (4d.)			4
Jerome Lemuy taylor (20s.) [a][61]		2	
Hector Cotier scholmaster (£3)		6	
John de Best taylor (20s.) [a]		2	
Jacob Martine goldsmith (£5) [a]		10	
John Barnardine bomfacio per poll (4d.) [a]			4
Henrick Speriche & Alicia Maria, servantes (8d.) [a]			8
Henrick Tarrishe per poll (4d.) [a]			4
Thomas Kirliche (4d.) [a]			4

60. E.359/52, r. 14 gives surname as de Gaffen.
61. E.359/52, r. 14 gives surname as Lenuye.

	£	s.	d
Phillipe Rutter per poll (4d.)			4
John Paine (20s.)		2	
Isack de Bridges (20s.)		2	
James van Holte per poll (4d.)			4
Ambrose Pavia (20s.)		2	
Charles Gubert per poll (4d.) [a]			4
John Roye per poll (4d.)			4
Math[?]ren Serins per poll (4d.)			4
Marie Pebrake per poll (4d.) [a]			4

191.　　　　SAINT ANDROWES UNDERSHAFTE
　　　　AND AL HALLOWES IN YE WALL PARISHES
　　　　　Englishmen

	£	s.	d
Sir Thomas Offley knight Comissioner			
(£340)	17		
Nicholas Wheler (£100)	5		
Sir Thomas Hinage knight in landes			
(£80) [a]	5	6	8
Mr Moile Finche in landes (£50)			
[x - Kent £3 6s. 8d.]	3	6	8
Mr Edward Wotton in landes (£100)			
[x - Kent £6 13s. 4d.]	6	13	4
Mr Thomas Wotton in landes (£100)			
[x - Kent £6 13s. 4d.][62]	6	13	4
Thomas Sares (£60)	3		
William Chester in landes (£40)			
[x - Bucks. 20s.]		53	4
Edward Barret in landes (£100)			
[x - Berks. £6 13s.4d.]	6	13	4
Edward Bacon in landes (£50)			
[x - Berks. £3 6s. 8d.]	3	6	8
Robert Beale in fees (£10) [a]		13	4
Henry Ofley in landes (£15)		20	

　　　　　　　Strangers

	£	s.	d
Nicholas Fountayne (£200)			
[b - Antwerp mer.]	20		
[r.8]			
John Hublone (£50) [b - Antwerp mer.]	5		

　　　　　　　Englishmen

	£	s.	d
Bartholmew Pickman chandler (£4)		4	
James Copland smithe (£3)		3	
John Genno tayllor (£4)		4	
John Starton tayllor (£3)		3	
John Mourton yeoman (£3)		3	
Symon Smyth yeoman (£4)		4	
Symon Burton waxchaundler (£25)		25	

62. 'Commissioner' in margin.

	£	s.	d
Henrye Lodge brewer (£6)		6	
Thomas Gillibrande (£3)		3	
Symon Shriefe wolman (£3) [a]		3	
Raphe Middleton inholder (£3)		3	
John Craddock butler (£3)		3	
Thomas Haslowe carpenter (£5)		5	
Paule Eaton carpenter (£3)		3	
John Silliard joyner (£3)		3	
William Hollidaie merchaunt (£15)		15	
Nevell Goodd gent (£3) [a]		3	
Robert Tarbock taylor (£3)		3	
John Legge brewer (£4)		4	
Robert Taylor cordwainer (£4)		4	

192.   Strangers in ye same parishe

Erasmus della Founteyne (£15)			
[b - Antwerp mer.]		30	
Peter Hubline merchaunt (£5)			
[b - Antwerp mer.]		10	
John Van Hales & Barbara his wife			
per poll (8d.)			8
Martin Vanion and his wife and Johan			
Devale theire servante per poll			
(12d.) [a]			12

Englishmen

Emanuell Franckline merchaunt (£8)		8	
Widowe Beamond (£3)		3	
Peter Austen cordwainer (£3)		3	
John Trulowe cowper (£3)		3	
William Iveson clothworker (£3)		3	
Thomas Awsten purser (£8)		8	
John Pattenson cordwainer (£3)		3	
Davye Parre joyner (£3)		3	
Gilbert Segar beareclark (£3)		3	
John Russell pewterer (£3)		3	
William Hunt cordwainer (£3)		3	
William Mace cordwainer (£4)		4	
Harvie Lonas tayllor (£4)		4	
Erasmus Bennet merchaunt (£5)		5	
Henry Bradshawe victuler (£3)		3	
Robert Moris (£4) [x - Mddx. 16s.]		4	

Strangers

Guillame Dellamere (20s.)		2	
Henry van Brasselles tailor (40s.)		4	
John Lewis tayllor (20s.) [a]		2	
Nicholas Bewett per poll (4d.)			4
Marie Hamett servant with Peter Egar (4d.)			4
Farnando Copin per poll (4d.)			4

	£	s.	d
Funger Johnson per poll (4d.)			4
John Ryley armorer per poll (4d.)			4
Peter Egar per poll (4d.)			4
Widowe Chamberline per poll (4d.)			4
Widowe Bloys per poll (4d.)			4

193. SAINT OLAVE PARISHE
Englishmen

	£	s.	d
Sir Fraunces Walsingham knight commissioner [Blank]	[Blank]		
Thomas Cletheroll (£50)		50	
William Painter gent (£120) [x - Q £1 6s. 8d.]	6		
Mistress Aylife in landes (£20) [a]		26	8
Dustane Anies (£80)	4		
Mr William Fitzwilliams in fees (£20) [a]		26	8
Nathaniell Partiche gent (£50) [x - Mddx. 16s.]		50	

Strangers

	£	s.	d
Jacob Verseline (£20)		40	
Innocent Comer (£20) [x - Q 64s.]		40	
Robert Briatt (£10)		20	
Innocent Lucatelli (£20)		40	
Augustine Bassany (£20) [x - Q 64s.]		40	

Englishmen

	£	s.	d
Robert Harris wolman (£3)		3	
John Organ wolman (£5)		5	
Fraunces Woodford wolman (£5)		5	
[r.9]			
Henry Bendishe (£3)		3	
John Thomas purser (£10)		10	
William Grigges (£3)		3	
Adam Raieshawe carpenter (£5)		5	
Thomas Aman carpenter (£3)		3	
George Rolf pewterer (£3)		3	
Robert Ayner cowper (£3)		3	
Peter Huningborne purser (£8)		8	
Thomas Hackett stacioner (£3)		3	
John Mouse skiner (£3)		3	
Robert Androwes frewterer (£3) [a]		3	
Richard Eversley silkeweaver (£3)		3	
Nicholas Johnson gardiner (£3)		3	
William Otwell porter (£3)		3	
Nicholas Weckes carpenter (£5)		5	
John Woodrofe packer (£3)		3	
William Petala broker (£3)		3	
Roger Holland clothworker (£3)		3	
Cesar Dolphin merchaunt (£10)		10	

	£	s.	d
194. Strangers in the same parishe			
Jesper Blancquet (20s.)		2	
Iwan de Forge & his wiffe per poll (8d.)			8
Vintrie Durrine post per poll (4d.)			4
Roger Nowell (4d.)			4
Nowell the scholmaster & his wife (8d.)			8
Nicholas Pettit broker (20s.)		2	
Arnold Grevans per poll (4d.)			4
Jarvis Rawlins per poll (4d.)			4
Peter de Parrye merchaunt (£5)		10	
Robert Howell Margaret de Rena et Margaret Moyna servantes with Peter Parre (16d.)			16
Marrie Parrie Peter Parries wife (4d.)			4
Nicholas Hollicott (20s.)		2	
Tuffyne de Valloys duth [sic] post (20s.)		2	
Anthony Johnson and Garret Parnell servantes with William Masse (8d.) [a]			8
Martine Close and Garrett van Gallo servantes with Richard Alline per poll (8d.) [a]			8
Garrett Fantroy with Henry Bradshawe (4d.)			4
Widowe Pickett per poll (4d.)			4
Angell Grisell [a] & John Luprine per poll (8d.)			8
Leven Clarke widowe per poll (4d.)			4
Nicholas Grafford & his wiffe per poll (8d.) [a]			8
Marie Brearde widowe (4d.) [a]			4
Agnes Fremend servant with John Tuppett (4d.)			4
Dominico Cassellere, Bastian Selmalle, Marco Guado, Vincent Celleoll, Camella Forrme [a], John Maria Surlaine [a] servantes with Jacob Vercelin (2s.)		2	
Nowell Roger and John Russell per poll (8d.)			8
195. CRECHURCH PRECINCT Englishmen			
Richard Bedo yeoman (£6)		6	
Robert Duland stacioner (£3)		3	
Brian Naylor baker (£3)		3	
Elise Harrison plasterer (£3) [x - Farringdon ward Without 5s. as Harris]		3	
Strangers their			
Remere Sergiante (20s.)		2	
Jacomyne his wife per poll (4d.)			4

	£	s.	d
William Rues, Nicholas Richardes, Habrick Fisher all per poll (12d.)			12
Haunce van Sivicote (20s.)		2	
Margaret his wife and Maria de Clock (8d.)			8
Peter Busher tayllor (£3)		6	
Hannikine his wife & Marie his servant (8d.)			8
Arnold Riche and his wife (8d.)			8
Jacobe van Noster and Jacomyne his wife (8d.) [a]			8
Haunce Stele & Dugine his daughter and Henrye Exendall his servante per poll (12d.)			12
[r.10]			
Symon Clarke per poll (4d.)			4
John Dent and Jane his wife per poll (8d.) [a]			8
Henry Rose and Maria his wiffe (8d.) [a]			8
Sibell Starke widowe per poll (4d.) [a]			4
Simon Tarrinton (40s.) [a]		4	
Margaret his wife, Dugine and Katherine, Strawen de Barr and Richard de More his servantes (20d.) [a]			20
Peter Screvell and Martine his wiffe (8d.)			8
John Nightingall Margaret his wiffe Jane his servante (12d.)			12
Garett Wattine Katherine his wife & Symon Durison (20s. 8d.)		2	8
196. Charle Utkey and Elizabeth his wiffe (8d.)			8
Margaret Johnson, Clara Johnson, Marie Johnson, Jane Vanderlinden, Tice Johnson & Peter Powell all servantes with Jacob Johnson per poll (2s.)		2	
Margaret Bechesine & Marke Bechesine (8d.) [a]			8
Harrian Pruse and Susana his wife (8d.)			8
William Mose Johan his wife and Appolonia Moyse, Giles de Boy & Pinkine his wif (20d.)			20
Gyles Cornelis, Garrett Florence and Arnold Harman (12d.) [a]			12
Jasper Bungle[63], Katherine Bungle, Philipp Lipton[64] & Nellykine Bungle[65] per poll (16d.) [a]			16

63. E.359/52, r. 14 gives this surname as Bingeley and Binigeley.
64. E.359/52, r. 14 gives this surname as Lupton.
65. E,359/52, r. 14 gives Mallakin as first name.

	£	s.	d
Andrewe Bussher, Lynckine his wife, Anthonye Peters and Dericke Venison his servauntes (16d.)			16
Lewis vander Caple, Margaret his wife, Katherine Johnson & True Mulline his servaunt (16d.)			16
Katherine Jander, Jane and Margaret Jander (12d.) [a]			12
Gilbert Garrett and Katherine his wife (8d.)			8
Glode Dutteney, Jane his wife, Barbara Gawde and Marie Cruce servauntes (41s.)		3	
John Billingey Anne his wife and Starr his servaunt (20s. 8d.)		2	8
Jane Cockes Piera Saloman widowes (8d.)			8
George Francke & Susanna his wife (8d.) [a]			8
Godfrey Winge & Katherine his wife (8d.)			8

	£	s.	d
THE COMPANIES			
The Iremongers in landes (£8)		10	8
The Tylers and Bricklaiers in landes (£4)		5	4
The Fletcher in landes (26s. 8d.)			20
[Endorsed] Summa	271	8	8

197. [r.17] BASSIESHAWE WARDE
Petty collectors: Robert Crosse, salter, and John Storer, baker.]

ST MICHAELLS
[English]

	£	s.	d
John Jackman (£60)	3		
Samuell Backhowse (£150) [x - Hants. 53s. 4d.]	7	10	
Amy Hobbes wydowe (£100) [x - Surrey 26s. 8d. by name of Robert Livesey][67]	5		
Thomas Cranefeild (£100)	5		
Wylliam Dummer (£30)		30	
George Stockmeade (£140)	7		
Anthony Calthorpp (£100)	5		
Thomas Rose (£100)	5		
Thomas Owen gent (£60) [x - Salop. 8s.]	3		
Wylliam Higges (£60)	3		
Wylliam Blunte (£100) [x - Kent 33s. 4d.]	5		
Wylliam Elkyn (£100)	5		
Symon Furner (£50)		50	
John Storer (£50)		50	
Nicholas Cotson (£50)		50	
Thomas Norton (£10)		10	
James Elwyck (£50)		50	

67. E.359/52, r. 14 gives Ann as first name.

140

	£	s.	d
Henry Holford (£50) [x - Westminster 10s.]		50	
Christofer Atkynson gent in fees (£10) [a]		13	4
Allayn Colley (£3)		3	
John Cotesford (£10)		10	
Robert Crosse (£12)		12	
John Tyffyn (£4)		4	
Thomas Welles (£3)		3	
James Harman (£6)		6	
John Robertes (£10)		10	
John Churchill (£15)		15	
John Yomans (£15)		15	
Wylliam Parris (£6)		6	
Gregory Wysdome (£15)		15	
John Humfrey (£10)		10	
198. Hugh Mantell (£5)		5	
Robert Conyers (£15)		15	
Richard Brock (£10)		10	
Wylliam Marryon (£5)		5	
Thomas Barnes (£5)		5	
Henry Dunston (£3)		3	
Wylliam Cobb (£8)		8	
Nicholas Leake (£6)		6	
John Ley (£3)		3	
Wylliam Myles (£3)		3	
John Guyle (£3)		3	
[r.18]			
James Robynson (£3)		3	
Anthony Webb (£3)		3	
Anne Ellyott (£3)		3	
Wylliam Bostock (£12)		12	
John Ince (£4)		4	
George Sory (£8)		8	
Thomas Shawe (£12)		12	
Wylliam Davies (£10)		10	
John Harlowe (£3)		3	
Thomas Farnaby (£4)		4	
George Swane (£3)		3	
John Wyllett (£3)		3	
John Tanner (£10)		10	
Raphe Crewe (£8)		8	
Clement Calthorpp (£5)		5	
Thomas Brende (£6)		6	
Raphe Bostock (£3) [a]		3	
Edward Ap John (£3)		3	
Straungers			
Peter Cannan (£3)		6	
Melchiar his wyfe per poll			4

	£	s.	d
Abraham Lekeever per poll			4
Companies			
The Cowpers in landes (£10)		13	4
The Gyrdlers in landes (£10)		13	4
The Weavers in landes (£6)		8	
The Masons (£5)		5	
[Endorsed] Summa	84	17	8

199. [r.60]   BILLINGESGATE WARDE
[Petty collectors: John Stubbes, fishmonger, and John Wylde, fishmonger.]

ST MARYE HILL PARISHE:
[English]

Thomas Blanck Alderman (£300)	15	
William Holstock (£100)	5	
Arthure Malbye (£160)	8	
John Hayward (£50)		50
Thomas Austell (£60)	3	
Richard Payne (£60)	3	
Michaell Bowthe (£50)		50
Marmaduke Spight (£60)	3	
Cutbert Buckle (£200)	10	
John Lemon (£50)		50
John Bassocke (£50)		50
Thomas Eve (£50)		50
Thomas Younge (£50)		50
William Hitchcock (£50)		50
Thomas Wattes (£50)		50
Nicholas Harrys (£20)		20
Richard Rogers (£3)		3
William Cortys (£3)		3
John Peterson (£3)		3
James Kerre (£3)		3
Richard Willys (£25)		25
Robert Carpinter (£10)		10
John Smythe (£3)		3
James Felles (£8)		8
Henrye Clarke (£5)		5
Richard Gote (£5)		5
John Harrison [Blank]	[Blank]	
John Gibbens (£6)		6
William Daves (£3)		3

200. Otwell Semper (£5)	5
Thomas Sulliard (£20)	20
John Sarres (£3)	3
Thomas Edward (£10)	10
Richard Tompkins (£10) [x - Q 10s.]	10

	£	s.	d
John Wotton (£3)		3	
Symon Galles (£5)		5	
John Draper (£8)		8	
Morrys Walker (£10)		10	
Richard Arnold (£6)		6	
John Stowers (£3)		3	
Thomas Bence (£10)		10	
William Jeston (£5)		5	
Thomas Standley (£3)		3	
Rowland Colley (£3)		3	
Raphe Claxon (£15)		15	
Thomas Nokes (£10)		10	
John Poulton (£3)		3	
Thomas Martyn (£6)		6	
Walter Bassocke (£3)		3	
Raphe Grene salter (£6)		6	
William Logyne (£10)		10	
Nicholas Wager (£3) [a]		3	
Richard Atkinson (£5)		5	
William Felles (£3)		3	
Tobye Edwyn (£3)		3	
Angell Gelles (£3)		3	
Christofer Johnson (£3) [a]		3	
John Dewe (£3)		3	
John Fermer (£3)		3	
Thomas Tompkyns (£8)		8	
Jasper Tynes (£3)		3	

201. [r.61]   Strangers:

	£	s.	d
Joice van Erpe (£50) [b - Antwerp mer.]	5		
Guilliam Curteine (£20)		40	
John Rosier (£20) [b - Antwerp mer.]		40	
Doctor Daniell (£10)		20	
Raphaell vande Pitt (£30)	3		
Fraunces Decoy (£3)		6	
Margeret the wyfe of Gillam Curtein, Joane			
& Margret his daughters and Haunce			
his servaunte poll		16	
Elizabeth a Duche woman within Angell Giles			
house poll		4	
Jane Farmen widowe, Marye and Jane his [sic]			
daughters poll		12	
Peter Foxe Silkin his wyfe Harman & Nicholas			
Duchmen poll		16	
Pullen the wyfe of Raphaell van de Pitt,			
John & Lewes there servauntes poll		12	
Jerman Galmottes, Barbary his wief, John			
Whetfronge a servaunte poll		12	

	£	s.	d
Elizabeth the wyef of Frances Decoy & Elizabeth his daughter poll			8
Helen the wyfe of John Rosser & Margrett his maide poll			8
Helen the wife of Joice van Erpe, Haunce, Alice and Elizabeth his servauntes poll			16

202. ST BUTTOLPHES PARISHE:
[English]

	£	s.	d
Nicholas Revell (£150)	7	10	
Edward Halle (£200)	10		
Edmund Baldroe (£50)		50	
John Stockes (£50)		50	
John Archer (£70) [x - Essex 13s. 4d.]	3	10	
Thomas Heynes (£50)		50	
Symon Stodderd (£50)		50	
Thomas Hacker fishmonger (£30)		30	
John Wilde (£40)		40	
John Stubbes (£70)	3	10	
Widowe Hacker (£50)		50	
Mistres Lucar in landes (£20)		26	8
Thomas Barber (£30)		30	
George Hamonde (£5)		5	
Richard Johnson (£5)		5	
Christofer Williamson (£5)		5	
John Hacker (£30)		30	
George Killingworthe (£5) [x Kent 13s.4d.]		5	
Thomas Parkherste (£3)		3	
Edmond Clyffe (£3)		3	
Robert Ellyott (£3)		3	
James Carter (£35)		35	
Robert Best (£3)		3	
Nicholas Brooke (£5)		5	
Henry Wolley (£3)		3	
Richard Pointell (£30)		30	
Thomas Widhope (£6)		6	
Thomas Hardinge (£6)		6	

	£	s.	d
203. William Homerton (£20)		20	
John Chapman (£3)		3	
Richard Marshall (£5)		5	
William Stooke (£3)		3	
Edward Dawe and Roberte Valler his partener (£6)		6	
Gilbert Thurston (£10)		10	
Christofer Lander (£3)		3	
Thomas Marret (£3)		3	
Thomas Abbott (£20)		20	

	£	s.	d
William Edwardes (£3)		3	
William Flowerdewe (£10)		10	
John Fitzwillams (£15)		15	
William Stockes (£5)		5	
Strangers:			
Peter Seres (£70)	7		
Mathew Lulles (£60) [b - Antwerp mer.]	6		
Garret Williamson (£30) [a]	3		
Martyn Vaversyn (£20)		40	
Haunce Wonters (£70) [b - Antwerp mer.][68]	7		
John Lodovike (£20)		40	
Jasper Selois (£20) [a]		40	
Martyn Strewsey (£20)		40	
Peter Godscall (£10)		20	
Denys de Mounte (£20)		40	
William Kyes (£3)		6	
Cornelius Jacobbe (£10)		20	
Widowes in the same parishe			
Widowe Stockmeade (£10)		10	
Widowe Willis (£3)		3	
Widowe Landethe (£5)		5	
Widowe Howe (£10) [a]		10	
[r.62]			

204. Strangers:

John Angelotta poll	4
Katherine Emery widowe poll	4
Mawdlyn ye wife of Martyn Vaversyn, Susan their daughter and Katherine poll	12
John Abell, Margaret his wife, Andrew his sonne and Mary Veragen their maide poll	16
Elizabeth the wyef of Peter Seres, Joyce his man & Jane his maide, servauntes poll	12
Jane the wife of Mathew Lulles, Dirick his man and Anna his maide, servauntes poll	12
Jane the wife of Cornelis Jacobson & Phillippe his maide poll	8
Katherine the wife of John Lodowick & Anthonie his sonne poll	8
Katherine the wife of Martyn Strewse & Jerome Goodson his servaunt poll	8
Ellys Maye and Tawnykyn his wyfe poll	8
Matheus Bowden & Jaques Bartell servauntes to Jasper Celosse & Tanekin their servauntes poll	12

68. Wonters was exonerated as an Antwerp merchant although there is no marginal notation to that effect in the assessment roll.

	£	s.	d
Haunce Demitter and Lamberd his boye poll			8
Tanykyn the wyfe of Denys Demount & Katherine his servaunt poll			8
Elizabeth the wife of Peter Godscall & Reynoldes their boye poll			8
Mathias Clowcarte servaunt to Garret Williamson poll			4
Daniell van Bussisen & Katherine his wyfe poll			8

205.   ST ANDREWE HUBBERTES PARISHE
[English]

Michaell Lyon (£50) [x - Mddx. 9s.]	50	
John Grene thelder (£3)	3	
William Redmar (£20)	20	
John Grene the younger (£10)	10	
John Ollyffe (£10)	10	
Barnaby Bestowe (£20)	20	
Andrew Adrianson (£15)	15	
Andrew Banbery (£10)	10	
Ellize Childersley (£3)	3	
Richard Giles (£3)	3	
Lawrence Addames (£3)	3	
George Freshingfilde cooke (£5)	5	
Richard Rode (£3)	3	
Ellize Merchaunt (£5)	5	
Richard Robinson (£8)	8	
John Johnson (£6)	6	
Thomas Haydon (£6)	6	
Thomas Burnley (£20)	20	
Raphe Graunte (£3)	3	
Thomas Grene (£6)	6	
William Holton (£3)	3	
John Meyden (£3)	3	
Michaell Horner (£3) [a]	3	
John Reynoldes (£3)	3	
George Bell (£3)	3	
Davy Phillippes (£3)	3	
William Browne (£3) [a]	3	
Edward Saunders (£3)	3	
Jerome Burton (£3)	3	
John Stevens (£3)	3	
John Turnor (£10)	10	
William Acheley (£10)	10	
Nicholas Langley (£10)	10	
Thomas Weaver (£12) [x - Q 24s.]	12	
John Kinge (£15)	15	
Davy Newball (£6)	6	

	£	s.	d
206. Strangers:			
Joyce van de Plancke (£40)	4		
Guilliam ver Maiden (£10) [b - Antwerp mer.]		20	
Peter Paliat (£10)		20	
Augustine Bewlewe (£30)	3		
Cristian van Strayse (£10)		20	
Petronille Vairmaiden wife of Guillam			
Vermaiden and Guillam Cornelle			
his man poll			8
Davy Mallen and Mary Cornelis within			
his house poll [a]			8
Cristian van Welter & Alice his wife poll			8
Katherine wife of Peter Pallett & Suzan			
de Morrey in his house poll			8
William Tilman within William Holton			
poll [a]			4
John Dilson & John Boone servauntes with			
John Johnson poll [a]			8
John Arnold servant with Richard Robinson			
poll			4
John Richardson servaunt with Richard			
Giles poll [a]			4
Katherine wife of Cristian van Strawson,			
Jakamyn Suzan his servaunt poll			8
Nicholas Williamson within Ellys Merchaunt,			
John Rookes, Giles Bedall in ye same			
house poll			12
Joyce van lan Boze, servaunt to Joyce			
van Planke poll			4
Agnes del Haye under Augustine de Beaulyen,			
& James Fallowe servaunte to the said			
Augustine poll			8
[r.63]			
Mary Bryet and Mary Bryet [sic] two sisters			
poll [a]			8
James Rounecont poll [a]			4
Lambert and John Hollibushe under John			
Olyff poll			8
207. ST GEORGES & ST MARGARETES PARISHES			
[English]			
Thomas Wilford (£50)		50	
Robert Howe (£80)	4		
Edward Rewe (£50)		50	
Peter Collett (£50)		50	
Thomas Gawyn gent (£70)			
[x - Wilts. £1 10s.]	3	10	
John Alden (£80)	4		

	£	s.	d
Robert Dalborne (£20) [ass. 2s. 8d.			
in Surrey]		20	
John Acheley (£3)		3	
Robert Proctor (£3)		3	
Richard Sadler (£3)		3	
John Bennett (£3)		3	
Gilbert Tomlinson (£10)		10	
Richard Clarke (£3)		3	
Robert Mylles (£3)		3	
Thomas Romney (£3)		3	
Humfry Cooke (£3)		3	
Edmond Ansell (£10)		10	
John Ball (£5)		5	

Strangers

	£	s.	d
Guiliame le Spera (£10)		20	
Peter Clement (£20)		20	[sic]
John Phenix (£60)	6		
John de Lanoye (£50)	5		
Walter Artson (£50) [b - Antwerp mer.]	5		
Henrick Voites (£15)		30	
William Browninge (£30)	3		
Haunce Gast (£20) [ass. 30s. in Langbourn			
Ward as John Guest]		40	
Paule de la Haye (£20)		40	
Joice Bowes (£3)		6	
Gabriel Vandeviver (£3)		6	
Giles Showmaker servaunt to Peter Clement,			
& Dino his maide servaunt poll [a]			8
Katherine ye wife of Henry Footes, Katherine			
a maide servaunt & Michell a boy poll			12

	£	s.	d
208. Margret the maide servaunt of Paule de la			
Haye poll [a]			4
Margaret the wife of Walter Artson, Michell &			
Elizabeth his maides & John Stripp his			
man poll			16
Trunkin the wife of John Phenix & Katherine			
his maide poll			8
Katherine Heydon & Jane her daughter poll			8
John Richardes within goodwife Crowe poll [a]			4
Margret Gueson a widowe poll			4
Anne ye wife of William Browninge, Quintyne			
his sister, John his manservaunt poll			12
Margret ye wife of Joyce Boues & his sister			
Katherine Beske poll			8
[Blank] the wife of Gabriell Vandiviver, Joice			
his daughter, Tobye Abberd & Agnes his			
wife within them poll			16

	£	s.	d
Katherine the wife of Haunce Gaste & Mary			
his maide poll			8
Joyce the wyfe of Gillam Lespeere & Conradus			
their man poll			8
Pawle Towbaste & Barbary a maide in the house			
of Haunce Hostat dwelled in poll			8

209.   ST MARGRET PATTEN:
[English]

Richard Porter (£3)		3
Robert Foyden (£3)		3
John Clyffe (£5)		5
John Russell (£3)		3
Dionys Brogden (£5)		5
John Martyn (£6)		6
James Lisbye (£10)		10
Richard Baker (£10)		10
Henry Unthanke (£20)		20
William Lucas (£10)		10
John Collier (£10)		10
Richard Lessett (£5)		5
John Martyn my L. Maiors officer (£5)		5
John Bradley (£5)		5
John Lisbye (£3)		3
Thomas Gryffyn (£6)		6
Augustine Soda (£5)		5
[Endorsed] Summa	269	17

210. [r.68]   BISSHOPPS GATTE
[Petty collectors: John Edwardes, draper, and Wyllyam Kerwyn, freemason.]

ALHALLOWES PARISHE

Mr Thomas Smith, Customer (£150)		
[x - Kent £4 13s.]	7	10
Henry Dale a Sessor (£70)	3	10
William Horne (£70)	3	10
Simon Horsepoole (£60)	3	
Richard Ibotson (£60)	3	
John Edwardes (£50)		50
Richard Thompson (£50)		50
Henry Hawghton (£50)		50
Henry Cneil stranger (£50)	5	

English

John Barton (£8)		8
John Finche (£5)		5
Christofer Peerte (£20)		20
Isbell Whittingham widowe (£25)		
[ass. 40s. in Mddx.]		25

149

	£	s.	d
Hughe Bullocke (£8)		8	
Robert Mason (£20)		20	
John Bearden (£3)		3	
Robert Hall (£6)		6	
John Adline (£20)		20	
Robert Mudesley (£30)		30	
Roger Preston (£3)		3	
Humfrey Parris (£3)		3	
John Wriothsley (£3)		3	
John Winge (£3)		3	
George Cooke (£3) [a]		3	
Elyzabeth Fyssher widowe (£6)		6	
John Bently (£3) [a]		3	
Richard Kinge (£8)		8	

Stranger

| Susan the servaunte of Henry Cneil per pol (4d.) | | | 4 |

211.   ST PETERS IN CORNEHILL PARISHE
[English]

	£	s.	d
Foulke Heath (£50)		50	
Percivall Hassold (£50)		50	
Edwarde Cawnte (£50)		50	
William & Thomas Walthall, partiners (£60)	3		
Hugh Golde (£50)		50	
Jozeph Birchet within William Dale in landes (£10)		13	4
Giles Hicfeilde, stranger (£10)		20	
John Inman (£3)		3	
Thomas Malyn (£5)		5	
John Rayment (£3)		3	
Richard Sturman (£3)		3	
Thomas Kenestone (£3)		3	
William Manor (£3)		3	
William Bromlye (£3)		3	
Melchisadecke Bennet (£3) [a]		3	
Lybias Swan (£4)		4	
John Dixon (£3)		3	
Thomas Galle (£3)		3	
William Foidone (£4)		4	
Richard Wille (£8)		8	
Widdowe Chatterton (£10)		10	
Salomon Bright (£10)		10	
Mighell Smithe (£10)		10	
Thomas Smithe (£10)		10	
Richard Pingle (£25)		25	
John Crant (£15)		15	
John Basforde (£15)		15	

	£	s.	d
Henrie Holdsworthe (£3)		3	
William Leycrofte (£3)		3	
Robert Warden (£8)		8	
Lybias Barnarde (£3)		3	
Widdowe Barber (£3)		3	
William Dethicke alias Yorke (£25) [b][69]		25	
Widdowe Satchfeilde (£8)		8	
Strangers			
John Rodmaker per pol (4d.) [a]			4
Widdowe Pryme per pol (4d.) [a]			4

212.   ST MARTINE OUTWICHE PARISHE
[English]

	£	s.	d
Dame Marie Rowe (£100)	5		
John Spencer (£300)	15		
Thomas Randall (£80)	4		
Christofer Hoddesdone (£100)	5		
[r.69]			
Simon Bowerman (£50)		50	
John Anwicke in fees (£20)		26	8
Henry Colthurst (£50)		50	
Strangers			
Lovies Fongle (£30)	3		
Adam Villert (£10)		20	
Englishmen			
Fernando Clutterbooke Reynold Kopcot			
partiners (£40)		40	
Widdowe Foster (£3)		3	
John Frostone (£5)		5	
Thomas Cozen (£3)		3	
Julinus Bemishe (£6)		6	
Thomas Bullocke (£3)		3	
Rychard Foxe (£15)		15	
Strangers			
Mary Villaris per pol (4d.) [a]			4
George Welton per pol (4d.) [a]			4
Garret Farringre per pol (4d.) [a]			4
John Huddenhewe per pol (4d.) [a][70]			4
Garret Crewse per pol (4d.) [a]			4
Phillip Mayhalt per pol (4d.) [a][71]			4
Saunders Singre per pol (4d.) [a]			4

69. Dethicke, as York Herald, was exonerated by virtue of letters patent of 4 June 1549 and writ to the treasurer and barons dated 1 July 1581 (E.359/52, r. 13).
70. E.359/52, r. 13 gives surname as Hedgedinghewe.
71. E.359/52, r. 13 gives surname as Mackall.

	£	s.	d
213. ST ETHELBOROWES PARISHE			
[English]			
Mathewe Harrison (£50)		50	
Mr John Cowper late alderman (£400)	20		
Elizabeth Stevens widowe in landes (£20)		26	8
Dame Anne Gressham in landes (£200)			
[x - Mddx. £13 6s. 8d.]	13	6	8
James Holmeleye in landes (£15)		20	
Thomas Collsell (£80) [x - Essex 40s.]	4		
Mistres Margaret Bonde widowe (£100)	5		
John Watson (£50)		50	
Daniell Bonde (£60) [ass. £3 6s. in Essex]	3		
Clement Kelke (£50)		50	
John Robinson (£50)		50	
William Reade gent in landes (£50)			
[x - Mddx. £2]	3	6	8
William Kerwine (£50)		50	
John Terrill gent in landes (£40) [a]		53	4
Henrye Paverser gent in landes (£40) [a][72]		53	4
Henry Owtred in landes (£50) [a]	3	6	8
John Gifforde in landes (£100)			
[x - Staffs. £2]	6	13	4
Richard Glascocke (£50)		50	
William Burde [Blank]	[Blank]		
Nicholas Gorge gent (£80)	4		
Strangers			
Peter Bowlters (£60)	6		
Jacob Saule (£40)	4		
Godfrey Canion alias Anthonie Jorrey (£80)	8		
Godfrey Canenocle (£20)		40	
Englishemen			
John Wells (£15) [x - Q 44s.]		15	
Edwarde Walker (£6)		6	
Mathewe Bucke (£15)		15	
John Stanton (£15)		15	
Arthure Norton (£3)		3	
214. John Messenger (£15)		15	
Robert Lewes (£10)		10	
Richard Bowelles (£3)		3	
Nicholas Williams (£3)		3	
Richard Clercke (£3)		3	
Thomas Dasone (£10)		10	
Robert Burton (£3)		3	
Robert Owldon (£3)		3	
George Kilmere (£3)		3	

72. E.359/52, r. 13 gives surname as Vavasour.

	£	s.	d
Thomas Millington (£10) [a]		10	
Strangers			
Stephan Segar, Fraunces his wife, Jane			
and Susan his dawghters per pol			16
Hubberd de Bowe, Mary his wife, James his			
sonne, Katherine & Anne his dawghters			
per pol [a - all except Hubberd]			20
John Graye (£6)		12	
Adryan Slablearte (£5) [a]		10	
Jane his wife, Ramens, Easter & Joyce his			
children per pol [a]			16
Peter Jacob per pol [a]			4
Simon Carrane & Jane his wife per pol			8
John Durant & Jane his wife per pol			8
Melcher Carrans dawghter per pol			4
Margaret Narke per pol [a]			4
Job Browyer (£3) [a]		6	
Jane his wife per pol [a]			4
Joyce Nighttingale (£5)		10	
Perren his wife, and John, his man per pol			8

215. ST ELLYNS PARISHE
[English]

	£	s.	d
Richard Wright (£5)		5	
John Mathewe (£20)		20	
Joan Skogges, widowe (£5)		5	
Edeth Hagar, widowe (£15)		15	
Robert Springe (£20)		20	
William Barbor (£6)		6	
Thomas Mundaye (£5)		5	
John Butcher (£15)		15	
Hugh Kenricke (£8)		8	
Robert Hubberd (£8)		8	
Joan Crayford, widowe (£10)		10	
Agnes Senter (£3)		3	
Peter Dood (£5)		5	
Edward Crayford (£3)		3	
[r.70]			
Jarman Cyoll (£3)		3	
Richard Rysbey (£3)		3	
Simon Smithe (£3)		3	
Thomas Sawnders (£10)		10	
Strangers			
Hance Carpre, Fraunces his wife, and			
Jerrome Vonschouse, their servaunt			
per pol			12
Sykin Bowltis his wife, Sara Boultis &			
Peter Boultis their children (12d.)			12

	£	s.	d
Anthony Cornellis, servant to Boultis			
per pol [a]			4
Barthilmewe de Some, Dominian his wife,			
and Lambard de Graye their servant			
per pol [a - Lambard de Graye]			12
Beter Burly (£3) [a]		6	
Jane Burly, his wife [a]			4
Agatha Saule, his wife, Anne Saule and			
Mary Saule (12d.)			12
Mary Cannion, his wife, Daniell Canion and			
Barbara, his mayden (12d.)			12
Margaret Iverye alias Cannion & Marie			
Iverye (8d.)			8
Margaret Fountayne, Marie Jones, & Jane			
Whitebreade per pol			12
Robert Master per pol [a]			4
Garret de Coner, Margarett his wife, and			
Julian theire Mayden (12d) [a]			12

216.   ST BOTOLPHES PARISHE
                         [English]

	£	s.	d
Nicholas Sawnders (£60) [a]	3		
William Campion, in Fees (£10)			
[x - Mddx. 21s. 4d.]		13	4
Agnes Johnson, widowe, in landes (£15)		20	
Robert Bestney, gent, in landes (£10)			
[x - Mddx. 13s. 4d.]		13	4
Henry Billingham, gent. (£50)			
[x - Q 14s. 8d.]		50	
John Banbury, in landes (£10)		13	4
William Waypoole, in landes and Fees (£10)			
[x - Suff. 26s. 8d.][73]		13	4
Mr. Edmunde Dimmocke, in landes (£100)			
[x - Lincs. £6 13s. 4d.]	6	13	4
John Roche, gent, in landes & Fees (£100)	6	13	4
Henrie Catline, in landes and Fees (£20) [a]		26	8
[Stranger]			
John Mountoye, stranger (£10)		20	
Englishmen			
Edwarde Hamonde (£10)		10	
Alice Robinson, widowe (£5)			
[ass. 8s. in Mddx.]		5	
Thomas Armestronge (£10)		10	
Henry Stacye (£15)		15	
Roger Gibsone (£6)		6	
Giles Griffine (£5)		5	

73. E.359/52, r. 13 gives surname as Walpole.

	£	s.	d
Thomas Cutler (£5)		5	
William Barnes (£3)		3	
Henry Bennet (£3)		3	
John Jefferye (£3)		3	
Robert Phillipps (£15)		15	
Robert Nicholles (£8) [a]		8	
Joane Wood, widowe (£30)		30	
Robert Foorde (£3)		3	
Simon Gardner (£3)		3	
John Grene (£5)		5	
Evan Ap Davie (£3)		3	
Anthonye Catcher (£3)		3	
Thomas Mason (£3)		3	
Richard Taylor (£3)		3	
Hillary Walpoole (£5)		5	
Hughe Pere (£3)		3	
John Burrowes (£3)		3	
Richard Walker (£3)		3	
Peter Collett (£3)		3	
John Coplestone (£3)		3	
Henrye Isham (£15)		15	
Ellis Stempe (£15) [a]		15	
John Austine (£10)		10	
Christofer Ysham (£10)		10	
Edward Isham (£10) [a]		10	
John Hall (£3)		3	
Kaphe Knighton (£10)		10	
Robert Wilson (£5)		5	
Anthony Hall, in landes (£6)		8	
217. Randall Bates (£3)		3	
Henry Ewarton (£5)		5	
Robert Eagles (£25)		25	
Robert Sutton (£4)		4	
Thomas Laughton (£5)		5	
John Lyffe (£10)		10	
Hughe Walker (£5)		5	
Amdrew Knight (£5)		5	
Marke Grymes (£3)		3	
Thomas Domvell (£3)		3	
John Dutton (£5)		5	
Rowland Sleyforde (£5)		5	

Strangers

Jarret de Nover (£3) [a]		6	
Catherine his wife and George his sonne			
per pol [a]			8
Jomary Pomforde per pol [a]			4
Joyffe Fever (40s.) [a]		4	

	£	s.	d
Jane his wife, John & Androwe his			
servauntes per pol [a]			12
Christofer Beane, Dericke, & Ronart,			
servauntes (12d.)			12
Charles Harris & Tonet his wife (8d.)			8
James Castaneell (£3)		6	
Mirchet his wife & Fraunces his			
dawghter (8d.)			8
Peter Mowberry (£3)		6	
Peter Dolly & Jane his wife (8d.) [a]			8
[r.71]			
John Lordain, Tonet his wife, Quint,			
servant per pol [a - John]			12
John Lorde (4d.)			4
Martine Bardye and Anne his wife (8d.)			8
Charles du Caine & Marret his wife (8d.) [a]			8
Arthure Oliffe (4d.) [a]			4
Widdowe Walle (4d.) [a]			4
Jacob Duprue (40s.)		4	
Jeane his wife (4d.)			4
Leonard Johnson (4d.) [a]			4

218.   BEDLAM
[Strangers]

	£	s.	d
Hawnce van Howden (20s.)		2	
Marie his wife, John his servaunte (8d.)			8
John Specocke, Catline his wife (8d.)			8
Dericke his servant (4d.)			4
Peter le Cate & Jane his wife (8d.)			8
James del Tower, Mary his wife, Daniell			
& Jane his servauntes (16d.)			16
Peter Favell (£5)		10	
Balthazar van Solle, Barbara his wife			
(8d.) [a]			8
Anthony Beane (20s.)		2	
Joyce his wife (4d.)			4
Mighell Wood, Antonet his wife (8d.)			8
William Le Sage (£3)		6	
Mary his wife, John and Robert his			
servauntes per pol			12
John de Prye, Mary his wife, Jackmine his son (12d.)			12
Jacob Stockeye (£3) [a]		6	
Mary his wife (4d.) [a]			4
Balthazar Covay, Tonnet his wife, Daniell			
his servaunt (12d.)			12
Guilliam de Roy, Emay his wife (8d.)			8
John Frettle (20s.) [a]		2	
Suzan his wife per pol [a]			4

	£	s.	d
John Le Fever, Jane his wife (8d.) [a]			8
John de Bewberrie, Loricke his wife (8d.)			8
Mari Workman & Nicholas her man (8d.)			8
Jacob Carpenter, Barbary his wife (8d.) [a]			8

219.   MR. OFFELEYES RENTES
[Strangers]

	£	s.	d
John Mensey (£3)		6	
Agnes his wife, Jesper and Martine his servauntes (12d.) [a - Jesper and Martine]			12
Mary Hickeye (4d.)			4
Michaell Cosshey (20s.)		2	
Mary his wife, Agnes his dawghter (8d.)			8
Phillip Farmasse and Jane his wife (8d) [a][74]			8
Piere Ashelye & Mary his wife (8d.)			8
Adrian Toopie (£3)		6	
Martine his wife, Nicholas & Abreham his servauntes per pol [a]			12
Betor Bekine (40s.)		4	
Jane his wife, Adam and Daniell his servauntes per pol			12
Luke Chambre, Antonet his wife (8d.)			8
Fraunces Edward (4d.)			4
John Lewe (20s.)		2	
Jane his dawghter (4d.)			4
John Stapperd, Jane his wife, and Peter [a - Peter] his sonne (12d.)			12
Paul Foorde and Marye his wife (8d.)			8
Jarrat de Noye & Katherine his wife & George his sonne (12d.) [a]			12
Androwe Jozeph (20s.)		2	

220.   HAWCKES ALLEY
[Strangers]

	£	s.	d
Florence Calwaye, Joyce his wife (8d.)			8
Stacie Turrie (20s.)		2	
Hubborde his wife and Florence his mayde (8d.)			8

SOPE HOWSE ALLEY
[Strangers]

	£	s.	d
Tybirt Mercie & Jane his wife (8d.) [a]			8
Anthonie Doble & Marie his wife (8d.) [a]			8

74. E.359/52, r. 13 gives surname as Fraunces.

	£	s.	d
Tonnet Hewberrie (4d.) [a]			4
Agnes Husbie (4d.) [a]			4
Elizabeth Clossey (4d.) [a]			4
Mentenet Drewe & Barbara her daughter per pol [a]			8
Clement Fountayne, Mary his wife per pol (8d.)			8
Widdowe Hewberd (4d.)			4
John de Rewe (4d.)			4
Jane Slatton (4d.)			4
Anne Leynemye (4d.) [a][75]			4
Fraunces de Saye & Marie his wife (8d.) [a]			8
Lewis Curtaine & Jackline his wife (8d.)			8
Mary Cherrye (4d.) [a]			4
John Phillor & Jackline his wife (8d.)			8
John de Cat & Sara his wife (8d.)			8

221.   HALFE MONE ALLEY
[Strangers]

	£	s.	d
John Le Swane (20s.)		2	
Anne his wife (4d.) [a]			4
Senton Mercie (4d.) [a]			4
Peron Carrey (4d.)			4

NETMAKERS ALLEY
[Strangers]

	£	s.	d
John Corney (4d.) [a]			4
George Norman and Marie his mother (8d.)			8
Gillian Bramfier, Marie his wife (8d.)			8
Bowne Prennoe (4d.)			4
Caro Trecar, Phillip his wife (8d.)			8
Larrant Prebounde, Jackline his wife per pol			8

MASES ALLEY
[Strangers]

	£	s.	d
Simon Hemawe & Jackmine his wife (8d.)			8
Lewen de Hevat, Tonnet his wife (8d.)			8
Messell Loticke & Susan his wife (8d.)			8

MADDOCKES ALLEY
[Strangers]

	£	s.	d
Mary Pattericke (4d.)			4
Jacob de Prye & Joyce his wife (8d.) [a]			8
Widdowe Gyles (4d.)			4

CROUNE ALLEY
[Strangers]

	£	s.	d
John Larrowe & Bennet his wife (8d.)			8

75. E.359/52, r. 13 gives surname as Leaminge.

	£	s.	d
The Lether sellers in landes (£12)		16	
Summa	279	9	8

222. [r.83]   BREDSTRETE WARDE
[Petty collectors: Hughe Hendley, merchant taylor, and Wylliam Bower, haberdasher.]

ALLHALLOWES PARISHE
[English]

William Albanye (£180)	9	
Hughe Hendley (£60)	3	
John Marden (£60) [x - Mddx. £1]	3	
Richard West (£120)	6	
Roger Wilcockes (£140)	7	
Alexander Everye (£100)	5	
Robert Howse (£200)	10	
Robert Appowell (£120)	6	
Thomas Tomlynson (£50)		50
William Bowre (£50)		50
Alexander Avenon (£250)	12	10
John Dunscomb (£50)		50
Robert Bye (£50)		50
William Lyntford (£60) [x - Mddx. £1]	3	
Mistres Hulson wyddow and John her sone (£50)		50
William Craven (£50)		50
William Pryce (£50)		50
William Hyll (£3)		3
Mathew Litchfeilde (£20)		20
Thomas Whitbroke (£3)		3
Robert Fido (£6)		6
Humfrey Sloughe (£5)		5
Roger Marson (£15)		15
John Dorchester (£5)		5
Richard Horsneale (£5)		5
Thomas Maye (£3)		3
John Pryce (£3)		3
David Lewes (£6)		6
David Cocke (£6)		6
Thomas Woordsworth (£25)		25
John Boren (£3)		3
William Wilkes (£10)		10
George Howson (£5)		5
John Marten (£6)		6
William Emmerton (£3)		3
John Venn (£12)		12
George Dunscombe (£16)		16

Strayngers

Anthonye Gother, straynger (£5)		10

159

	£	s.	d
Wulfrett Vanbile, strainger (£3)		6	

223. [r.84]   ST MILDREDES PARRISHE
                         [English]

	£	s.	d
Dame Elizabeth Nicholas wyddow (£100)	5		
William Thwaytes (£50)		50	
Robert Sole (£150)	7	10	
Richard Packington (£50)		50	
John Ireland (£60)	3		
Thomas Boxe (£50)		50	
Thomas Langham (£60)	3		
Regnald Barker (£100)	5		
Stephen Woodford (£50)		50	
Edmond Taverner in landes & fees (£30)			
[x - Oxon. 13s. 4d]		40	
Thomas Procter (£3)		3	
John Jaxson (£15) [ass. 15s. in Mddx.]		15	
William Prest (£8)		8	
William Williamson (£3)		3	
Ambrose Gillatt (£6)		6	
John Sutton (£20) [x - Oxon. 21s.]		20	
John Mownslowe (£6)		6	
Thomas Calles (£6)		6	
Phillipp Francklyn (£3)		3	
David Gyttons (£4)		4	
Thomas Harkar (£10)		10	
Thomas Arte (£3)		3	
Adam Chatterton (£12)		12	
Edmond Owen (£6)		6	
Robert Waynam (£20)		20	
Roger Tylor (£3)		3	
William Graunte (£3)		3	
William Alcocke (£3)		3	
Roger Warde (£3)		3	
Robert Cawsey (£10)		10	
John Thecher (£4)		4	

Straingers

	£	s.	d
Hubert Mertyn, strainger (£3)		6	

224.   ST PETERS & ST MARYE MAGDALEN
                  [Milk Street] PARRISHES
                  [English]

	£	s.	d
Richard Martyn Alderman (£260)[76]	13		
Richard Rogers (£50) [ass. 26s. in Mddx.]		50	
Thomas Blackwaye (£100) [a]	5		

76. 'Officiar infra turr' London' in margin. Exonerated by virtue of letters patent dated 23 June 1581 (E.359/52, r. 14).

	£	s.	d
Richard Peacocke (£300) [a]	15		
Thomas Skynner (£300)	15		
Baptyst Hixe and Mistres Penne his			
mother (£50) [Mrs. Penne ass.			
10s. in Castle Baynard ward]		50	
Rowland Martyn (£50)		50	
Stephen Durant (£40)		40	
George Martyn (£20) [ass. 6s. in Essex]		20	
Henrie Bannyster and Sparroo (£15)		15	
Walter Smythe (£5)		5	
Richard Harper (£5)		5	
Morgan Pope (£5)		5	

ST AUGUSTYNES PARRISHE
[English]

	£	s.	d
John Churchman (£70)	3	10	
Robert Cowper (£60) [ass. £1 10s. in Mddx.]	3		
Henrie Hunlocke (£70)	3	10	
Edward Kempton (£60)	3		
Robert Brett (£120) [ass. £5 in Mddx.]	6		
Raphe Porter (£50)		50	
John Sutton, merchaunttailor (£60)	3		
Gabriel Colstonne (£150) [x - Essex £2)	7	10	
John Allott, Alderman (£200)	10		
John Chaundler (£100)	5		
James Amerie (£60)	3		
Roger Clarke (£120)	6		
Randolphe Cambe (£70) [ass. £1 10s.			
in Mddx.]	3	10	
Hughe Woodcocke (£50)		50	
Raphe Amerye (£10)		10	
Nichdolas Cullom (£20)		20	
Edward Vickars (£3)		3	
Humfrey Walsingham (£15)		15	
[r.85]			
John Harrison (£18)		18	
Henrie Page (£15)		15	
John Langley (£20)		20	
Thomas Hublethwaite (£10) [a]		10	
William Conyers (£3)		3	
Andrew Osborne (£12)		12	
John Johnson (£12)		12	
Thomas Lawson (£10)		10	
Randall Wooley (£5)		5	
Allen Gardyner (£4)		4	
John Beaste (£3)		3	
Raphe Menley (£4)		4	
Fraunces Priscott (£3)		3	

	£	s.	d
Thomas Smythe (£20)		20	
Robert Fiz Richardes (£3)		3	
Thomas Browne (£3)		3	
Gilbert Ryddeo (£3)		3	
Thomas Pasmutche (£3)		3	
William Steevenson (£3)		3	

Straingers

Gilbert Barnes, strainger per pole			4

225. ST MARGARET MOYSES PARISHE
[English]

Henrie Blower and Jeffery Owen (£3)		3	
John Hey (£6)		6	
John Wright (£4)		4	
John Wheler (£4)		4	
Thomas Pollen (£6)		6	
John Perte (£6)		6	
John Howland (£4)		4	
John Smythe (£3)		3	
Humfrey Dunkin (£3)		3	
John Meyr (£6)		6	
Bartilmew Sutton (£3)		3	
Hughe Jones (£3)		3	
Roger Ofell (£10)		10	
Mistres Scott wyddow (£20)		20	
Richard Bushe (£8)		8	
Humfrey Feelde (£8)		8	

Straingers

Godfrey Portey, strainger per pole			4

ST NICHOLAS COLDABBEY &
ST MARY MAGDALEYNE [Old Fish Street] PARISHES
[English]

William Heynes (£50) [x - Q 20s.]		50	
William Gryffyn (£80) [x - Berks. 5s.]	4		
John Cowper (£40) [x - Q 6s. 8d.]		40	
Leonard Smythe (£30)		30	
Robert Benn (£20) [ass. 10s. in Farringdon			
ward Within]		20	
Thomas Atkyns (£5)		5	
William Burford (£3)		3	
Robert Todd (£3)		3	
Richard Richardson (£3)		3	
William Glover (£10)		10	
Richard Grene (£3)		3	
Thomas Kowdale & his partener			
John Haines (£15)		15	
John Wulffe (£3)		3	

	£	s.	d
Thomas Wendell (£3)		3	
William Chapman (£3)		3	
Richard Elmer (£4)		4	
William Richardson (£3)		3	
Richard Saker (£3)		3	
John Sharpe (£3)		3	
William Pennyngton (£12)		12	
Edward Burges (£3)		3	
Thomas Cokes (£4)		4	
Robert Colman (£4)		4	

Straingers

| John Large, strainger (£3) | | 6 | |

226.   ST JOHN EVANGELIST PARISHE
[English]

William Kempton, Alderman, Sessor			
(£260) [ass. £2 13s. 4d. in Mddx.]	13		
[r.86]			
William Cleyton (£50)		50	
Richard Johnson (£100)	5		
Richard Woodward (£50)		50	
Edward Redman & Edward Sayne (£50)		50	
William Stytche (£8)		8	
William Askew (£6)		6	
George Smythe (£4)		4	
Thomas Dowtye (£4)		4	
Arthur Rainscraft (£3)		3	
Thomas Bennet & Thomas Rolte (£3)		3	
Robert Hopkyns (£3)		3	
Dennys Fisher (£3)		3	
Henrie Heyton (£3)		3	
Richard Nyccoles (£3)		3	
Edward Puckerynge (£3)		3	
William Pettye (£4)		4	
Richard Duckynton (£12)		12	
Edward Archer (£5)		5	

ST MATHEWES PARISHE
[English]

Mistres Gamage wyddowe (£140)	7		
Thomas Wade (£70)	3	10	
Richard Centman (£50)		50	

COMPANIES

The Salters in landes (£71)	4	14	8
The Cordweyners in landes (£15)		20	

[English]

| Charles Havers (£6) | | 6 | |

	£	s.	d
Wyddow Chapman & Edward Lightfoote (£12)		12	
Thomas Wygges (£4)		4	
Thomas Bosworth (£4)		4	
Peter Robinson (£20)		20	
Thomas Rudd (£10)		10	
Robert Coomes (£12)		12	
Raphe Damporte (£20)		20	
Richard Craiford (£10)		10	
Robert Shepperd (£4)		4	
Thomas Makepease & Roger Deakyn (£6)		6	
[Endorsed] Summa	339	12	4

227. [r.54]   BRIDGE WARDE WITHIN

[Petty collectors: Richard Atkynson, haberdasher, and John Rogers, grocer.]

ST OLAVES PARISHE:

	£	s.	d
Richard Atkinson (£50)		50	
John Audley (£50)		50	
William Dossett (£10)		10	
Robert Draper (£10)		10	
Richard Norton (£3)		3	
Richard Denman (£25)		25	
Thomas Payne (£3)		3	
James Blancher (£3)		3	
Thomas Burson (£5)		5	
Lawrence Williams (£10)		10	
Patrick Borne (£10)		10	
Henry Mudd (£3)		3	
Thomas Awdley (£3)		3	
Randall Hankye (£3)		3	
Widowe Elkyn (£10)		10	
George Salthouse (£10)		10	
Thomas Abbott (£3)		3	
Richard Brackley (£15)		15	
Anthonie Lether (£5)		5	
Thomas Bulman (£10)		10	
Thomas Horner (£10)		10	

ST MAGNUS PARISHE:

	£	s.	d
John Seeger (£50)		50	
Robert Taillor (£60)	3		
John Rogers (£70)	3	10	
Richard Walters (£60)	3		
Widowe Cater (£50)		50	
Robert Stockes (£50)		50	
Widowe Lowe in landes (£20)		26	8
Anthonie Wolhouse (£100)	5		
Robert Bilbroughe (£60)	3		

	£	s.	d
Michael Blake (£100)	5		
John Langham (£50)		50	
Thomas Grene (£50)		50	
Robert Halle (£50)		50	
James Rowbotham (£50) [x - Essex 20s.]		50	
228. John Palmer (£50)		50	
Clement Buck (£10)		10	
James Lusher (£3)		3	
Thomas Bullock (£8)		8	
Allen Russell (£5)		5	
Widowe Lever (£8)		8	
Thomas James (£5)		5	
William Cleyton (£8)		8	
Widow Redman (£3)		3	
Widowe Dernelley (£3)		3	
Richard Odie (£3)		3	
Thomas Coe (£12)		12	
John Bright (£3)		3	
Christofer Puckeringe (£3)		3	
Walter Ridgley (£3)		3	
Robert Letchworthe (£5)		5	
John Smythe (£15)		15	
Thomas Vole (£5)		5	
George Norton (£3)		3	
William Tedcastle (£10)		10	
Thomas Shute (£5)		5	
Edward Johnson (£3)		3	
Robert Sherley (£5)		5	
John Woller (£5)		5	
Edward Wilde (£5)		5	
Thomas Hickman (£10)		10	
David Rogers (£3)		3	
Henry Mutchshotte (£3)		3	
John Turnor (£15)		15	
John Damport (£5)		5	
[r.55]			
Thomas Constantyne (£5)		5	
Thomas Champney (£3)		3	
Hamond Grene (£6)		6	
Peter Cooke (£10)		10	
James Stapers (£20)		20	
George Powell (£3)		3	
Richard Ick (£3)		3	
229. William Owen (£10)		10	
Thomas Thomas (£10)		10	
Thomas Bagnall (£15)		15	

	£	s.	d
John Challoner (£20)		20	
Samuell Brabam (£3)		3	
Richard Hadley (£15)		15	
Fraunces Barnes (£15)		15	
Henry Lawrence (£3)		3	
Thomas Armatredinge (£5)		5	
Richard Ballard (£3)		3	
William Perte (£3)		3	
Lawrence Mole (£15)		15	
Thomas Bagshawe (£20)		20	
William Chambers (£3)		3	
Henry Hemynge (£3)		3	
William Adames (£3)		3	
Charles Wilde (£20)		20	
George Drewe (£3)		3	
Lawrence Greene (£5)		5	
Robert Prannell (£5)		5	
William Swingfild (£5)		5	
John Meryfeild (£6)		6	
John Williamson (£5)		5	
John Fynche (£20)		20	
John Vans (£20)		20	
William Saunderson (£10)		10	
Velentyne Walden (£5)		5	

Strangers:

	£	s.	d
Cornelis Franke (£20)		40	
Alexaunder de Cone (£40)	4		
Nicholas Langulion (£20) [a]		40	
Vincent Camiora (£5)		10	
John Stockman (poll)			4
John Nitingale (poll) [a]			4

230.   ST BENETTES PARISHE ATT GRACESHURCHE
[English]

	£	s.	d
Robert Offley (£200)	10		
William Drought (£80)	4		
William Penyngton (£50) [ass. 60s. in Mddx.]		50	
John Chalinor (£70) [x - Mddx. £1 10s.]	3	10	
John Gonne (£3)		3	
Thomas Bennet, ironmonger (£3)		3	
Henry Rainscrofte (£3)		3	
John Cadye (£5)		5	
James Isaack (£8)		8	
Christofer Oswyn (£3)		3	
Richard Smythe (£3)		3	
Richard Burrell (£5)		5	
Thomas Garret(£3)		3	
Thomas Owin (£3)		3	

	£	s.	d
Hughe Doxye (£5)		5	
John Pyggyn (£3)		3	
John Scofeild (£10)		10	
George van Hooke (£3)		3	
William Dalborne (£5)		5	
Peter Syndrell (£3)		3	
Thomas Taillor (£15)		15	
Thomas Fetiplace (£15)		15	
Robert Fote (£3)		3	
William Ratclif (£10)		10	

Strangers:

Phillip and Bartholomewe Cursynye (£150)	15		
Jerome Jeryne, Barnard Jeryne, Benedict			
Bartholomue & Nycholas Cheifedostell (poll)		[sic]	4
Gillam Mort (poll) [a][77]			4

231. ST MICHAELS IN CROKED LANE
[English]

Thomas Ware (£110)	5	10	
Robert Hilson (£120) [ass. £1 10s. in Mddx.]	6		
Robert Gurney (£100)	5		
Stephen Swingfild (£50)		50	
James Dixon (£50)		50	
George Spencer (£8)		8	
William Sone (£10)		10	
William Barham (£3)		3	
John Westwray & Thomas Allott,			
coparteners (£6)		6	
Emanuell Turnbull (£3)		3	
Edmound Andrewes (£3)		3	
Peter Whitnold (£3)		3	
William Stanes (£3)		3	
[r.56]			
John Wattes (£15)		15	
Paule Leyton (£3)		3	
Symon Gardiner (£30)		30	
James Gardiner in landes (£20)			
[ass. 33s. 4d. in Herts.]		26	8
Thomas Beckylles (£3)		3	
Edmound Harvye (£3)		3	

ST MARGARETES PARISHE:
[English]

Richard Brabon (£70)	3	10	
Giles Garton (£200)	10		
William Francklyn (£50)		50	

77. E.359/52, r. 13 gives surname as Moore.

	£	s.	d
Clement Howlet (£6)			
[ass. 14s. in Mddx. as Howley]		6	
Thomas Dutton (£3)		3	
Rowland Stockes (£10)		10	
William Hicson and his parteners (£3)		3	
William Salisburie (£3)		3	
Henry Sled (£10) [x - Q 3s.]		10	
John Bybye (£10) [x - Q 5s.]		10	
Symon Tailbye (£3)		3	
John Waller (£3)		3	
John Taillor (£5)		5	
Widowe Wallys (£30)		30	
George Gippes (£15)		15	
Nicholas Grace (£3)		3	
Richard Garthe (£3)		3	
Widowe Penyfather (£10)		10	
James Langford (£5)		5	
Edward Richardson (£3)		3	
John Emnes (£3)		3	

232. ST LEONARDES PARISHE
[English]

	£	s.	d
Richard Morrys (£150)	7	10	
William Plasden (£60)	3		
Thomas Martyn (£50)		50	
Thomas Morrys (£60)	3		
Henry Leighe (£3)		3	
William Scalehorne (£3)		3	
William Heskett (£3)		3	
Richard Powntes (£15)			
[ass. 30s. in Candlewick ward]		15	
Widowe Cowley (£5)		5	
John Hilliard (£3)		3	
John Bennet (£10)		10	
John Brooke (£20)		20	
John Skote (£3)		3	
Owen Morgan (£10)		10	
Thomas Bynnell (£8)		8	
Henry Scotte (£3)		3	
Rychard Gowrde (£5)		5	
Henry Baker (£8)		8	
Richard Powle (£3)		3	
William Hamond (£10)		10	
Leonard Lodge (£10)		10	

ALLHALLOWES PARISHE:
[English]

	£	s.	d
Widowe Whalley (£50)		50	

	£	s.	d
Marke Warner (£50)		50	
Thomas Walker (£80)	4		
Phillippe Bonde (£5)		5	
Thomas Feild (£5)		5	
William Gallys (£5)		5	
Edward Skegges (£5)		5	
Edward Bartley (£5)		5	

ST MARTYNS PARISHE:
[English]

	£	s.	d
John Edmondes (£50)		50	
Reynold Robertes (£10)		10	
William Weaver (£5)		5	
Thomas Parke (£10) [ass. 5s. in Mddx.]		10	
Olliver Curtes (£3)		3	
Austyn Garland (£8)		8	
Thomas Mawe (£3)		3	

Strangers:

	£	s.	d
Jasper de Catte (£10)		20	
Nicholas La Barte (£10)		20	
James More (poll) [a]			4

COMPANIES

	£	s.	d
The Fyshmongers in landes (£96)	6	8	
[Endorsed] Summa	224	6	

233. [r.113]   BROADE STRETE
[Petty collectors: Gyles Howlande, grocer, and Rychard Bowdler, draper.]

ST MILDREDES AND [St. Mary] WOLCHURCH PARISHE
[English]

	£	s.	d
John Best (£70)	3	10	
Edward Homden (£60)	3		
Robert Hungate (£50) [x - Coleman Street ward 25s.]		50	
Nicholas Stanes (£50)		50	
Wolstane Dixe Alderman, sessor (£300)	15		
Henry Becher (£200)	10		
Nicholas Barnesley and Coxe (£50)		50	
Fraunces Gunter (£50)		50	
William Welden in landes & fees (£20)		26	8
Henry Tappeffeild (£50) [x - Mddx. 20s.]		50	

Strangers

	£	s.	d
Peter Veiglman (£10)		20	
John and Fraunces Dingins (£60) [b - Antwerp mer.]	6		
Bartholmew Shore (£20)[a]		40	

Englishmen

	£	s.	d
John Pownsonby (£15)		15	

	£	s.	d
Richard Westwoode (£15)		15	
Fraunces Puckeringe and John Bruerton (£3)		3	
Fraunces Longeworth (£10)		10	
Cuthbert Bonthe (£10)		10	
John Bodleigh (£3)		3	
William Hunt (£3)		3	
John Bowthe (£3)		3	
Mongey Pirson (£5)		5	
Laurenc Harrison (£3)		3	

ST BARTHOLMEWES PARISHE
[English]

	£	s.	d
Sir John Rivers, knight commissioner (£300)	15		
Thomas Dansier (£100)	5		
Anthony Radclife (£200)	10		
William Mounsey (£120)	6		
Anthony Garrard (£60)	3		
Richard Bowlder (£80)	4		
John Dent (£150)	7	10	
William Onslowe (£70)	3	10	
Simon Laurence (£50)		50	
Mistres Elizabeth Bowyer widowe (£100)	5		
Giles Howland (£50)		50	
Barnard Pigott (£20)		20	

234. Strangers

	£	s.	d
Giles Harblocke (£60)	6		
Paule Tipottes (£10)		20	
Jaques Whitfrongell (£40)			
[b - Antwerp mer.]	4		

Englishmen

	£	s.	d
William Baynam (£3)		3	
Henry Evans (£20)		20	
Richard Coxe (£10)		10	
George Flinte (£8)		8	
John Crafford (£6)		6	
John Perry (£3)		3	
Evangelist Johnson (£3)		3	
Elizabeth Canne (£20)		20	
Christopher Southowse (£20)		20	
Roger Parratt (£5)		5	
William Atkinsone (£3)		3	
Thomas Winington (£8)		8	
Stephen Burton (£3)		3	
[m.114]			
Robert Harrison (£10)		10	
William Brooke (£8)		8	
Hughe Rogers (£5)		5	

	£	s.	d
Thomas Hutton (£8)		8	
John Olmsted (£10)		10	
Incent Goodman (£10)		10	
Cornelis Fishe (£3)		3	
William Yardley (£3)		3	
Thomas Lancaster (£3)		3	
Hughe Grave (£5)		5	
Edmond Roby merchaunt lieinge at the			
house [of] Rafe Crose (£5) [a]		5	
Henry Calthorpe (£5) [a]		5	

Strangers

	£	s.	d
Joan Harblocke dawghter of Giles			
Harblock per poll (4d.)			4
Katherine Harblocke (4d.)			4
Playne her mayde (4d.)			4
Denys Veale (£3)		6	
Jacob Wittewrongill the yonger (4d.)			4
Cornelys Spiermek servant unto Paule			
Tipotes (4d.)			4
Aron Denys servant with the said Pawle			
Tipottes (4d.)			4

235. ST MARTINES OUTWICHE
Englishmen

	£	s.	d
George Southerton (£70)	3	10	
John Westwraye (£100) [x - Essex £1]	5		
Richard Stapers (£90)	4	10	
Mistres Mabell Brighte widowe (£60)	3		
Hughe Wygmill and widowe Warrin (£3)		3	
William Midgley (£3)		3	
John Pasfeild (£10)		10	
Laurence Leake (£5)		5	

ST BENNETES FINKE PARISHE

	£	s.	d
Oliver Geldner (£50) [a]		50	
James Alkines (£50)		50	
Thomas Croftes (£80)	4		
Rowland Eldrington (£80)	4		
Robert Warner (£50)		50	
Thomas Bennet (£50)		50	
Sir Edward Mountacute in landes (£100)			
[x - Norfolk £4 8s. 10d.]	6	13	4
George Holman (£30)		30	
David Holliland (£30)		30	

Strangers

	£	s.	d
Baptiste de Puys (£30)	3		

Englishmen

	£	s.	d
James Rowe (£3)		3	

	£	s.	d
Richard Wasse (£20)		20	
Elizabeth Dodd (£3)		3	
John Phillipes (£3)		3	
Peter Worliche (£10)		10	
Edward Dawson (£20)		20	
Richard Sissell (£3)		3	
Richard Prince (£6)		6	
John Williams (£3)		3	
Richard Neale (£10)		10	
Richard Hottoffe a lawyer (£20)		20	
Richard Willett (£10)		10	
John Gibson (£3)		3	
Thomas Frier (£8)		8	
236. Lawrence Walker (£3)		3	
John Sede (£3)		3	
John Roper (£3)		3	
William Borradale (£10)		10	
Johan Ricksman (£15)		15	
Stephen Treackle (£8)		8	
John Norton (£5)		5	
William Norffolke (£6)		6	
Raphe and James Bradshawe (£20)			
[a - James Bradshawe]		20	
John Monger (£10) [ass. 6s. 8d. in			
Kent]		10	
Fraunces Wight (£3)		3	
William Conradus (£10)		10	
Robert Bladewell (£3)		3	
Michael Parker (£3)		3	
William Walmesley (£20)		20	
Henry Stockton (£3)		3	
Erasmus Sandesbury (£3)		3	
[r.115]			
Henry Sharewood (£5)		5	
John Kempton (£3)		3	
John Wall (£5)		5	
Gregory Shorter (£5)		5	
William Crowe (£5)		5	
Thomas Hearon (£3) [a][78]		3	
John Carwell lawyer at John Maylors			
house (£5)		5	
Strangers			
Fabian Niphio (£5)		10	
Hercules Fraunces his wife and a servant per			
poll (12d.)			12

78. E.359/52, r. 14 gives surname as Herne.

	£	s.	d
Davie Langelie and Mary his wife &			
Josikin his wifes mother (12d.)		12	
John Eke and Johan Hidonce per poll (8d.)			8

237.   ST PETERS THE POORE &

          ALHALLOES IN THE WALL PARISHES

Englishmen

	£	s.	d
Martine Calthrop Alderman (£300)	15		
William Coles (£150)	7	10	
William Garrawaye (£120)	6		
Mistres Quarles widow (£100)	5		
Mistres Garraway widowe (£120)			
[x - Mddx. £2]	6		
John Catcher (£150)	7	10	
Thomas Altham (£120)	6		
Nicholas Garnons (£80)	4		
Thomas Alline (£50)		50	
Sir Thomas Kitson knight in landes			
(£200) [x - Suffolk £13 6s. 8d.]	13	6	8
Mathewe Dale (£80) [x - Surrey 13s. 4d.]	4		
Charreles Bond (£70)	3	10	
William Cockine(£200)	10		
The Ladie Sanders in landes (£100)			
[x - Mddx. £4 8s.]	6	13	4
Lucke Lane (£80)	4		
William Gage in fees (£10) [x - Lincs. 8s.]		13	4
Richard Peter (£50) [x - Herts. 12s.]		50	
Thomas Webbe (£50)		50	
Richard Maningham (£50)		50	
William Cooke in landes & fees (£20)		26	8

Stranger

John Papworth alias Vanderbeck (£50)			
[b - Antwerp mer.]	5		

Englishmen

	£	s.	d
John Stephens (£3)		3	
Martin Calthorpe junior (£35)		35	
Michell Freston (£5)		5	
John Palmer (£10)		10	
Thomas Catcher (£3)		3	
Richard Hull (£10)		10	
Thomas Frethern (£5)		5	
William Typper (£3)		3	
John and William Browne (£10)		10	
Mathew Sturdivante (£5)		5	
John Willis (£3)		3	
Benedick Browne (£5)			
[x - Q 24s.]		5	
Roger Coram gentleman (£10) [a]		10	

	£	s.	d
William Skinner lyeinge at the house of			
Roberte Richardes (£3) [a]		3	
Walter Turner lyeinge at ye house of ye said			
Richardes (£3) [a]		3	

238. Strangers

	£	s.	d
Mighell Nowon & Isabell his wife and			
Debra his maide per poll (12d.)			12
Robert Gilles his servant per poll			
(4d.) [a]			4
Anthoney Desvilles, Jane his wife and			
Marie Cornely maid (12d.)			12
Barbara Poppottes daughter of John Poppotes			
Marry Standon his mayde and George			
Cornelo (12d.)			12
George Carvelo per poll (4d.)			4
William Dyamond musicion per poll (4d.)			4

Englishmen

	£	s.	d
James Dodson (£20)	20		
Laurence Wilson (£4)	4		
Arthur Goldinge (£20)	20		
John Nicholson (£4)	4		
Hughe Stanley (£3)	3		
William Flanninge (£4)	4		
William Osborne (£3)	3		
Thomas Cockes (£15) [x - Q 8s.]	15		
Oliver Woodlife (£3)	3		
Adrian Thorpe (£3)	3		
John Symondes (£3)	3		
Peter Streate (£3)	3		
John Burton (£6)	6		
William Padge (£6)	6		
Richard Smythe (£10) [x - Q 32s.]	10		
[r.116]			
William Jackson (£3)	3		
John Bland (£3)	3		
Elizabeth Skalton (£5) [a]	5		
James Kinge (£3)	3		
Robert Moose (£3)	3		
Richard Peter wolwynder (£3)	3		
Arthur Rogers (£3)	3		
Richard Ireland (£3)	3		
John Mounson which lodgeth at Mr Gages			
house (£40) [a]	40		

239. Strangers

	£	s.	d
John Gaby and his wife & a child per			
poll (12d.) [a]			12

	£	s.	d
Tamet Garden widowe per poll (4d.) [a]			4
Mary a widowe, Joyce Farnone & his wife &			
two servantes per poll (20d.) [a - Mary]			20
Adrian See and his wife per poll (8d.)			8
Marke Mountaine widowe & her maide per			
poll (8d.)			8
Joyce Yonker and his wife per poll (8d.)			8
Barnard Fander and his wife per poll (8d.) [a]			8
John Dayse and his wife per poll (8d.)			8
Anthony Blakell and his wife per poll (8d.)			8
Christopher de Pester and his wife & one			
Child per poll (12d.)			12
Peter Bayley and his wife & a servant per			
poll (12d.)			12
John Clikerd (£3)		6	
Towe servantes of the said John Clikerd per			
poll (8d.)			8
Peter Foye (£3)		6	
Two servantes of the same Peter Foye per			
poll (8d.)			8
Balthaser Carryman and his wife per poll (8d.)			8
Jarret Lytte and his wife (8d.)			8
Fraunces Marshall (£3)		6	
Two Children & fower maides of the said			
Marshall (2s.)		2	
Arnold Beard (£3)		6	

240.   ST MARGARET IN LOTHBURYE
Englishmen

	£	s.	d
William Killigrew in landes (£60)			
[x - Q £1 6s. 8d.]	4		
John Pelsant (£50)		50	
Thomas Bramley (£60)	3		
Robert Fleton (£50)		50	
William Nodes (£10) [a]		10	
Edward Duncombe (£20)		20	
Richard God (£3)		3	
Edward Fawkener (£15)		15	
John Coggen (£5)		5	
Christofer Humfrey (£10)		10	
Robert Waldoe (£15)		15	
Richard Rowdinge (£10)		10	
Leonard Hinchepoole (£3)		3	
Nicholas Sanders (£10) [a]		10	

Strangers in ye said parishe

	£	s.	d
Denys Blanke, his wife & a maid per			
poll (12d.)			12
Albred Sporoke & his wife per poll (8d.)			8

	£	s.	d
THE PARISHE OF CHRISTOPHERS			
Englishmen			
Robert Oudner (£3)		3	
Thomas Taylor (£20)		20	
Richard Candler (£10) [ass. 40s. in			
Mddx. as Cadler]		10	
Geffrey Leonard (£5)		5	
Thomas Turnor (£10)		10	
George Grave (£5)		5	
John Heathe (£3)		3	
Thomas Spragge (£5)		5	
Henry Suger (£30)		30	
Richard Robinson (£3)		3	
Fowlke Piggott (£5)		5	
Thomas Randall (£3)		3	
Strangers in the said parishe			
Adrian Davelew servant unto John Dinghens			
per poll (4d.)			4
Cornelis Candora (£3)		6	
James Cooke and his wife per poll (8d.)			8
John Strohand (£5)		10	
THE COMPANIES			
The Carpenters in landes (£11)		14	8
The Merchaunttayllors in landes (£49)	3	5	4
The Drapers in landes (£46)	3	1	4
[Endorsed] Summa	368		4

241. [r.11]   CANDLEWYCKESTREETE WARDE
[Petty collectors: Wyllyam Barnard, draper, and Wyllyam Evans, clothworker.]

[St. Mary] ABCHURCHE PARRYSSHE			
[English]			
Sir John Braunche knight (£260)			
[x - Essex £3 6s. 8d.]	13		
Wyddowe Evans (£60)	3		
Morgan Awbrey (£50)		50	
Humphrey Brooke (£60)	3		
Wyllyam Carowe (£60)			
[x - Kent 17s. 4d.]	3		
John Owldham (£50)		50	
Edwarde Hyde (£50)			
[x - Essex 10s. 8d.]		50	
Henry Hubblethwayte (£50)		50	
Roberte Streete (£15)		15	
Wyllyam Godfrey (£10)		10	
Thomas Busbye (£10)		10	

	£	s.	d
Nycholas Haddocke (£3)		3	
Wyllyam Edwardes (£3)		3	
John Evans shomaker (£3)		3	
Thomas Whythorne (£3)		3	
Chrystopher Dyckynson (£3)		3	
Roberte Chaser (£3)		3	
Edmond Baker (£3)		3	
Thomas Hussey (£15)		15	
Austen Whalle wythin Hussey (£10)			
[x - Norwick 10s.]		10	
Edward Sinnyor (£3)		3	
Rychard Myller (£3)		3	
Wyllyam Harwood (£3)		3	
John Merydeth (£3)		3	
Jerom Dalton (£10)		10	
Lawrence Monnes (£5)		5	
Wyddowe Pownd (£5)		5	
Thomas Bynd (£15)			
[x - Cordwainer ward 3s.]		15	
Rychard Cooke (£3)		3	
Wyllyam Osborne (£6)		6	
Thomas Barfoote (£8)		8	
Henrye Kempton (£6)		6	
Roger Robotham (£5)		5	
Wyllyam Wythers (£6)		6	
Roger Cowper (£3)		3	
Straungers			
Wyddowe Raymond (£10)		20	
Cornellys Drodger (£10)			
[ass. 10s. in Farringdon ward			
Within as Dregg]		20	
[r.12]			

242.   ST LAWRENCE PAROCHE
[English]

	£	s.	d
Rychard Wyseman (£60)	3		
Randall Symmes (£50)		50	
John Ownsted gen. (£150)			
[x - Q 13s. 4d.]	7	10	
James Wylkenson (£3)		3	
Reygnold Parke (£3)		3	
Rychard Alderton (£3)		3	
Peter Monne (£5)		5	
Edwarde Torner (£3)		3	
Roberte Mempryse (£3)		3	
Straunger			
Symon Johnson per poll			4

177

	£	s.	d
ST MARTYN ORGAN PAROCHE			
[English]			
Henrye Hewett (£170)	8	10	
Edmund Moore (£50)		50	
Dyanys Burton wyddowe (£40)		40	
John Hawys (£50)		50	
Wyllyam Barnarde (£80) [ass. £4 in Mddx.]	4		
John Garrard (£100)	5		
John Whyte (£70) [x - Southwark £1]	3	10	
Mychaell Pennyngston (£50)		50	
Thomas Clyffe (£50) [x - Essex 15s.]		50	
Rychard Scofylde (£100)	5		
Wyllyam Evans (£50)		50	
Hugh Platt in Landes (£10)		13	4
George Marburye (£5)		5	
Roberte Bate (£10)		10	
Water Toll (£5)		5	
Thomas Burgesse (£5)		5	
Wyllyam Hewett in Landes (£10)		13	4
Humphrey Burton (£10)		10	
Walter Cade (£20)		20	
Rychard Butler (£5)		5	
Henrye Wollyston (£5)		5	
Roberte Thomas (£25)		25	
Thomas Morrys (£10)		10	
Thomas Hasell (£3)		3	
Edward Dartenoll (£3)		3	
Henry Smarte (£3)		3	
James Bonevant (£3)		3	
Thomas Lateware (£5)		5	

243.   Straungers

	£	s.	d
Martyn de la Falia (£300)			
[b - Antwerp mer.]		30	
Charles Deburgrave (£10)		20	
Guillyaume de Best (£50)	5		
Peeter Moore (£20)		40	
Arnolde Arnoldson (£40)	4		
Joyce Vandenstene (£15)			
[b - Antwerp mer.]		30	
Hauns Vandenstene per poll			4
Nicholas Vandenstene per poll			4
Jacob Yeoman (£40)			
[b - Antwerp mer.][79]	4		
Jaques Yeoman per pol			4
Adrian de Bronkere per pol			4
in Peeter Mores howse			

79. E.359/52, r. 14 gives surname as Jenian.

	£	s.	d
Warner Wychelhenson per pol			4
Wyllyam Moore per pol			4
in Martyn de Lafalia his howse			
James Narratt per pol			4
Adryan Narrott per pol			4
in Guilham de Best his howse			
Frauncys Vanstrasse per pol			4
in Nycholas Jones howse			
Conrade Reynoldes per pol			4
Mesias Quinten per pol			4
Straungers in Abchurche paroche			
Garrett Joyse (£3)		6	
Cornellius de Busye (£3)		6	
Peter de Brewer per pol		.	4

244. [r.13] ST CLEMENTES, ST NYCHOLAS &
ST MYCHAELLES PAROCHES
[English]

	£	s.
Elizabeth Hewett wyddowe (£60)	3	
Wyllyam Keble (£50)		50
Robert Wythens (£150)	7	10
Edwarde Pylseworthe (£40)		40
Rychard Reynoldes (£10)		10
Stephen Dallemond (£10)		10
Wyllyam Robson (£3)		3
Evans Gryffyn (£3)		3
Henrye Newton (£3)		3
Robart Aragon (£3)		3
Willyam Dawkes (£10)		10
John Fox (£6)		6
John Evans (£6)		6
Rychard Janson (£3)		3
John Walden (£3)		3
John Mare (£3)		3
Symon Leverett (£3)		3
James Elye (£20)		20
Thomas Pawle (£3)		3
Henrye Lewys (£20)		20
Roberte Elkington (£5)		5
Wyllyam Nettelles (£5)		5
Thomas Frend (£3)		3
John Kinge (£5)		5
Nycholas Manlye (£5)		5
Henrye Bowres (£20)		20
Wyllyam Scott (£15)		15
Rychard Pountys (£30)		
[x - Bridge ward 15s.]		30
Wyllyam Androse (£18)		18

	£	s.	d
Wyddowe Wolstone (£3)		3	
John Dudlye (£3)		3	
Josephe Hadwell (£5)		5	
Thomas Arnold (£5)		5	
Wyllyam Peacke (£5)		5	
Nycholas Dalton (£20)		20	
245. Rychard Bingham (£20)		20	
Thomas Wryght (£20)		20	
Raphe Kynge (£20)		20	
Leonerd Smythe (£10)		10	
Roberte Kerkeham (£5)		5	
John Spencer (£5)		5	
Rychard Horner (£3)		3	
Mr Doctor Becken (£20) [a]		20	
Rychard Dantson (£3)		3	
Wyllyam Ingram (£10)		10	
Roger Brome (£3)		3	
John Hallye (£3)		3	
Peter Wryght (£3)		3	
Nycholas Harryson (£3)		3	
Nycholas Jeffreys (£3)		3	
George Russell (£3)		3	
Edward Bagshawe (£8)		8	
Roger Gathorne (£3)		3	
Thomas Scott (£3)		3	
Wyllyam Lewter (£3)		3	
Thomas Bannester (£3)		3	
Roberte Crucheley (£3)		3	
James Jackeson (£10)		10	
Henrye Weste (£3)		3	
Wylliam Cotton (£12)		12	
John Gurley (£5)		5	
Wyddowe Allyn (£3)		3	
Henrye Castell (£3)		3	
Thomas Lightfoote (£3)		3	
Christofer Bruce (£3)		3	
Straungers			
Gyles Bowntenacle (£80)			
[b - Antwerp mer.]		8	
Henrye Hoche per pol			4
Arnold Varhove per pol			4
Cornellys Varhove per pol			4
Mychell Straband per pol			4
[endorsed] Summa	198		16

246. [r.28]   CASTLEBAYNARDE WARDE
[Petty collectors: Wyllyam Kelsycke, grocer, and Rychard Smyth, woodmonger.]

SAYNT BENNETTES PARISHE
[English]

	£	s	d
Doctor Lewes (£60)			
[x - Monmouthshire?]	3		
Doctor Martyn (£70)			
[x - Cambs. 40s.]	3	10	
Sir Gilbert Dethick in fees (£50)[80]	3	6	8
Norrey Herault [William Flower] in			
fees (£20)		26	8
Lancaster Herault [John Cooke] in			
fees (£10)		13	4
Chester Herault [Edmund Knight] in			
fees (£10)		13	4
Doctor [Bartholomew] Clark, Deane (£60)			
[x - ?][81]	3		
Doctor Mowse (£50)			
[x - Process][82]		50	
Doctor Stanhope in fees (£20)			
[x - Process][83]		26	8
Doctor [William] Clerke (£50)			
[x - Mddx.?][84]		50	
Doctor Joans (£50)			
[x - Process, denied][85]		50	
Doctor Cawdwell in landes (£20)		26	8
John Lewes proctor (£70) [x - Surrey £1 10s.]	3	10	
Davyd Smyth (£50)		50	
John Baker (£50)		50	
John Cobham gen in landes (£10)			
[x - Kent 26s. 8d.]		13	4
Thomas Brande in landes (£150)			
[x - Surrey £3 6s. 8d.]	10		

80. Sir Gilbert Dethick, Garter King of Arms; William Flower, Norroy King of Arms; John Cooke, Lancaster Herald; and Edmund Knight, Chester Herald were exonerated by virtue of letters patent of 4 June 1549 and writ from the queen to the treasurer and barons of the exchequer dated 1 July 1581 (E.359/52, r. 14). 'Herald' is written in the margin next to each of these names.
81. E.359/52, r. 14 gives Bartholomew as first name.
82. Mowse was exonerated from payment by process; as rector of East Dereham in the diocese of Norwich he paid towards the clerical subsidy more than his assessment for the lay subsidy (E.359/52, r. 14).
83. Stanhope was exonerated on the same basis as Dr. Mowse, above. Stanhope was prebendary of the prebend of Botevant in the cathedral church of York (E.359/52, r. 14).
84. E.359/52, r. 14 gives William as first name.
85. Jones's claim to exoneration by virtue of his payment toward the clerical subsidy was denied (E.359/52, r. 14).

	£	s.	d
Jelbert Hill gent (£20) [x - Herts. 20s.]		20	
Edmonde Moore (£25)		25	
Richerd Ashby (£15)		15	
James Alston (£3)		3	
Thomas East (£3)		3	
Richerde Florence (£3)		3	
Rycherd Moore (£4)		4	
Symon Lee (£3)		3	
Edwarde Rodes (£3)		3	
John Edridge (£5)		5	
Christofer Dickenson (£3)		3	
Thomas Moore (£3)		3	
William Replye (£3)		3	
Ambrose Kyster (£6)		6	
Rowland Mallard (£20) [x - Surrey 6s. 8d.]		20	
George Nockes (£3)		3	
Roger Blynckerne (£3)		3	
John Rice (£16)		16	
Dyonys Kempe (£15)		15	
Stephen Stringer (£3)		3	
Robert Nicholles (£10)		10	
Henrye Bynnyman (£10)		10	
Richerde Berrye (£3)		3	
John Parre (£12)		12	
Roger Robbet (£3)		3	
Thomas Rosse (£5)		5	
Wydowe Earsley (£5)		5	
George Heager (£8)		8	
[r.29]			
John Osborne (£3)		3	
George Pynder (£5) [a]		5	

Summa [Blank]

247. ST ANDROWES PARISH
[English]

	£	s.	d
Sir Thomas Walsingham knight in landes (£60) [x - Kent?]	4		
John Fortescue in landes (£80) [x - Staffs. £4 8s. 8d.]	5	6	8
Thomas Manninge in fees (£10)		13	4
Anthonye Walker (£60) [ass. 14s. 8d. in Q]	3		
Mistress [Margaret] Blackwall wydowe (£100) [x - Sussex £2 10s.][86]	5		
Edmonde Hill (£70)	3	10	
Robert Lewesley (£50)		50	
Thomas Lytchfelde in landes and fees (£40) [a][87]		53	4

86. E.359/52, r. 14 gives Margaret as first name.
87. E.359/52, r. 14 gives surname as Leyffeld.

	£	s.	d
James Gardener (£50)		50	
Doctor Skevington in fees			
(£20)		26	8
Josselyn Turnor (£3)		3	
John Tapley (£3)		3	
Owen Tedder (£3)		3	
John Bryan (£16)		16	
Thomas Peacock (£5)		5	
Thomas Bowlinge (£3)		3	
Brice Blackman (£3)		3	
Robert Bleamore (£5)		5	
Barnabye Money (£3)		3	
Robert Brigges (£3)		3	
Richerd Edwardes (£5)		5	
Laurence Puddle (£8)		8	
John Goddard (£20)		20	
John Westley (£3)		3	
Richerde Smyth (£20)		20	
Roger Bell (£3)		3	
Richerd Wattes (£5)		5	
Frauncys Harryson (£3)		3	
Leonarde Mapes (£10)		10	
John Irelande (£5)		5	
Mathewe Greene (£3)		3	
William Onyon (£3)		3	
John Warren (£3)		3	
Thomas Hanforde (£5)		5	
John Emerye (£3)		3	
John Poke (£4)		4	
Richerde Becket (£3)		3	
Hugh Granawaye (£3)		3	
Henrye Browne (£10)		10	
Richerde Cattell (£3)		3	
Mark Byrde (£3)		3	
Robert Welton (£3)		3	
John Gryffen (£3)		3	
James Rutter (£3)		3	
John Tute (£3)		3	
Thomas Payne (£5)		5	
Robert Tyas (£5)		5	
William Symons (£3)		3	

Strangers

Haunce Farbarne per pol			4
Aobert Foxe			4
John Gybson (£10)		20	
Garret Uncle			4

Summa [Blank]

	£	s.	d
248. ST GREGORYES PARISH [English]			
Mr. Justice Southcot Comissioner in landes (£60)	4		
Doctor [Valentine] Dale (£100) [x - Hants. £5][88]	5		
John Harrington gen in landes (£20)		26	8
Doctor [Robert] Forth (£60) [x - Surrey £1 6s. 8d.][89] [r.30]	3		
Doctor Creake in fees (£10)		13	4
Doctor Bartlet (£50) [x - Sussex 26s. 8d.]		50	
Mistress Yale wydowe (£50) [x - Essex?]		50	
Edwarde Barker in fees (£10)		13	4
Adam Bland (£50)		50	
William Cooper (£80)	4		
Anthonye Hyggyns (£100)		100	
William Whyttle (£50)		50	
Richerde Thornburye (£3)		3	
Joseph James (£3)		3	
Richerd Ray (£3)		3	
Tytus Westby (£8)		8	
Michaell Shawller (£4)		4	
Robert Pavye (£3)		3	
Robert Kelly (£15)		15	
John Forde (£3)		3	
Doctor Farrand (£5)		5	
Proctor Wheler (£40) [x - Mddx. 13s. 4d.]		40	
William Hornblow (£10) [x - Farringdon ward Without 10s.]		10	
Geoffrey Gurley (£3)		3	
George Honor (£3)		3	
Thomas Pulforde (£5)		5	
Henrye Marshe (£3)		3	
Arthure Medlicote (£15)		15	
John Hayes taylor (£10)		10	
William Willson (£3)		3	
Richerde Boulton (£3)		3	
Thomas Platt (£3)		3	
249. Thomas Dale (£3)		3	
Thomas Fynche (£3)		3	
John Bolton (£3)		3	
Henrye Rastall (£3)		3	
Richerde Bennet (£5)		5	

88. E.359/52, r. 14 gives Valentine as first name.
89. E.359/52, r. 14 gives Robert as first name..

	£	s.	d
Symon Martyn (£5)		5	
Rycherde Cure (£3)		3	
James Janson (£15)		15	
Robert Calthropp (£5)		5	
Richerde Laurence (£3)		3	
Peter Burton (£3)		3	
James Turnor (£5)		5	
Laurence Swyngborne (£5)		5	
Thomas Forrest (£3)		3	
William Wright (£3)		3	
William Brooke (£3)		3	
Robert Applebye (£3)		3	
Lavyn Babyngton (£3)		3	
William Tasker (£5)		5	
John Wales (£3)		3	
John Hawarde (£25)		25	
John Starkye (£3)		3	
William Mallowes (£8)		8	
John Ellegde (£3)		3	
Roger Armitage (£3)		3	
Stephen Rowley (£3)		3	
John Watson (£5)		5	
John Ryckarde (£25)		25	
William Savell (£5)		5	
Robert Gryffen (£20)		20	
Thomas Sharples (£3)		3	
Edwarde Carter (£3)		3	
Thomas Greene (£20) [x - Q 6s. 8d.]		20	
250. Walter Williams (£3)		3	
James Redferne (£49)		49	
Thomas Nicholson (£5)		5	
Henrye Ranckell (£15)		15	
Phillippe Morgan (£12)		12	
John Hays barbor (£8)		8	
John Berrye (£20) [a]		20	
John Pount (£20)		20	
Richerde Smyth (£20)		20	
[r.31]			
Richerd Dysney (£5)		5	
Leonard Mylles (£40)		40	
John Thompson (£4)		4	
Laurence Rogers (£6)		6	
William Ceeres (£20)		20	
James Farrington (£10)		10	
Edwarde Halfacer (£3)		3	
Thomas Spencer (£3)		3	
John Lambert (£5)		5	

	£	s.	d
Roger Justin (£3)		3	
Raph Hamon (£5) [ass. 50s. in Mddx.]		5	
Richerd Sympson (£5)		5	
Raph Brooke (£5)[90]		5	
John Barwys (£12)		12	
William Dodde (£5)		5	
Thomas Wayght (£15)		15	
Thomas Porter (£15)		15	
John Francklyn (£3)		3	
Edwarde Taylor (£3)		3	

Straunger

| Albert the Hare per pol | | | 4 |

Companye

| The Companye of Stacyoners (100s.) | | 6 | 8 |

Summa [Blank]

251. ST MARYE MAGDALENS PARISH
[English]

	£	s.	d
Mr. Thomas Randolfe in landes and fees (£50) [x - Kent?]	3	6	8
Doctor [William] Drurye (£70) [x - Mddx. 50s.][91]	3	10	
Barnarde Randolfe in landes and fees (£50) [x - Mddx. 66s. 8d.]	3	6	8
Arthure Hall in landes (£30) [x - ?]		40	
George Sotherton in fees (£10)		13	4
Doctor Gylbert in fees (£20)		26	8
John Cotton (£4)		4	
Thomas Berrye (£8)		8	
Thomas Hanley (£12)		12	
Edwarde Bodye (£3) [a]		3	
William Corbet (£4)		4	
William Blewe (£4)		4	
Wydowe Cole (£5) [a]		5	
John Readinge (£3)		3	
Hamlet Wythington (£3)		3	
Peter Ogdon (£3)		3	
Wydowe Penne (£10) [x - (with Baptist Hicks) Bread Street ward 50s.]		10	
Clement Bryan (£3)		3	
John Harwood (£3)		3	
George Morlyn (£3)		3	
John Browne (£4)		4	
Warner Kinge (£14)		14	

90. Brooke, as Rouge Croix pursuivant, was exonerated by virtue of letters patent to the heralds of 4 June 1549 and the queen's writ to the treasurer and barons dated 1 July 1581. 'Herald' is written in the margin next to his name.
91. E.359/52, r. 14 gives first name as William.

		£	s.	d
Edwarde Fryer (£6)			6	
John Thrayle (£20)			20	
Thomas Pyforde (£3)			3	
Anthonye Smyth (£3)			3	
Thomas Baker (£3)			3	
252. William Frognoll (£3)			3	
Thomas Barlowe (£5)			5	
Symon Beswick (£5)			5	
John Schotcher (£3)			3	
Thomas Wilson (£20)			20	
Humfreye Axshawe (£8)			8	
Cutbert Fetherstone (£3)			3	
Richerd Pickeringe (£3)			3	
John Peerson (£3)			3	
John Frowme (£3)			3	
John Delawoode (£3)			3	
	Straungers			
Gyles Gyllam				4
Derick Derickson (20s.)			2	
	Summa [Blank]			

[r.32]   CHRISTES CHURCH AND ST FAYTHES PARISHES
[English]

Edmonde Stewarde gent in landes (£40)		£	s.	d
[x - Cambs. 40s.]			53	4
Frauncys Clark in fees (£10) [ass. 20s. in Surrey]			13	4
William Kelsick (£50)			50	
Doctor Awbrey (£60) [x - Surrey £1 10s. 8d.]	3			
George Bynneon (£20)			20	
Wydowe Best (£3)			3	
Henrye Lorde (£3)			3	
John Osborne (£3)			3	
George Brookesby (£3)			3	
The Ladye Rytch (£49) [a]			49	
John Burrowes (£5)			5	
Robert Haselwood (£3)			3	
Thomas Parkes (£3)			3	
William Sadler (£5)			5	
Summa [Blank]				
[Endorsed] Summa	202			16

253. [r.102]   CHEAPE WARDE
[Petty collectors: Thomas Gyles, haberdasher, and William Cowper, mercer.]

ST MARYE BOWE PARISH
[English]

Richard Grainger (£60)	3

187

	£	s.	d
William Laier (£60) [x - Mddx. 16s.]	3		
William Cowper (£80)	4		
Raphe Carkett (£50)		50	
William Dowgle (£50)		50	
Kelham Shrawley (£50)		50	
William Ormeshawe (£70)	3	10	
Thomas Harbert (£50)		50	
John Robynson in fees (£20)		26	8
Anthonye Blunte (£50)		50	
Robert Jackson (£50)		50	
Henrie Hungate (£50)		50	
Morrys Blunte (£15)		15	
Mistres Bonner wyddow (£20)		20	
Thomas Bonner (£3)		3	
George Huis (£12)		12	
William Bonner (£5)		5	
Henrie Page (£5)		5	
Andro Moore (£5)		5	
Roger Tanner (£3)		3	
John Beswell (£8)		8	
Thomas Phillippes (£5)		5	
Thomas Vesye partner with Mr Lare (£10)		10	

254.   ALHALLOWES IN HONY LANE
[English]

	£	s.	d
Richard Barnes (£250)	12	10	
Anthony Cage (£350)	17	10	
Mistres Braunche wyddowe (£160)	8		
Thomas Giles (£80)	4		
Humfrey Wilde (£60)	3		
James Cullymore (£50)		50	
Vincent Norrington (£50)		50	
William Smythe (£50)		50	
Thoms More (£50) [x - Mddx. 16s.]		50	
James Collyns (£3)		3	
Thomas Pecke (£5)		5	
Thomas Sotherne (£3)		3	
William Borname (£3)		3	
Thomas Cage (£3)		3	
William Loftys (£3)		3	
Thomas Rollande (£20)		20	
Roger Heylye (£10)		10	
Thomas Framton (£5)		5	
Nicholas Holder (£3)		3	
Thomas Mercer (£3)		3	
John Hasellwood (£3)		3	
Richard Lamberton (£3)		3	
Henrie Fylde (£13)		13	

	£	s.	d
Adam Holland (£3)		3	
Myles Hubbert (£5)		5	
John Wadhoope (£3)		3	

255.   ST LAWRENCE PARRISHE
[English]

	£	s.	d
John Crowche (£80)	4		
Edward Elmer (£200)	10		
William Stone (£120)	6		
Richard Colmer (£60)	3		
Mistres Hardie wyddowe (£50)		50	
Barthilmew Dodd (£50) [ass. 40s. in Mddx.]		50	
John Niccolles (£70)	3	10	
[r.103]			
Thomas Grymes (£120)	6		
Edward Fisher (£60)	3		
Stephen Some (£70)	3	10	
Richard Wythers (£50)		50	
William Quarleys (£70)	3	10	
William Froste (£70)	3	10	
Henrie Dewise (£50)		50	
Henrie Rooffe (£50)		50	
Thomas Owsleye (£50)		50	
John Winckes (£50) [x - Q 32s.]		50	
Thomas Dobson (£50)		50	
Richard Claiton (£50) [ass. 20s. in Mddx.]		50	
William Becher (£100)	5		
John Hewes (£60)	3		
John Purvey gentleman in landes &			
fees (£50) [x - Herts.?]	3	6	8
Harrie Rowe (£50)		50	
Gilles Hollden (£5)		5	
Thomas Pennyngton (£3)		3	
William Gooffe (£10) [ass. 6s. in Mddx.]		10	
Richard Pyatt (£5)		5	
Edmond Stephens (£5)		5	
Lawrence Gremsdiche (£3)		3	
John & Samuell Greye (£3)		3	
John Raynes (£10)		10	
Stephen Crosse (£10)		10	
Thomas Sherman (£40)		40	
John Hyde (£3)		3	
William Boothbye & his brother (£10)		10	
Edward Florrye (£5)		5	
Fulke Laye (£5)		5	
John Foord (£3)		3	
Charles Hobsonn (£3)		3	

	£	s.	d

256. CATTETON STRETE IN YE PARISHE OF ST LAWRENC LANE
[English]

	£	s.
William Cope (£5)		5
Thomas Esterbe (£5)		5
Thomas Page (£10)		10
William Otmer (£3)		3
William Middleton (£20)		20
John Pattsonn (£10)		10
Edward Bagnall (£10)		10
Raffe Holmes (£3)		3
Robert Edward (£3)		3
John Kente (£3)		3
Edward Kynge (£3)		3
Thomas Ellyott (£5)		5
Thomas Symes (£3)		3
John Rayneshawe (£5)		5
Wyddow Byllings (£3)		3
Robert Shore (£3)		3
Robert Vayle (£5)		5
Ambrose Woodcocke (£15)		15
George Allyn (£10)		10

ST STEPHENS & ST BENNETTES PARISHES
[English]

	£	s.
John Newman (£120)	6	
Olyver Style (£50)		50
Roger Warefeilde (£50)		50
William Poveye (£50)		50
Edward Buckey (£50)		50
Thomas Heaton (£70) [x - Surrey £1 6s. 8d.]	3	10
William Thompson (£50)		50
Richard Western (£50)		50
John Bodnam (£10)		10
Robert Chauntrell (£20)		20
Robert Sybtharpe (£6)		6
William Brockbanck (£80) [x - Mddx. £1 12s.]	4	
Raphe Grene (£6) [x - Q 32s.]		6
Edmond Brockbancke (£10)		10
Raffe Morrys (£10)		10
Edward Gennynges (£3)		3
Robert Storyes (£5)		5
Lawrence Tynes (£10)		10
Edward Gwyne (£5)		5
William Terell (£10)		10
Wyddow Heward (£10)		10
Robert Smythe (£25)		25
William Caldycot (£3)		3

	£	s.	d
257. ST MARTYNES PARISHE			
[English]			
John Colmer (£70) [x - Essex £1]	3	10	
John Alsopp (£100)	5		
Richard Bradgat (£50)		50	
John Bowerman (£50)		50	
Robert Walkeden (£50)		50	
James Smythe in fees (£10)		13	4
John Ellyottes (£50)		50	
James Mownsey (£70) [x - Surrey £1]	3	10	
[r.104]			
Straingers of St Martynes parishe			
Fraunces Bishopp (£70) [b - Antwerp mer.]	7		
[English]			
John Stoddart (£6)		6	
James Battes (£3)		3	
Baldwyn Castleton (£3)		3	
Hughe Boyle (£3)		3	
William Dennys (£3)		3	
Humfrey Theare (£15)		15	
Thomas Ryder (£10)		10	
Phillip Tenche (£5)		5	
Jerrome Page (£10)		10	
Fraunces Grigges (£10)		10	
Symon Standyche (£3)		3	
John Lockwood (£10)		10	
Thomas Wood (£5)		5	
Jonas Fryndge (£5)		5	
William Madoxe (£5)		5	
Mathew Paryshe (£5)		5	
John Bontinge (£10)		10	
Straingers in St Martyns parishe in ye howse of Fraunces Byshopp			
Phillip Byshopp straynger per poll			4
John Byshopp per poll			4
Anne Byshopp per poll			4
Marytt Derrock per poll			4
Lyskyne Dawson per poll			4
258. ST MARY COLECHURCHE PARISHE			
[English]			
Thomas Muffett (£80)	4		
John Cheke (£90)	4	10	
Thomas Godbye (£70)	3	10	
Henrie Bishopp (£50)		50	
John Cage (£60)	3		
Robert Cutt (£70)	3	10	
Lawrence Hewett (£40)		40	

	£	s.	d
John Pynder (£50)		50	
Raffe Bressie (£60)	3		
Thomas Garrawaye (£50)		50	
Mistres Chapman wyddowe (£100)	5		
William Baye (£25)		25	
John Napper (£3)		3	
Gregorie Pilkinton (£15)		15	
Thomas Stede (£3)		3	
Nicholas Badger (£15)		15	
Henrie Worthye (£3)		3	
Mistres Jacob (£3)		3	
Peter Galthorpe (£20)		20	
William Borne (£3)		3	
Godfrey Isbart (£10)		10	
William Isbert (£3)		3	
Wyddow Maston (£10)		10	
Nicholas Slanye (£5)		5	
Robert Boyer (£3) [ass. 5s. in Mddx.]		3	
Edward Dawkes (£15)		15	
Lawnclott Burton (£10)		10	
William Parsons (£3)		3	
Robert Morar (£5)		5	
George Forrest (£3)		3	
Richard Goodinge (£30)		30	
William Pycheford (£5)		5	
Marke Dinglye (£5)		5	
John Nashe (£10)		10	
John Terrell (£8)		8	
Nicholas Chapman (£3)		3	
Nathanyell Byshopp (£5)		5	

259.   ST MILDREDES PARRISHE
                              [English]

	£	s.	d
George Hawes (£50)		50	
Richard Haille (£100)	5		
John Hudson (£50)		50	
Mistres Mylls wyddow (£100)	5		
Nicholas Raynton (£80) [x - Gloucs. £1 1s. 4d.]	4		
John Wylde (£80)	4		
Robert Tudnam (£50)		50	
Richard Taileford (£60)	3		
William Milles (£50)		50	
Robert Gyttons (£50)		50	
John Hobson (£60)	3		
Barthilmew Hobson (£50)		50	
Wyddow Hobson & her sonne William (£60)	3		
Raynold Trype (£5)		5	

	£	s.	d
Thomas Chambers (£3)		3	
Richard Gryne (£3)		3	
William Besse (£3)		3	
Thomas Ikyne (£5)		5	
Trynyon Shortus (£8)		8	
Richard Ikyne (£3)		3	
Lenard Thwaytes (£3)		3	
[r.105]			
Roger Eayre (£3)		3	
John Haselldone (£3)		3	
John Chadock (£3)		3	
William Shingleton (£5)		5	
George Othersall (£15)		15	
John Othersall (£5)		5	
James Norman (£15)		15	
Wyddow Cornyshe (£5)		5	
William Ramse (£3)		3	
James Meller (£3)		3	
John Goottes (£5)		5	
Thomas Lane (£25)		25	
Edward Lane (£3)		3	
Edward Dobson (£3)		3	
Richard Stockwood (£8)		8	
Wyddow Codner (£3)		3	

260. ST PANCRAS PARRISHE
[English]

	£	s.	d
Ambrose Smythe (£250)	12	10	
James Huishe (£100)	5		
John Castlyn (£50)		50	
Richard Wright (£80)	4		
Thomas Lawrence (£100)	5		
William Hewett (£250)	12	10	
Robert Turveyle (£50)		50	

Companyes

	£	s.	d
The Mercers hall in landes (£69)	4	12	
The Grocers hall (£55)		55	

[English]

	£	s.	d
William Lynnagers (£10)		10	
Nicholas Pendleberry (£10)		10	
Harry Laye (£5)		5	
Thomas Smythe (£8)		8	
Henrie Anthonye (£3)		3	
Thomas Chapman (£3)		3	
William Walker (£3)		3	
Humfrey Sownde (£3)		3	
John Parkyns (£10)		10	
James Borton (£3)		3	

	£	s.	d
Thomas Taller (£5)		5	
Edward Goodwyn (£10)		10	
Hughe Holme & Augustyne Digbye (£8)		8	
George Richardson (£3)		3	
Richard Gloceter (£3)		3	
Straingers			
In the howse of Lewys Byshopp strainger			
Henrie Monyr strainger per poll			4
Barpotane Straung strainger per poll			4
Arnold Begman howsholder & strainger (20s.)		2	
Godfrey Heckeks strainger per poll			4
Myghell Mychellsome per poll			4
In the howse of Georg Richardson Englishman			
Harman Lowdwexson strainger per poll			4
Hobbart Albarte strainger per poll			4
[Endorsed] Summa	413	12	4

261. [r.57]   COALEMANSTREETE WARDE
[Petty collectors: John Taylor, haberdasher, and Edward Turfutt, longbow-string maker.]

ST STEPHENS PAROCHE IN COALEMANSTREETE
[English]

	£	s.	d
John Taylor (£150)	7	10	
Stephen Skydmore (£200)	10		
Robert Chrystofer (£100)	5		
Wyllyam Danyell (£50)		50	
Wyddowe Beston in landes & fees (£20)		26	8
Nycholas Tucke (£50)		50	
John Whyte (£100)	5		
Elizabeth Lowe wyddowe (£150)	7	10	
Doctor [William] Lowen in landes and fees			
(£20) [x - Essex 26s. 8d.][92]		26	8
Edward Clerke in landes (£40) [ass. 66s.			
8d. in Suff. and 53s. 4d. in Mddx.]		53	4
George Horsey in landes (£40)			
[x - Heref. 53s. 4d.]		53	4
Wyllyam Ellecar (£50)		50	
Thomas Wrothe in landes & fees (£10)		13	4
Robert Maunsell (£50)		50	
Walter Coppynger (£50)		50	
Thomas Raynscrofte in landes (£15)		20	
John Baker in landes (£20) [x - Kent 40s.]		26	8
Edward Yates gent in landes (£40) [a]		53	4
Wyllyam Smythe (£50) [x - Norf. 20s.]		50	
John Tassett in landes & fees (£40) [a]		53	4

92. E.359/52, r. 13 gives name as William Lewen.

194

	£	s.	d
Edward Turffett in landes (£15)		20	
Mistres Browne wyddowe (£50)		50	
Gregorye Charlett (£50) [x - Kent 6s. 8d.]		50	
George Smythe (£60) [a]	3		
George Goldinge in landes (£15)		20	
John Harryson (£50)		50	
John Tufton in landes (£30) [x - Kent 80s.]		40	
Wyddowe Borne (£3)		3	
262. Wyddowe Warde (£3)		3	
Wyddowe Wythers (£3)		3	
Thomas Tether merchaunt (£3)		3	
Wyddowe Malthus (£8)		8	
John Gardner porter (£3)		3	
Thomas Hulme haberdasher (£3)		3	
Gyles Duncombe merchaunt (£20)		20	
Rychard Morrys (£3)		3	
James Leather inholder (£3)		3	
Wyllyam Teysdale farrier (£3)		3	
Wyllyam Deade, Mr Cordelles clerke (£3)		3	
Rychard Rydge farrer (£3)		3	
Edward Wrothe merchaunt (£10)		10	
John Osbaston merchaunt (£10)		10	
Frauncys Walton merchaunt (£6)		6	
John Maunsfyld gent (£15)		15	
John Sutton (£5)		5	
Nycholas Trott powlter (£3)		3	
Wyllyam Browne curryor (£3)		3	
Thomas Barnes curryor (£15)		15	
Robert Wheatley hackeneyman (£5)		5	
John Whyte curryor (£3)		3	
Thomas Stanbacke curryor (£3)		3	
John Ben hackneyman (£3)		3	
John Rolf typler (£5)		5	
Wyllyam Johnson gent (£10)		10	
Wyllyam Stere vyntner (£5)		5	
Thomas Crompe fletcher (£5)		5	
Wyllyam Wyllson armorer (£3)		3	
Robert Hungate merchaunt (£25) [ass. 50s. in Broad Street ward]		25	
Raphe Bettes plasterer (£8)		8	
263. Peter Hunsdon gent (£15)		15	
Mathew Sutclyfe gent in landes (£10) [a]		13	4
Rychard Wrenche attorney (£15)		15	
John Sheryffe barborsurgeon (£3)		3	
Geoffrey Duckett mercer (£20)		20	
[r.58]			

195

	£	s.	d
John Twysse sadler (£10) [x - Q 12s.]		10[93]	
Thomas Shenbroke brycklayer (£4)		4	
Rychard Paskyns freemason (£3)		3	
Thomas Sadd glasyer (£3)		3	
Thomas Maddocke bagmaker (£3)		3	
Thomas Paskins freemason (£3)		3	
Rychard Wootton clotheworker (£5)		5	
Davye Floodd cordwayner (£3)		3	
Rychard Brygges plasterer (£5)		5	
John Myles woolman (£3)		3	
Wyllyam Bottom plasterer (£3)		3	
John Ramrydge in fee (£1)			16
John Wyllyams (£3)		3	
Mychell Cobb (£20) [x - Q 24s.]		20	
Thomas Heathe merchaunt (£5)		5	
Wyllyam Axe plumber (£5)		5	
John Flower merchaunt (£3)		3	
Gregorye Smythe merchaunt (£40)		40	
Leonerdo Poare merchaunt (£10)		10	
Drewe Clerke cooke (£3)		3	
Mathewe Twyford (£8)		8	
John Hunt merchaunt (£5)		5	
Robert Hoddye hackeneyman (£3)		3	
Wyllyam Hyllman (£5)		5	

264. ST MARGARETTES PAROCHE
[English]

	£	s.	d
Aunsell Beckett (£70)	3	10	
Thomas Weekes in landes (£20)		26	8
Sir Thomas Ryvet knight in landes (£200) [x - Cambs. £6 13s. 4d.][94]	13	6	8
Mychell Warner (£50)		50	
Thomas Sylvester (£50) [ass. 20s. in Surrey]		50	
Thomas Grymes (£50)		50	
Thomas Denman (£50)		50	
Rychard Warham merchaunt (£10)		10	
Rychard Hubbert upholster (£3)		3	
Wyllyam Palmer fownder (£4)		4	
Wyddowe Stephenson (£3)		3	
James Lambert fownder (£3)		3	
Wyllyam Aunsell (£3)		3	
Rychard Fabott (£3)		3	
Thomas Garthe clotheworker (£3)		3	
Rychard Stubbes whytebaker (£5)		5	

93. E.359/52, r. 13 erroneously gives assessment of 26s. 8d.
94. E.359/52, r. 13 gives Henry as first name.

	£	s.	d
Wyllyam Coale merchaunt (£10)		10	
Henrye Terry surgeon (£3)		3	
Thomas Harton fownder (£3)		3	
John Dymmocke gent (£4)		4	
Rychard Kynge pewterer (£4)		4	
Walter Hunt fownder (£3)		3	
John Sleygh gent (£5)		5	
Christofer Sherlocke barborsurgeon (£3)		3	
John Symons fownder (£3)		3	
Wyllyam Lyester fownder (£3)		3	
[Blank] Chamber merchaunt (£3) [a]		3	
Wyllyam Dove (£3)		3	
Roberte Smythe merchaunt (£3)		3	
Thomas Brudenell merchaunt (£40) [a][95]		40	
Thomas Morrys merchaunt (£40) [a]		40	

265.   ST OLAVES PAROCHE
[English]

	£	s.	d
Dame Elizabeth Lee wyddowe (£200)	10		
Margaret Chamberleyn wydowe (£110)	5	10	
Robert Chamberleyn (£70)	3	10	
Henry Isham (£60) [ass. £1 6s. 8d. in Mddx.]	3		
Thomas Cambell (£100)	5		
Henrye Anderson (£100)	5		
Arthur Breame in landes (£30)			
[x - Surrey 13s. 4d.]		40	
Nycholas Maken sadler (£3)		3	
Humfrey Nycholls brownbaker (£5)		5	
Martyn Archedale (£40)		40	
Edward Tydder (£5)		5	
Rychard Wood armorer (£5)		5	
Edmond Burlas merchaunt (£10)		10	
Cutbert Lee talloughchaundler (£5)		5	
Augustyne Fulkes merchaunt (£10)		10	
Thomas Nycholles (£10)		10	
Rychard Hill lynnendraper (£3)		3	
Wyllyam Daunser merchaunttaylor (£5)		5	
Peter Durant clotheworeker (£4)		4	
Patrycke Ward grocer (£6)		6	
Wyllyam Sharpe vintener (£5)		5	
Frauncys Whyte grocer (£8)		8	
Anthonye Stanlacke (£10)		10	
Jonas Thomson cooke (£3)		3	
Wyllyam Seager (£3)		3	
Gylberte Spycer millener (£5)		5	
Mistres Jennynges wyddowe (£8)		8	

95. E.359/52, r. 13 gives Brudenell's first name as Robert.

197

	£	s.	d
John Calcott merchaunt (£10)		10	
Companye			
The Fownders hall (£6)		6	
The Armorers hall (£21)		21	
Straungers			
Lewes Raymond (£20)		40	
Nicholas Remye (£6)		12	
John Dewaye (£6)		12	
Christofer Frederycke (£5)		10	
Hubbert Reygnoldes (£3)		6	

266.   ST STEPHENS PAROCHE
[Strangers]

Nycholas Frend	4
Adryan his wife	4
Adryan hys daughter	4
Jane Landers his mayd	4
Margarett Wybest hys mayd	4
James Turwen	4
Luce hys wyfe	4
Adam Bovenge	4
John Galye	4
Cypryan Valeria	4
Anne hys wyfe	4
Izacke Cypryan	4
John Rowe minister	4
Luca hys wyfe	4
John Rowe hys sonne	4
Martyn Marshall	4
Jane hys wyfe	4
Wyddowe Lowdyoves	4
Peter Potalyan	4
Arthur hys wyfe	4
John Marvod his servaunt	4
John Adams his servaunt	4
Peter Byssey	4
Elizabeth his wyfe	4
Elizabeth Gowtey his mayd	4
Christofer Vanderslyde	4
Jane hys wyfe	4
John Baptiste	4
Jane hys wyfe	4
George Wolfe	4
Duram hys wyfe	4
Agnes Wolfe	4
Alyce Venyan	4
Elizabeth Casett	4
Marye Evans	4

	£	s.	d
George Turwen			4
Shonett hys wyfe			4
Jaquelyne Turwyn his mother			4
servauntes to John Dewaye			
James Cowlas			4
James Jacobes			4
John Vandercan			4
James Vandercan			4
Marye Caffes			4
Seme Vandercan			4
Peter Cupp servaunt with Hubert Reygnoldes			4
Phillypp Reymond servaunt with Lewes Reymond			4
Mathewe Bolte			4
[Endorsed] Summa	186	18	4

267. [r.45]   CORDWAYNERSTRETE WARDE
[Petty collectors: Robert Cobb, girdler, and George Cullymore, draper.]

ST ANTOLYNES PARRISHE
[English]

Thomas Pullison, alderman, sessor (£250)	12	10
The Lady Martyn (£350)	17	10
Robert Dickenson (£50)		50
Walter Fyshe (£70)	3	10
William Thoroughgood (£200) [x - Herts. £2]	10	
Henrie Silles (£50) [a]		50
Henrie Jaye (£60)	3	
John Lucas (£50)		50
Humfrie Corbett (£70) [x - Mddx. 16s.]	3	10
Roger Gamadge (£50)		50
Fraunces Higham (£50)		50
Thomas Archedale (£50)		50
George Staynsmore & William Spratt		
coparteners (£10)		10
Stephen Scarborow (£15)		15
Raynold Guye & Humfrey Downe		
coparteners (£6)		6
Thomas Ludwell (£10)		10
William Gryffyn (£25)		25
John Pecke (£6)		6
Edwyn Babington (£25)		25
John Slater (£5)		5
Thomas Allablaster & Hughe Ley		
coparteners (£6)		6
William Harreat (£20)		20
Robert Wright (£5)		5
John Allington (£6)		6
William Horne (£3)		3

	£	s.	d
John Exton & Nicholas Exton			
merchaunttes (£10)		10	
Anthonye Marler (£8)		8	
Thomas Rawlyns (£6)		6	
Straingers			
Giles Ewen (£5)		10	
Jacolyn his mayde servaunte per poll			4
John Rossell strainger (£3)		6	
Jacobb Bloet his servaunte per poll [a]			4

268. [St. Mary] ALDERMARYE PARRISHE
[English]

	£	s.	d
Sir Richard Pype knighte (£350) [a]	17	10	
William Marsham (£200)	10		
Robert Hawes (£100)	5		
Mistress Dawbney wyddowe (£50)		50	
Henrie Palmer (£50)		50	
Thomas Watterhowse (£50) [x - Herts. 6s.]		50	
John Rooe (£50)		50	
Richard Roddewaye (£50)		50	
Thomas Fletcher (£50)		50	
John Warter & Fraunces Brampton			
coparteners (£6)		6	
Robert Herne (£5)		5	
Symon Wrenche (£6)		6	
Stephen Mabb & Jeffery Hosier			
coparteners (£6)		6	
Robert Genney (£8)		8	
Robert Dorram (£10)		10	
Edward Catcher (£6)		6	
William Garrett (£12)		12	
Thomas Eyre (£3)		3	
[r.46]			
William Cole (£3) [ass. 8s. in Mddx.]		3	
Symon Tewke (£6)		6	
Jasper Lamberte (£15)		15	
Rauff Radclyffe (£10)		10	
David Jones (£20)		20	
Henrie Sambrooke (£3)		3	
Danyell Elmesmore (£3)		3	
Richard Farryngton (£10)		10	

	£	s.	d
269. Leonard Pedock (£3)		3	
Margaret Hollygrave wyddowe (£6)		6	
Richard Goslynge (£10)		10	
John Hoskyns (£20)		20	
Henrie More (£3)		3	
Michael Newark (£3)		3	

	£	s.	d
Raffe Worthington (£3)		3	
Thomas Blande (£6)		6	
Richard Constantyne (£6)		6	
Richard Hudson & William Shorley his			
partener (£3)		3	
John Sympson (£5)		5	
George Nevell (£8)		8	
Robert Bornam (£5)		5	
John Kybblewhyte (£3)		3	
William Withenell (£8)		8	
Henrie Borne (£3)		3	
John Gymlett (£3)		3	
John Hayes (£20)		20	
John Meres (£3)		3	
Evan Thomas (£5)		5	
Robert Austen (£8)		8	
Alexander Barton (£3)		3	
Richard Gore (£20)		20	
John Thompson (£4)		4	
Peter Swynlerst (£3)		3	
Henrie Chevall (£10)		10	
Thomas Bynde (£3) [ass. 15s. in			
Candlewick ward]		3	

270. ST MARYE BOWE PARISHE
[English]

	£	s.	d
Thomas Lamton & Richard Freman (£50)		50	
John Woodward (£60) [x - Sussex £1 10s.]	3		
Nicholas Elcocke (£50)		50	
William Phillippes (£80)	4		
Richard Smythe (£200) [x - Herts. £1 6s. 8d.]	10		
George Collymore (£50)		50	
Peter Baker (£60)	3		
Thomas Browne (£70) [x - Mddx. 10s.]	3	10	
Robert Cobb (£50)		50	
John Sympcott (£80) [x - Essex £1 10s.]	4		
George Owgnell (£50) [ass. 17s. 9 1/2d.			
in Bucks.]		50	
Henrie Parvys (£80)	4		
Hughe Jones (£50)		50	
Nicholas Breamer (£50)		50	
Charles Hoskyns (£120)	6		
Richard Bradshawe (£70)	3	10	
John Reve (£3)		3	
John Scott (£15)		15	
Edmond Robynson (£3)		3	
Edmond Pierson (£10)		10	
John Edwardes (£8)		8	

	£	s.	d
John Barnes (£20)		20	
Symon Cruxton (£10)		10	
William Beere (£8)		8	
William Howland (£15)		15	
John Whytehand (£4)		4	
William Powell (£3)		3	
William Jones (£12)		12	

271. ST BENNET AND ST PANCRASH PARRISHES
[English]

	£	s.	d
Richard Warren gentleman (£200)			
[ass. £4 8s. in Mddx.]	10		
John Watson (£50)		50	
[r.47]			
John Blunte (£60)	3		
Cuthbert Brande (£50)		50	
William Gamadge (£200)	10		
Nicholas Moseley (£100) [x - Kent 8s.]	5		
Thomas Cutler (£50)		50	

Straingers

	£	s.	d
Peter Vallor (£50)	5		
Lewys Bishopp (£60)	6		

ST PANCRASSE PRECINCTE

	£	s.	d
Alice Middleton wyddowe (£3)		3	

ST BENNET SHERHOGGES PRECINCTE

	£	s.	d
Thomas Nicholas (£4)		4	
Richard Foster (£8)		8	

Straingers in the same precincte

	£	s.	d
Henrie Mony servaunte to Lewes Biskopp			
strainger per poll			4
Barbe Potean his maide servaunte per poll			4

ST JOHNS PRECINCTE

	£	s.	d
William Banckes (£3)		3	
Thomas Duffeilde (£3)		3	
Alexander Lockwood (£3)		3	
William Pecock (£4)		4	
Henrie Leye (£5)		5	
Gryffyn Robartes (£3)		3	
Ellynor Mylls wyddowe (£6)		6	

Straingers in the same precincte

	£	s.	d
Christofer Derrycke (£6)		12	
Prudens Harsey his maide servaunte per poll			4

272. TRYNITYE PRECINCTE

	£	s.	d
Evan Gryffyn (£3)		3	

	£	s.	d
Christofer Noddinge (£4)		4	
Richard Newman (£3)		3	
Straingers			
Thomas Ireland a strainger per poll			4

ALLHALLOWES PARRISHE

	£	s.	d
Richard Maye (£180)	9		
John Tapp (£150)	7	10	
Roger Abdye (£120)	6		
John Davenet (£50)		50	
Richard Benyon (£70) [ass. £3 in Essex]	3	10	
Arthur Hewet (£50)		50	

ALLHALLOWES PRECINCTE

	s.
John Povey (£3)	3
Richard Colley (£3)	3
Christofer Dunscomb (£10)	10
Thomas Hawes (£10)	10

ST THOMAS APOSTLES PARRISHE

	£	s.	d
Nicholas Spenser in landes (£20)		26	8
William Salter (£70) [x - Bucks. £1 10s.]	3	10	
James Cayne in landes (£20)		26	8

S THOMAS APOSTLES PRECINCTE

	£	s.	d
Henrie Mowmford (£3)		3	
Richard Powell & Humfrey Hyde coparteners (£3)		3	
John Poker (£10)		10	
Henrie Gasset (£3)		3	
John Stacye (£3)		3	
Isack Hallywaye (£4)		4	
Richard Skynner (£5)		5	
Thomas Mylls (£3)		3	
[Endorsed] Summa	290	16	4

273. [r.15]   CORNEHILL WARDE
[Petty collectors: Morgan Rychardes, skinner, and Wyllyam Ryder, haberdasher.]

ST MYCHELLS ST CHRISTOFERS
& ST MARYE WOLCHURCHE PAROCHES
[English]

	£	s.
Thomas Tyrryll (£70)	3	10
Wyddowe Wayght in landes (£15)		20
Edmond Pygott (£60)	3	
Thomas Allyn skynner (£80)		
[x - Kent £1]	4	

	£	s.	d
Bryan Caverley (£50)		50	
John Harbye (£50)		50	
Phyllypp Gunter (£300)	15		
John Lute (£50)		50	
Morgan Rychardes (£50)		50	
Edmond Aunsell (£80)	4		
John Wheeler (£60)	3		
Nycholas Fuller (£50) [ass. 20s. in Essex]		50	
Edward Thorne in landes (£20)		26	8
Thomas Forman (£100)	5		
Wyllyam Ryder (£70)	3	10	
Rychard Milles (£50)		50	
Gyles Crowche (£50)		50	
George Kevall (£50)		50	
Cornellys Corne estraunger (£10)		20	
John Bull (£5)		5	
Thomas Burdett (£20)		20	
Wyllyam Chappman (£5)		5	
Wyllyam Hamond (£6)		6	
Rychard Maye (£3)		3	
John Bowltinge (£8)		8	
Thomas Porche (£5)		5	
Thomas Evans (£5)		5	
Edward Barbor (£25)		25	
John Wythers (£15)		15	
Nycholas Abraham (£3)		3	
Wyllyam Flewett (£6)		6	
Wyllyam Lanam (£10)		10	
Wyddowe Luter (£3)		3	
Rychard Saunderson (£3)		3	
Thomas Fygge (£3)		3	
274. Robert Westley (£8)		8	
Thomas Stowe (£10)		10	
James Cannon (£5)		5	
Thomas Colfe (£6)		6	
Nycholas Pudsey & John Ryddlesdon (£5)		5	
Percyvall Burton (£3)		3	
John Ryckeford (£3)		3	
Thomas Doncaster (£6)		6	
John Jones (£5)		5	
John Gryffyn (£3)		3	
Mychell Crowche (£5)		5	
Wyllyam Keltrydge (£30)		30	
George Hall (£3)		3	
George Walker (£5)		5	
Gylberte Godfrey (£3)		3	
Cutbeart Creeckeplace (£3)		3	

	£	s.	d
Thomas Palmer (£5)		5	
John Brokebanke (£12)		12	
John Warner (£3)		3	
Rychard Levans (£5)[96]		5	
Robert Wyllcoxe (£3)		3	
Wyllyam Shambrooke (£5)		5	
Wydowe Bales (£6)		6	
Nycholas Nenton grocer (£5)		5	
John Shambrooke (£3)		3	
Rychard Marcam (£8)		8	
Thomas Wythers (£3)		3	
Gabryell Curtys (£3)		3	
Hugh Sponer (£3)		3	
Alexander Sharpe (£3)		3	
Henrye Rychardson (£3)		3	
Raphe Bynckes (£6)		6	
Samuell Monger (£5)		5	
[r.16]			
Lawrence Caldwall (£10)		10	
Thomas Holmes (£6)		6	
Thomas Thornehill (£5)		5	
Meredyth Hughes & John Cooper (£5)		5	
275. Rychard Dodd (£10)		10	
Wyllyam Browne (£40)		40	
Edmond Jarvys (£3)		3	
Ellys Some (£20)		20	
John Nokes (£15)		15	
Wyddowe Yomans (£3)		3	
Robert Stephens (£10)		10	
James Crucheley (£5)		5	
Peter Hardlowe (£20)		20	
Wyddowe Merrycke (£6)		6	
John Marshall (£10)		10	
George Dale (£12)		12	
Anthonye Sodye (£5)		5	
John Eldrydge (£5)		5	
Thomas Foxe and Thomas Bruce (£6)		6	
Edward Phillyppes (£3)		3	
Robert Sallysburye (£3)		3	
George Smythe (£6)		6	
John Stephens (£3)		3	
Israell Owen (£6)		6	
Roger Rygbye (£15)		15	
Thomas Paradyne & John Paradyne (£40)		40	

96. A marginal mark (+) indicates that Levans was exonerated of payment in Cornhill ward, but I did not find a corresponding entry for this exoneration in the enrolled accounts, E.359/52.

	£	s.	d
Edward Ryder (£5)		5	
Humfrey Streete (£12)		12	
Henry Ayleward (£12)		12	
Davye Wythers (£3)		3	
Wyddowe Boweyer (£10)		10	
Luke Bedford (£3)		3	
Thomas Smythe (£5)		5	
Arnold Rychardson (£5)		5	
John Jaques (£20)		20	
John Thompson (£8)		8	
Rychard Gylmore (£5)		5	
Danyell Androwes (£10)		10	
John Maskall (£5)		5	
Thomas Lyllye (£5)		5	

276.   ST PETERS PAROCHE IN CORNEHILL
[English]

	£	s.	d
Thomas Pygott (£40)		40	
Phillipp Jones (£50)		50	
Thomas Gardyner (£60) [ass. £3 in Mddx.]	3		
Gamalyell Woodford (£50)		50	
Wyddowe Hylles in landes (£15)		20	

Straunger

	£	s.	d
Waldron Pope (£10)		20	

ST PETERS PAROCHE

	£	s.	d
Frauncys Lambert (£5)		5	
Doctor Preyst (£10)		10	
Theophylye Adams (£30)		30	
George Gunbye (£3)		3	
Rychard Hodge (£8)		8	
Rychard Carlehill (£3)		3	
Davyd Evans (£10)		10	
Roberte Gunston (£6)		6	
Rowland Rayleton (£15)		15	
John Malyn (£3)		3	
	115	7	8
[Endorsed] Summa	115	8	8

277. [r.76]   CREPLEGATE
[Petty collectors: Richard Cotton, leatherseller, and Frauncys Quarles, draper.]

ST MARY MAGDALYNS PARISHE
[English]

	£	s.	d
John Lacey (£200)	10		
Michaell Boyle (£60)	3		
Oliver Rowe (£80)	4		
Thomas Egerton in fees (£20)		26	8

	£	s.	d
Thomas Alderseye (£100)	5		
Baldwine Dereham (£80)	4		
Thomas Bayarde (£250)	12	10	
Richarde Procter (£100)	5		
Roberte Sadler (£60)	3		
Thomas Maye (£50)		50	
Leonarde Hollydaye (£80)	4		
Robert Fountayne (£50)		50	
Richard Loftes (£50)		50	
Arthure Wright (£50)		50	
William Rowe alderman (£200)	10		
John Parkines (£50)		50	
Gerrard Goore a Sessor (£260)	13		
John Hunte (£30)		30	
Richard Hickman and Richarde Haywarde			
partiners (£10)		10	
William Cartor (£20)		20	
Robert Wake (£4)		4	
Thomas Henshawe (£3)		3	
Thomas Bankes (£3)		3	
Randall Foster (£3)		3	
William Pyke (£20)		20	
Thomas Elliott (£3)		3	
Leonarde Dorchester (£4)		4	
John Altam (£3)		3	

278.   [St. Mary] ALDERMANBURY PARISHE
[English]

	£	s.	d
Ralphe Woodcocke alderman a Sessor (£200)	10		
Sir William Damsell knight (£400)	20		
John Bourne (£70)	3	10	
Clement Paston in landes (£60)			
[x - Norfolk £5 2s. 8d.]	4		
James Dalton in landes (£20)		26	8
Fraunces Dodde (£50)		50	
Robert Davies in fees (£20)			
[x - Surrey 20s.]		26	8
John Barnes in landes (£25)		33	4
Mistres Coise widowe (£100)			
[x - Mddx. 26s. 8d.]	5		
Oliver Godfreye in landes (£20)			
[ass. 26s. 8d. in Kent]		26	8
John Rawlyns in fees (£20)			
[x - Monmouthshire 13s. 4d.]		26	8
Mistres [Joyce] Francklyn widowe (£150)			
[x - Herts. 40s.][97]	7	10	

97. E.359/52, r. 14 gives first name as Joyce.

	£	s.	d
John Swinerton (£60) [x - Mddx. 20s.]	3		
Mistres Burnell widowe in landes (£20) [a]		26	8
Mr Clarenciaulx herault [Robert Cooke]			
in landes & fees (£20)[98]		26	8
Mr [John] Pomfrett in landes & fees (£20)			
[x - Dorset?][99]		26	8
Robert Butler in landes & fees (£20)		26	8
Mistres Beatrix Gressham widowe (£60)			
[x - Surrey £5)	3		
[r.77]			
Sampson Meverell in landes (£30)			
[x - Staffs. 40s.]		40	
William Thompson (£5) [a]		5	
Richard Newton (£3)		3	
Richard Blagne (£5)		5	
Nicholas Warner (£6)		6	
Roberte Mascall (£5) [x - Lime Street			
ward 5s.]		5	
Gregory Newland and Robert Penruddock (£6)		6	
Mathew Chamberlin (£3)		3	
Thomas Kendon (£5)		5	
George Bowes (£3)		3	
William Bygmore (£3)		3	
279. John Dodson (£6)		6	
Robert Whippe (£3)		3	
Richard Brigges (£6)		6	
Walter Williams (£10)		10	
Thomas Hulmes (£5)		5	
Ellice Parrie (£3)		3	
Mighell Lenton (£5)		5	
William Brigg (£3)		3	
Simon Bedall (£3)		3	
Robert Harrington (£3)		3	
Roger Busshe (£3)		3	
William Vincent (£3)		3	
William Patten (£10) [b][100]		10	
Addam Cooper (£3)		3	
John Rice (£4)		4	
Thomas Atkinson (£3)		3	
William Simpson (£6)		6	

98. 'Harald ad arm' ' is written in the margin. Robert Cooke, Clarenceux King of Arms, was exonerated by virtue of letters patent of 4 June 1549 and writ from the queen to the treasurer and barons dated 1 July 1581 (E.359/52, r. 14).
99. E.359/52, r. 14 gives first name as John.
100. 'Myneralls per bre' ' in margin. William Patten claimed, and was apparently denied, exemption on the basis of letters patent of 1 May 1577 to Thomas Thurland and Daniel Houghstetter and their partners in the Company of Mines Royal (E.359/52, r. 14).

	£	s.	d
Richard Foxe (£5)		5	
John Bacon (£3)		3	

ST ALBONES PARISHE

	£	s.	d
Richard Cotton (£50)		50	
John Tidcastle (£50)		50	
Assabell Partridge (£100) [x - Mddx. 40s.]	5		
Robert Tailor (£50)		50	
John Leake (£100) [x - Notts. 18s. 8d.]	5		
John Freston in landes (£20) [x - Yorks.?]		26	8
John Sibthorpe (£50)		50	
John Martine (£70)	3	10	
Charles Browne in landes (£20)		26	8
Fraunces Wotton (£50)		50	
Fraunces Quarles (£50)		50	
280. Doctor Smithe in fees (£10)		13	4
Doctor Marbecke in fees (£10)		13	4
Mistres Backhowse widowe (£100)	5		
Bettrice Gardiner widowe (£8)		8	
Humfrey Baker (£3)		3	
Henrie Watson (£3)		3	
George Cabell (£3)		3	
George Bedford (£3)		3	
Richard Lytchfeilde (£5)		5	
William Yonge (£10)		10	
Alexander Peele (£3)		3	
Edward Wotton (£10)		10	
Bryan Ellam (£4)		4	
Arthure Cutler (£3)		3	
Anthonye Medcalfe (£10)		10	
Christofer Tyson (£3)		3	
Fraunces Leeche (£6)		6	
Gilbert Ramsey (£3)		3	
Robert More (£3)		3	
Tymothe Farmer (£3)		3	
Thomas Savage and John Spilsberie (£3)		3	
Richard Brooke gent (£15)		15	
Thomas Tailor (£3)		3	
Fraunces Greneham (£3)		3	
Allyn Downer (£3)		3	
John Pollard (£3)		3	
Mistres [Elizabeth] Multon widowe (£10) [x - Surrey 15s.][101]		10	
John Hilles gent (£10) [x - Surrey 10s.]		10	
Barnabas Hilles (£3)		3	

101. E.359/52, r. 14 gives Elizabeth as first name.

	£	s.	d
Henry Downer (£6)		6	
[r.78]			
Simon Farnell (£10)		10	
Nicholas Hurdis (£3)		3	
Mawrice Ekeholte stranger (£6)		12	
William Piggott Englisshman (£6)		6	

281.   ST MICHAELLS PARISHE
[English]

	£	s.	d
Fraunces Heaton (£60)	3		
Elizabeth Williamson in landes (£10)			
[ass. 6s. 8d. in Lincs.]		13	4
Anthony Keye (£50)		50	
Henrye Deacon (£60) [x - Q 34s. 8d.]	3		
John Jenninges (£60)	3		
Lancelot Yonge (£50) [x - Q 24s.]		50	
Walter Browne (£50) [x - Farringdon			
ward Within 20s.]		50	
William Warren in landes & fees (£20)			
[x - Mddx. 20s.]		26	8
Henry Barre in fees (£10)		13	4
Robert Raynson (£120) [a]	6		
Abraham Lynce (£10)		10	
Joyce Williamson widowe (£20)		20	
Richard Handburye (£80)	4		
Robert Sawnders (£5)		5	
John Hall (£5)		5	
Robert Stone (£3)		3	
Nicholas Morgan (£3)		3	
John Everitt (£5)		5	
Richard Bannister (£3)		3	
Henry Cowly (£3)		3	
Hughe Ingrome (£12)		12	
Thomas Simons (£3)		3	
Widowe [Alice] Marshe (£10) [ass. 14s. in			
Mddx.][102]		10	
Edwarde Glover (£3)		3	
John Toolys (£6)		6	
John Cartor (£6)		6	
Lawrence Warner (£3)		3	
Alice Woodwarde widowe (£6)		6	
William Hudson (£3)		3	
Gawin Wilson (£3)		3	
William Harvye (£20)		20	
Richard Browne (£15)		15	
William Roomley (£4)		4	

102. E.359/52, r. 15 gives Alice as first name.

	£	s.	d
Straungers			
John Williamson (£3)		6	
Miles Godfreye (4d.)			4

282. ST LAURENCES PARISHE
[English]

	£	s.
Thomas Cordell (£80)	4	
Edmunde Hogen (£80)	4	
John Withers (£60)	3	
Robert Rowe (£70) [x - Mddx. 40s.]	3	10
John Foxe (£50)		50
Martine Trotte (£80)	4	
Thomas Lowe (£70)	3	10
Mistres Hodgeson widowe (£50)		50
William Williamson (£3)		3
Edwarde Hearne (£6)		6
Robert Goodwine (£5)		5
John Byttenson (£3) [a]		3
George Pyckmere (£3)		3
Robert Bate (£3)		3
William Style (£6)		6
Edwarde Swayne (£15)		15
Edmond Maye (£5) [x - Q 16s.]		5
Mighell Crowche (£5)		5
George Hunte (£5)		5

283. ST PETERS PARISHE

	£	s.
Sir Lionell Duckett knight Commissioner (£300) [b][103]	15	
Lawrence Palmer (£150) [x - Surrey £3 6s.8d.]	7	10
Richarde Brereton (£50)		50
Edward Palmer (£80)	4	
Richard Trayforde (£50)		50
Brian Savell (£5)		5
William Whitehorne (£5)		5
George Waddington (£5)		5
John Tottle (£3)		3
William Martine (£3)		3
[r.79]		
Thomas Boyer (£3)		3
George Robertes (£10)		10
Richard Brooke (£3)		3
Nicholas Moore (£3)		3
John Barnes (£3)		3

103. 'Myneralls per bre' ' in margin. Duckett claimed, and was apparently denied, exemption on the basis of letters patent of 1 May 1577 to Thomas Thurland and Daniel Houghstetter and their partners in the Company of Mines Royal (E.359/52, r. 14).

	£	s.	d
Goodwiffe Widgington widowe (£20)		20	
William Sawnders (£8)		8	
Nicholas Lawrence (£3)		3	
Gabriell Newman (£20)		20	
Tristram Walter (£3)		3	
Jerome Savage (£3)		3	
William Dale (£3)		3	
John Baker stranger (4d.)			4

284. ST ALPHAGE & ST OLAVES PARISHES

	£	s.	d
Sir Rowland Haywarde knight Comissioner (£400)	20		
Doctor Master in fees (£50) [x - Q £3 6s. 8d.]	3	6	8
Doctor Atslowe (£60) [x - Essex 30s.]	3		
The Ladye Cordell (£60) [a]	3		
Henry Townesende in landes (£20) [a]		26	8
Thomas Griffine (£50)		50	
Edwarde Kinge (£50) [a]		50	
Christofer Fulkes in fees (£20)		26	8
John Gilpine in fees (£10) [x - Mddx. 15s.]		13	4
Andreas Bircrofte stranger (£10) [b - Antwerp mer.]		20	

Englishmen

	£	s.	d
Widowe Fawcet (£3)		3	
John Tailor (£3)		3	
Harrie Seamer (£3)		3	
Anne Fraunces widowe (£6)		6	
Alexander Barnardine (£3)		3	
William Howe (£3)		3	
Richard Richardson gent (£5) [a]		5	
John Webrome gent (£10) [x - Kent 53s. 4d.][104]		10	
Anthonie Spencer (£3)		3	
Richard Holden gent (£5)		5	
John White gent (£20)		20	
Anthonye Ratseye (£10) [x - Essex 4s.]		10	
William Washeford (£3)		3	
John Nicholls (£3)		3	
William Dewsberie (£3)		3	
Thomas Rapier (£3)		3	
Thomas Clea (£3)		3	
Ambrose Lupo (£10) [x - Q 32s.]		10	
Thomas Norris (£5) [x - Q 6s.8d.]		5	

104. E. 359/52, r. 14 gives surname as Wyborne.

	£	s.	d
Thomas Baker (£3)		3	
Richarde Lea (£5)[105]		5	
285. Thomas Phillipps (£3)		3	
James Sherman (£5)		5	
Thomas Commyn (£3)		3	
Peeter Coole (£3)		3	
Robert Newland (£3)		3	
John Reade (£6)		6	
Fraunces Hitchecocke (£10) [x - Q 64s.]		10	
John Kinge (£3)		3	
Thomas Whelor (£20)		20	
Peeter Cobbe carpenter (£10)		10	
Richard Benson (£3)		3	
William Snealinge (£5)		5	
Thomas Thomkines (£3)		3	
Thomas Rosemond (£3)		3	
Jeames Dagger (£3)		3	
William Stayner (£5)		5	
Shippe Alley			
Richard Ottewell (£3)		3	
John A Rye (£3)		3	
Thomas Thrusshe (£10)		10	
Thomas Marcant (£3)		3	
Richard Penne (£4)		4	
Robert Pantlin (£3)		3	
Thomas Selbie (£10)		10	
Henrie Flicke (£3)		3	
John Preston (£5)		5	
Mistres Hudson widowe (£10) [x - Essex 5s.]		10	
[r.80]			
Thomas Wotton (£3)		3	
Strangers			
John Debois (4d.)			4
Thomas Waltrop (4d.)			4
Jeames Boorce (4d.) [a]			4
286. ST JOHN ZACHARIES PARISHE			
[English]			
Jefferie Griffine (£3)		3	
Robert Graye (£3)		3	
John Smithe (£3)		3	
George Aylewaye (£6)		6	
Lambart Osbolston (£3)		3	

---

105. 'Pursuiant ad arm' ' in margin. Lee, as Portcullis pursuivant, was exonerated by virtue of letters patent of 4 June 1549 and writ from the queen to the treasurer and barons dated 1 July 1581 (E.359/52, r. 14).

	£	s.	d
ST GILES PARISHE			
Thomas Smithe in landes & fees (£30) [a]		40	
John Hiliard (£80)	4		
Robert Tailor in landes & fees (£50)			
[x - Kent 40s.]	3	6	8
Henrie Finche in landes & fees (£20)			
[x - Mddx. 5s.]		26	8
Mathewe Smithe gent (£100)			
[x - Somerset 53s. 4d.]	5		
Richard Lovelas in landes & fees			
(£20) [a]		26	8
John Stubbs in landes (£10)			
[x - Norfolk 10s. 8d.]		13	4
Helene Raper widowe (£50)		50	
Thomas Floudd in landes & fees (£20)			
[x - Kent 13s. 4d.]		26	8
Roger Townsende in landes (£100)			
[x - Mddx. £5 6s. 8d.]	6	13	4
John Glascocke in landes & fees (£20)			
[x - Essex 13s. 4d.]		26	8
John Povie (£50)		50	
Edward Vanham in fees (£10)		13	4
Martine Harlakington in landes & fees (£20)			
[ass. 40s. in Kent]		26	8
John Fuller gent (£140)			
[x - Mddx. 53s. 4d.]	7		
Doctor Hamond (£50)		50	
Thomas Bradshawe (£50)		50	
Edwarde Wilson in landes (£10) [a]		13	4
Thomas Hanburie (£10) [x - Hants. 10s.]		10	
Edward Pooly in landes & fees (£10)		13	4
William Dalbye in landes & fees (£20)			
[ass. 26s. 8d. in Mddx.]		26	8
William Gressham gent in landes (£100)			
[x - Kent £4 8s. 8d.]	6	13	4
David Simpson in landes and fees (£20)			
[x - Essex 13s. 4d.]		26	8
William Latham in landes & fees (£20)			
[x - Essex 53s. 4d.]		26	8
Thomas Foster in landes & fees (£20)		26	8
Simon Terrington stranger (£10)		20	
287. Companies			
The Haberdasshers in landes (£21)		28	
The Bruers in landes (£21)		28	
The Waxchaundlers in landes (£8)		10	8
The Curriors in landes (£13)		17	4
The Plaisterers in landes (20s.)			16

	£	s.	d
The Scriveners in landes (£10)		13	4
Redcrosse Streete			
Davie Mopted (£3)		3	
John Cooper (£3)		3	
John Armorer (£3)		3	
Charles Langley (£3)		3	
John Eckles (£6)		6	
Sir Humfrey Jylbert knight (£40)		40	
Robert Bellonne (£10)		10	
Jeane Cox widowe (£10)		10	
Fraunces Tirar (£3)		3	
Richard Barlo (£15)		15	
Reanald Dent (£6)		6	
Arthure Gardner (£5)		5	
Richard Miller (£15)		15	
Robert Streeche (£3)		3	
John Whinniarde (£6) [x - Q 6s. 8d.]		6	
Edward Thickines (£10)		10	
John Russell (£5)		5	
Barbican			
Margaret Cade widowe (£3)		3	
John Bambridge (£3)		3	
John Charlewood (£3)		3	
Robert Bellomye (£5) [a]		5	
Robert Ap Thomas (£5)		5	
John Spencer (£5)		5	
Thomas Gardner (£30)		30	
John Favor (£3)		3	
Edmond Bull (£5)		5	
William Wantlin (£5)		5	
Robert Newman (£6)		6	
Gyles Hodgeson (£6)		6	

288. Golding Lane

	£	s.	d
Roger Sherman (£3)		3	
Christofer Colman (£3)		3	
Robert Allyson (£13)		13	
Thomas Cotton (£3)		3	
Henrie Evans (£6)		6	
[r.81]			
Jeames Heyborne (£3)		3	
Whitecrosse Streete			
Nicholas Browne (£3)		3	
Peter Merrye (£3)		3	
Robert Burbridge (£3)		3	
William Baxter (£3)		3	
Anthonye Bonden (£3)		3	
John Taylor (£3)		3	

	£	s.	d
Stephen Wilkinson (£3)		3	
Fraunces Bowes widowe (£5) [a]		5	
Robert Fynche (£3)		3	
Joyce Barlo widowe (£10)			
[ass. 13s. 4d. in Mddx.]		10	
Johan Lorde widowe (£3)		6	[sic]
Stephen Barton (£3)		3	
John Harrison (£3)		3	
John Grange (£5)		5	
Phillip Garland (£4)		4	
Henrie White (£3)		3	
Fraunces Putman (£3)		3	
Richard Mawrice (£3)		3	
Thomas Lee (£8)		8	
John Cartor (£3)		3	
Griffine Robert (£3)		3	
John Browne (£3)		3	
Henrie Willis (£3)		3	
John Crookes gent (£10)		10	
Thomas Benson (£3)		3	
Christofer Todde (£3)		3	
Chrostofer Butler (£6)		6	
John Corbyn (£3)		3	
Thomas Browne (£3)		3	

289. Forstreate

	£	s.	d
John Evans (£3)		3	
Richard Grymes (£3)		3	
John Brand (£5)		5	
Anthonye Tindall (£3)		3	
Cutbert Race (£3)		3	
Christofer Cartor (£3)		3	
William Streatton (£5)		5	
John Erethe (£3)		3	
William Barker (£3)		3	
Richard Pawson (£3)		3	
John Granger (£4)		4	
John Ashemore (£5)		5	
William Thorpe (£3)		3	
Richard Gregorie (£3)		3	
Thomas Bettes (£5)		5	
Richard Haynes (£3)		3	
John Clyfforde (£3)		3	
Widowe Belhowse (£10)		10	
Nathaniell Tracie (£10) [ass. 16s. in Essex][106]		10	

106. Tracie and Rowland Smart are bracketed in the margin with the notation 'both in one house.'

	£	s.	d
Rowland Smart (£5)		5	
Raphe Adlington (£3)		3	
Grubstreete			
Thomas Ilove (£3)		3	
Thomas Coole (£3)		3	
Thomas Gravelyn (£3)		3	
Hughe White (£5)		5	
Edward Starr (£3)		3	
Thomas Bradshawe goldsmith (£5)		5	
George Towers (£3)		3	
Henrie Parrie (£3)		3	
William Thompson (£5)		5	
Edward Fearefax (£3)		3	
Thomas Frampton (£3)		3	
John Egleston (£15) [ass. 40s. in Mddx.]		15	
Davie Warde (£3)		3	
George Richardson (£3)		3	
John Hodgekinson (£3)		3	

290. Moorelane

	£	s.	d
Robert Goram (£5)		5	
Edmond Stanfeelde (£5)		5	
John Moodie (£5)		5	
Nicholas Rydar (£3)		3	
Henry Convarse (£3)		3	
Thomas Samforde (£5)		5	
Anne Preston (£5)		5	
Thomas Butler (£3)		3	
Jefferie Yonge (£3)		3	
John Stanton (£3)		3	
[r.82]			
Martine Burrall (£5)		5	
Thomas Harrison (£3)		3	
William Bradshawe (£3)		3	
Richard Dyer (£5)		5	

[Strangers]
Strangers in Redcrosse streete

	£	s.	d
Walter Moyses (4d.)			4
Bingam Vandornicke (4d.)			4
Catheren Pelt, Stephen Debear [and]			
Richard Demorye, his servauntes (12d.)			12
Barbican			
Noy Jeparte (£3)		6	
John Dewent, Gillam Matteres [and]			
Jacob Garrett, his servauntes (12d.)			12
Yonbaldma Pretuses (£3) [a][107]		6	

107. E.359/52, r. 14 gives Yewbalman as first name.

	£	s.	d
Garter Place			
Arnold Cooke (4d.)			4
John Bilbo (4d.)			4
Leefes Yarde			
Dennis Demaster (£4)		8	
Golding Lane			
Emery Durant (£3)		6	
Catheren Decon his servaunt (4d.)			4
In Whitecrosse Streete			
Peter Savage (£40)	4		
Simon Semon [and] Samuell Senapatt,			
his servauntes (8d.)			8
Jeames Wilforde (4d.)			4
John Melom (£5)		10	
Leonard Melom, his servaunt (4d.)			4
Gerven Mahew (4d.)			4
291. In Grubstreete			
Samuell Barker (4d.)			4
Mighell Westen (4d.)			4
John Anthony his servaunt (4d.)			4
John Wyer (4d.)			4
John Garwawghe (4d.)			4
Davie Rokines, Charles Vanderwarde, John			
Laventie, Hance Cocourte [and] Katherine			
Sminyers, his servauntes (20d.)			20
In Doctor Bullines Yarde			
Anthony Lambert (4d.)			4
Pockey Mussen, Valentine Cursen [and]			
John Corner, his servauntes (12d.)			12
Perden Depere (4d.)			4
Arnold Depere his sonne (4d.)			4
Jacklini Depere his daughter (4d.)			4
Cornellis Loles (£10) [a]		20	
Jeames Dodegay, his servaunt (4d.) [a][108]			4
Betwene Grubstreete & More Lane			
Peter Marcage (4d.) [a][109]			4
In Moore Lane			
Peter Terrintine (£4)		8	
Peter Antus, Martine Myes [and] Marie			
Myes, his servauntes (12d.)			12
Almon Mutton (£3)		6	
Peter Clarke, his servant (4d.)			4
Copt Hall in Moore Lane			
Charles Treswer (4d.)			4

108. E.359/52, r. 14 gives surname as de Gage.
109. E.359/52, r. 14 gives surname as Marriage.

	£	s.	d
Fraunces Peter (4d.)			4
Moore Feildes			
John Stephens (4d.)			4
Abraham Shenyshawe (40s.)		4	
Balwine Flemin, his servaunt (4d.)			4
[Endorsed] Summa	476	19	4

292. [r.64]   DOWGATE WARDE

[Petty collectors: Arnold Rutton, brewer, and Wyllyam Shawcrofte, girdler.]

ALHALLOWES THE GREATE PAROCHE
[English]

	£	s.	d
Henry Campyon a Sessor (£150)	7	10	
Christofer Swaldell (£50)		50	
George Querneby (£60)	3		
John Cressye in landes (£10)		13	4
Arnold & Mathue Rutton (£100)	5		
William Hamersley (£15)		15	
Abraham Campyon (£10)		10	
William Pystor (£10)		10	
Widdow Washe (£10)		10	
William Tanfield gent (£20) [a][110]		20	
John Kiddyare (£10)		10	
William Bisley (£10)		10	
William Moyzer (£10) [x - Kent 3s.]		10	
John Wardall (£20) [x - Tower ward 10s.]		20	
Edward Chapman (£10)		10	
Thomas Kiddye (£25)		25	
Rychard Brooke (£20)		20	
Widdow Parkinson (£10) [a][111]		10	
Thomas Morgan (£10)		10	
Humffrey Veiron (£15)		15	
Gyles Fludd (£20) [x - Kent 10s.]		20	
Clement Devyck (£20)		20	
William Hobson (£15)		15	
John Sweetinge (£3)		3	
Nycholas Chestre (£3)		3	
Alexandre Warde (£5)		5	
William Dupper (£5)		5	
Richard Ellyfe (£3)		3	
John Teball (£3)		3	
George Dowsse (£3)		3	
Thomas Person (£3)		3	
John Hall (£3)		3	
John Growme (£3)		3	

110. Marginal notation: 'habitat ad Quenehith.'
111. Marginal notation: 'apud Paddyngton.'

	£	s.	d
293. Thomas Russell (£5)		5	
Wyddow Ellyatt (£3) [a][112]		3	
John Armorer (£3)		3	
Roberte Davys (£3)		3	
Thomas Farbar (£3)		3	
Thomas Savage (£3)		3	
John Coxe (£3)		3	
George Idell (£3)		3	
John Boyse (£3)		3	
Thomas Byledge (£3)		3	
Roberte Partridge (£5) [a][113]		5	
Adam Pylsworth (£6)		6	
Widow Marshall (£3)		3	
James Beydell (£4)		4	
Henry Andsworth (£5)		5	
Salamon Sproute (£5)		5	
John Cooke (£5)		5	
John Browne (£3)		3	
Rychard Route (£6)		6	
Thomas Gilberte (£8)		8	
Humfrey Cartwright (£3)		3	
Laurence Wansley (£3)		3	
Willyam Hodges (£5)		5	
[r.65]			
Patrick Royton (£6)		6	
John Woode (£3)		3	
Widow Dawse (£5)		5	
Steven Jeffrey (£3)		3	
Henry Palmer (£3)		3	

Straungers:

	£	s.	d
John Dewkin (£10)		20	
Hubert Francklin (£10)		20	
Garrett Tryon (£7)		14	
Alard Starte (£5)		10	
Widdow Garratt (£10)		20	
John Burgrave (£3)		6	

294.

ALHALLOWES THE LESSE
SCT LAWRENCE POWNTNEY &
SCT JOHNS PAROCHES
[English]

	£	s.	d
Thomas Rygges (£100)	5		
William Offley (£70)	3	10	
Richard Cowper & William Glover (£60)	3		
Richard Morrys (£50)		50	

112. Marginal notation: 'apud Reigate in Sur'.'
113. Marginal notation: 'apud Edelmeton.'

	£	s.	d
William Shacrofte & Richard Venables (£80)	4		
Edward Lawson & Niccholas Barry (£60)	3		
Richard Bourne (£110)	5	10	
Edward Ireland (£20)		20	
John Cowper (£15)		15	
John Browne (£10)		10	
Syrack Rosse (£10)		10	
William Hudson (£10)		10	
Henry Peyton (£20)		20	
Thomas Gyles (£8)		8	
Owen Jones (£10)		10	
Christofer Bouldrye (£15)		15	
Andrew Phones (£10)		10	
Roberte Swyster (£3)		3	
William Keling (£3)		3	
Edmond Bowby (£3)		3	
William Yerley (£3)		3	
Philipp Bardfield (£3)		3	
Thomas Johnson (£5)		5	
Robert Puckell (£3)		3	
Thomas Langton (£5)		5	
Symon Webb (£4)		4	
Robert Younge (£3)		3	
295. John Moorton (£3)		3	
John Warall (£5)		5	
Arthure Goodgame (£3)		3	
John Eldrick (£5)		5	
Richard Flecknall (£3)		3	
William Anthonie (£3)		3	
Mathue Gravenor (£5) [a]		5	
Arthure Heskinges (£3)		3	
Humffrey Nailor (£5)		5	
William Beswick (£10)		10	
Thomas Burte (£25)		25	
William Tenche (£25)		25	
John East (£20)		20	
Richard Baker (£20)		20	
Henry Smythe (£10)		10	
John Tompkins (£5)		5	
Adam Davys (£3)		3	
Davis Tregron (£3)		3	
Bright Stoner (£3)		3	
Raphe Simpson (£5)		5	
Richard Handmore (£5)		5	
John Fleminge (£3)		3	
John Grene (£3)		3	
Thomas Fountaine (£6)		6	

	£	s.	d
Jonas Ludbrooke (£5)		5	
Ryce Gryffyn (£3)		3	
Thomas Bartridge (£5)		5	
Anthonie Playforth (£5)		5	
John Manners (£3)		3	
William Large (£3)		3	
John Whytby (£10)		10	
296. Rychard Handcocke (£10)		10	
Thomas Gylborne (£20)		20	
Thomas Jaxson (£10)		10	
Adam Johnson (£3)		3	
William Sherd (£5)		5	
Robert Snelling (£3)		3	
Laurence Cooke (£3)		3	
[r.66]			
Arnold Dunkin (£3)		3	
John Brownesmythe (£3)		3	
Thomas Prest (£3)		3	
John Pryce (£3)		3	
George Gillman (£3)		3	
Henry Glover (£6)		6	
Thomas Barry (£8)		8	
James Lockerson (£3)		3	
Thomas Adams (£5)		5	
Willyam Runyon (£5)		5	
Gryffin Evans (£3)		3	
Anthonye Etheridge (£3)		3	

Straungers:

	£	s.	d
Dyrick James (£40) [x - Southwark £3 14s.]	4		
Laurence Dondino (£20)		40	
Michael Gryffin alias Corsellis (£50)	5		
Roger van Payne (£50)	5		
John Billilng (£10) [a]		20	
John Bellewe (£10)		20	
Charles van Payne (£50) [b - Antwerp mer.]	5		
Alexaunder Buggard (£5)		10	
Henry Arnold (£3)		6	
Widow Dormere (£10)		20	
Niccholas Kinge (£5)		10	

297.   Straungers and straungers servauntes per poll

	£	s.	d
John Closse [a]			4
Garratt Crane [a]			4
Severin Swere			4
Roger Shornback			4
Jacob Elson			4
Richard Evans [a]			4

	£	s.	d
Servauntes dwelling within widow Dormers			
Jane Gorgrave			4
A servaunt dwelling with Michell Corsellys			
Segar Corsellys			4
Servantes dwelling with Niccholas Kinge			
Sarah Kinge			4
Lewys Angine			4
Reke Armose			4
Niccholas Johnson			4
Servauntes dwelling with Alexaunder Buggard			
Parnell Langswere			4
Haunse Boger			4
Joseph Kanowne			4
Servauntes dwelling within Dyrick James			
Hubett Dryson			4
Tyse Otten			4
Peter Driskye			4
Peter Heyner			4
Dirrick Mache			4
Poulse Cremer			4

298. A servaunt dwelling within Mr Campyon

	£	s.	d
Joseph Tapp			4
Servauntes dwelling within John Burgrave			
Anthony Reneare [a]			4
John Hudd [a][114]			4
Mathue Kinge [a]			4
Daniell Isling [a]			4
Leven Kinge [a]			4
A servaunt dwelling within Garratt Tryon			
Austen Vandorse			4
Servauntes dwelling within James Elsom			
Aron Caldron			4
John Ballyn			4
[r.67] Servauntes dwelling within Arnold Rutton			
Milker Johnson			4
Henry Luper			4
Niccholas Lyncklea			4
Garlyn Vanmouse			4
Peter Coune			4
Harbar Graunte			4

COMPAYNIES WITHIN THE SAYD WARD

	£	s.	d
The Dyers in landes (£16)		21	4
The Skinners (£100)	5		
The Inholders (£8)		8	

114. E.359/52, r. 13 gives surname as Wood.

	£	s.	d
The Tallowchaundlers in landes (£21)		28	
The Joyners (100s.)		5	
[Endorsed] Summa	127	15	8

299. [r.106]   FARINGDON WITHIN
[Petty collectors: Henry Mathewe, grocer, and John Ballett, goldsmith.]

ST PETERS IN CHEPE
[English]

Androwe Palmer in fees (£25)		33	4
Richard Morley, skynner (£60)	3	
Fraunces Langley belongong to Blackwell Hall (£6)		6
John Walker (£3)		3
William Harcott (£12)		12
William Skynner (£3)		3
Thomas Coke (£10)		10
Richard Mathewe (£3)		3
Thomas Stock (£5)		5

Straunger

Mathey Leyners (£4)		8

ST MATHEWES PARISHE
[English]

John Clark (£100)	5	
John Mabb thelder (£80)	4	
John Mabb thonger (£100)	5	
James Banckes (£100)	5	
George Warren (£3)		3
George Gatchett (£10)		10
Henry Eyre (£10)		10
Symon Edmondes (£10)		10
William Bereblock (£10)		10
Robert Elder (£3)		3
Thomas Covell (£6)		6
John Bradishe (£15)		15
William Snowe (£7)		7
Gaius Newman (£3)		3
Robert Dighton (£3)		3
Hanibal Gamon (£3)		3
Fraunces Morley (£3)		3
Henrye Sherland (£10)		10

300.   ST FOSTERS[115] & ST OLAVES PARISHES
[English]

William Denham (£150) [x - Surrey £3]	7	10

115. St. Vedast Foster Lane.

	£	s.	d
Robert Brandon (£120)	6		
William Dixson (£150) [a]	7	10	
Richard Howe (£100)	5		
Henry Gilbert (£160)	8		
Christofer Wasse (£100)	5		
Wydowe Lanyson (£50)		50	
Robert Wynch (£80)	4		
Henry Caulton (£70)	3	10	
Hughe Morgan Sessor (£150)	7	10	
Thomas Clerk (£60)	3		
Thomas Pope (£60)	3		
Robert Marshe (£60)	3		
Anthonye Bate (£50)		50	
Thomas Robertes (£50)		50	
Thomas Hartopp (£50)		50	
John Ballet (£100)	5		
Clement Skidmore (£60)	3		
Robert Medley (£50)		50	
Thomas Marshe gen (£100) [x - Mddx. £2]	5		
[r.107]			
Richard Foxe (£5)		5	
Robert Aske (£20)		20	
Robert Durant (£15)		15	
Roger Samuell (£5)		5	
James Pemberton (£15)		15	
James Nuthed (£5)		5	
William Webb (£5)		5	
Isaack Sutton (£18)		18	
Nicholas Hericke (£40)		40	
John Cockes (£10)		10	
Thomas Townley (£5)		5	
Richard Eales (£3)		3	
James Sharpuls (£3)		3	
Henry Whitacres (£3)		3	
William Furtho (£12)		12	
301. Robert Farington (£3)		3	
John Mothe (£3)		3	
John Hassall (£3)		3	
George Gardyner (£3)		3	
Manasses Stockton (£10)		10	
Nicholas Hilliard (£5)		5	
Robert Hutchen (£6)		6	
John Togood (£15)		15	
William Willis (£3)		3	
Fraunces Allen (£5)		5	
Robert Benne (£10) [x - Bread Street ward 20s.]		10	

	£	s.	d
Richard Wollaston (£18)		18	
John Worley & Ditton his partiner (£10)		10	
George Coles (£3)		3	
William Morrys (£7)		7	
Thomas Sympson (£3)		3	
Edward Parke (£3)		3	
William Lee (£3)		3	
John Coke & Want his partyner (£3)		3	
Walter Merell (£3)		3	
Christofer Merell (£8)		8	
Jerard Anderson (£3)		3	
Hughe Cotgrave alias Ritchemond (£10)[116]		10	
Edmonde Wheler (£10)		10	
Fraunces Roltes (£3)		3	
William Baldrey (£3)		3	
Robert Cowper (£3)		3	
Richard Harbert (£15)		15	
Richard Williams (£7)		7	
Christofer Corey (£15)		15	
William Awder (£6)		6	

Straungers per poll

Gilbert Johnson per pole			4
Mathewe Reynoldes per pole [a]			4

302.   ST OLAVES PARISHE IN MUGWELL STREAT
[English]

John Feild (£5)		5	
Stephen Fulwell (£15) [x - Q 8s. 4d.]		15	
Thomas Spight (£10)		10	
John Curwyn (£5)		5	
Fraunces Johnson (£10)		10	
Mathewe Chamberleyn (£3)		3	

ST AUGUSTYNES PARISHE
[English]

Edward Broke (£3)		3	
Fraunces Birde (£3)		3	
Launcelott Corbett (£3)		3	
John Crane (£15)		15	
Henry Jernegan esquier (£49) [a]		49	
Henry Barrowe gen (£15) [a]		15	
John Kyndon (£6)		6	
Robert Salter (£3)		3	
Peter Pereson (£3)		3	
Richard Halsey (£3)		3	

116. 'Harald ad arm' in margin. As Richmond herald, Cotgrave was exonerated by virtue of letters patent of 4 June 1549 and writ from the queen to the treasurer and barons dated 1 July 1581.

	£	s.	d
Symon Clynt (£3)		3	
Richard Hawley (£3)		3	
John Edwardes (£5) [a]		5	

ST MICHAELLS IN THE QUERNE
[English]

	£	s.	d
Henry Prannell (£200)	10		
Thomas Awdeley (£120)	6		
Thomas Bancke (£100)	5		
Robert Coggen (£50)		50	
Hughe Fairecloughe (£60)	3		
William Peake (£70) [x - Mddx. £1 10s.]	3	10	
Peter King (£12)		12	
Thomas Smith (£3)		3	
[r.108]			
John Browne (£5)		5	
Lawraunce Hawes (£5)		5	
William Serch (£5)		5	
Richard Sprignall (£12)		12	
Edward Marshall (£3)		3	
Richard Wynder (£10) [x - Surrey 8s. 4d.]		10	

	£	s.	d
303. William Brome, stacioner (£3)		3	
Walter Browne (£20) [ass. 50s. in Cripplegate ward]		20	
John Dicons (£3)		3	
Richard Bacon (£3)		3	
Henry Denham (£6)		6	
John Harryson thelder (£25)		25	
Robert Peacock (£5)		5	
Richard Wattes (£3)		3	
Richard Cornewell (£20)		20	
William Alleyn (£3)		3	
Fraunces Morgan (£6)		6	
Henrye Foster (£5)		5	
Henrye Mathewe (£8)		8	
John Mackerithe (£3)		3	
Nicholas Layfeild (£3)		3	
Thomas Modye (£15)		15	
Richard Amyas (£5)		5	
John Tyroe (£7)		7	
Richard Block (£3)		3	
Thomas Nedeham (£15)		15	
Richard Bradshawe (£3)		3	
Thomas Lee (£7)		7	
John Warde (£10)		10	
Christofer Sprentall (£6)		6	
Edward Flete (£10)		10	

	£	s.	d
Stephen Porter (£5)		5	
Thomas Wynter (£10)		10	
Richard Adams (£10)		10	
Anthonie Bingham (£8)		8	
John Ledham (£3)		3	
John Nott (£5)		5	
Owen Lloyde (£10) [a]		10	

Straunger

| Peter Marrowe straunger (£10) | | 20 | |

304.   ST FAITHES PARISHE
[English]

	£	s.	d
William Norton (£70)	3	10	
Peter Osborne esquier (£70)]			
[x - Westminster?]	3	10	
Sir Gyles Alyngton in landes (£150)			
[x - Cambs. £8 16s.]	10		
John Wyght (£50)		50	
Thomas Willet (£50) [x - Essex 20s.]		50	
Christofer Robynson (£50)		50	
Christofer Smith in fees (£20)		26	8
William Babham (£20)		26	8 [sic]
William Harbert in landes (£15) [a]		20	
John Walley (£3)		3	
Doctor Cesar (£10)		10	
Henrye Kynnersley (£3)		3	
William Mountjoye gen (£40) [x - Essex 5s.]		40	
Justinian Kidd (£15)		15	
William Geare (£10) [ass. 7s. in Kent]		10	
Phillipp Harryson (£5)		5	
William Bedill (£20)		20	
Paule Whitehorne (£10)		10	
George Langdale (£5) [x - Q 16s.]		5	
Thomas Golde (£3)		3	
Fraunces Phipps (£3)		3	
John God (£5)		5	
William Blackwell (£30)		30	
Robert Walker (£3)		3	
William Shatteswell (£3)		3	
Anthonie Lawe (£5) [ass. 10s. in Mddx.]		5	
Doctor Hone (£10)		10	
Thomas Lynne (£5)		5	
Richard Ward (£5)		5	
Andrewe Mansell (£3)		3	
Arthure Wilmott (£10) [a]		10	
Edward White (£3)		3	
Androwe Bower (£3)		3	
Olyver Wilkes (£3)		3	

	£	s.	d
305. Richard Veale (£3)		3	
John Burles (£5)		5	
Abraham Veale (£3)		3	
John Lynne (£6)		6	
Thomas Byrde (£5)		5	
Thomas Woodcock (£5)		5	
[r.109]			
Thomas Stirropp (£3)		3	
Richard Collyns (£3)		3	
Richard Watkyns (£10)		10	
Garret Dewes (£15)		15	
Abraham Kitson (£3)		3	
Gabriell Cawood (£5)		5	
Fraunces Coldock (£7)		7	
Stephen Smith (£3)		3	
William Emerey (£5) [a]		5	
George Bysshopp (£10)		10	
William Ponsonby (£3)		3	
Thomas Chaire (£5)		5	
Richard Glover (£3)		3	
Humfrey Cole (£3)		3	
Myles Jenynges (£3)		3	
John Hankynson (£6)		6	
Thomas Parke (£3)		3	
Thomas Rawlyns (£25) [a]		25	
William Sugden (£30) [a]		30	
Doctor Byngham (£10)		10	
Richard Smith (£5) [a]		5	
Straungers			
Arnold Brickman (£20)		40	
Martyn Harderetes (£20)		40	
Cornelis Dregg (£5) [x - Candlewick ward			
20s. as Drodger]		10	
Robert Fountayne (£10) [a]		20	
Claudius Holliband (£5) [a]		10	
Morrys Mabell (£25)		50	
James Coorte per pole [a]			4
306. ST MARTENS PARISHE WITHIN LUDGATE			
[English]			
Doctor Hussey (£60)	3		
John Blemor (£80)	4		
John Glascock (£50)		50	
Edward Brockett in landes (£40)			
[x - Bucks. 53s. 4d.]		53	4
Richard Tarleton (£10)		10	
Thomas Watton (£10)		10	
John Robynson (£20)		20	

229

	£	s.	d
John Hartford (£3)		3	
Thomas Gee (£20)		20	
Walter Bullock (£3)		3	
John Mascall (£20)		20	
William Dermer (£30)		30	
John Kiddye (£10)		10	
Nicholas Turnor (£3)		3	
Richard Maskall (£5)		5	
Edward Cowper (£3)		3	
Richard Nicolson (£35)		35	
Henrye Tayleford (£40)		40	
Thomas Coke (£5)		5	
John Hollingshead (£10)		10	
William Redston (£10)		10	
John Corket (£5)		5	
Thomas Standishe (£3)		3	
Roger Smithson (£6)		6	

Straungers

	£	s.	d
Rocko Bonetto (£6) [a]		12	
Roger Staffote (40s.)		4	
Andrewe Robynson por pole			4

307. CHRISTES CHURCH PARISHE
[English]

	£	s.	d
Thomas Fanshawe esquier in landes & fees			
(£40) [x - Herts.?]		53	4
Dorothye Maskall widowe (£50)		50	
John Short (£50)		50	
George Crowther (£170) [x - Mddx. £2]	8	10	
John Southwall (£80)	4		
Gamaliell Pye (£70)	3	10	
John Jackson (£100)	5		
John Laund (£100)	5		
John Incent (£50) [x - Essex 26s. 8d.]		50	
Michael Flemmyng in landes & fees (£5)		6	8
Doctor Smith in fees (£10)			
[ass. 50s. in Surrey][117]		13	4
Thomas Haselwood (£90) [ass. 13s. 4d.			
in Surrey]	4	10	
Fraunces Grene (£50)		50	
Robert Adams (£50)		50	
Raphe Fiche (£50)		50	
Robert Payne (£60)	3		
Edward Bigges in landes & fees (£20)		26	8
George Burgoigne in landes and fees (£20)			
[ass. 40s. in Herts.]		26	8

117. Identified as doctor of medicine in E.359/52, r. 10.

	£	s.	d
Richard Broughton in landes and fees (£20)		26	8
John Baker in landes & fees (£20)			
[x - Kent 21s. 4d.]		26	8
Thomas Baker in landes & fees (£20)			
[x - Kent 16s.]		26	8
Arthure Lee (£50)		50	
John Robotham (£10) [a]		10	
[r.110]			
Gilliam Treasourer (£10) [x - Q 8s. 4d.]		10	
Robert Lynne (£5)		5	
Robert Lorkyn (£3)		3	
John Clouney (£3)		3	
Thomas Mylner (£12)		12	
William Benson (£3)		3	
Thomas Page (£12)		12	
308. William Crowder (£5) [a]		5	
William Shearles (£15)		15	
Richard Atkynson (£5)		5	
Richard Letsham (£5) [x - Mddx.?]		5	
George Noden (£3)		3	
Richard Adamson (£5)		5	
Richard Parkyns (£5)		5	
William Dewes (£10)		10	
James Haselwood (£3)		3	
John Wiginton (£3)		3	
John Stockwood (£3)		3	
Thomas Goodyson (£8)		8	
John Hunter (£6)		6	
Edward Orwell (£30)		30	
Robert Sey (£10) [x - Mddx. 13s. 4d.]		10	
John Somers gen (£20) [x - Q 26s. 8d.]		20	
Godfrey Fanshawe (£10) [x - Essex 10s.]		10	
William Grey (£10)		10	
John Howe (£5)		5	
John Slye (£3)		3	
John Judson (£6)		6	
Robert Keare (£5)		5	
Martyn Parker (£3)		3	
Edward Holmes (£5)		5	
Edward Bysshopp (£3)		3	
William Thurlowe (£3)		3	
William Love (£3)		3	
Richard Waldyng (£6)		6	
William Povye (£3)		3	
John Povye (£25)		25	
Raff Jaxson (£3)		3	
Thomas Jaxson (£15)		15	

	£	s.	d
309. Henrye Boden (£3)		3	
Andrewe Walton (£3)		3	
Thomas Worshipp (£3)		3	
Arthure Parkyns (£7)		7	
Symon Lynche (£5)		5	
Robert Nixson (£3)		3	
Olyver Mason (£5)		5	
Hughe Bramley (£3)		3	
Martyn Stodderd (£3)		3	
Anthonye Wolcock (£6)		6	
Wydowe Ebden (£3)		3	
Richard Siberye (£3)		3	
Robert Barnard (£3)		3	
Thomas Sturman (£3)		3	
Christofer Dunkyn (£10)		10	
Henry Ellis iremonger (£15)		15	
John Hewson (£3)		3	
William Smalwood (£5)		5	
Thomas Blundell (£5)		5	
Richard Scales (£20)		20	
John Lawce (£5)		5	
Thomas Woster (£3)		3	
Henrye Shawe (£20) [ass. 20s. in Surrey]		20	
Richard Merin (£3)		3	
Wydowe Jugg (£10)		10	
Mighell Prior (£5)		5	
Rauff Heyward (£3)		3	
John Stapleford (£10) [x - Q 8s. 4d.]		10	
Fraunces Blithe (£10)		10	
John Turnor (£30) [x - Mddx. 11s.]		30	
Wydowe Fletcher (£3)		3	
John Walter (£20)		20	
310. William Maskall (£10)		10	
John Harryson (£10)		10	
Thomas Brayfeild (£5)		5	
Thomas King (£5)		5	
Hugh Knott (£6)		6	
Samuell Dole (£3)		3	
James Baylye (£3)		3	
John Bates (£10)		10	
John Ward (£5)		5	
Rauff Scull (£3)		3	
William Richardson (£20)		20	
John Hatter (£5)		5	
Wydowe [Joan] Best (£10) [x - Mddx. 8s.][118]		10	

118. E.359/52, r. 14 gives Joan as first name.

	£	s.	d
Walter Garnett (£5)		5	
Isaack Bing (£6)		6	
Thomas Harryson silkweaver (£3)		3	
Thomas Foxe (£5)		5	
William Pye (£20)		20	
Thomas Perye (£3)		3	
[r.111]			
Fraunces Clarke (£3)		3	
William Lawnde (£5)		5	
John Scrogges (£3)		3	
Robert Wood (£3)		3	
Thomas Ward (£8)		8	
Henrye Wyndridge (£6)		6	
Rice Hickes (£40)		40	

Straungers

	£	s.	d
Harmon Garretson (40s.)		4	
John Thompson straunger (40s.) [a]		4	

311.   ST ANNES AT BLACK FRYERS
[English]

	£	s.	d
Sir William More knight in landes (£70)			
[x - Surrey £3 6s. 8d.]	4	13	4
Anthonie Kempe gen in landes (£40) [a]		53	4
Robert Creswell (£10) [a]		10	
Vincent Skynner in landes & fees (£20)			
[x - Mddx. 26s. 8d.]		26	8
John Hare (£50)		50	
Sir Thomas Browne in landes (£70)			
[x - Surrey £5 6s. 8d.]	4	13	4
The Ladye Saunders in landes (£15)		20	
Sir George Carewe knight in landes (£40) [a]		53	4
William Cornewallis gen in landes (£20) [a]		26	8
Nicholas Hare gen in landes (£50)			
[x - Norfolk £2 13s. 4d.]	3	6	8
Sir Thomas Sherley knight in landes			
(£70) [x - Sussex £4]	4	13	4
John Lee gen (£20)		20	
William Honys in fees (£10) [a]		13	4
Mr Cote gen sewer in fees (£20) [a]		26	8
Robert Willowes gen in landes & fees			
(£20) [a]		26	8
Richard Browne esquier in landes (£20)			
[x - Surrey 26s. 8d.]		26	8
Robert Hewes (£3)		3	
Peter Swallowe (£5)		5	
Robert Dunkyn (£3)		3	
Robert Asheton (£3)		3	
John Wood (£3)		3	

	£	s.	d
George Barwick (£5)		5	
Andrewe Lyon (£3)		3	
Richard Alford (£5)		5	
Garret Sawcie (£5)		5	
Owen Lother (£3)		3	
Symon Prelio (£30) [a]		30	
John Dolling (£3)		3	
Bonaventure Eno (£3)		3	
William Joyner Mr of Defence (£3)		3	
Richard Fitzwater (£3)		3	
James Chedelton (£3)		3	
Edward Lane esquier (£40) [a]		40	
Mr [Blank] Hampton gen (£10) [a]		10	

312.   Straungers

	£	s.	d
John de Horse (£10)		20	
Askanius Reynolde (£10)		20	
Sebastian Bonfoy (£25)		50	
Martyn Garret (£10)		20	
Richard Buffo (£10)		20	
John de Mere (£20)		40	
Robert La Howlla (£10)		20	
Richard Tanfeild (£10)		20	
Angelo Victoria (£3)		6	
James More (£3)		6	
Hericke Almayne (£5)		10	
James Morgan (40s.)		4	
Jerome Hawley (£5)		10	
John Edwardes (£10)		20	
Nicholas Dewit (40s.)		4	
John Baptist (40s.)		4	
John Lewes (£5)		10	
Thomas Vantrolier (£15)		30	
Jerom Pipes (40s.)		4	
James Surmoyes (£7) [a]		14	
Henry Fowlewater (40s.)		4	
Peter Orman (£3)		6	
Michell Blanke (20s.)		2	
Glod Bevoys (20s.)		2	
Robert Baheire (£3)		6	
Reynold Buff (£5)		10	
Abraham Mighell (20s.)		2	
Peter Sage (20s.)		2	
Mathewe Garret (£5)		10	
Frauncis Nowey (£3)		6	
Peter Harvy (£3)		6	
Peter Segar (40s.) [a]		4	
Fraunces Rugo (40s.)		4	

	£	s.	d
John King (40s.)		4	
John Henrick (£3)		6	
[r.112]			

313.　　　　Black Fryers straungers per pole

Charles servaunt to James More per pole			4
Anthonoe Vanbright servaunt to Martyn			
Garret per pole			4
John Moreton & Barnard Bodwyn his man per pole			8
Gyses Hassell & Stephen Brewer servauntes to			
Henry Almayne per poles [a]			8
Christofer Lordynaeres goldsmith per pole			4
Harmon Buckhold goldsmith per pole			4
James Waterson & John Writyng servauntes to			
John Henrick per pole			8
Peter Latillier servaunt to James Morgan			
per pole			4
Peter de Giles servaunt to Bastyan Bonfoy			
per pole [a]			4
John Gasker fetherdresser per pole			4
Peter Bonevall fetherdresser per pole			4
Fraunces Lectuary perfumer per pole			4
Huble Garret, Garret Johnson, & William Fowke			
servauntes to Robert la Howlla per pole			12
Atkyn Dyviner [and] William Lewes servauntes			
to Nicholas Dewit per pole			8
Harman Boremaster [and] Peter Vandeclete			
servauntes to John Baptist per poles			8
Symon Brewer goldsmith & two men children			
per poles			12
Peter Oryng pynker per pole			4

314. Thomas Whitherspon servaunt to Henry

Fowlewater per pole			4
Peter Peck servaunt to Glode Bevoys per pole			4
Gillam the lame French preacher & iii men			
children per poles [a - 2 children]			16
Godfrey servaunt to Reynold Buff per pole			4
Lewes de Mayne cutler per pole [a]			4
Charles de Glasse & William Jacob servauntes			
to Abraham Mighell per poles [a]			8
Malcas Mentley goldsmith per pole			4
Peter Boys buttonmaker per pole			4
Gillam Anwick servaunt to Mathewe			
Garret per pole			4
Giles Bullenger & Anthonie Vernell			
servauntes to John de Horse per poles			8
Mr Fownteyne French preacher per pole			4

	£	s.	d
James Johnson servaunte to Fraunces Noway			
per pole			4
Bennett le Preter scholmaster per pole			4
Peter Peto taylor per pole			4
Nicholas Hatont cobler per pole			4
Guy Dybdale goldsmith & James Sotherland			
his man per pole			8
Anthonie Gero shoemaker per pole			4
Nicholas de Brewen servaunt with Askanius			
Reynaldo bokeseller per pole			4
Nicholas de Bars gilder per pole			4
Anthonie Garret cutler per pole [a]			4
Harman Copleman silversmith per pole			4
[Endorsed] Summa	435	18	8

315. [r.87]   FARRINGTON WITHOUT
[Petty collectors: Thomas Allyn, haberdasher, and Rychard Arnold, haberdasher.]

ST DUNSTONES PARISHE
[English]

	£	s.	d
Edwarde Cordell in landes and fees (£50)			
[x - Mddx. £2 13s. 4d.]	3	6	8
Thomas Powle in landes and fees (£70)			
[x - Essex £2 13s. 4d.]	4	13	4
Francis Alforde (£50)		50	
Margaret Draper widowe (£70)	3	10	
Sir Gilbert Garrat knight comissyoner			
in landes (£50)	3	6	8
John Croke in landes and fees (£50)			
[x - Bucks £4]	3	6	8
John Eve gent in landes and fees (£20)		26	8
Richard Bowser (£50)		50	
Christofer Whitchecock (£50)		50	
Henry Webbe (£60)	3		
William Salte (£50)		50	
Peter Legart (£40)		40	
Richard Tottle (£100)			
[ass. £2 13s. 4d. in Mddx.]	5		
Myles Doddinge in landes and fees (£10)		13	4
Henry Garnet (£50) [x - Mddx. 20s.]		50	
Richarde Garthe (£80)			
[x - Southwark £2]	4		
Anthony Burbage (£50)		50	
Christofer Downe (£50)		50	
Thomas Marshe (£60)	3		
Widowe ap Thomas (£50) [ass. 10s. 8d. in			
Mddx. as Margaret Morgan, widow]		50	

	£	s.	d
Thomas Powle the yonger in fees (£10) [ass. 16s. in Surrey]		13	4
Henry Dyner in landes (£20) [ass. 26s. 8d. in Norf.]		26	8
Thomas Gorge gent in landes (£40) [x - Q?]	2	13	4
Raffe Shelden esquier in landes (£150) [x - Worcs. £4]	10		
Sir Thomas Marvyn knight in landes (£67) [x - Q £4 8s.]	4	9	4
Sir Rowland Clarck knight in landes (£40) [a]	2	13	4
Mr John Popham Comissyoner in landes (£40) [x - Somerset 66s. 8d.]		40	[sic]
Robert Atkinson (£50) [x - Mddx. 40s.]		50	
Mistres Dister widowe (£40)		30	[sic]
John Martyn (£50)		50	
Charles Morison gen in landes (£40) [x - Herts. £2 13s. 4d.]	2	13	4
Thomas Roper gen in landes and fees (£100) [x - Kent £6 13s. 4d.]	6	13	4
Henry Jones in landes and fees (£10)		13	4
316. Mistres [Elizabeth] Alford widowe in landes (£30) [x - Bucks 40s.][119]		40	
William Gosnall in landes (£20) [ass. 5s. in Farringdon ward Without as Gosnold]		26	8
Thomas Johnson (£3)		3	
John Williams (£3)		3	
John Hill (£10)		10	
George Sydgeweke (£3)		3	
Daniel Botham (£3)		3	
Humfreye Wood (£3)		3	
Richard Hawse (£5)		5	
Dorothie Dalton widowe (£3)		3	
William Allen (£3)		3	
Thomas Cartwrighte (£6)		6	
Mr Buttes gent in Cartwrightes howse (£5) [a]		5	
Robert Fyxer (£3)		3	
[r.88]			
John Redman (£3)		3	
William Forrest gent (£16) [ass. 30s. in Mddx.]		16	
The Ladye Sherington (£30) [a]		30	
Edward Rust gent (£5)		5	

119. E.359/52, r. 14 gives Elizabeth as first name.

	£	s.	d
Mr Doctor Johnson (£10)		10	
Symon Penyall (£3)		3	
Thomas Westesse (£3)		3	
William Balle (£3)		3	
Robert Spatchurste (£3)		3	
Raffe Allinson (£5)		5	
James Berrye (£3)		3	
Henrye Tottye (£3)		3	
Richard Catcher (£5)		5	
Thomas Catcher (£25)		25	
Nicholas Brome (£3)		3	
George Colburne gent (£35)		35	
Robert Westwood (£3)		3	
Richarde Wistowe (£3)		3	
John Hedge (£3)		3	
Thomas Hollowaye (£25) [x Q 20s.]		25	
John Howle (£3)		3	
William Crowche (£6)		6	
317. Henry Knowles (£3)		3	
John Morgaine (£3)		3	
John Hinson (£3)		3	
Peter Hardcastell (£5)		5	
Christofer Hunt (£3)		3	
William Turner (£5)		5	
Henrye Carpenter (£13)		13	
Elizabethe Kennett (£3)		3	
John Horner (£5) [a]		5	
Mistres Newton widowe (£12)		12	
Thomas Welche in Mistres Newtons howse (£30)		30	
John Cokxe (£15)		15	
Richard Greene (£15)		15	
Henrye Midleton (£8)		8	
Edward Pittes in Greenes howse (£45) [x - Worcs.?]		45	
Deonize Armes (£5)		5	
Richard Hughes (£5)		5	
George Bull (£10)		10	
Thomas Dawson (£3)		3	
George Allen (£5)		5	
Thomas Smithe (£3)		3	
Henrye Robinson (£25)		25	
Thomas Lloyde (£3)		3	
Raffe Crowe (£3)		3	
John Adeson (£3)		3	
Mistres Lockey wydowe (£10)		10	
Henrye Payne (£12)		12	
Mistres Ellsinge widowe (£30)		30	

	£	s.	d
Edward Turrell (£5)		5	
Doctor Dodding in Ellsinges howse (£10)		10	
John Roman (£3)		3	
Raffe Jackson (£3)		3	
Thomas Sandes (£16)		16	
Widowe Garlike (£8)		8	
Richard Rogers (£3)		3	
Mistris Millesent (£10)		10	
318. Walter Meredithe (£4)		4	
William Cooke (£10)		10	
Roger Aldriche (£3)		3	
Widowe Hodgeson (£3)		3	
John Warde (£3)		3	
Humffreye Leighton (£5)		5	
Thomas Bland (£10)		10	
John Marshall (£10)		10	
[r.89]			
William Pascall (£3)		3	
Raffe Rogers (£10)		10	
Richard Brewster gent (£30)		30	
Walter Brumall (£3)		3	
John Walker (£20)		20	
Emanuell Maunsell (£16)		16	
Edward Wayland (£3)		3	
Henrye Leyke (£10)		10	
William Howe (£10)		10	
Symon Cannon (£5)		5	
John Dalton (£10)		10	
Richard Holdernes (£5)		5	
Christofer Goore (£6)		6	
Walter Goore (£10)		10	
Richard Fowlkes (£30) [x - Q 44s.]		30	
John Clarke (£3)		3	
Henrye Beverley (£3)		3	
William Kingseleye (£25)		25	
Martyne Garrett (£3)		3	
Thomas Nogaye (£8)		8	
John Welles (£5)		5	
Edward Whittingham (£8)		8	
William Emes (£35)		35	
Lawrence Holdon (£10)		10	
John Barnard (£5)		5	
Richard Warren (£5)		5	
319. CHAUNCERIE LANE			
Thomas Harris (£8)		8	
William Bovee (£6)		6	

	£	s.	d
John Newsame (£5)		5	
Thomas Caper (£3)		3	
Humfreye Dalleye (£3)		3	
William Campe (£3)		3	
Paule Conington (£3)		3	
William Pratt (£5)		5	

CROWNE COURTE

Wydowe Martynne (£6)	6
John Collere (£10)	10

CHAUNCERY LANE ABOVE THE
FIELD GATES AND IN THE FIELDES

Symon Williams (£3) [a]	3
George Carter (£3) [x - Mddx. 4s.]	3
Humfreye Aplegate gent (£20)	
[x - Mddx. 12s.]	20
Peter Richardson (£5)	
[x - Mddx. 3s.]	5
Fraunces Kempe (£40)	
[x - Mddx. 20s.]	40
John Foorde gent (£45) [x - Sussex 40s.]	45
Roger Marvyn gent (£5) [x - Mddx. 5s.]	5
Roger Tysdale (£3) [x - Mddx. 3s.]	3
John Bavington (£5) [x - Mddx. 4s.]	5
Henrye Sacheverell (£3) [x - Mddx. 3s.]	3
John Yonge (£3) [x - Mddx. 4s.]	3
Thomas Partridge (£3) [x - Mddx. 4s.]	3
Roger Pratt (£5) [x - Mddx. ?]	5
Mr [John] Rotheram one of the Sixe Clarkes	
(£30) [x - Mddx. 20s.][120]	30
Mr Doctor Carye (£30)	
[x - Mddx. 20s.]	30
Mr Moolenoxe (£10) [x - Notts. 40s.]	10
Sir Edward Herbertt (£40) [a]	40
Thomas Manlye gent (£10) [a]	10
Mr Waldron gent (£10) [x - Somerset	
26s. 8d.]	10
Mr Lowe gent (£20) [x - Staffs. 4s.]	20

320.   FEWTER LANE

Mistris Vynes wydowe (£5) [x - Oxon.?]	5
Mr John Thomas (£5)	5
George Dyer gent (£6)	6
Michaell Forde gent (£5) [ass. 15s. in	
Mddx.]	5

120. E.359/52, r. 14 gives John as first name.

	£	s.	d
George Pyttes gent (£3)		3	
Mr Ferrys (£6) [a]		6	
Richard Rooke gent (£3)		3	
Thomas Bysseye (£8)		8	
Thomas Pagett gent (£10)			
[x - Northants. 8s.]		10	
Arthure Corye gent (£10)		10	
[r.90]			
Richard Ryder gent (£10)		10	
John Taylor (£10) [ass. 6s. 8d. in Surrey]		10	
William Hollowaye (£3)		3	
Robertt Johnson (£3)		3	
Thomas Gryffyn (£5) [a]		5	
John Cotton gent (£40) [a]		40	
Mr Radforthe one of the Pregintories			
(£40) [a]		40	

THE WHITE FRYERS

	£	s.	d
Mr George Hayes (£20)		20	
Thomas Staunton (£10)		10	
William Gosnold (£5) [x - Farringdon ward			
Without 26s. 8d. as Gosnall]		5	
Gentill Greenfield (£12) [ass. 20s.			
in Mddx.]		12	
John Burden (£20)		20	
Thomas Lucas (£10)		10	
William Gunter (£5)		5	
Thomas Newton (£5) [a]		5	
Thomas Payne (£5)		5	
Margarett Browne widowe (£3)		3	
Edward Gryffythe (£5)		5	

Straungers

Sampson Morden jeweller (£10)		20	

Strangers in the White Fryers

John Asson servaunt with Mistris			
Draper poll			4
John van Champenhant servant with John			
Tandye poll			4

321. ST BRIDES PARISHE
[English]

	£	s.	d
John Stone (£60)	3		
Paule Pope (£60)	3		
Edmond Bragge (£50)		50	
Richard Crowche (£50)		50	
William Baynam gent in landes (£40)			
[x - Kent?}	2	13	4
John Hyde (£60)	3		

	£	s.	d
Mr William Hanbye gent in Hydes house			
in landes (£40) [a]	2	13	4
Robert Walker (£50)		50	
Widowe [Frances] Sanbatche in landes and			
fees (£20) [ass. 26s. 8d. in Kent][121]		26	8
Henrye Jones in landes and fees (£20)		26	8
Bryan Onslowe gent in landes (£40) [a]	2	13	4
Mary Frenche widowe in landes (£15)		20	
Mistris [Elizabeth] Snowe in landes (£20)			
[x - Beds. 33s. 4d.][122]		26	8
George Kempe in fees (£10) [x - Suffolk?]		13	4
Sir Christofer Allyn in landes (£40)			
[x - Kent £2 13s. 4d.]	2	13	4
John Fernham in landes and fees (£30)			
[x - Q 40s.]		40	
Edward Fisher in landes and fees (£20) [a]		26	8
Edward Tirrell in landes (£20) [ass. 80s. in Essex]		26	8
Michael Harcot in landes and fees (£20)			
[x - Bucks 32s.]		26	8
The Lady [Elizabeth] Goldinge in landes (£40)			
[x - Kent £2 13s. 4d.][123]	2	13	4
Hierome Westone in landes and fees (£20)			
[x - Essex 26s. 8d.]		26	8
Doctor Salisburye (£50) [a]		50	
Henrye Studleye (£6)		6	
William Howson (£6)		6	
Mistris Stafford widowe (£10)		10	
Nicholas Maddoxe (£8)		8	
Margaret Crathorne widowe (£20)		20	
James Kenvyne (£5)		5	
322. Peter Noxton (£15)		15	
John Yeardelye (£8)		8	
Richarde Mathewe (£10)		10	
Henrye Peacher (£10)		10	
John Hill (£5)		5	
Edward Trussell (£3)		3	
Anthonye Pryor (£3)		3	
Nicholas Hawkefford (£5)		5	
Davie Gryffithe (£3)		3	
John Okelye (£3)		3	
Lawrence Hill (£10)		10	
Hughe Willson (£5)		5	
Ellis Harris (£5) [ass. 3s. in Aldgate			
ward as Harrison]		5	

121. E.359/52, r. 6 gives Frances as first name.
122. E.359/52, r. 14 gives Elizabeth as first name.
123. E.359/52, r. 14 gives Elizabeth as first name.

	£	s.	d
[r.91]			
William Horneblowe (£10) [ass. 10s. in			
Castle Baynard ward]		10	
William Robinson (£20)		20	
Thomas Midlebrooke (£3)		3	
John Marshe (£8)		8	
John Dixson (£3)		3	
Peter Frenche (£5)		5	
Roger Knowles (£5)		5	
William Thatcher (£10)		10	
William Sutton (£5)		5	
Richard Saunders (£3)		3	
William Negoose (£3)		3	
Christofer Huson (£15)		15	
John Pickevans (£3)		3	
William Cowdrye (£5)		5	
Richard Attkinson (£8)		8	
John Dodgeson (£5)		5	
323. Cuttbertt Edone (£20)		20	
Edmond Lested (£8)		8	
Robertt Parramore (£5)		5	
William Yomans (£5)		5	
Henrye Trussell (£10)		10	
Thomas Fartlowe (£3)		3	
Humfrey Wemmes (£15)		15	
Henrye Alderseye (£10)		10	
Peter Koe (£5)		5	
John Nightingale (£8)		8	
Raffe Balle (£10)		10	
Nicholas Blasedon (£5)		5	
Robertt Plowman (£3)		3	
Richard Veale (£20)		20	
Walter Fytchett (£3)		3	
Gregorye Heathe (£3)		3	
George Tuke (£3)		3	
Richard Freeman (£5)		5	
Walter Gunter (£5)		5	
Bryan Holmes (£3)		3	
Edmund Austyne (£5)		5	
Roger Yonge (£5)		5	
Bartholomewe Quynie (£25)		25	
Phillipp Williams (£5)		5	
Thomas Foulkes (£3)		3	
Hughe Brawne (£25)		25	
Thomas Swynton (£10) [x - Beds. 10s.]		10	
Thomas Masham (£3)		3	
William Allett (£5)		5	

	£	s.	d
324. Mr. Larke gent (£20) [x - Essex 26s. 8d.]		20	
Richard Foxe (£5)		5	
Robert Johnson (£3)		3	
Thomas Fielde (£5)		5	
Lawrence Cotton (£3)		3	
Robert Stanger (£8)		8	
Mr Bluntt (£10)		10	
Robert Richardson (£8)		8	
Nicholas Kinge (£8)		8	
Roger Allenson (£3)		3	
Nicholas Burton (£6)		6	
John Eaton (£5)		5	
Thomas Stothard (£8)		8	
Frauncis Stubbinge (£10)		10	
Frauncis Farrowe (£15)		15	
Thomas Hill (£3)		3	
Valentyne Penson (£5)		5	
Edward Sleepe (£10)		10	
Edmond Harryson (£3)		3	
[r.92]			
Robert Jenkinson the elder (£20)		20	
John Hill brewer (£10)		10	
Robert Furneys (£3)		3	
Mr Stoninge (£5) [a]		5	
John Skott (£3)		3	
William Harveye (£3)		3	
Raffe Newberye (£12)		12	
James Taylor (£10)		10	

325. SALISBURYE COURT WITHIN AND WITHOUT

	£	s.	d
Hughe Russell (£10)		10	
John Robins (£3)		3	
Thomas Sallett (£3)		3	
John Treavor (£20)		20	

THE WOOD WHARFE

	£	s.	d
Thomas Andrewes (£5)		5	
John Blande (£10)		10	
Myles Berrye (£3)		3	

SHOOE LANE

	£	s.	d
Robert Yonger (£5)		5	
John Foster (£3)		3	
Edward Marten (£3)		3	

THE FLEETE LANE AND THE FLEETE RENTES

	£	s.	d
Edward Mathewe (£3)		3	
Leonard Lockeye (£3)		3	

	£	s.	d
Straungers in the Fleete Rentes			
Anthonye Squeerre poll			4
Symon Shevaler poll			4
Oliver Eskirke poll			4
Nicholas Sermoyes (20s.)		2	
Anthonye Herringe (20s.)		2	
Michael Saroe (20s.)		2	
John Marya (20s.)		2	
Barbara Lymberger (20s.)		2	
Venissynt Grushe poll			4
WITHIN BRYDEWELL			
Mistris Gybson wydowe (£5)		5	
George Grymes (£5)		5	
William Goulde (£5)		5	
William Kinge (£5)		5	
Straungers within Brydwell			
Marten Pynnoxe (20s.)		2	
Gillam Latten poll			4
326. **GRENES RENTES**			
John Monyngton (£3)		3	
Richard Guye (£3)		3	
Humfreye Armitage (£3)		3	
Rowland Allen (£3)		3	
Wyllyam Woode (£3)		3	
Straungers in Greenes Rentes			
Ellis Brewyn (20s.)		2	
Mason Johnson (40s.)		4	
Gillam Bargett poll			4
James Drassinge poll			4
James Delonge poll			4
Romayne Myndemer poll			4
SAYNCTE BRYDES CHURCHE YEARDE			
Arthure Faunte (£5)		5	
George Pyttes (£3)		3	
Straungers in Popingey Alleye			
Peter Cherytree poll			4
John Palmer poll			4
John Fraunces poll			4
James his sonne poll			4
Straungers in Blacke Horse Allye			
Peter Glamore poll			4
Arnolde Smythe (20s.)		2	
[r.93]			
Peter Horson poll			4
Gillam Countt poll			4

	£	s.	d
Florence Debocke poll [a][124]			4
Michaell Borsham poll [a][125]			4
Straungers in Shooe Lane			
Peter Dowsett (20s.)		2	
Hughe Hubbard de Vele (20s.)		2	
John Wetherspoone poll			4
Collsell Maugham poll			4

327.   ST MARTYNS PARISHE
[English]

	£	s.	d
Sir Thomas Bromley knight Lord Chaunccellor of England in landes (£50)	3	6	8
Thomas Allyn (£60)	3		
Richarde Elesworth in landes and fees (£10)		13	4
Jasper Chlmdley [sic] (£50) [x - Mddx. 40s.]		50	
Thomas Spackman (£60) [x - Essex £1]	3		
Richard Arnold (£30)		30	
John Savage gent in landes (£20)		26	8
Mistris Alington widowe (£100)	5		
Mr George Carie in Mistris Allingtons house in landes (£40) [x - Devon £2 13s. 4d.]	2	13	4
Sir Henry Woodhouse knight in landes (£40) [a]	2	13	4
Hughe Overend (£3)		3	
Robert Newman (£3)		3	
James Willmore (£3)		3	
Richard Wilkinson (£5)		5	
Fordinando Maline (£8) [ass. 10s. in Mddx. as Malinge]		8	
John Leighton (£5)		5	
Thomas Antrobus (£10)		10	
Florence Cawldwell (£20)		20	
Nicholas Wolleye (£12)		12	
Anthonie Tryme (£3)		3	
Thomas Lee (£3)		3	
Walter James (£5)		5	
John Graunge (£25)		25	
John Richardson (£5)		5	
Charles Wodmyster (£10)		10	
Henrye Leythelye (£3)		3	
Edmond Beningefilde (£40) [x - Suffolk 53s. 4d.][126]		40	
John Studseburye (£3)		3	

124. E.359/52, r. 14 gives surname as de Hece.
125. E.359/52, r. 14 gives surname as Bersham.
126. E.359/52, r.14 gives surname as Beddingfeld.

	£	s.	d
328. Richard Hatcheman (£3)		3	
Henrye Naylor (£6)		6	
John Higginson (£3)		3	
Jeoffrye Ponde (£15) [x - Q 24s.]		15	
John Leeche (£5)		5	
William Gilbertt (£3)		3	
Richard Swifte gent (£30) [x - Essex 12s.]		30	
Humfreye Huntt (£12)		12	
Thomas Flaskett (£6)		6	
John Elles (£5)		5	
Robertt Ibatson (£5)		5	
Thomas Goodman (£5)		5	
John Warrenor (£10)		10	
Thomas Taylor (£5)		5	
Edward Gryffithe (£12)		12	
Rowland Collson (£3)		3	
Christofer Lambertt (£12)		12	
Roger Walker (£6)		6	
Robert Broughe (£6)		6	
William Eardelye (£8)		8	
John Bladon (£6)		6	
Walter Westmerland (£5)		5	
Edmond Hasellwood (£5)		5	
William Cleybrooke (£8)		8	
Robert Newdicke (£20)		20	
William Frythe (£3)		3	
Richard Frythe (£10)		10	
Edward Branden (£5)		5	

329. ST BARTHOLOMEWES THE LESSE PARISHE
[English]

	£	s.	d
Hierome Hawley (£60) [x - Mddx. £1 6s. 8d.] [r.94]	3		
William Burcher (£10)		10	
Mistris Hone widowe in landes (£10)		13	4
Doctor Turner in fees (£10)		13	4
Robert Collette gent (£20)		20	
Thomas Martyn lawyer (£3)		3	
Mistris Frauncis Pryce gentylwoman (£20)		20	
William Knight (£5)		5	
Albone Clerck gent (£10) [a]		10	
Robert Nicolas blackesmythe in landes (£10)		13	4
Elizabeth Byckenton widowe (£3)		3	
Ellyn Kettelborowe widowe (£3)		3	
John Marryat taylor (£3)		3	
Myles Haward coppersmythe (£5)		5	
Thomas Baker taylor (£3)		3	
George Etheridge gent (£3)		3	

	£	s.	d
John Henry glover (£3)		3	
Straungers			
Balteser Bucke (£3)		6	
Maryan Delamus poll			4
Peter Grave poll			4
Thomas Dyshane and his wife poll			8
Mathewe Johnsan poll			4

330. ST BARTHOLOMEWES THE GRETE
[English]

	£	s.	d
Sir Walter Mildmaye knight Comissyner			
[Blank]	[Blank]		
The Lorde Chefe Baron [Sir Roger Manwood]			
in landes (£100) [x - Kent			
£3 6s. 8d.][127]	6	13	4
The Lady Catlyn in landes (£40)	2	13	4
William Neale Auditor (£100) [x - Hants. £2]	5		
Philip Skidmore (£100) [x - Bucks. £1 5s.]	5		
William Colsell in fees (£10)		13	4
Richarde Spurlinge (£10) [x - ? 10s.]		10	
William Brande in landes and fees (£10)			
[ass. 42s. 8d. in Surrey]		13	4
Rychard Brokman in landes and fees (£15)			
[x - Surrey 20s.]		20	
Laurence Argall in landes and fees (£20)			
[x - Mddx. 26s. 8d.]		26	8

THE LIBERTYE AND CLOSSE OF GREATE ST BARTHOLOMUES
[English]

	£	s.	d
Nycholas Wyllye gent (£6 13s. 4d.)		6	[sic]
Ursula Garret widowe (£5)		5	
Katheryne Durant widowe (£5)		5	
Henry Fynche fyshmonger (£6 13s. 4d.)		6	
Morrys Spleman tayllor (£5)		5	
Thomas Shepard tayllor (£6 13s. 4d.)		6	
Jhon Shawe scrivener (£4)		4	
Roger Jones tayllor (£4)		4	
Morrys Thomas tayllor (£4)		4	
Straungers			
John Symondes poll			4

331. ST SEPULCERS PARISHE
[English]

	£	s.	d
Edward Basshe esquier in landes (£150)			
[x - Herts. £4 8s.]	10		
Augustine Stuart in landes and fees (£20)		26	8

127. E.359/52, r. 14 gives the chief baron's name.

	£	s.	d
Robert Baltroppe in fees (£30)			
[x - Q 66s. 8d.]		40	
Mathew Martyn (£50)		50	
Mistris Averie widowe (£60)	3		
William Fitzwilliams in landes (£20)		26	8
George Monox gent in landes (£30)			
[ass. 44s. in Essex]		40	
Thomas Lodge in fees (£15) [ass. 10s. in Essex]		20	
Henry Spence (£50)		50	
William Herrynge (£50) [x - Essex 10s.]		50	
Edmond Morrant in fees (£15)		20	
William Gardyner (£200) [x - Surrey			
£1 6s. 8d.]	10		
Thomas Hollingshed (£50)		50	
Gregory Newman (£40)		40	
Hughe Stewkley gent in landes (£60)			
[x - Somerset £2 13s. 4d.]	4		
William Gomersall (£100) [x - Mddx.£1 6s. 8d.]	5		
Rowland Hynde (£120) [x - Bucks. £1 6s. 8d.]	6		
Thomas Digges in landes and fees (£20)		26	8
Thomas Crompton (£50) [x - Essex 20s.]		50	
Richarde Warde in landes (£40) [x - Q			
£1 14s. 8d.]	2	13	4
Francis Ram in landes and fees (£10)			
[x - Essex 10s. 8d.]		13	4
John Horssey in landes (£10)		13	4
[r.95]			
Christofer Haiefield in landes (£10)[128]		13	4
Doctor Barnesdale in fees (£10)		13	4
Richarde Branthwaite in fees (£10)		13	4
Doctor [Thomas] Hall in fees (£10)			
[ass. 5s. in Mddx.][129]		13	4
John Skynner in landes and fees (£20) [a]		26	8
Thomas Burgen gent in landes (£30) [a]		40	
Richard Swifte in landes and fees (£20)			
[x - Essex 12s.]		26	8
Strangers			
Guilliaume Lamadie (£16)		32	

332.   SMYTHEFILDE QUARTER
                          [English]

	£	s.	d
James Rolf (£3)		3	
Roger Charleton (£4)		4	
Willyam Webbe (£7) [x - Q 8s.]		7	

128. A marginal notation O [oneratur] indicates that Haiefield was discharged in another place and remained liable for the present assessment, but I did not note a corresponding entry in the enrolled accounts, E.359/52.
129. E.359/52, r. 13 gives Thomas as first name.

	£	s.	d
John Warde (£6)		6	
Thomas Townley (£5)		5	
John Hawkefford Clerke of the Exchequer			
(£6) [ass. 10s. in Essex as Hawkeswell]		6	
John Johnson (£3)		3	
William Allyn (£10)		10	
Mychaell Owen Clerke of the Exchequer (£10)		10	
Mistris Wilbraham widowe (£5)		5	
Robert Secoll (£3)		3	
Arnolde Aprice (£5) [a]		5	
John Cheswick (£3)		3	
John Lune the Common Hunte (£4)		4	
John Gaskyn (£6)		6	
William Fulwood (£12)		12	
Master Dewe (£3)		3	
Bartylmewe Yardley (£3)		3	
William Rock (£3)		3	
Stephan Taylor (£3)		3	
Richard Bradshawe (£3)		3	
Leonard Smythe (£5)		5	
Thomas Garret (£4)		4	
Thomas Watwood (£3)		3	
Robert Whawley (£3)		3	
Nycholas Scryvenor (£5)		5	
Widowe Wood (£20)		20	
William Ireland (£5)		5	
Thomas Atkinson (£10)		10	
Humfrye Pountney (£5)		5	
333. Edward Fletcher (£6)		6	
William Borne (£8)		8	
Bryan Garvey (£5)		5	
James Gonnell (£10)		10	
Robert Rolf (£6)		6	
Christofer Hatfeild (£8) [ass. 6s. 8d. in Surrey]		8	
Thomas Spivye (£3)		3	
Arthure Mewes stranger poll			4
Thomas Kingeffeld (£5)		5	
William Freman (£8)		8	
Richard Wright (£3)		3	
William Buerdsell (£3)		3	
John Hunnynge (£3)		3	
Humfry Winington Clarke to the Chamber (£8)		8	
James Browne serjeant (£10)		10	
Henry Callowaye (£3)		3	
William Allyn yoman (£3)		3	
Richard Walker apperteyninge to Justice			
Southcote (£3)		3	

	£	s.	d
John Waters Sir Christofer Hattons man (£10)		10	
John Avasene (£4)		4	
John Webster (£5)		5	
John Bowland (£3)		3	
John Scarlet gent (£12)		12	
Mr Scott (£10)		10	
Mr Wyatt (£10)		10	
Mr Carden (£10) [x - Q 32s.]		10	
Edward Powell (£4)		4	
Raffe John, Judge Southcotes man (£3)		3	

334. Rychard Payne (£4)   4
Thomas Rogerson (£4)   4
William Shawe (£4)   4
Stephen Horton (£3)   3
[r.96]
John Stephens (£20)   20
Walter Rypond (£15) [x - Q 13s. 4d.]   15
John Harryat (£5)   5
John Hawkyns (£5)   5
John Bygges (£3)   3
John Rolfe (£5)   5
Henry Androwes (£3)   3
Arthure Agar Clarke of thexchequer (£5)   5
John Myller (£4)   4
Thomas Idle (£7)   7
Thomas Robertes (£3)   3
Thomas Broke (£5)   5
Thomas Maryatt (£3)   3
Thomas Browne trumpiter (£3)   3
James Edwardes (£3)   3
Allexaunder H̃ytchin (£4)   4
John Odwaie (£3)   3
John Gryffyn (£3)   3
Richard Matyson (£10)   10
John Shawe merchauntt (£3)   3

ST SEPULCHERS PARISHE HOLBORNE CROSSE QUARTERS
[English]
Raffe Smythe (£3)   3
Richard Payne (£3)   3
George Sharples (£8)   8
Nicholas Robertes (£6)   6
Christofer Beettes (£4)   4
Widowe Cowper (£3)   3
James Boytell (£3)   3

335. Henry Bradshawe (£3)   3

	£	s.	d
John Horsley (£3)		3	
Symon Bentley (£3)		3	
Edward Harper (£10)		10	
John Kylbye (£3)		3	
Powell Rychards (£3)		3	
Richard Williams (£3)		3	
Fraunces Bybson (£3)		3	
Anthony Bere (£20)[130]		20	
Robert Mylles (£3)		3	
Richard Waight (£3)		3	
William Norton (£5)		5	
Stephen Rogers (£5)		5	
Cornelis Caters (£14)		14	
Richard Smythe (£10)		10	
Thomas Ladam (£3)		3	
Thomas Sharpe serjeant (£3)		3	
William Mason (£3)		3	
Thomas Willson (£3)		3	
Thomas Peake (£3)		3	
William Downes (£3)		3	
John Anokes (£5)		5	
Richard Jones (£4)		4	
Robert Showre (£3)		3	
Roger Caron (£20)		20	
John Thompson (£3)		3	
Thomas Osborne (£4)		4	
Hughe Olliver (£3)		3	
Thomas Wattes (£5)		5	
John Gravener (£3)		3	
Henry Parker (£3)		3	
336. Fraunces Adames (£3)		3	
Molher Gallowaie (£3)		3	
John Cleyton (£15)		15	
Edward Owin (£3)		3	
Henry Parkins (£3)		3	
Hughe Lewes (£5)		5	
John Mattingley (£8)		8	
[r.97]			
William Freman and his sonne, strangers poll			8
Humfrey Foxall (£5)		5	
Ellys Boystell (£3)		3	
Fraunces Labroyle straunger (£5)		10	
Mr Quille one of the quenes majestes garde (£10) [x - Q 24s.]		10	

130. 'Offic inf' turr' London' in margin. Exonerated by virtue of letters patent dated 23 June 1581 (E.359/52, r. 14).

	£	s.	d
Henry Stapleforthe (£3)		3	
Mr. [John] Kelley (£20) [x - Q 24s.][131]		20	
Edward Riddowe (£3)		3	
George Newell (£3)		3	
Peter Duckanoye stranger (£3)		6	
Christofer Kellett (£3)		3	
John Saxbey (£8)		8	
Davye Powell (£5)		5	
William Jarden (£16)		16	
Christofer Ladan (£3)		3	
John Pyper (£12)		12	
Robert Kytchin (£3)		3	
Thomas Downer (£6)		6	
Willyam Ley (£4)		4	
Zacharye Collier (£18)		18	

337.   THE CHURCHE QUARTER ST SEPULCHERS PARISHE

	£	s.	d
Thomas Warren (£20) [ass. 10s. in Essex]		20	
Davye Jones (£3)		3	
William Parratt (£5)		5	
Widowe Bettes (£3)		3	
Oliver Duchey de la Villa poll [a]			4
Robert Slater (£3)		3	
Robert Peacocke (£5)		5	
George Strange (£5)		5	
Ellys Jones (£12)		12	
John Stokes (£3)		3	
Richard Alestree (£3)		3	
John Hobson (£3)		3	
Richard Lawrence (£5) [a]		5	
Jarvys Dunbery (£3)		3	
William Conwaye (£12)		12	
Leonerd Johnson stranger poll			4
Mathewe Austyn (£5)		5	
Edward Owyn (£3)		3	
Robert Aldred (£30)		30	
Willyam Symcocke (£10)		10	
Garrett Boyce (£3)		3	
Mr Cason gent (£12)		12	
Rychard Shepard (£8)		8	
Widowe Downes (£4)		4	
Thomas Martyn (£5)		5	
Gabriell Martyn straunger (£4)		8	
John Mahewe (£4)		4	
Thomas Hatfeild (£8)		8	
William Powell (£3)		3	

131. E.359/52, r. 14 gives John as first name.

	£	s.	d
Widowe Strange (£3)		3	
Raffe Rogers (£3)		3	
James Armorer gent (£15) [x - Mddx. 6s.]		15	
William Johnson Clarke of Newgate (£6)		6	

338. Thomas Goodman (£6) | | 6 |
Richard Lowden (£3) | | 3 |

338. Thomas Goodman (£6)		6	
Richard Lowden (£3)		3	
William Lambert (£3)		3	
Hughe Evans (£3)		3	
Leonard Kinge (£10)		10	
Thomas Fuller (£5)		5	
John Hewes (£5)		5	
Thomas Hampton (£5)		5	
[r.98]			
Jerome Greneham (£3)		3	
Roger Horsall (£3)		3	
Thomas Johnson vintener (£15)		15	
Enoveck Chamber (£3)		3	
Roger Barrett (£3)		3	
Henry Kynge (£14)		14	
Anthony Spadman (£3)		3	
George Lucas (£3)		3	
Thomas Burridge (£25)		25	
William Burley (£8)		8	
Widowe Lofton (£12)		12	
Edward Lightmaker (£5)		5	
James Bynckes (£3)		3	
Richard Abbott (£6)		6	
John Swetinge (£3)		3	
William Dane (£3)		3	
Lawrence Howson (£3)		3	
Mr Lowe lawier (£10)		10	
Edmond Kingffeild fremason (£3)		3	
Mr Walker Doctor in Phisicke (£10)		10	
John Gater (£4)		4	
John Hipworthe (£3)		3	
Martyn Allyn (£3)		3	
William Walker pewterer (£3)		3	

339. THE OLDE BAILYE QUARTER ST SEPULCHERS PARISHE

Rychard Kellytt (£4)		4	
William Towley (£10)		10	
Richard Delworthe (£4)		4	
John Best cutler (£3)		3	
John Nicholas (£5)		5	
Mr Taillor gent in Mr Gyffordes house (£15)		15	
James Thornton (£3)		3	
John Filde (£12)		12	

	£	s.	d
Thomas Stafferton attorney (£3)		3	
Raffe Smythe (£3)		3	
Widowe Rilley (£3)		3	
Thomas Snellinge (£3)		3	
Nicholas Cole pursivant (£3)		3	
John Axton (£3)		3	
William Rowlyf (£12)		12	
William Cooke (£3)		3	
Thomas Clatterbock (£3)		3	
Mr Goldwell gent (£3)		3	
Mr Walton broker (£5)		5	
Anthonie Justinene a stranger (£3)		6	
Anthonie Goodenere a stranger (£8)		16	
Widowe Stamford (£3)		3	
Thomas Burshe (£3)		3	
Edward Gryffin (£5)		5	
Widowe Farmer (£3)		3	
Richard Wright (£3)		3	
Jane Rolffe (£3)		3	
Cutberd Sparke (£3)		3	
Michell Cowborne baker (£3)		3	
340. Henry Parkyns gent (£5)		5	
Garrett Johnson straunger (£5)		10	
John Cornylle (£6)		6	
Leonard Cloughe (£3)		3	
Mr Legge gent (£10)		10	
John Bell (£3)		3	
Androwe Starkey (£3) [a]		3	
John Halle hacneyman (£5)		5	
William Coverdall hacneyman (£3)		3	
Henry Smythe (£12)		12	
William Killingworth (£3)		3	
Thomas Sabb (£3) [a]		3	
[r.99][132]			
Thomas Lutwiche serjeant (£12)		12	
John Williams (£3)		3	
Frances Gryffin gent (£5)		5	
Robert Aley (£3)		3	
Thomas Cooke serjeant (£3)		3	
Thomas Franke (£5)		5	
John Lambert (£4)		4	
Richard Kinge (£10)		10	

132. In the left margin of the membrane nearest the name of John Richardson is written 'Flete Lane.' It is not clear whether this applies to all those persons listed under the Old Bailey Quarter up to Seacole Lane; to those persons in the left hand column on m. 99 next to which the words are written (i.e. Thomas Lutwiche to John Symondes); or to all those from John Richardson to William Wilson.

	£	s.	d
Thomas Brokenbery (£3)		3	
John Etheridge drawer (£3)		3	
Edward Henson scriviner (£6)		6	
Mr Ramefforth an attorney (£4)		4	
William Handslippe (£10)		10	
Humfry Kinge (£5)		5	
John Richardson (£3)		3	
Richard Brankle (£3)		3	
Richard Page (£3)		3	
Mychaell Ladyman (£3)		3	
Fraunces Caverley (£3)		3	
341. Jane Doone (£3)		3	
Widowe Camden (£3)		3	
William Lordinge serjeant (£6)		6	
William Wade (£4)		4	
Robert Excellent (£5)		5	
Widowe Harvye (£3)		3	
Peter Olliver stranger poll			4
Nicholas Sonderland (£3)		3	
John Hodgson (£3)		3	
William Baglaghe (£3)		3	
Thomas Parrett (£3)		3	
John Edwardes (£3)		3	
John Waters (£3)		3	
John Symondes stranger poll			4
William Wilson (£3)		3	

SECOLE LANE

Thomas Hewson (£3)		3	
John Eveason (£3)		3	
Hughe Younge (£3)		3	

IN GEORGE ALLEY

Giles Bushert stranger and his wife poll			8
William Crowe (£3)		3	
Thomas Bradley (£12)		12	

IN BERE ALLEY

William Percivall (£3)		3	
Henry Kennex a stranger (£8)		16	
Peter Gagney (£5)		5	
Thomas Hasilwood (£3)		3	
Peter Tramplore stranger (£3)		6	
John Boulton (£10)		10	

342.　　　　ST ANDREWES PARISHE IN HOLBORNE

Sir Christofer Hatton knight Comissioner [Blank]　　　　[Blank]

	£	s.	d
John Roper esquier in landes and fees (£80)			
[x - Kent £3 13s. 4d.]	5	6	8
Rychard Payne esquier (£200) [x - Kent?]	10		
Edward Bartlett (£20) [x - Ipswich 13s. 4d.]		20	
Anthonye Bartlett (£20)		20	
George Harison in landes (£20) [x - Mddx. 24s.]		26	8
John Cowper in landes and fees (£10)		13	4
Fraunces Stiche (£50) [ass. 13s. 4d. in Surrey]		50	
Assheton Ailesworth in landes (£20)		26	8
Edmound Standen in fees (£20) [x - Surrey			
13s.4d.]		26	8
John Talbot gent in landes (£40) [a]	2	13	4
John Brograve esquier in landes (£30)			
[x - Herts. 26s. 8d.]		40	
John Cowell (£50)		50	
Henry Phillipps in landes (£20) [a]		26	8
Godfrey Fulgem in landes and fees (£10) [a]		13	4
Anthonie Knevett in landes and fees (£20)		26	8
William Copcot in landes and fees (£20)		26	8
[r.100]			
John Bland (£3)		3	
Roger Snowden (£3)		3	
Thomas Wilson (£4)		4	
Hughe Yardley (£4)		4	
William Woodfall (£3)		3	
Assheton Showen stranger (£3)		6	
Thomas Stuckey (£4)		4	
William Gardinar (£3)		3	
Edward Saunders (£16)		16	
John Crowson (£5)		5	
William Richard (£7)		7	
343. Alexander Cockes (£3)		3	
John Fotheringill (£8)		8	
Thomas Eaton (£16)		16	
John Forest (£3)		3	
Robart Foxe (£4)		4	
Raffe Isott (£6)		6	
Thomas Bigges (£3)		3	
Jeames Lambart stranger (20s.)		2	
Lucas Ban his servante poll			4
Roger Showen stranger (£3)		6	
Baptist Giles his servant poll			4
William Cotton (£3)		3	
Richard Alderworth (£4)		4	
Hughe Wadilowe in landes (£6)		8	
Richard Pettye (£4)		4	
Thomas Bartilmeue (£3)		3	

	£	s.	d
Thomas Baldwine (£3)		3	
Thomas Hill (£3)		3	
John Davis (£4)		4	
Bonyface Rankyn (£3)		3	
Stephen Wright (£3) [a]		3	
Richard Scarlet (£3)		3	
John Greene (£3)		3	
Fraunces Flower in fees (£10) [a]		13	4
John Homes (£4)		4	
Thomas Badcoke (£3)		3	
George Hall (£8)		8	
Ellin Comes widowe stranger poll [a]			4
John Whitt (£4)		4	
Thomas Bullocke (£3)		3	
344. John Clarke (£3)		3	
Edward Dent (£3)		3	
John Mesell stranger poll			4
Morris Cockshed (£3)		3	
Paule van Sekerfull stranger poll [a]			4
Thomas Price (£3)		3	
John Bowyer (£4)		4	
Robart Walwyn (£5)		5	
Thomas Perin (£9)		9	
John Wigan (£10)		10	
Nicholas Clapham (£3)		3	
John Warmyngham (£3)		3	
John Buckett and Jacomyn his wife strangers poll			8
William Streetes (£3)		3	
John Garrarde (£5)		5	
Thomas Assher (£4)		4	
Humfrey Parkes (£5)		5	
Robart Ladyman (£3)		3	
Thomas Thorny (£3)		3	
John Hynche (£4)		4	
Thomas Stantlye (£4)		4	
John Dewell (£7)		7	
George Langford (£3)		3	
Edmond Alkins (£3)		3	
Tristram Alsoppe (£4)		4	
Hamond Parkes (£6)		6	
Thomas Frenche (£3)		3	
[r.101]			
Gillam Cochebray & Mary his wife strangers poll			8
345. Edmond Parton (£4)		4	

	£	s.	d
Humfry Johnson (£3)		3	
Rychard Hunt (£6)		6	
Rychard Alderidge (£3)		3	
Roger Morgan (£4)		4	
Walter Wallys (£3)		3	
Thomas Higgyns (£10)		10	
Daniell Swartes stranger (£5)		10	
Henry Lanman (£10) [x - Q 24s.]		10	
Oliver Pluckett (£3)		3	
Thomas Rawson (£3)		3	
Richard Barker (£4)		4	
Rubyn Carr (£4)		4	
Edward Dalby (£5)		5	
William Biggleskert (£3)		3	
Edward Brand (£4)		4	
Henry Lambert (£3)		3	
William Knight (£6)		6	
Thomas Martyn (£4)		4	
Robert Rodes (£3)		3	
Mistres Massye (£5)		5	
John Slynehed (£6)		6	
Gilbert Gest (£3)		3	
Robert Tyson (£3)		3	
Rychard Faringdon (£3)		3	
George Isaack (£3)		3	
Thomas Banckes (£3)		3	

[Endorsed] Summa   562

346. [r.36]   LANGEBURNE WARDE
[Petty collectors: Thomas Gray, grocer, and Thomas Thompson, haberdasher.]

SAYNT MARYE WOLNOTHES PARISH AND [St. Mary] WOLCHURCH PARISH
[English]

	£	s.	d
Sir Thomas Ramsey knight, Comissioner (£400)	20		
William Abraham (£120)	6		
John Hawkyns (£50)		50	
Hugh Keale (£60)	3		
Roger Tasker (£50)		50	
Nicholas Style (£50)		50	
John Alderson (£50)		50	
Peter Dewes (£10)		10	
Robert Rase (£3)		3	
Luke Smyth (£3)		3	
Patrick Brewe (£6)		6	
John Wylkyns (£3)		3	
Frauncys Kydde (£4)		4	
Richerd Brook (£3)		3	

	£	s.	d
William Rawlynson (£3)		3	
John Kettlewoode (£6)		6	
Henrye Kettlewoode (£4)		4	
Rowland Broughton (£6)		6	
George Newbolde (£15)		15	
Elizabeth Wetherhill (£8)		8	
Emanuell Cole (£20)		20	
Gyles Sympson (£7)		7	
Thomas Sympson (£12)		12	
Thomas Francklyn shopkeeper (£3)		3	
William Frank (£5)		5	
Richerd Leversage (£8)		8	
Thomas Corbet (£15)		15	
William Cocknedge (£10)		10	
Uxor Balangier (£3)		3	
Thomas Clark (£3)		3	
Thomas Walker (£3)		3	
Edwarde Crosshawe (£10)		10	
Doctor Muffet (£8)		8	
Uxor Atkynson (£5)		5	
347. Frauncys Barnarde (£10)		10	
Walter Boulton (£3)		3	
Edwarde Gryffen (£20)		20	
William Indee (£6)		6	
Edwarde Horwood (£6)		6	
Edmonde Greet (£3)		3	
Thomas Ridge (£3)		3	
Uxor Pykeringe (£8)		8	
Nicholas Caldwell (£3)		3	
William Warde (£5)		5	
Thomas Wattes (£20)		20	
Robert Bysshopp (£3)		3	
Rowlande Okeover (£20)		20	
George Samwell shopkeeper (£3)		3	
[r.37] Strangers			
John Ferne (£30)	3		
James Goddescall (£50)	5		
Jacob Wilhelmo (£10) [a]		20	
Fredrick Frederigo (£20)		40	
In the house of John Ferne			
James Ferne per pol			4
Hierom van Asse per pol			4
Frauncis Merando [a]			4
Michaell Barret and Marye his wyfe			8
James Johnson			4
In the howse of James Goddescall			
Uxor Sye per pol			4

	£	s.	d
Mathewe Sye and Marye Sye her children			8
In the house of Hugh Keale			
Hugh Lynsey a Scott per pol			4
In the house of William Franck			
Davyd Gylbert per pol			4
Danyell Fever			4
Summa	[Blank]		

348.   SAYNT NICHOLAS ACONS PARISH
[English]

	£	s.
John Hall (£70)	3	10
John Lucas (£60)	3	
John Mason (£6)		6
John Luter (£3)		3
Uxor Lyvers (£10)		10
Thomas Short (£8)		8
Richerd Hughes (£3)		3
William Dove (£5)		5
Raph Hamor (£5)		5
John Nokes (£10)		10
Richerd Mylwarde (£3)		3
Edwarde Banester (£10)		10
Robert Rogers in Banisters house (£30)		30
William Shores (£3)		3
Nicholas Hussey (£5)		5
Roger Hamor (£5)		5
Humfrey Evans (£3)		3
Robert Petit (£3) [a]		3
Thomas Adamson (£6)		6
William Towes (£4)		4
Richerde Gwyn (£3)		3
John Thomas (£3)		3

349.   Strangers

	s.		d
John Goddescall (£120)	12		
Peter Tryon alias Truyne (£130)	13		
Simon de Starky (£30)	3		
Melchior Vanhasse (£70)	7		
Haunce Walters (£60) [b - Antwerp mer.]	6		
In the house of Thomas Adamson			
Walforde Rothermaker (£3)		6	
John Loy his servant per pol			4
In the house of John Holden			
Andreas Farnandes per pol			4
James Poole and his wyfe			8
Arthure Brenkhers and his wyfe Sara			8
Bastian his servant			4
In the house of Melchior Vanhasse			

	£	s.	d
John van Presson his servant per pol			4
In the house of Haunce Walters			
Martyn Walters his servant			4
Anne Goddes his mayde			4
In the house of Peter Tryon			
Jacob Tryon per pol			4
Summa [Blank]			

350.   SAYNT EDMONDES AND ST CLEMENTES PARISHES
[English]

George Barne Alderman (£240)	12	
Thomas Butcher (£80)	4	
[r.38]		
William Whytmore (£200)	10	
Thomas Russell (£60)	3	
Mistress Barnham wydowe (£210)	10	10
Robert Dowe (£60)	3	
George Gynne in landes (£15)		20
Thomas Thompson (£50)		50
Benedick Barnham (£50)		50
Otwell Bestowe (£50)		50
John Jolles (£50)		50
William Feake (£30)		30
Robert Bate (£6)		6
Richerde Reade (£5)		5
Uxor Lowe (£20)		20
Richerd Dixson (£8)		8
John Hyggyns (£12)		12
George Taylor (£10)		10
Richerd Maryot (£5)		5
William Crosseley (£5)		5
Phillypp Curtys (£16)		16
Robert Goodwyn (£3)		3
George Richerdson (£3)		3
John Bylbey (£10)		10
John Goodwyn (£15)		15
Henrye Banes (£8)		8
John Malyn (£5)		5
Thomas Kingman (£3)		3

351. John Draper (£3)		3
John Poole (£10)		10
Thomas Hill (£6)		6
John Decrowe (£10)		10
John Laughton (£3)		3
Richerd Agar (£6)		6
Frauncys Barnham (£6)		6
Peter Smyth (£3)		3

	£	s.	d
William Drywood (£12)		12	
John Parret (£3)		3	
John Varnam (£20)		20	
Thomas Eveley (£5)		5	
Richerd Wilkinson (£15)		15	
John Phelpes (£5)		5	
John Smyth (£5)		5	
John Tucker (£5)		5	
Raph Rotherham (£8)		8	
Richerd Haskynson (£3)		3	
Thomas Cathorne (£3)		3	
Thomas Bycroft (£5)		5	
Vincent Lounde (£5)		5	
Christofer Bracy (£12)		12	
Edmond Hill (£30)		30	
John Evans (£3)		3	
William Watson (£5)		5	
Peter Evans (£3)		3	
Richerde Baylye (£3)		3	
Raph Baylye (£6)		6	
Mark Kydde (£6)		6	

352.   Strangers

	£	s.	d
Peter Vandewall (£50) [b - Antwerp mer.]	5		
John Bruges (£30)	3		
John de Cunynge (£20)		40	
Peter de Coster (£40) [b - Antwerp mer.]	4		
In the house of Peter de Coster			
Vyncent Loyelet per pol			4
Anne de Coster			4
Margaret Henrickes			4
In the house of Peter Vandewall			
Agnes his mayde servant			4
Walter Janson his manservant			4
In the house of John Bruges			
Victoryne his maydeservant			4
In the howse of the saide Peter Vandewall			
Joyce Vanbush (£3) [b - Antwerp mer.]	6		
[r.39] In the house of William Hayward			
Barnarde Renish and his wyfe per pol			8
Uxor van Blanbargen per pol			4
Summa [Blank]			

353.   ALL SAYNTES PARISH IN LUMBERDSTREET
[English]

	£	s.	d
Martyn Woode (£50)		50	
Peter Symons (£50)		50	
George Haynes (£3)		3	

263

	£	s.	d
Richerd Osborne (£20)		20	
Robert Jackson (£3)		3	
John Allen (£3)		3	
John Pyttoll (£3)		3	
Dyonys Lennet (£3)		3	
William Albert (£10)		10	
Leonerde Coxe (£15)		15	
John Parker (£3)		3	
John Laycock (£5)		5	
Uxor Burde (£4)		4	
John Brygges (£5)		5	
Thomas Higbed (£16)		16	
Eloy Echarde (£6)		6	
Richerde Etthell (£3)		3	
John Bees (£5)		5	
William Foote (£3)		3	
Baptist Hasell (£5)		5	
John Turpin (£20)		20	
Anthonye Whittfeilde (£5)		5	
Mathewe Keyne (£3)		3	
Walter Hill (£8)		8	
Shopkeepers John Dobbes and William			
Alsop iii li a pece (£6)		6	

Strangers

Arnolde Verne and his wyfe per pol			8
William Tronster his servant			4
John Lyon and Dionys Bartholmewe his servant			8
James Bartholl & his wyfe, and Brissell			
their maydservant [a - Brissell]			12
Summa	[Blank]		

354.   SAYNT DYONYS BACKCHURCH PARISH
[English]

	£	s.	d
Sir James Harvy, Lord Maior, Commissioner			
(£340)		17	
William Sherington (£80)		4	
Edwarde Osborne, Alderman, Sessor (£250)		12	10
William Curtesse (£60)		3	
Thomas Grey (£60)		3	
Thomas Bressy, Sessor (£200)			
[ass. £6 in Mddx.]		10	
John Reade in landes (£15)		20	
Robert Man (£3)		3	
John Pywell (£3)		3	
Nicholas Collyer (£3)		3	
Richerde Cooper (£12)		12	
Arthure Nedeham (£12)		12	
Richerde Poynter (£20)		20	

	£	s.	d
Martyn Stockwell (£3)		3	
Phillipp Swallowe (£3)		3	
James Redmore (£5)		5	
William Casey (£3)		3	
Andrewe Marsh (£20)		20	
Edwarde Godfrey (£3)		3	
James Batty (£7)		7	
John Woodward (£35)		35	
Roger Tyndall (£6)		6	
Richerd Carington (£4)		4	
Thomas Gray the yonger (£4)		4	
Goodluck Cott (£3)		3	
Robert Sadler (£3)		3	
John May (£15)		15	
Thomas Fleet (£3)		3	
Martyn Harbert (£3)		3	
George Noone (£5)		5	
355. William Weston (£5)		5	
Humfrey Revell (£35)		35	
Hughe Parke (£8)		8	
Owen Rydley (£15)		15	
Thomas Wood (£15)		15	
Robert Bringborne (£10)		10	
Richerd Smyth (£3)		3	
[r.40]			
Robert Preston (£3)		3	
Danyell Peterson (£20)		20	
John Knight (£3)		3	
Robert Lant (£5)		5	

Straungers

	£	s.	d
Peter Samyne (£50)	5		
Nicholas Delanoy (£30) [b - Antwerp mer.]	3		
Abraham Vandeldon (£30) [b - Antwerp mer.]	3		
James Cole (£50)	5		
Peter Typot (£5)		10	
Emanuell Demetris (£40) [b - Antwerp mer.]	4		
John Bewgram (£10)		20	
Alexander de Myllyn (£20) [b - Antwerp mer.]		40	
William Whytebread (£30) [b - Antwerp mer.]	3		
Vincent Le Barre (£40)	4		
Agatha Vanhill (£10)		20	
Sara Vanhill (£10)		20	
Michael Mannet (£20) [b - Antwerp mer.]		40	
Hipolito Beaumont (£20) [ass. 20s. in			
Mddx. as Epolita]		40	
In the house of Peter Samyne			
Reynolde Richerdes his manservant			4

	£	s.	d
Alice Garret his maydservant			4

356.   In the house of Nicholas Delanoy
Anthonye Tryfarfe, Jane Carpenter and

Dyonyse Jarbranch his servantes pol			12

In the house of Abraham Vandelden

John Rounce his servant pol			4
Marye Clementes his mayde servant pol			4

In the house of James Cole

James Cole his sonne per pol			4
Elizabeth Cole his daughter			4
Eve Sayence his maide pol			4

In the house of Hipolito Beaumonti

Scipio Beaumonti			4
Horatio Fransato (£3)		6	
John Lupryn and James Roomcom,[133] servantes pol [a]			8
Henrick Neigburgh and Margaret his wyfe			8
Adryan Cornelius and James Heawith servantes per pol			8
John Peen (£5)		10	
Haunce Wygell, William Herninge, Joyce Crumbrogram and Lewis Alnick his servantes per pol			16
George Vandall and Janekyn his wyfe and Marye Vantropyn his servant			12

In the house of Peter Tippot

Cornelis ne Vanhoven per pol			4

357.   In the house of Emanuell Demetris

Danyell Etiler his manservant			4
Elizabeth Frende his maydservant			4
Harman van Hambach (£3)		6	
Abraham Vanharwick (£3) [b - Antwerp mer.]		6	
Anne Bounyers their mayde [a][134]			4
Garret van Awken [a]			4
John Waternyell (£3)		6	

In the house of Laurence Cartwright
James Jeringe, Laurence Dorough and

Martyn Gossen per pol			12

In the house of William Whytebreade
James Mawse and Margaret Hosse his servantes

per pol			8
Geoffrey Pryor (£3)		6	

In the house of Alexander Millen

133. E.359/52, r. 7 gives surname as Rancome.
134. E.359/52, r. 7 gives surname as Bovers.

	£	s.	d
Uxor Judick per pol			4
Nicholas Lenhart and his wyfe per pol			8
In the house of John May			
John Larde per pol			4
In the house of John Bewgrom			
[r.41]			
Margaret Vandevall and Anne Plattfoot			
servantes per pol			8
In the house of John de la Barre			
John Vincent and one Marye servantes per pol			8
In the house of wydow Cotton			
Garrat and Jerrat two strangers pol			8

Summa   [Blank]

358.   ST GABRIELL FANCHURCH PARISH
[English]

	£	s.	d
Robert Cambell (£50)		50	
Doctor Taylor in fees (£10)		13	4
William Towerson, Sessor (£80)	4		
Seth Lacy (£20) [ass. 40s. in Tower ward]		20	
Laurence Smyth (£12)		12	
Davyd George (£5)		5	
Thomas Harryson (£4)		4	
William Parrat (£3)		3	
Thomas Spencer (£6)		6	
John Wanton (£10)		10	
Nicholas Farrer (£6)		6	
William Clowes (£6)		6	
John Bayworth (£12)		12	
George Cooper (£4)		4	
Henrye Bowdeler (£10)		10	
Danyell Perrye (£5)		5	
Anthonye Moorcroft (£12)		12	
William Greenwell (£11)		11	
Michaell Sycklemore (£3)		3	
Nicholas Pystor (£5)		5	
Henrye Richerdson (£6)		6	
Richerd Powell (£3)		3	
John Nicholson (£3)		3	
William Boddye (£3)		3	
Roberte Applegate (£3)		3	
In the house of Robert Applegate			
John Poole (£10)		10	
Thomas Eaton (£3)		3	
William Hill (£3)		3	

359.   Strangers

| Lewes Sayes (£40) | 4 | | |

	£	s.	d
John Guest (£15) [x - Billingsgate ward			
40s. as Haunce Gast]		30	
Alexander Tybantee (£70)	7		
Henrye Lambertson (£3)		6	
Godfrey Lynse and Garret Pynson			
his servantes			8
In the house of Lewes Sayes			
Wallerin Sayes, Anne Gomort and Flipot			
Virgilot servantes per pol			12
In the house of Alexander Tybanty			
Panpilio Golito per pol			4
Guido Bust			4
Syloe Pichen per pol			4
Marcus Laurence and Gotred his wyfe [a]			8
In the house of Marcus Laurence			
Tobias and Suzan Vynce servantes pol			8
Alcue Mure			4
Andryan Pylyn and Janekyn his wyfe			8
Janikin Caveles their servant			4
John Palmer			4
Summa [Blank]			

360.   ALL SAYNTES STAYNINGES PARISH
[English]

	£	s.	d
John Layvenham (£3)		3	
Cornelys Hande (£5)		5	
Roger Payne (£3)		3	
[r.42]			
George Laurence (£3)		3	
John Bayforth (£3)		3	
Humfrey Walker (£10)		10	
Thomas Benynge (£3)		3	
Humfry Grymshawe (£4)		4	
John Saunders (£15)		15	
John Mongomery (£8)		8	
Robert Carre (£3)		3	
John Yeoman (£3)		3	
Thomas Hyggens (£3)		3	
John Warde (£4)		4	
Thomas Greene (£3)		3	
Thomas Jones (£3)		3	
Andrew Walker (£3)		3	
Strangers			
John Baptista Sambitores (£20) [a]		40	
Lewin Vantilt (£20)		40	
Alanso de Basurto (£10)		20	
In the house of John Baptista Sambitores			
Thomas the servant of Alanso de Basurto [a]			4

	£	s.	d
John Atrice per pol [a]			4
Fardinando a Blackamore			4
Margaret a maydservant [a]			4

361.   In Culver Alley

	£	s.	d
Glode Paynter per pol			4
Ellyn his servant [a]			4
Tannykyn a Douchwoman			4
Magdalen her servant			4
In Starre Alley			
Thomas Bysshoppe per pol			4
In the house of wydowe Lewys			
Albert and Herman two Douchmen, botchers [a]			8
John Garretson (£3)		6	
Bonyface Face (£5)		10	
In the house of Thomas Jones			
Lambert Vandeback and his wyfe			8
Peter Flemyn and Cathery his syster			8
In the house of Levyn Vantilt			
John Raywarde per pol			4
Mathewe Stylton			4
Sara Barrell a mayde servant			4

COMPANYE

	£	s.	d
The Pewterers in landes (£13)		17	4
Summa [Blank]			
[Endorsed] Summa 363		8	4

362. [r.43]   LYME STREETE WARDE
[Petty collectors: Mathewe Dolman, haberdasher, and Gregory Yonge, grocer.]

ST PETERS AND ST ANDREWES PAROCHES
[English]

	£	s.	d
Sir Nicholas Woodroff knight,			
Commyssioner (£270) [x - Mddx. £5]	13	10	
Gregory Yonge (£50)		50	
Lawrence Gough (£50)		50	
Wylliam Phillipps in landes and fees			
(£20) [ass. 20s. in Mddx.]	26		8
Doctor Penny in fees (£10)	13		4
Wylliam Wrothe (£80) [x - Herts. 17s. 4d.]	4		
Wylliam Mylward (£50)		50	
Hughe Offeley (£120)	6		
Edmond Bressy (£60)	3		
Thomas Starkye, Alderman (£220)	11		
Mathewe Dolman (£50)		50	
Henry Gylmyn in fees (£20)	26		8

	£	s.	d
Peter Haughton (£50)		50	
Henry Bradbridge in landes (£20)			
[x - Sussex 13s. 4d.]		26	8
Raphe Sares (£3)		3	
David Powell (£3)		3	
Wylliam Tyboll (£5)		5	
Richard Lockson (£5)		5	
Robert Mascall (£5) [ass. 5s. in			
Cripplegate ward]		5	
Wylliam Hartridge (£5)		5	
Wylliam Fowler (£6)		6	
George Speringe (£3)		3	
[Blank] Richardes (£3)		3	
Wydowe Perpoynte (£3)		3	
Wylliam Phillipps, taylor (£3)		3	
John Copland (£3)		3	
Richard Hadlowe (£3)		3	
George Dove (£4)		4	
[r.44]			
John Whyte (£6)		6	
John Stowe (£3)		3	
Peter Towers (£3)		3	
Thomas Fytche (£3)		3	
John Weste (£3)		3	
Thomas Danyell (£3)		3	
Wylliam Pearch (£10)		10	
Wylliam Handbury (£15)		15	
Edward Cox (£5)		5	
Mathewe Fleer (£10)		10	
Rowland Richardson (£3)		3	
Robert Wright (£3)		3	
Lawrence Otwell (£20)		20	
363. John Wielde (£5)		5	
John Rooper (£3)		3	
Thomas Warbee (£3)		3	
Robert Cox (£3)		3	
John Reymond (£5) [x - Q 6s. 8d.]		5	
Robert Donkerley (£3)		3	
Richard Baynes (£5)		5	
Richard Bonde (£3)		3	
Thomas Playne (£3)		3	
Robert Kyngslonde (£5)		5	
Christofer Thatcher (£10)		10	
Jane Dutton (£10) [x - Essex 5s.]		10	
John Stanfeild (£5)		5	
Lancellott Ottorborne (£3)		3	
John Carowe (£5)		5	

	£	s.	d
Edmond Rowley (£5)		5	
Nicholas Speringe (£10)		10	
Straungers			
Peter Buskell (£100) [b - Antwerp mer.]	10		
Adrian de Porter (£60) [b - Antwerp mer.]	6		
John Pedericons and Katheryn his wyfe			
per poll		8	
Cornelius Johnson & Henry Johnson his man			
per poll		8	
Troiolus de Crete and Sara his wyfe,			
Magdalen his daughter, Katheryn			
Falkener a servante per poll		16	
In Peter de Bosquells howse, Jane his wyfe,			
Tanekyn Mason, Mary Ballenger, Lambert			
Joye, Nicholas Hobloyn per poll		20	
In Adryan de Porters howse, Francys his wyfe,			
Haunce van Seelde, Cely Lapson per poll		12	
In Robert Kingslons howse, James Fox per poll		4	
In John Langleys howse, Helyn Cornelis per poll		4	
[Endorsed] Summa	82	6	4

364. [r.48]   PORTSOKEN WARDE
[Petty collectors: John Barnard, skinner, and Frauncys Shyngewell, ironmonger.]

ST BUTTOLPHES PAROCHE
[English]

	£	s.	d
Sir William Pelham knighte in landes			
(£100) [x - Bucks. £4 13s. 4d.]	6	13	4
Thomas Goodman (£60) [x - Essex £1 15s.]	3		
William Wood (£50) [x - Mddx. 25s.]		50	
Anthony Duffield (£80) [x - Mddx. £1 10s.]	4		
George Kirkham in fees (£10) [x - Q 10s.]		13	4
William Gray in landes (£15)			
[x - Essex 13s. 4d.]		20	
Thomas Beane in fees (£20)		26	8
William Coche in fees (£18) [x - Q 24s.]		24	
William Jorden in fees (£20)		26	8
Henry Trochell in fees (£10) [x - Q 32s.]		13	4
William Skipwith in landes & fees (£10)		13	4
William Maperley in fees (£10) [x - Q 14s. 8d.]		13	4
James Harding in fees (£10) [x - Q 64s.]		13	4
Gawen Smythe in fees (£18) [x - Q 24s.]		24	
Thomas Davyes (£5)		5	
Leonerd Murffen in fees (£8)			
[x - Mddx. 8s.][135]		10	8

135. E.359/52, r. 7 gives surname as Smurfett.

	£	s.	d
Humffrey Scragg (£10)		10	
William Parlaby (£5)		5	
Henry Conwey (£10)		10	
Richard Jaques (£5)		5	
Henry Tunston (£5)		5	
Thomas Dowsing in fees (£8)[136]		10	8
William Nawton (£10)		10	
John Jones (£5)		5	
John Harvy (£5)		5	
Richard Casey (10s.) [sic]		10	
John Ansell (£8)		8	
Anthony Bell (£3)		3	
Edward Waple (£3)		3	
Thomas Crowchley (£3)		3	
Fraunces Shingwell (£3)		3	
Roberte Austen (£7)		7	
Christofer Tysdall (£3)		3	
365. Raffe Wekes (£3)		3	
Pierse Conway (£5)		5	
John Syllies (£3)		3	
John Golson (£5)		5	
Adam Ryder (£3)		3	
Thomas Parker (£5)		5	
Richard Peake (£3)		3	
Henry Browne (£3)		3	
Christofer Carleton (£3)		3	
John Sprignell (£8)		8	
John Barnerd (£3)		3	
Phillipp Goodman (£5)		5	
Christofer Walker (£3)		3	
Thomas Baker (£3)		3	
Toby Wood (£15)		15	
Widow Lawson (£5)		5	
Edward Bendlowes (£10)		10	
George Fawlkener (£6)		6	
Niccholas Raynolds (£8)		8	
[r.49]			
William Dorner (£5)		5	
John Wallys (£5)		5	
Robarte Preist (£4)		4	
George Clarck (£8)		8	
Oswall Bate (£5)		5	
Widow Soda (£5)		5	
William Sylvester (£3)		3	

136. Marginal notation: 'offic' infr' tur' in London.' Dowsing, as moneyer at the mint, was exonerated by privy seal directed to treasurer and barons dated 23 June 1581 (E.359/52, r. 7).

	£	s.	d
George Elken (£7)		7	
Leonerd Fryer (£3)		3	
John Baker (£3)		3	
John Phillipps thelder in fees (£6)		8	
John Phillypps the younger in fees (£6)		8	
John Balderston (£3)		3	
John Cook (£3)		3	
Phillipp Roythsby (£5)		5	

366.   Straungers

	£	s.	d
John Waterskott (£10)		20	
Marck Anthonie Galiardeto in fees (£24)			
[x - Q £3 4s.]	3	4	
Marten de Custer (£5)		10	
Cornellys van Essen (£5)		10	
Guillam le Roy (£4)		8	
Guillam Bury in fees (£18) [x - Q 64s. as			
Guillam Vandebarro]		48	
John Gounner in fees (£18) [x - Q 64s. as			
Gom van Osterwicke]		48	
Peter Lupo in fees (£18) [x - Q 64s.]		48	
Fraunces Marcus (40s.)		4	
James Mott (£3)		6	
Pasquell Browell (40s.)		4	
John de Howsey (£3)		6	
James de Messynes (£3)		6	

Straungers by poll

	£	s.	d
Saunder Ingrave and his wief and iiii			
servantes		2	
Gyles Vander Ogen and his wief			8
John van Haynes and hys wief			8
John de Vyniers and his wief & his mother			12
Joyse Owchyer and hys wief			8
Marten van Barenbargh & hys wief and			
ii servauntes			16
John Rychardson and hys wiefe			8
Adrian Laman and his wief and one			
servaunt [a]			12
Jacob Follio and one servaunt			8
James, Marten de Custers servaunt			4
Cornellys van Essen hys iiii servauntes			16
Lewyn Timberman and his wief and one servaunt			12
Marten Vanderlinger & his wiefe, iiii			
Children & one servaunt		2	4
Godfrey Lambright			4

	£	s.	d
367. John de Grave and his wiefe and one servaunt			12
Peter Shatlyne			4

	£	s.	d
Guillam le Roy hys iiii servauntes			16
Gtorge [sic] Cooke			4
William Wickers and hys wief and			
ii servauntes			16
Fraunces Marcus his iiii servauntes			16
John Haynes			4
Harry Hunter			4
Rowland Brooke			4
John de Housey hys servaunt			4
Marten de Camber and his wief & his brother			
[a - brother of Marten de Camber]			12
Rowland Samford and hys wief			8
Gabriell Savegrave and his wief			8
[r.50]			
Peter Bayllett and hys wief and			
iii children [a]			20
Jaques Dennett and hys wief and ii children			16
[Blank] Raynoldes hys wief and one sonne			8
Jaques Rabye and his wief			8
Mr Thomas			4

THE MYNORYES

	£	s.	d
John Skinner in fees (£8)		10	8
John Jones (£6)		6	
Christofer Newcome (£3)		3	
Anthonie Eaton (£3)		3	
Avery Arsnell (£3)		3	
John ap Morgan alias Pryse (£3)		3	
Thomas Colnes (£3) [a]		3	
Lewys Williams (£3)		3	
[Endorsed] Summa	57	11	4

368. [r.51] QUENEHITH WARDE
[Petty collectors: Humfrey Huntley, ironmonger, and Robert Harryson, salter.]

ST PETERS PAROCHE

	£	s.	d
Frauncys Throgmorton gent in landes			
(£40) [ass. 100s. in Kent]		53	4
Doctor Vulpe (£10)		10	
Robert Holte (£15)		15	
Roger Pearte (£18)		18	
Thomas Bell (£4)		4	
John Apryce (£5)		5	
Edmond Rawlinges (£6)		6	
Wylliam Rowth (£4)		4	
Humfrey Felstede (£5)		5	

	£	s.	d
Frauncys Warner (£3)		3	
Alexander Benett (£3)		3	
Rychard Wyatt (£5)		5	
Wylliam Jenkinges (£3)		3	
Raffe Rodes (£3)		3	
John Mynors (£5)		5	
John Pedd (£3)		3	
Esdras Fayrmaners (£3)		3	
Thomas Kyngslaye (£5)		5	
Thomas George (£3)		3	
John Floraunce (£3)		3	
Wylliam Wylcockes (£3)		3	
Ryce Rogers (£3)		3	
John Byll (£10) [x - Essex 8s.]		10	

Straungers

| Guylliam Bryscoe (£5) | | 10 | |

369.   ST MICHAELLS, ST MYLDREDES, ST OLAVES
AND TRYNYTIE PAROCHES
[English]

Mr Edward Fenner, sergeante at the lawe			
(£30) [x - Surrey 26s. 8d.]		30	
Wylliam Shelley gent in landes (£100)			
[x - Sussex £6 13s. 4d.]	6	13	4
Anthony Maynie gent in landes (£40)			
[x - Sussex 56s.]		53	4
Thomas Randoll (£50)		50	
Wylliam Wydnell (£70)	3	10	
Robert East and Wylliam Skydmore			
partners (£180)	9		
Doctor Symynges (£200)	10		
Humfrey Huntley (£50)		50	
Roger Hole (£15)		15	
Steven Hardwyck (£3)		3	
John Vayze (£15)		15	
John Howse (£8)		8	
Humfrey Rassor (£8)		8	
John Cox (£15)		15	
George Dytton (£6)		6	
Henry Swynnerton (£15) [ass. 18s. 8d.in Kent]		15	
Wylliam Hathorne (£6)		6	
Thomas Harryson (£3)		3	
Frauncys Clarke (£5)		5	
John Rooper (£6)		6	
Frauncys Brigges (£3)		3	
Steven Fytche (£3)		3	
John Androwes (£3)		3	
Thomas Pakington (£3) [x - Q 24s.]		3	

	£	s.	d
Thomas Wylliams (£3)		3	
Edward Sympson (£5)		5	
John Smyth (£5)		5	
John Allyn (£5)		5	
Wydowe Waynewright (£5)		5	
Robert Fuller (£3)		3	
Raffe Wheler (£4)		4	
Anthony Clarke (£3)		3	
John Dayssey (£3)		3	
[r.52]			
William Holligrave (£3)		3	
Charles Newell (£6)		6	
Morgan Jones (£6)		6	
John Whetton (£3)		3	
Caleb Trewe (£8)		8	
John Fenn (£6)		6	
Richard Chestre (£3)		3	
370. Henry Battill (£3)		3	
Thomas Field (£12)		10	[sic]
Robarte Susan (£8)		8	
John Trafton (£8)		8	
Richard Lecolte (£10)		10	
Widow Savage (£3)		3	
Widow Foyster (£3)		3	
Roberte Chambers (£3)		3	
Niccholas Willson (£3)		3	
Clement Homes (£4)		4	
James Hill (£3)		3	
Richard Thorpe (£8)		8	
Thomas Niccholson (£3)		3	
Edward Jackson (£3)		3	
William Tope (£3)		3	
Roberte Postell (£3)		3	
Leonerd Brownsword (£3)		3	
Thomas Faysse and Richard Sandes (£3)		3	
Roberte Peacock (£20)		20	
John Chambers (£10)		10	
Raffe Strave (£12)		12	
James Batson (£3)		3	
Richard Drewe (£3)		3	
Walter Harbert (£3)		3	
Thomas Brownrick (£10)		10	
Straungers			
John van Holst alias Haunce (£100)	10		
Anthonie de Vigo (£30) [a][137]	3		

137. Marginal notation: "f' process' ad wardam de Castelbaynard."

	£	s.	d
John Debins his sonne per poll			4
George Jane his servant per poll			4
Fydt Dome hys servaunt per poll			4
Helgar Alden his servaunt per poll			4
Adam Brane his servaunt per poll			4
Guillyam Marry his servaunt per poll			4
George Camby his servaunt per poll			4
Tyse Lenerd per poll			4
Jacob Nelking per poll			4
Cornellys Nellman (20s.)		2	
Peter Bennett per poll			4
John Debavoy (20s.)		2	
Elling Debavoy his daughter per poll			4
Susan Debavoy his daughter per poll			4

371.   SCT NICCHOLAS AND SCT MARY SOMERSETTES PAROCHES
[English]

	£	s.	d
John Heynes, Sergeaunt cator (£60)			
[x - Q £1 6s. 8d.]		3	
Humfrey Moseley (£60)		3	
Thomas Browne in fees (£30)			
[x - Heref. 26s. 8d.]		40	
John Leak (£50)		50	
James Keley (£80)	4		
Thomas Sewell (£50)		50	
Roberte Harryson (£50)		50	
Henry Pierson (£15)		15	
Reignold Stone (£15)		15	
Edmund Brigges (£3)		3	
John Gittinges & Richard Newton (£6)		6	
John Lawson (£3)		3	
John Walton (£3)		3	
Hughe George (£3)		3	
John Holstock (£3)		3	
Richard Harrys (£25)		25	
William Dent (£3)		3	
William Nedeham (£8)		8	
Richard Gill (£6)		6	
Alexander Rowth (£8)		8	
Edward Sucklay (£3)		3	
John Carter (£4)		4	
John Kent (£4)		4	
Evans Gryffin (£3)		3	
John Kirrye (£5)		5	
Edward Joanes (£3)		3	
Thomas Grantam (£3)		3	

	£	s.	d
372. Nicholas Padye alias Dragon (£3)[138]		3	
John Pascall (£5)		5	
Davyd Fludd (£3)		3	
John Daffye (£3)		3	
Henry Browne (£4)		4	
[r.53]			
John Farmor (£3)		3	
Phillipp Rowth (£3)		3	
John Nokes (£3)		3	
Anthony Abbott (£4)		4	
James Newham (£3)		3	
Thomas Cocksetter (£3)		3	
George Nailer (£5) [x - Q 6s.]		5	
Richard Wiggins (£3)		3	
John Fletcher (£6)		6	
Roberte Griffinn (£3)		3	
Niccholas Clarke (£3)		3	
William Willes (£3)		3	
John Ball (£4)		4	
Robart Rowse (£3)		3	
John Heges & Lewes Randall (£5)		5	
Anthony Piersey (£3)		3	
Edward Fartlow (£6)		6	

Straungers

	£	s.	d
Bargott Miller (20s.)		2	
John Massey (£3)		6	
Anthony Vas per poll			4

COMPANIES

	£	s.	d
The Smythes hall (£10)		10	
The Paynter Hall (£6)		6	
[Endorsed] Summa	108	16	4

373. [r.117] TOWER WARDE
[Petty collectors: Paule Bannynge, grocer, and John Hyghlord, skinner.]

SAINT DUNSTONES, ST MARYE BARKINGE,[139]
ST OLAVES, AND ALHALLOWES[140] PARISHES
[English]

	£	s.	d
Mr William Webbe, alderman (£160) [ass. 13s. 4 in Herts. and 13s. 4d. in Berks.]		8	
Sir George Harte, knight, in landes (£150) [x - Kent £4 8s.]		10	

138. Marginal notation: 'pursuiant ad arm'.' Paddy, as Rouge Dragon pursuivant, was exonerated by virtue of letters patent of 4 June 1549 to the heralds and writ from the queen to the treasurer and barons dated 1 July 1581 (E.359/52, r. 7).
139. Allhallows Barking.
140. Allhallows Staining.

	£	s.	d
Roberte Coxe (£60)	3		
Thomas Hunte (£80)	4		
John Hide (£50)		50	
William Sebrighte (£20)		20	
The Ladie [Mawdlin] Chester, in landes			
(£40) [x - Herts. 20s.][141]		53	4
William Lewson (£50)		50	
Richard Saltonstall (£200) [ass. £1 6s. 8d.			
in Essex and 2s. 8d. in Mddx.]	10		
John Hawkins, esquier (£150) [x - Kent			
£3 6s. 8d.]	7	10	
Lawrence Mellowes (£50)		50	
Thomas Wycken (£70)	3	10	
Sir William Allyn, knight (£100)	5		
John Lowen, in landes (£20)		26	8
Mistres Gonston, widowe, in landes (£20)		26	8
Mr. John Barker (£300) [x - Ipswich			
£3 6s. 8d.]	15		
Paule Bannynge (£100)	5		
Buttolphe Holder (£60) [a][142]	3		
John Highlorde (£60)	3		
Thomas Towneson, in fees (£12)		16	
John Herdson (£160)	8		
Thomas Herdson (£200)[143]	10		
William Haines (£50)		50	
William Page (£80)	4		
John Collett (£50)		50	
Martyn Archdale (£80) [a]	4		
John Carryll (£150) [x - Surrey £1 10s.]	7	10	
William Chelsam (£70) [x - Surrey 13s. 4d.]	3	10	
George Allyn (£50)		50	
Jasper Swifte, in fees (£15)		20	
Andrewe Joyner (£70) [ass. £1 6s. 8d.			
in Essex]	3	10	
374. William Longe (£150)	7	10	
John Porter (£100)	5		
Mistres Polsted, widowe, in landes (£20)			
[x - Surrey 26s.]		26	8
Richard Hewson (£130)	6	10	
Roger Fludde (£100)	5		
William Barker (£100)	5		
Edward Dychar, in landes (£20)		26	8
George Hanger (£60)	3		

141. E.359/52, r. 14 gives Mawdlin as first name.
142. E.359/52, r. 14 gives surname as Holden.
143. Herdson was exonerated as a resident of the Cinque Ports, in accordance with the terms of the subsidy act (E.359/52, r. 14).

	£	s.	d
Henrye Cletherowe (£80)	4		
Richard Bowland (£50) [ass. 24s. in Mddx.]		50	
Humfrye Browne (£50)		50	
John Edwardes (£50)		50	
Jeffry Turvile, gent., in fees (£10)		13	4
Henrie Richardsone (£50)		50	
William Watson (£50)		50	
Lewes Writzey (£60)	3		
Nicholas Agar (£60) [x - Essex 10s.]	3		
Giles Flemynge (£50)		50	
Oliver Skinner (£60)	3		
William Hopkyns (£60) [x - Tower of London, Mddx. £1 10s.]	3		
John Daniell (£60) [x - Kent 16s.]	3		
Thomas Morrys (£60)	3		
Arthure Midleton, in fees (£20) [x - Q 5s.]		26	8
Widowe Somers, in fees (£10)		13	4
Thomas Writtington (£50)		50	
Robert Prowe, in landes and fees (£20) [a]		26	8
Strangers			
Balthezar Ruttes (£30) [b - Antwerp mer.]	3		
Nicasius de Glase (£20)		40	
Anthonie Anthonison (£40) [b - Antwerp mer.]	4		
Augustine Bolle (£10) [b - Antwerp mer.]		20	
Widowe Fortre (£10) [b - Antwerp mer.]		20	
Horatio Pallavisino (£350)	35		
375. Cornelis de Nawie (£10)		20	
Haunce Pyke (£20)		40	
Andreas de Loo (£70)	7		
Paule Justiniano (£40)	4		
Doctor Hector Nonnez (£20)		40	
Lewes de Paize (£10)		20	
John de Revera (£30)	3		
Acerbo Velutelli (£40)	4		
John de Swigo (£20)		40	
John Agapito (£30)	3		
Augustine Graffigna (£20)		40	
Marke Anthonie Bassanie (£20) [a]		40	
Jerome Benalio (£40)	4		
Roger James (£300)	30		
Tice Rutton (£150)	15		
Jaques Garrett (£10) [b - Antwerp mer.]		20	
Godfrey Mosanus (£10)		20	
Nicholas de Gottze (£100) [r.118]	15	[sic]	
Jacob Hugoberte (£50)	5		
Arthure Bassaynie (£20) [a]		40	

	£	s.	d
Edward Bassanie (£20) [a]		40	
Andrewe Bassanie (£20) [a]		40	
Hierome Bassanye (£20) [a]		40	
Giles Malapert (£40) [a]	4		
John Lavare (£10) [a]		20	
Israell Huckle (£20)		40	
Jaques and John Garbye (£20)			
[b - Antwerp mer.]		40	
Barnard Lewis (£30)	3		
Allard la Mere (£10) [a]		20	
Fraunces de Venero (£10)		20	
Ambrosse Grasso (£10) [x - Q 64s.]		20	
Jeffrey Brownsman (£10)		20	
Companies			
The Clothworkers, in landes (£71)	4	14	8
The Bakers (£20)		20	

376.   [English]

	£	s.	d
Robert Chawner (£3)		3	
Robert Beamond (£10)		10	
Thopmas Clyffe (£8)		8	
Robert Goodwin (£6)		6	
John Hardware (£3)		3	
William Buckley (£15)		15	
George Pixley (£4)		4	
Zacharie Marshall (£3)		3	
Margerye Holte, widowe (£5)		5	
Edward Parker (£15) [x - Kent 10s.]		15	
Thomas Sherlocke (£4)		4	
Nicholas de la Marshe (£5)		5	
William Bolton (£3)		3	
John Williams (£5) [a]		5	
James Cudnar (£6)		6	
John Clarcke (£3)		3	
Henrye Bullington (£4)		4	
Thomas Wansworthe (£4)		4	
John Holbroke (£3)		3	
John Standley (£3)		3	
Thomas Gaye (£3)		3	
Richard Wood (£3)		3	
Hughe Walley (£8)		8	
Arthure Tilley (£4)		4	
William Webbe (£4) [a]		4	
John Wansworthe (£5)		5	
Thomas Sympson (£3)		3	
Giles Frethren (£3)		3	
Elizabeth Coxton, widowe (£5)		5	
Henrie Sutton (£10)		10	

	£	s.	d
377. Richard Sharpe (£6) [ass. 5s. 4d. in Mddx.]		6	
Helen Chapman, widowe (£8)		8	
Robert Awgar (£5)		5	
William Goldringe (£3) [x - Walbrook ward			
3s. as Golderidge]		3	
Gilbert Kerbye (£3)		3	
Launcelot Jon (£3)		3	
Thomas Frampton (£3)		3	
Christofer Dodson (£3)		3	
Seth Lacye (£40) [x - Langbourn ward 20s.]		40	
Robert Wright (£5)		5	
Richard Travell (£3)		3	
William Harrys (£3)		3	
John West (£4)		4	
Richard Rowhed (£5)		5	
Erasmus Harbye (£12)		12	
Thomas Middleton (£6)		6	
Alice Goldwell (£8) [a]		8	
Thomas Farrington (£6)		6	
Robert Kerbye (£3)		3	
Grace Bradshawe, widowe (£3)		3	
William Bradshawe (£3)		3	
Andrew Hewett (£3)		3	
Thomas Newton (£8)		8	
James Hanscombe (£5)		5	
William Reve (£8)		8	
William Diett (£3)		3	
Daniel Dymarse (£3)		3	
Robert Wilton (£5)		5	
William Golwier (£10)		10	
Nicholas Carnabie (£3)		3	
Roger Rafe (£3)		3	
378. William Myller (£4)		4	
Thomas Willson (£3)		3	
Hughe Ireland (£3)		3	
George Tubman (£4)		4	
Edmond Puckle (£12)		12	
Raffe Quernbye (£6)		6	
John Wardall (£10) [ass. 20s. in			
Dowgate ward]		10	
George Jackson (£12)		12	
Nycholas Atkyns (£8)		8	
John Webbe (£12)		12	
William Younge (£3)		3	
Thomas Clynche, in Mr. William Barkers			
house (£10) [a]		10	
John Newton (£25)		25	

	£	s.	d
George Dodson (£8)		8	
John Williamson (£5)		5	
Thomas Parker (£20)		20	
Henrye Smythe (£10)		10	
James Grafton (£3)		3	
John Davison (£5)		5	
George Mownffeild (£3)		3	
[r.119]			
Henrye White (£3)		3	
Jerome Beale (£25)		25	
Guy Bowers (£3)		3	
Thomas Clarke (£3)		3	
Fraunces Clarke (£4)		4	
Robert Holdborowe (£8)		8	
William Wiggyns (£20)		20	
Edmond Warner (£8)		8	
William Page the younger (£3)		3	
Robert Puckle (£6)		6	
379. Anthonie Williamson (£5)		5	
William Clarke (£12)		12	
Rychard Frenche (£5)		5	
Richard Startop (£5)		5	
Robert Madocke (£3)		3	
Mathew Drinkill (£3)		3	
Richard Bate (£8)		8	
Dionise Gallowaye (£3)		3	
William Cowrtney (£3)		3	
Richard Thomson (£15)		15	
Henry Bourne (£20)		20	
John Gyles (£3)		3	
Hughe More (£3)		3	
Marye Bully, widowe (£5)		5	
Edward Goodman (£5)		5	
Edmond Holte (£25) [x - Q 24s.]		25	
Robert Hutchinson (£4)		4	
Phillipe Watkyns (£5)		5	
Jeffry Nettleton (£15)		15	
John Woodcoke (£3)		3	
John Newton (£8)		8	
John Turck (£6)		6	
Humfry Baker (£3)		3	
Robert Clarke (£12)		12	
Davie Atkinson (£3)		3	
Richard Bowers (£3)		3	
John Byngam (£8) [a]		8	
Richard Frevell (£8)		8	
Thomas Hopton (£8)		8	

	£	s.	d
Mathew Colecloth (£10) [x - Q 6s. 8d.]		10	

380. Richard Lea (£10) 10
John Houghe (£25) 25
Thomas Ashmore (£8) 8
John Braye (£4) 4
Brian Twisilton, in Richard Blouth
    house (£8) [a] 8
William Stafford, in John Lewes
    house (£8) [a] 8
Thomas Arondell (£20) 20
John Gathorne (£5) 5
James Carter (£3) 3
William Hackell (£3) 3
William Dickinson (£3) 3
Richard Barrett (£3) 3
John Fysher (£20) 20
John Wilborne (£3) [a] 3
Thomas Brewyn (£10) 10
Thomas Parkyns (£3) 3
William Quinton (£10) [a] 10
Robert Longe (£10) [a] 10
Thomas Stephens (£10) 10
Edward Wilkinson (£13) 13
Richard Vincent (£10) 10
William Flower (£3) 3
John Hodland (£4) 4
John Shewte (£15) [x - Q 13s. 4d.] 15
William Williamson (£3) 3
Stephen Aborrowe (£20) [a] 20
Thomas Androwes (£10) 10
Albert Atkinson (£3) 3

381. John Wostenham (£9) [x - Mddx. 9s.] 9
Andrewe Peble (£3) 3
Marmaduke Withens (£3) 3
Thomas Royden (£3) 3
John Clarke (£3) 3
Thomas Eaton, in a gardein (£20)
    [x - Q 26s. 8d.] 20
Roger Easton (£3) 3
William Cockes (£3) 3
John Stephinson (£3) 3
Cutbert Rowles (£10) [x - ?] 10
Thomas Valantine (£3) 3
John Hopkyns (£3) 3
Martyn Hopkyns (£5) 5
Roger Greene (£5) 5

	£	s.	d
Henrye Wynter (£3) [a]		3	
Richard Parson (£3)		3	
Robert Smythe (£8)		8	
Mathew Kyrk (£3)		3	
Thomas Herne (£8) [a]		8	
Edmond Riddall, in Rolles house (£3) [a]		3	
Henry Pantry (£3)		3	
Robert Denham (£3)		3	
Robert Forster (£3)		3	
Richard Wright, botson (£3)		3	
Henry Stockley, mason (£3)		3	
Thomas Carter (£10)		10	
George Leonard (£3)		3	
Edward Tilman (£3)		3	
Nicholas Beane (£3)		3	
Thomas Jesson (£8)		8	
William Nicolson (£3) [a]		3	
382. John Walle, a barbor (£3)		3	
Launcellott Grenewood (£3)		3	
Evans Flood (£5)		5	
[r.120]			
Thomas Icoppe (£3)		3	
William Blower (£6)		6	
Benedict Haynes (£3)		3	
Richard Lewes (£10)		10	
Andrew Furstlande (£20)		20	
Richard Earlye (£5) [a]		5	
Andrew Brome (£5)		5	
John Wood (£10)		10	
Edmond Watson (£3)		3	
Thomas Perke (£5)		5	
George Nedeham (£30)		30	
John Bennett (£8)		8	
Widowe [Elizabeth] Smythe (£3)			
[ass. 6s. 8d. in Surrey][144]		3	
Christofer Berrye (£3)		3	
John Fulwood (£6)		6	
John Kymber (£10)		10	
Thomas Jones, a baker (£3)		3	
John Nottingham (£3)		3	
William Kymber (£3)		3	
Mr. Basford, in Ryans house (£5) [a]		5	
Robert Palmer (£4)		4	
Widowe Jeffrey (£3)		3	
Robert Hopton (£3)		3	

144. E.359/52, r. 7 gives Elizabeth as first name.

	£	s.	d
383. Straungers			
Lawrence Farrant (£3)		6	
Bartholomewe Harrison (40s.)		4	
Cornelys Garryson and William Baker, his			
servaunt, poll			8
Giles Barex & John Familfow, servauntes			
with George Pixlex, [*recte* Pixley?], poll			8
Johan Powle, widowe (£10)		20	
her fower children, poll			16
Anthonie de Lyne, in William Biltons house (20s.)		2	
John Baptist, in Pitchers house, poll			4
Jacob Mynistralis, in widowe Eatons house (20s.)		2	
Jasper Augustines cosyn, in the same house, poll			4
Anthonie Pouncell (£5)		10	
and in his house			
Nicholas Haunsman (£10) [b - Antwerp mer.]		20	
Pierre Drumes (£10) [b - Antwerp mer.]		20	
Jaques Bowdett (£10) [a]		20	
Thomas Forten (20s.)		2	
Raphaell Zeet (40s.)		4	
Anne Fisher, Rebecca Lamota, Elizabeth Lamota,			
servauntes with Anthonie Pouncell, poll			12
Giles Bultiell (£20) [b - Antwerp mer.]		40	
James Natigall and Angnes Martien, his			
servauntes, poll			8
John Lambrighte (20s.)		2	
John Fortrye (£5) [b - Antwerp mer.]		10	
384. Margerett Fortre, Elizabeth Tefre, Elizabeth			
Scolett, Samuell Fortre & Margarett			
Fortre, in the house of widowe Fortree, poll			20
Lewen Sarto & Elizabeth Warde, servauntes with			
Mr. Pallavisino, poll			[8]
Jakemyn van Sleper, Cornelis de Neva, Katherine			
de Neves, in the houses of Cornelis de			
Neva, poll			12
Lawrence de Lewis, Hance Walskeret, Derick			
Lynckill, servauntes with Erasmus Harbie,			
poll			12
Haunce Spike, Jarmyn Spike, Aunys Spike,			
Jasper Walscott, Peroune Gesens, in the			
house of Haunce Spike, poll			20
John Warren, poll			4
Jaques de Rewe (£20) [b - Antwerp mer.]		40	
Peter Forman, Charles Carewe & Cristian, in			
the house of Jaques Rewe, poll			12
Alice Rose, servaunt with Anthonie			
Anthonison, poll			4

	£	s.	d
Arthure Fountaine and Isaack, servauntes with			
Nicholas de Glasse, poll			8
385. Allard Farrinewe (40s.)		4	
Katherine de Fore, Joyce Manson, Johan Josue,			
his servauntes, poll			12
John Pyffer (20s.)		2	
Katherine Edwardes, widowe, in Pyffers house,			
poll			4
John Gabriell, Fraunces Gabriell, Judithe le			
Poynere and Susan Gabriell, in Jaques			
Gabriell his house, poll			16
Lambert [Blank] and Katherine [Blank] in James			
Hanscomes house, poll [a]			8
John Calveta (£5)		10	
Stephen de John, poll			4
Peter de Sebean (£10)		20	
Lokes, his man, poll			4
Dionise Fryrie, widowe (£5)		10	
Agnes Alberye, her mayde, poll			4
Peter Apple (£3)		6	
Gosarte Vanderbecke (40s.)		4	
Anthonie Mace, Leon Rosse, Henry Foke, Frances			
Fick, his servauntes, poll			16
Peter Sweter (£5)		10	
Isae Brome, Nicholas Bromesnerthe, servauntes			
with Jeffry Broman, poll			8
386. Thomas Hackett, poll			4
John Varry (£3)		6	
Anthonie Gomes (£3)		6	
Phillippe Machievelli (£3)		6	
Augustine Leveto, poll			4
Fraunces Benalio, servaunt with Jerome Benalio,			
poll			4
Arnold Penyon (£3) [a]		6	
Hector Harte (£3)		6	
Richard Didainer, John Johnson, servauntes in his			
house, poll [a - John Johnson]			8
Stephen de Grace (40s.)		4	
Jane, sister to Mr. Brewen, & Margret his			
maide, in Thomas Brewen's house, poll			8
Martyn Broke (£8)		16	
John Regall, poll			4
George Crewsman (20s.)		2	
Nicholas Lome his servaunt, poll			4
Martyn de la Ut (20s.)		2	
John Martyn, servaunt to John Hopkins, poll			4

	£	s.	d
John Longate (40s.)		4	
[r.121]			
Phillipe del Mall, Perow del Mall, his			
servauntes, poll			8
Adrian Oblee (£3)		6	
Thomas Bosse and John Mase, his servauntes,			
poll			8
Peter Mannock (20s.)		2	
Alice William, servaunt with Mrs. Somers, poll			4
Christofer Williams (20s.)		2	
Edithe Browe, servaunt with John Walt, poll [a]			4
Harman Pike, poll			4
Godfrey Caste (£3)		6	
387. John Grave in the said Godfrey's house, poll			4
Peter Beck (20s.)		2	
Powle Ticle within the said Peter's house			
(£3) [a]		6	
Nicholas Berry (£3)		6	
Sara Myssen his mayde, poll			4
John Davis (20s.)		2	
Gartrid his maide, poll			4
Jerom Uppard, Frances Alvas, Frances Pape,			
Grace, in Mr. Doctor Hector his house, poll			16
Barnard Denys (£3) [a]		6	
Ares Daviga, Jerom, his servauntes, poll			8
Evangelista Constantine, Nicholas Gabito,			
servauntes with Lewes Ryse, poll			8
Jerome, servaunt with John de Revera, poll			4
Joseph Seminarye, Alexander Tirille, Merine			
de Gottes, Addrine Tyne, servauntes			
with Nicholas de Gootes, poll			16
Agustine Piene, Jacob Avale, servauntes with			
Augustine Grafigna, poll			8
Uslye Melinbeck, Uslie Melinbeck, Mary Lewes in			
Richard Lewes' house, poll			12
Trikinge Somers, servaunt with William Blower, poll			4
Thomas Portener, servaunt with Andrew de Loo, poll			4
Veronne Martyn, servaunt with Pawle Justinian, poll			4
James Johnson, Christian Reinoldes, Vanse Mewse,			
John Thomas, Jacob Johnson, servauntes with			
Roger James, poll			20
Guinkin Godfrey, Gord Gaste, Derick Starken,			
Tylman Tunman, John Morrey, servauntes with			
William Longe, poll			20
Jacob Mason, Susan Mason, John Harrof, Peter			
Burlinge and Jane his wyef, in the house of			
Godfrey Mason, poll			20

	£	s.	d

[Total £487 8s.]
[The Summa for this ward has either faded
so far that it is indiscernible or it was
obliterated when the document was repaired.]

388. [r.73]   VYNTRIE WARDE
[Petty collectors: Nycholas Poare, vintner, and Raffe Rydley, vintner.]

ST MARTYNS PARISHE
[English]

	£	s.	d
William Maynard (£50) [x - Mddx. 20s.]		50	
Thomas Serle in landes (£20)			
[x - Essex 20s.]		26	8
Richard Hilles (£60)	3		
Richard Culverwell (£60)	3		
Richard Woar (£60)	3		
Nicholas Poore (£50)		50	
Elizabeth Culverwell (£25)		25	
Elizabeth Roche (£25)		25	
Robert Lee (£30)		30	
Robert Molde (£12)		12	
Marcye Birde widowe (£15)		15	
Thomas Penne (£12)		12	
Barnard Windover (£10)		10	
Thomas Bedwolfe (£10)		10	
Raffe Ridley (£10)		10	
Robert Peacocke (£6)		6	
John Awdry (£6)		6	
John Dardes (£8)		8	
Thomas Ruddock (£6)		6	
George Kirwyn (£6)		6	
Johanne Goody widowe (£6)		6	
John Cosen (£5)		5	
Thomas Dawson (£5)		5	
Henry Damport (£3)		3	
William Mascall (£3)		3	
Edwyn Love (£3) [a]		3	
Thomas Birde (£3)		3	
John Branche (£3)		3	
389. John Culverwell (£3)		3	
William Gonne (£3)		3	
Reginald Walker (£3)		3	
Peter Hutchinson (£3)		3	
John Yates (£3)		3	
Thomas Payne (£3)		3	
William Robinson (£3) [x - Mddx. 10s. 8d.]		3	
William Pursell (£3)		3	

	£	s.	d
Alice Luntlowe widowe (£3)		3	
Ambrose Watson (£3)		3	
John Baker (£3)		3	
James Farrell (£3)		3	
Edmond Bracye (£6)		6	
Richard Dardes (£3)		3	
William Yemans (£3)		3	
Raufe Garfeild (£3)		3	
Strangers			
John Calland thelder poll			4
Barbara Calland his wyfe poll			4
Bartholomewe Maybrand (20s.)		2	
[Blank] Wrenche his servante poll			4
Nicholas Fevar (20s.)		2	
Andrew Rosse poll			4
Harman Johnson poll			4
Allard Linell (£3)		6	
Jane Lineall his wyfe poll			4
Mary Stringer [and] Elizabeth Stringer,			
her daughters poll [a - Mary]			8
Lewis Greney poll			4
Dennys Bacheler poll			4
Mary Pringey poll			4

390.   ST JAMES PARISHE
[English]

	£	s.	d
Richard Platt (£200)	10		
Edmond Chapman (£120) [x - Q £1 4s.;			
ass. £1 12s. in Mddx.]	6		
[r.74]			
Richard Skippe (£120)	6		
Thomas Alworth (£50) [ass. 20s. in Berks.]		50	
Thomas Agar in fees (£20)		26	8
Joanne James widowe (£50)		50	
Elizabeth Hackett widowe in landes (£10)		13	4
Anthonie Holmeade (£30)		30	
Thomas Bland (£10)		10	
William Powle (£10)		10	
John Robotham (£10)		10	
James Shelton (£10)		10	
Roger Jones (£20)		20	
Simon Dewens (£10)		10	
Robert Mudge (£10)		10	
Jhoanne Smarte widowe (£5)		5	
Sebastian Briskett (£10)		10	
Fraunces Evington (£6)		6	
Anthonie Culverwell (£5)		5	
John Darke (£6)		6	

	£	s.	d
William Warren (£6)		6	
Thomas Nokes (£5)		5	
John Person (£5)		5	
Thomas Bentley (£5)		5	
William Woodam (£3)		3	
John Davenaunte (£5)		5	
Robert Peterson (£5)		5	
Thomas Gillett (£3)		3	
William Gardiner (£3)		3	
Thomas Carter (£3)		3	
391. Thomas Stacye (£3)		3	
William Nixon (£3)		3	
Thomas Newton (£3)		3	
Nicholas Honor (£3)		3	
John Richardes (£5)		5	
Thomas Kere (£3)		3	
Thomas Norman (£3)		3	
John Painter (£3)		3	
Henrie Bedle (£3)		3	
Robert Shawe (£3)		3	
Lawrence Arryan (£3)		3	
Phillipe Tradenuyck (£3)		3	
Thomas Robinson (£3)		3	
William Hudson (£3)		3	
Thomas Horton (£3)		3	
Richard Warde (£5)		5	
John Hybby (£3)		3	

Strangers

	£	s.	d
Henrick Bickman (£5)		10	
Alkin his wyfe poll			4
John Harman, Peter Weboo, Gilbert			
Williamson, Mynce his mayde [and]			
Edward Fisher, his servantes poll			20
Arnold Potman, Garrett Edwardes, John Quack,			
Henrick Bootes, servauntes with William			
Hudson & Thomas Robinson poll			16

392.   ST THOMAS APOSTLES
                          [English]

	£	s.	d
Henry Killigrew esquier in landes (£20)		26	8
Richard Shepham (£70)	3	10	
Arthure Dawbeney (£10)		10	
Richard Lister (£20)		20	
Edmond Calthrope (£25)		25	
Peter Saintlowe (£15)		15	
Robert Fysher (£10)		10	
William Taylor (£5)		5	

	£	s.	d
Richard Scales (£12)		12	
Thomas Fletcher (£8)		8	
George Smythehurst (£8)		8	
Raffe Burrowes (£6)		6	
John Bowthe (£5)		5	
John Pendlebury (£5)		5	
William Wood (£3)		3	
John Cocley (£3)		3	
John Cooke (£3)		3	
Nicholas Cooke (£3)		3	
Wylliam Gymber (£3)		3	
John Bolton (£3)		3	
William Robinson (£3)		3	
Roger Bestowe (£3)		3	
Johanne Abbott widowe (£3)		3	
John Abbott (£3)		3	
John Digges (£10)		10	
Margarett Fulmer (£3)		3	
Richard Walton (£3)		3	
Galfrid Abbott (£3)		3	

Strangers

Guilliaune Cantilion (£10)		20	

393. [r.75] ST JOHNES PARISHE
[English]

William Doddesworthe (£80)	4		
Henry Bennett (£3)		3	
Thomas Jones (£3)		3	

TRINITIE PARISHE
[English]

Hughe Floode (£3)		3	
Edward Clarvaux (£3)		3	
Clement Burles (£3)		3	
William Hallatt (£3)		3	
Marye wyfe to Guilliam Cantillion poll			4

ST MICHAELLES PATER NOSTER PARISHE
[English]

John Heydon (£200) [ass. £5 in Mddx.]	10		
John Bodley (£200)	10		
Thomas Knowles (£60)	3		
Samuell Knowles (£60)	3		
Richard Bodley (£50)		50	
Peter Blundell (£80) [x - Devon £1]	4		
Thomas Castlyn (£20) [x - Suff. 9s. 4d.]		20	
Anthonie White (£20)		20	
Humfrey Watson (£10)		10	

	£	s.	d
Raffe White (£3)		3	
Thomas Trippe (£3)		3	
Richard Eture (£5)		5	
Thomas Monslowe (£3)		3	
Straungers			
Nicholas Cowper (£40) [b - Antwerp mer.]		40	[sic]
Abraham Knodder his servaunt poll			4

COMPANIES			
The Companie of Vinteners in landes (£20)		26	8
The Companie of Cutlers (£40)		40	
The Companie of Plombers (£5)		5	
[Endorsed] Summa	133	15	8

394. [r.33]   WALBROOKE WARDE
[Petty collectors: Henry Fawx, grocer. A blank space is left for the second name.][145]

ST SWYTHENS PARRISHE
[English]

	£	s.	d
John Harte, Alderman, Sessor (£260)	13		
Stephen Slanye (£160)	8		
Nicholas Luddington (£60)	3		
John Mansbridge (£50)		50	
Fraunces Bradborne (£50)		50	
Robert Hampson (£50)		50	
Randolph Mannynge (£50)		50	
John Travys (£50)		50	
Edward Osborne (£50) [ass. 8s. in Kent]		50	
Richard Egerton & Samuell Porter (£50)		50	
Walter Plommer (£50)		50	
Barthilmew Barnes (£60)	3		
Thomas Delacar (£50)		50	
Gefferye Elwayes (£50)		50	
Thomas Hill (£3)		3	
John Stone (£8)		8	
Edward Asheby (£3)		3	
John Rushall (£20)		20	
Alexander Hickes (£40)		40	
John Hille (£25)		25	
Hughe Apparrey (£5)		5	
John Powell (£3)		3	
William Weberton (£6)		6	
Richard Randall (£3)		3	
William Redman (£5)		5	

145. The second petty collector was Walter Plummer, who, with Henry Fawx, signed and sealed the indenture.

	£	s.	d
John Prentice (£8)		8	
Henrie Parpoynte (£15)		15	
Raffe Daelle (£3)		3	
Edward Cage (£20)		20	
John Walker (£3)		3	
Christofer Porter (£3)		3	
Fraunces Godd (£20)		20	
Thomas Amyes (£3)		3	
John Bonner (£5)		5	
John Gilborne (£20)		20	
395. Raffe Hasile (£5)		5	
Fraunces Lodge (£3)		3	
William Weekes (£3)		3	
John Sympson (£4)		4	
Nicholas Sympson (£6)		6	

Straingers

	£	s.	d
John Brewer per poll			4
[r.34]			
Inglebarr Kinton per poll			4
John Freemounte (20s.)		2	

ST MARYE WOOLCHURCHE PARISHE
[English]

	£	s.	d
John Ritche (£150) [x - Q £2]	7	10	
Henrie Allington (£150)	7	10	
Robert Brooke (£120)	6		
Robert Smythe (£50)		50	

Straingers

	£	s.	d
Balthesar Sanches (£100)			
[ass. £1 14s. in Mddx.][146]		10	

[English]

	£	s.	d
Robert Kennyngham (£10)		10	
Richard Large (£3)		3	
John Sharpe (£3)		3	
Thomas Hille (£3)		3	
Robert Perpoynte (£3)		3	
William Sherlie (£6)		6	
Peter Beckman (£3)		3	
Raffe Cheke (£3)		3	
William Greanebancke (£3)		3	
Thomas Davies (£3)		3	
William Smythe (£5)		5	
John Kettlewood (£3)		3	
John Selwyne (£3)		3	

146. Marginal notation: 'mediet.' Sanches, the queen's comfit maker, was allowed by privy seal dated 4 July 1581 to pay at the same rate as English (E.359/52, r. 7; E.208/25).

	£	s.	d
Henrie Butler (£20)		20	
Leonard Page (£5)		5	
Richard Horton (£15)		15	
Richard Hunte (£5)		5	
Edward Hunte (£3)		3	
Clement Webster (£10)		10	
Raffe Kynge (£6)		6	
Richard Wade (£3)		3	
John Hille (£3)		3	
William Spencer (£3)		3	
John Whetstone (£3)		3	
Edward Noble (£5)		5	

396.   ST STEPHENS PARRISHE
[English]

	£	s.	d
George Bonde, alderman (£260)	13		
Thomas Goore (£250)	12	10	
John Spenser (£60)	3		
William Brokebancke (£70) [x - Mddx. £1 10s.][147]	3	10	
Sir Richard Baker knight in landes (£100)			
[x - Kent £6 13s. 4d.]	6	13	4
John Watson (£50)		50	
William Bonde (£50)		50	
George Baker (£5)		5	
George Hickeson (£5)		5	
Wyddow Ludford (£5)		5	
George Fenn (£5)		5	
Richard Dickenson (£12)		12	
William Comber (£10)		10	
Gryffyn Jones (£3)		3	
Ellies Owyne (£3)		3	
Roger Brewar (£8)		8	
William Melton (£3)		3	
John Hearne (£4)		4	
Tymothie Cockerell (£3)		3	
John Maie (£3)		3	
John Teyte (£4)		4	
Thomas Jenx (£5)		5	
William Muschampe (£3)		3	
Edward Collyns (£3)		3	
Richard Cheryott (£3)		3	

397.   ST JOHNS PARRISHE
[English]

	£	s.	d
John Trott (£120)	6		
Wyddow Trott (£50)		50	

147. E.359/52, r. 7 gives surname as Broodbank.

	£	s.	d
[r.35]			
John Leger (£60)	3		
Nicholas Pierson (£50)		50	
William Jackson (£12)		12	
John Palmer (£8)		8	
Phillip Dye (£8)		8	
John Ratclyffe (£4)		4	
John Burd (£3)		3	
Robert Meate (£5)		5	
Launcelott Patricke & Thomas			
Wright, partners (£3)		3	
Richard Palmer (£3)		3	
John Isard (£3)		3	
Robert Francke (£3)		3	
William Prestman (£3)		3	
William Raiener (£3)		3	
Henrie Modye (£3)		3	
Robert Pinchebacke (£3)		3	
John Borne (£3)		3	
Raffe Holte (£3)		3	

ST MARYE BUTTOLPHES PARISHE
[English]

	£	s.	d
Henrye Faulke (£50)		50	
Richard Sleford (£100)	5		
Lawncelot Batherst (£70)	3	10	
John Osborne (£60) [x - Mddx. £1]	3		
Robert Gabbett (£50)		50	
Olyver Gilner (£50)		50	
Gryffyn Kenricke (£3)		3	
John Barlowe (£3)		3	
William Baxter (£30)		30	
Robert Dove (£6)		6	
John Colbye (£5)		5	
Peter Cartwright (£15)		15	
Robert Careles (£6)		6	
Peter Scales (£10)		10	
William Golderidge (£3) [ass. 3s. in			
Tower ward]		3	
William Prynce (£3)		3	
Wyddow Hewett (£5)		5	
Georg Bowlles (£15)		15	

398.　　　　ST MARYE ABCHURCH PARISHE
[English]

	£	s.	d
Rychard Yonge (£70)		70	

		£	s.	d
John Burnell (£50)			50	
John Mansbridge thelder (£140)		7		
Roger Mountagne (£60)		3		
	Straingers			
Peter Bowtell (£50) [b - Antwerp mer.]		5		
	[English]			
William Grove (£10)			10	
Edward Weberton (£10)			10	
John Ellies (£20)			20	
William Marshe (£5)			5	
Edward Clarke (£5)			5	
Wyddowe Perte (£3)			3	
William Clarke (£3)			3	
Martyn Leather (£10)			10	
William Joanes (£3)			3	
Richard Parname (£3)			3	
Richard Kynge (£3)			3	
Roger Reigenoldes (£15)			15	
John Beaver (£10)			10	
John Leke (£10)			10	
	[Endorsed] Summa	220	11	

297

THE 1541 ORPHANS' BOOK

[The last rotulet (r.26) of the 1541 subsidy roll is the certificate of assessment of the estates of orphans of citizens of London. The certificate is an estreat of an indenture between the subsidy commissioners for London and George Medley, Chamberlain of the City of London, whom the commissioners named petty collector of the assessments on orphans' estates. (On the assessment of orphans, see the Introduction, pp. xviii, xxxvi.) Many parts of this rotulet are too faded to be legible.]

	£	s.	d.
399. Thomas Maynde, sh[ ]an, Richard [ ], draper, for the Orphan of William Blund[ ] Shoman[?] (£92 22d.)		46	1
400. John Symson, haberdasher, Henry Brayn, merchauntaylor, for thorphan of Lawrence Bradshawe, taylor (£36)		18	
401. Robert Wollworth, grocer, John Nevell, iremonger, Symon Webbe, dyer, for thorphan of Nicholas Whit sky[ ] (£92 12s. 6d.)		46	4
402. John Hargatson, brewer, Henry Bawly, skynner, for the Orphan of Richard Remo[ ], letherseller (£37 12d.)		19	
403. Elyzabeth Stathom, vid., Richard Gervis, mercer, for thorphan of William Stathom, mercer (£741)	18	10	6
404. Thomas Wattes, draper, Thomas Curtes, pewterer, for thorphan of John Maydenhed, draper (£27 3s. 6d.)		13	7
405. Thomas Bowyer, John Lane, grocers, for the Orphan of John Maydenhed, draper (£55 11s. 6d.)		27	6
406. Jamys Page, haberdasher, John Wyndman, or', for thorphan of John Maydenhed, draper (£113 11d.)		56	6

298

	£	s.	d
407. Thomas Whit, Robert Melyshe, taylors, for thorphan of Rychard Blakgrave (£87 15s.)		43	11
408. Roger Whaplod, draper, John Jakes, mercer for thorphan of Robert Hansard, taylor (£54 9s. 6d.)		27	3
409. John Baynton, grocer, George Foyster, corier, of thorphan of William Howe, broderer (£23 2s. 6d.)		11	7
410. Henry Brayn, taylor, William Uxley, grocer, for thorphan of Henry Pykman, bowyer (£37 7d.)		18	6
411. John Sturgion, haberdasher, John F[ ]ing, taylor, for the orphan of Hughe Fyliok (£165 5s. 7d.)	4	2	7
412. Robert Barfot, mercer, Henry Wyncot, taylor, for thorphan of Richard Haydon, brewer (£87 15s.)		43	10
413. Edward Burlace, mercer, William Bikner, haberdasher, for the orphan of Jamys Marston, mercer (£196 12d.)	4	18	
414. Roger Chan', mercer, Thomas Maynerd, clothworker for thorphan of William Courtman alias Clerke, vynterer (£157 8s. 4d.)		78	8
415. Richard Buttle, Richard Holte for thorphan of Thomas Lee, merchant taylor (£185 5s.)	4	12	7½
416. John Smyth, Thomas Whilt, merchauntaylors, for thorphan of Thomas Lee, merchantaylor (£185 5s.)	4	12	7½
417. John Lewen, Edmund Pyrry, drapers, for the Orphan of Thomas Mannysworth alias Manser (£81 10s. 3d.)		40	10
418. Ambrose Barker, grocer, Thomas Lyncoln, pan', for thorphan of Robert Lacy, grocer (£88 17s.)		44	6

	£	s.	d
419. Nicholas Sympson, barbor surgion, Thomas Philippes for the Orphan of Rychard Aron, draper (£23 3s. 3d.)		11	6
420. Robert Milles, Raulf Foxley, merchaunt, for the Orphan of Alyxander Hillton (£185 5s.)	4	12	7½
421. Edward North, gent., Thomas Burnell, mercer, for thorphan of Edward Myrfyn, skynner (£210 12s. 5d.)		105	4
422. Elyzabeth Wade, wydow, Richard Holte, taylor, for thorphan of Robert Wade, merchauntaylor (£72 2s. 6d.)		36	
423. Robert Barton, Aur', Robert Norton, iremonger, for the orphan of John Tynley (£37 12d.)		18	6
424. Nicholas Bulle, Thomas Callton, aur', for the orphan of Thomas Welles, haberdasher (£62 7½d.)		31	
425. Ambrose Barker, grocer, Robert Allford, draper, for thorphan of Hughe U[mp]ton[?], draper [ ]		[ ]	
426. John Sadler, draper, William Castlyn, mercer, for thorphan of Hughe Umpton[?], draper (£193 13s. 9d.)	4	16	9
427. William Dauntesey[?], John Garrardes, woollpakker, for thorphan of Hughe Umpton[?], draper (£224 5s.)		112	1
428. Agnes Smyth, wydow, Richard Pykering, brewer, for thorphan of Robert Smyth, iremounger (£148 4s.)		74	
429. Thomas Trappes, John Chaundelor, aur', for the Orphan of Thomas Gadbury, aur' (£40)		20	
430. Agnes Best, vid., Robert Hamond, wodmounger, for thorphan of Thomas Best, baker (£53 17s. 9d.)		26	11

	£	s.	d
431. John Pace, draper, Raulf Bowryn, clothworker, for thorphan of John West, taylor (£27 15s. 6d.)		13	11
432. George Barne, haberdasher, David Jonys, baker, for thorphan of Richard Rolfe (£37 12d.)		18	6
433. Elyzabeth Browne, vid., William Robyns, mercer, for thorphan of Thomas Browne, mercer (£68 5s.)		34	1
434. Henry Sukley, William Harper, merchauntaylors, for the orphan of Richard Fletcher, taylor (£253 12d.)	6	6	6
435. Robert Herdes, merchauntaylor, Thomas Maynard, clothworker, for thorphan of John West, merchauntaylor (£39 12s. [ ])		19	10
436. Thomas Doughtie, stokfyshemounger, Nycholas Cosen, taylor, for thorphan of William Dokket, grocer (£211 9s. 8d.)		105	9
437. Nicholas Allwyn, Thomas Bavyn, aur', for thorphan of John Wathouse, vyntener (£37 12d.)		18	6
438. Thomas Hedley, draper, William Rigeley, merchaunt taylor, for thorphan of Wyllyam Sympson, skynner (£46 2s. 7d.)		23	1
439. Raulf Aley, grocer, William Gresham, mercer, for the orphan of Rychard Croupton, mercer (£242 7s. 8d.)		6	14
440. John Lute, Raulf Hamersley, clothworkers, for thorphan of John Hemyngway, draper (£36 10s. 5d.)		18	3
441. William Hewetson, Henry Polstede, merchauntaylors, for thorphan of William Nycollson, draper (£103 2s. 10d.)		51	8
442. Olyver Leder, fyshemonger, Henry Wymot, merchauntaylor, for thorphan of John Rudston, Aldermen (£37 3s.)		18	7

	£	s.	d
443. John Ascue, draper, William Gresham, mercer, for the Orphan of John Rudston, Alldreman (£216 5s.)		108	1½
444. John Warner, skynner, Thomas Abraham, letherseller, for thorphan of Henry Lodington, grocer (£148 4s.)		74	1
445. John Cokkes, sen., John Cokkes, jun., for thorphan of John Lane, tawlowchaundelor (£27 14d.)		13	6
446. Richard Jervis, mercer, Roger Horton, aur', for the Orphan of Henry Lodyngton, grocer (£222 6s.)		111	1
447. Richard Ferror, grocer, Thomas Cosen, inholder, for thorphan of John Johnson (£50 9s. 3d.)		25	3
448. Richard Hart, baker, Hamo'd Amcotes, stokfyshemonger, for thorphan of John Pyne, scryvener (£47 7s. 9d.)		23	8
449. John Bekyngham, stokfyshemonger, Leonard Johnson, stokfyshemonger, for thorphan of Walter Palley, stokfyshemonger (£144 7s. 2d.)		72	2
450. Roger Chalyoner, mercer, John Charley, cowper, for the Orphan of John Wendoner, skynner (£40 8s.)		20	2
451. Jefferay Chamber, merchauntaylor, Edward Stuard, sadler, for the Orphan of John Rudston, Alldreman (£123 4s. 10d.)		60	19
452. Margery Allpart, vid., Thomas Marbery, haberdasher, for thorphan of Edward Allpart, aur' (£277 17s. 6d.)	6	19	
453. Hughe Eglesfyld, letherseller, William Robyns, mercer, for the Orphan of Thomas Eglesfyld, letherseller (£149 7s.)		74	8
454. Ambrose Wolley, grocer, John Davy, clothworker, for thorphan of Nicholas Pynchon (£48 17s. 10d.)		24	5

	£	s.	d
455. William Beale, Willyam Carket, skynners for the Orphan of Nicholas Pynchon (£48 17s. 10d.)		24	6
456. John Canon, Rychard Bottole, taylors, for thorphan of Nycholas Pynchon (£48 17s. 10d.)		24	6
457. Richard Gervis, mercer, for thorphan of Thomas Cryspe, mercer (£85 16s.)		42	11
458. John Egleston, grocer, William Myrry, grocer, for thorphan of John Barton, mercer (£96 18s.)		48	5
459. William Harper, Thomas Howe, merchauntaylors, for thorphan of Fewtor Doctor, vyntener (£40 3s. 11d.)		20	
460. Leonard Johnson, Thomas Pawley, stokfyshemongers for the Orphan of Nycholas Pynchon, bocher (£48 17s. 10d.)		24	6
461. John Margatson, brewer, for thorphan of Humfray Rogerson, inholder (£28 7s. 10d.)		14	2
462. Anthony Maler, Rychard Grymes, haberdasher, for thorphan of John Broke, mercer (£197 6s. 8d.)	4	18	8
463. John Wyllford, William Wilford, merchauntaylors for thorphan of Guye Rawlynson, merchantaylor (£69 7s. 6d.)		34	8
464. Robert Allford, George Brugg, drapers, for thorphan of John Permenter, clothworker (£125 13s. 4d.)		62	10
465. Anna Plesaunce, vid., Stephin Kyrton, merchauntaylor, for the Orphan of John Plesaunce, brewer (£178 3s. 6d.)	4	9	1
466. Robert Chapman, draper, Robert Lorde, Aur', for thorphan of Robert Bromsted, haberdasher (£32 8s. 4d.)		16	2

	£	s.	d
467. Agnes Hill, vid., Davyd Wodrof, haberdasher, for the Orphan of John Hill, haberdasher (£25 6s. 9d.)		12	8
468. Walter Younge, Thomas Whit, merchaunt, for thorphan of Peter Cave, draper (£78)		39	
469. Walter Younge, Raulf Foxley, for thorphan of Thomas Kytson, knyght (£300)	7	10	
470. Nicholas Fuller, Thomas Fuller, for thorphan of Rowland Edwardes, mercer (£161 8s. 5d.)	4		8
471. Agnes Tolle, vid., Thomas Bysshop, mercer, for thorphan of Robert Tolle, taylor (£25)		12	6
472. Lady Pecok, for thorphan of John Hasyllfote (£390)	9	15	
473. Executors of Humfray Cheshire, bocher, for the Orphan of the said Humfray (£87)		43	6
474. Thomas Chamberleyn, draper, Thomas Vycary, barbor surgion, for thorphan of Peter Cave (£39)		19	6
475. Thomas Wyvell, John Machelle, clothworkers, for thorphan of John Rudston, Alldreman (£58 10s.)		29	3
476. William Monslow, Henry Polstede, mercers, for thorphan of Alyxander Plymley (£35 5s. 7d.)		17	7¹/₂
477. Humfray Beche, salter, Christofer Campion, mercer, for thorphan of Alyxander Plymley, mercer (£97 10s.)		48	9
478. Robert Long, William [ ], mercers, for thorphan of John Coping, [ ] [ ]		78	
479. Rowland Shake[ ], John Hare, mercers, for thorphan of [ ] Ha[ ]ngton, mercer (£202 18s. 8d.)		100	18

	£	s.	d
480. Richard Brog[ ], [ ] Henry [ ], grocer, for thorphan of Walter[?] Martyn[?], grocer [ ]		27	
481. Edward Lacy[?], merchaunt taylor, Thomas [ ], skynner, for the Orphan of [ ] [ ]		[ ]	

[The next six entries in the manuscript, being almost entirely lost, are omitted here.]

	£	s.	d
482. George Crowche, skynner, Jamys Pag[ ], haberdasher, for thorphan of William Turnor, skynner (£230 10s.)	5	15	3
483. William Bele, pallipar', William Crumpton, [ ], for thorphan of [Ralph] Dodmer, Aldreman (£102 7s. 6d.)		51	2
484. Edmund Cokerell, grocer, Henry Polstede, taylor, for thorphan of Raulf Dodmer (£292 10s.)	7	6	3
485. George [ ], pellipar, William Hobson, haberdasher, for thorphan of Raulf Dodmer, Aldreman (£97 10s.)		48	9
486. [ ] [ ], [ ], Roger Welles, [ ] for thorphan of John Stephins, clothworker [ ]		19	4
487. Nicholas Cosen, taylor, Elyzabeth Hynde, vid., for thorphan of Robert Hynde, haberdasher (£58 10s.)		29	3
488. Thomas Browne, aur', Robert Mellyse [?], merchaunt for thorphan of Thomas Godfray, aur' (£30 10d.)		15	
489. Agnes Hatton, vid., William Raynold, bowyer, for thorphan of William Hatton, ferror (£47 16s.)		23	11
490. John Rawlyns, skynner, John Berde [?], taylor, for thorphan of Walter Wright, merchaunt (£26 13s. 4d.)		13	4

	£	s.	d
491. Thomas Trappes, [ ], Robert Mellyshe, merchaunt, for thorphan of Raulf Dodmer, Aldreman (£98 10s.)		49	3
492. Cristofer Payne, brewer, William Clerk, skynner, for thorphan of Hughe Hatton, brewer (£30)		15	
493. Margaret Browne, vid., Henry Sukley, merchaunt, for thorphan of Edward Browne, merchauntaylor (£143)		71	6
494. Margaret Goore, vid., John Watson, Inholder, for thorphan of John Goor, inholder (£33 3s.)		16	7
495. Elyzabeth Smyth, vid., John Byrde, barbor, for thorphan of William Smyth, barbor surgion (£58 10s.)		29	3
496. Edward Borlace, Humfray Pakyngton, mercers, for thorphan of Jamys Balney, mercer (£400 9s. 6d.)	10		3
497. William Smyth, [ ], Thomas Marbery [?], for thorphan of Raulf Dodmer, Aldreman [ ]		48	9
498. Letys [ ], vid., Edward Sa[ ], [ ], for thorphan of Henry [ ], [ ] [ ]		19	10
499. [ ] Carow, wydow, [ ] Skyd[ ], mercer[?], for thorphan of [ ] Carow, clothworker (£390)		9	15
500. Margar[ ] [ ], vid., Thomas Broke, merchaunt, for thorphan of David[?] Jard[ ], cowper (£55 18s.)		28	
501. Roger Himyng[?], Edward[?] Warner, pisc', for the Orphan of John Henry, merchaunt (£34 2s.)		17	
502. Nicholas Revell, grocer, Richard Williams, [ ], for thorphan of Richard Atkyns, [ ] (£48 10s.)		24	3

	£	s.	d
503. John Milles[?], [ ], John Sweteman[?], grocer, for thorphan of John[?] Richard, draper (£333 18s.)	8	7	
504. John Juxson, John [ ], merchaunt, for thorphan of John Smyth, merchaunt (£195)	4	17	6
505. Humfray Pakyngton, Edward Burlace[?], [ ], for thorphan of Robert Pakyington, mercer (£713 19s.)	17	17	
506. Robert Smyth, grocer, Thomas Cheyny, saltor, for thorphan of Thomas Barley, grocer (£244 14s.)	6	2	4
507. John Machell, clothworker, John Maynard, mercer[?], for thorphan of Lawrence Carow, clothworker (£316 17s.)	7	18	5
508. Raulf Lathom, Nicholas Allwyn, aur', for the Orphan of John Twysellton, Alldreman (£148 13s.)		74	4
509. William Caylewaye, aur', William Bonham, stacioner, for thorphan of William Robynson, sadler (£50 14s.)		25	4
510. Giles Brugge, Antony Fabyan, drapers, for the Orphan of Humfray Monmouth, Aldreman (£221 6s. 6d.)		110	8
511. Alyxaunder Perpoynt, Thomas Perpoynt, drapers, for thorphan of Humfray Monmouth, Aldreman (£195)	4	17	10
512. John Fayry, John Carway, mercers, for thorphan of William Whit, letherseller (£410)	10	5	
513. Hughe [ ]nos, Robert Smyth, brewers, for thorphan of Robert Warner, brewer (£97 2s.)		48	6
514. Margaret Shaklok, vid., John God, tailor, for the Orphan of Jamys Shaklok [ ] (£63 16s.)		31	11

	£	s.	d
515. Ambrose Barke[r], grocer, Raulf Devenet, taylor, for thorphan of Humfray Monmouth, Aldreman (£195)	4	17	6
516. Joanne Hodder, wydow, Nicholas Bark[er?], armorer, for thorphan of Arthure Hodder, taylor (£23 11s.)		11	9
517. Thomas Fysher, draper, Richard Povy, bowyer, for thorphan of Humfray Monmouth, Alldreman (£195)	4	17	6
518. Thomas Rowe, William Mery, grocer, Walter Younge, merchaunt, for thorphan of Robert Rowe, merchaunt (£221 11s. 8d.)		110	9
519. Thomas Rowe, Roger Hamyng[?], fyshemonger, Robert Smyth, clothworker, for the orphan [of] Robert Rowe, merchaunt (£221 11s. 8d.)		110	9
520. William [ ], George Robynson, [ ], for the orphan of John Mondy, Knyght, Alldreman (£159 3s. 10d.)		79	8
521. William Harding, mercer, William Southwodde, Aur', for thorphan of Thomas Brewester, pisc' (£118 19s.)		59	6
522. Thomas Rowe, Thomas Wanles, skynner, Christofer Nicollson, merchaunt, for thorphan of Robert Rowe (£221 11s. 8d.)		110	9
523. William Taylor, haberdasher, Ewstane Ripeley, taylor, for thorphan of John Hasylfote, haberdasher (£180 8s.)	4	10	3
524. George Heton, taylor, William Tukker, grocer, for thorphan of John Hasyllfote, haberdasher (£180 8s.)	4	10	3
525. John Yareley, John Lunde, haberdashers, for thorphan of John Hasillfote (£226 18s.)		113	6
526. William Goodhew, grocer, Edmund Baker, cordwainer, for thorphan of Roger Walker, wollman (£39)		19	6

		£	s.	d
527.	Margaret Long, wydow, Thomas Blank, haberdasher, for thorphan of John Long, late Alldreman (£85 15s. 9d.)		42	11
528.	John Blundell, John Hare, mercers, for the Orphan of Hewe Mothwolde, mercer (£97 10s.)		48	9
529.	Agnes Cachemayde, wydow, Henry Brayn, merchaunt, for thorphan of John Cachemayd (£292 10s.)	7	6	3
530.	Executors of Robert Deane, grocer, for the orphan of the said Robert Deane (£298 3s. 4d.)	7	9	2
531.	Executors of John Burnam, corier, for thorphan of the said John Burnam (£94 8s.)		47	2
532.	Executors of John Smyth, baker, for thorphan of the sayd John Smyth (£39)		19	6
533.	Executors of John Hoke, bocher, for thorphan of the sayd John Hoke (£42)		21	
534.	Executors of Robert Lyng for thorphan of the same Robert (£160)	4		
535.	Letyse Worshop, vid., John Garret, salter, for thorphan of John Worshop, scryvener (£35)		17	6
536.	Henry Awsten, haberdasher, Nicholas Cosen, merchaunt, for thorphan of Raulf Dodmer, Knight, late Alldreman (£195)	4	17	6
537.	Anne Inglyshe, wydow, William Wyllford, jun', merchaunt, for thorphan of Mighell Inglyshe, mercer (£170 10s.)	4	5	3
538.	John Chaunterell, Thomas Gyttons, vyntenor, for the Orphan of Richard Harris, haberdasher (£250 12s.)	6	5	4
539.	William Newman, draper, Walter Astelyn, peuterer, for thorphan of Richard Harris, haberdasher (£125 6s.)		62	8

	£	s.	d
540. Isabell Witlok, wydow, John Bowhen, brewer, for thorphan of Christofer Whitlok, brewer (£82 9s.)		41	3
541. Thomas Bower, draper, Robert Clerke, baker, for thorphan of Thomas Grafton, draper (£65)		32	6
542. Edmund Ascue, draper, Richard Rede, salter, for thorphan of William Pratt, grocer (£282 10s.)	7		15
543. Henry Awsten, haberdasher, John Charley, cowper, for thorphan of Nicholas Denys, skynner (£185 12s.)	4	12	10
544. Thomas Spencer, clothworker, Rychard Bowle, barbor surgion, William Peter, lynen draper, for thorphan of John Molle breuer (£89 8s.)		44	8
545. John Guylbert, haberdasher, Edward Saunders, letherseller, for the orphan of Thomas Bayly, bowyer (£21 9s.)		10	9
546. Rychard Ascue, John Ascue, drapers, for thorphan of William Pratt, grocer (£349 8s. 4d.)	8	14	
547. Richard Ascue, John Ascue, drapers, for thorphan of William Pratt, grocer (£123 15s.)		[ ]	
548. Katheryn Parker, wydowe, John Armestrong, pastelor for thorphan of Rychard Parker, Coke (£26 16s.)		13	6
549. John Chaundelor, Aur', Morgan Wolf, Aur' for thorphan of Nicholas Jenyns, Aldreman (£68 5s.)		34	1 1/2
550. Jamys Hynshall, broderer, Henry Vaughan, draper, for the orphan of Richard Gates, paynter stayner (£56 14s.)		[ ]	
551. Laurence Ja[ ]on, fyshemonger, William [ ], [ ], for the orphan of John Pet[ ], [ ], [ ]		11	8

	£	s.	d
552. Edmund Ascue, draper, Richarde Rede[?], salter, for thorphan of William Pratt, draper (£182 12s.)	4	11	7
553. Anne Harper, wydow, John Watsone, Inholder, for thorphan of Thomas Harpenny [?], taylor [ ]		32	6
554. [ ] Wodde, cowper, [ ] [ ], clothworker, for thorphan of John Hall, draper (£81)		40	6
555. Christofer Draper, Iremounger, Stephyn Tego, mercer, for the orphan of Nicholas Jenyns, skynner (£78)		39	
556. Antony Elderton, Leonarde Johnson, Stokfyshemongers, for thorphan of Nycholas Jenyns, Allderman (£30 2s. 8d.)		15	1
557. Thomas Offeley, merchauntaylor, Davyd Wodruf, haberdasher, for the Orphan of William Comaunder, brewer (£140 10s. 6d.)		70	3
558. John [ ], merchaunt, Thomas Percy, skynner, for thorphan of Richard Lany, scryvener (£58 10s.)		29	3
559. Olyver Dawbnew, Rychard Eve, Talowchaundlers, for thorphan of Walter Thomas, letherseller (£72 8s.)		36	2
560. Thomas Bowyer, grocer, Richarde Osborn, grocer, for thorphan of William Cely, grocer (£65)		32	6
561. Sensa[?] Campion and Robert [ ], merchauntaylors, for the orphan of Thomas [ ], merchaunt (£130)		65	
562. John [ ], merchauntaylor, Peter [ ], [ ], for the orphan of Henry Grave, draper (£52 18s.)		26	6
563. Wallter Jobson, William Howet, clothworkers, for thorphan of William Page, clothworker (£204 15s.)		102	5

	£	s.	d
564. Robert Ashehurst, Edmund Lee, Aur', for thorphan of Edmund Hatcombe, Aur' (£145 10s. 6d.)		72	9
565. Anne Nalyn, vid., Christofer Nering, mercer, for thorphan of John Nalyn, grocer (£103 5s. 4d.)		51	7¹/₂
566. Elyzabeth Walton, vid., William Lantman for the orphan of Rychard Wallton, wollpakker (£73 2s.) discharged bycause it is more charge in Middelsex by xiid.		36	6
567. Henry Fysher and Androw Judde, pellipar' for thorphan of William Pratt, draper (£300)	7	10	
568. Thomas Acon al[alien], Akune Plummer, John Twyford, vyntener, for thorphan of William Clementes (£40)		20	
569. William Wilkynson, mercer, William Hobson, haberdasher, for the orphans of John Smyth, baker (£120)		60	
570. Robert Staly, George Foyster, curriers, for thorphan of John Blaklok, curryer (£27 13s.)		13	10
571. Katheryn Wyllcokes, vid., Mathew Dale, haberdasher, for thorphan of Thomas Lewes, haberdasher (£260)	6	10	
572. Robert Trappes, Nicholas Trappes, Aur', for thorphan of Edmund Shaw, haberdasher (£278 11s. 6d.)	6	19	[ ]
573. John Traves, George Crowche, pellipar', for thorphan of Richard Traves, merchauntaylor (£137 6s. 8d.)		68	8
574. Rychard Farr[ ], draper, William Clerke, [ ], for thorphan of Rychard Traves (£68 13s. 4d.)		34	4
575. Joanne Harris, vid., Robert Smythe, brewer, for thorphan of Adam Harris, Tawlowchaundlor (£40 6s.)		20	2

	£	s.	d
576. Denys Leveson, vid., for the orphan of Nicholas Leveson, mercer (£258 18s. 11d.)	6	9	6
577. Denys Leveson for the orphan or Nicholas Leveson, Mercer (£517 17s. 10d.)	12	19	
578. Denys Leveson, vid., for thorphan of Nycolas Leveson, mercer (£517 17s. 10d.)	12	19	
579. William [ ], grocer, John [ ], [ ], for the orphan of Robert Redman (£145)		72	6
580. Margaret Culley, vid., John Gray, clothworker, for thorphan of Raulf Cullen, talowchaundler (£36)		18	
581. Elizabeth Paxton, vid., George Baldok, bowyer, for thorphan of Thomas Paxton, founder (£30 10s.)		15	1¹/₂
582. Myles Wymbyshe, mercer, Robert Kycheyn, sadler, for thorphan of Robert Mannyng, Iremonger (£54 10s. 8d.)		27	3
583. John Langley, John Chaundeler, Aur', for the orphan of Robert Alen, Aur', discharged bycause the 1xiiiˡⁱviiˢ is devided amonge v childeryn			
584. John Farthing Raulf Foxley, merchauntaylors, for theorphan of John Raynoldes, mercer (£50)		25	
585. Elizabeth Alen vid. Robert Redmer, bocher, for the orphan of Robert Alen, bocher (£20 13s. 4d.)		10	4
586. Alyce Davell, wydow, Richard Turnor, taylor, for the orphan of John Davell, waxchaundeler (£27 4s. 6d.)		13	7
587. William Robyns, mercer, Androwe Judde, pellipar', for the orphan of William Collsell, mercer (£179 3s. 4d.)	4	9	7

	£	s.	d
588. Rychard Wylkynson, mercer, William Burrey, draper, for thorphan of William Collsell, mercer (£179 3s. 4d.)	4	9	7
589. Nicholas Bacon, mercer, Henry Fysheer, pellipar', for the orphan of William Collsell, mercer (£358 6s. 8d.)	8	19	2
590. Elizabeth Whit, wydow, John Halse, clothworker, for the orphan of Thomas Whit, sen', merchaunt (£66 5s.)		33	1½
591. Alyce Barley, wydow, John Curtes, letherseller, for the orphan of Walter Barley, brewer (£65 3s. 4d.)		32	7
592. Joanne Trom, wydow, Thomas Adams, stacyoner, for the orphan of William Trom, taylor (£25 8s.)		12	8
593. Robert Mellyshe, merchauntaylor, Richard Hall, dyar, for thorphan of John Willcokkes, haberdasher (£113)		56	6
594. Katheryn Wyllcokkes, vid., John Edwardes, haberdasher, for thorphan of John Wyllcokkes (£113)		56	6
595. Jamys Leveson, mercer, Denys Leveson, vid., for thorphan of William Clerke, mercer (£250)	6	5	
596. Jamys Leveson, mercer, Denys Leveson, vid., for thorphan of William Clerke, mercer (£250)	6	5	
597. Richard Fylde, draper, William Parker, draper, for the orphan of Clementes Towne, baker (£80)		40	
598. Olyver Dawbney, tawlow chaundler, Androw Yarley, merchaunt, for the orphan of Thomas Serles, bocher (£38 9s.)		19	3
599. Antony Elyot, Robert Chapman, pannar', for thorphan of Thomas Kytson, knyght (£300)	7	10	

	£	s.	d
600. Nicholas Alldy, Thomas Alldy, grocers, for the orphan of John Hill, merchauntaylor (£100)		50	
601. Kymburghe Pykman, vid., John Foster, pann', for thorphan of Thomas Pykman, draper (£78 9s.)		39	3
602. Raulf Foxley, Antony Cole, merchauntaylors, for thorphan of John Coke, marchauntaylor (£49 7s.)		24	8
603. John Machell, clothworker, John Blundell, mercer, for thorphan of Thomas Kytson, knight and Alldreman (£300)	7	10	
604. Joanne Westmore, vid., Robert Westmore, taylor, for thorphan of Rychard Westmore, iremounger (£106)		53	
605. Robert Curson, gent., Robert Hamond, wodmounger, for thorphan of Rychard Gybson, marchauntaylor (£98)		49	
606. Thomas Trappes, aur', Davyd Jonys, baker, for thorphan of Edward Coke, aur' (£55 10s.)		27	9
607. Thomas Whit, John Jenkyns, merchauntaylors, for thorphan of Peter Cave, draper (£39)		19	6
Summa Totalis pro parte dominus Regis	£696	14s.	8½d.

INDEX OF PERSONS

Roman figures refer to page numbers in the introduction, arabic figures to the numbers of sections in the text. All names are indexed, but obvious variants of a single surname are collected under the standard or most common form. Given the variability of sixteenth-century spelling, it may be necessary when searching for an individual to look under more than one possible variant forms of his or her name.

317

319

Index of persons

331

Index of persons

333

342

343

345

Index of persons

357

363

Index of persons

Mare, Meyr, John, 225, 244; *see also*
  Maare
Margatson, Margetson, Margettson:
  John, 139, 461
  Thomas, 189
Maria, Alicia, 190; *see also* Marya
Mariet, Marryat, Maryatt, Maryot:
  John, 329
  Richard, 130, 131, 350
  Thomas, 334
Marinis, Morysyne de, 134
Marlar, Marler, Anthony, 66, 77,
  267
Marliart, John, 15
Marlowe, Mistress Alice, 77
Marre (*see also* Mare):
  Henry, 67
  John, 67
Marret, Thomas, 203
Marriage, Peter, 291n
Marrowe:
  John, 183
  Peter, 303
  William, 18
Marry, Guillyam, 370
Marryat, *see* Mariet
Marryon, William, 198
Marse, Hugh, 163
Marsh, Marshe, Marsshe:
  Alice, widow, 281
  Andrew, 354
  Henry, 248
  John, 89(2), 322
  Nicholas, 81
  Nicholas de la, 376
  Robert, 300
  Thomas, 300, 315
  William, 398
Marshall:
  —, widow, 293
  Edward, 302
  Francis, 239(2)
  Jane, 266
  John, 275, 318
  Martin, 266
  Ralph, 36
  Richard, 203
  Thomas, 127, 128
  Zachary, 376
Marsham, William, 268
Marson, Roger, 222
Marston, James, 413
Martenson, Mighell, 156
Marten, Martien, Martine, Martyn,
  Martynne, Martyn:
  —, widow, 319
  Doctor —, xxxix n, 246
  The Lady —, 267
  Angnes, 383
  Edmund, 19

Edward, 325
Gabriel, 337
Garard, 13
George, 224
Guylham, 128
Hubert, 223
Jacob, 190
James, 142
John, xxxviii, 9, 10, 105, 138, 142, 163,
  170, 209(2), 222, 279, 315, 386
Mathew, 331
Nicholas, 37
Peter, 188
Ralph, 174
Richard, 120
Richard, alderman, 1 n, 224
Roger, 20
Rowland, 224
Simon, 249
Sybell, widow, 16
Thomas, 106, 200, 232, 329, 337, 345,
  387
Walter, 480
William, 283
Marvell, Saunders, 133
Marvod, John, 266
Marvyn:
  Roger, 319
  Sir Thomas, 315
Marya, John, 106, 325; *see also*
  Maria
Maryne:
  Anthony, 135
  Nicholas, 135
Maryot, *see* Mariet
Mascall, Maskall:
  Dorothy, widow, 307
  John, 275, 306
  Richar, 306
  Robert, 278, 362
  William, 310, 388
Mase, *see* Mace
Masewelo, Antony, 49
Masham, Thomas, 323
Maskrye, Richard, 104
Mason:
  Agnes, 46
  Alexander, 101
  Egbert, 7
  Godfrey, 387
  Jacob, 387
  John, 145, 348
  Oliver, 309
  Robert, 210
  Stephen, 103
  Susan, 387
  Tanekyn, 363
  Thomas, 216
  William, 335
Masse, William, 194

380

381

Index of persons

Neale:
  Richard, 235
  William, 330
Neapolye, Nicholas de, 136
Necton, William, 178
Nedeham:
  Arthur, 354
  George, 382
  James, 156
  Thomas, 303
  William, 371
Negoose, William, 322
Negro, Dyego, 128
Neighburgh:
  Henrick, 356
  Margaret, 356
Nelking, Jacob, 370
Nell, Mistress —, widow, 151
Nellman, Cornellys, 370
Nelson, John, 169, 175; *see also*
  Nallson
Nenton, Nicholas, 274
Nepper, James, 183; *see also* Napper
Nering, Christopher, 565
Neryat, Marriat, 152
Nese, Richard, 46
Neskyn, Henry, 140
Nettelles, William, 244
Nettleton, Geoffrey, 379
Neva, Cornelis de, 384(2)
Nevell, Neveyll:
  Anthony, 98
  George, 269
  John, 120, 401
  Nicholas, 163
  William, 140
Neves, Katherine de, 384
Neveson, Alexander, 20
Newark, Michael, 269
Newball, *see* Newbolde
Newberye, Ralph, 324
Newbolde, Newball:
  Davy, 205
  George, 346
Newcome, Newcom:
  Christopher, 367
  Richard, 73
Newdicke, Robert, 328
Newell:
  Charles, 369
  George, 336
Newes, Newys, Nowyes:
  Clement, 37
  Peter, 117
  Roger, xxxv, 59, 103
Newham, James, 372
Newland:
  Francis, 150
  Gregory, 278
  Robert, 285

Newman:
  —, *uxor* Newman, 95
  Gabriel, 283
  Gaius, 299
  Gregory, 121, 331
  Herman, 128
  John, 54, 256
  Richard, 272
  Robert, 287, 327
  Thomas, 187
  William, 61, 539
Newport, Richard, 135
Newsame, John, 319
Newton:
  Master —, 57
  Mistress —, widow, 317
  Henry, 244
  John, 378, 379
  Richard, 278, 371
  Robert, 149(2), 174
  Thomas, 320, 377, 391
Newyngton, William, 68
Nicholas, Nicolas:
  Doctor —, xxxix n, 13
  Courte, 158
  Dame Elizabeth, 223
  Gregory, 36
  Henry, 6
  John, 339
  Peter, 23
  Robert, 73, 329
  Thomas, 271
Nicholls, Niccolles, Nicholles, Nicolles,
  Nyccoles, Nycholles, Nycholls,
  Nycolles, Nycols:
  Cornelis, 33
  Dennis, 117
  Humphrey, 265
  John, 33, 117, 163, 175, 255, 284
  Richard, 226
  Robert, 72, 216, 246
  Roger, 69
  Simon, 7
  Thomas, 265
Nicholson, Niccholson, Nickelson,
  Nicollson, Nicolson, Nycholson,
  Nycollson:
  Christopher, 37, 522
  John, 173, 238, 358
  Paul, 141
  Richard, 306
  Thomas, 64, 250, 370
  William, 381, 441
Nichosmus, —, 52
Nidigat, John, 152
Nightingale, Nightingall, Nighttingale,
  Nitingale:
  John, 195, 229, 323
  Joyce, 214
  Margaret, 195

389

Index of persons

Poynere, Judithe le, 385
Poynter, Poyntor, Richard, 72, 354
Poyster, Jacob, 173
Prannell:
  Henry, 309
  Robert, 229
Prate, Roger de, xlv, 165
Pratt, Prat, Pratte:
  Cuthbert, 43
  Edward, 61
  John, 149
  Roger, 319
  Thomas, 29
  William, 319, 542, 546, 547, 552, 567
Prebounde:
  Jackline, 221
  Larrant, 221
Preist, Preyst (see also Prest):
  Doctor —, xxxix n, 276
  John, 83
  Robert, 365
Prelio:
  Mathew, 55
  Simon, 311
Prennoe, Bowne, 221
Prentice, John, 394
Presson, John van, 349
Prest (see also Preist):
  Thomas, 296
  William, 223
Prestman, William, 397
Preston:
  Anne, 290
  Edward, 161
  John, 285
  Ralph, 76
  Robert, 355
  Roger, 210
  Thomas, 102
Prestwick, John, 187
Prestwood, John, 187
Preter, Benett le, 314
Pretrell, Johan, 17
Pretuses, Yonbaldma, 290
Prevall, Richard, 84
Preyst, see Preist
Price, Pryce, Pryse:
  Frances, 329
  John, 222, 296
  John ap Morgan, alias, 367
  Morgan, 170
  Thomas, 344
  William, 222
Prince, Prynce:
  John, 64
  Richard, 235
  William, 397
Princell:
  Adryan, and wife, 172
  Gregory, and wife, 171

Pringey, Mary, 389
Prior, Pryor:
  Anthony, 322
  Geoffrey, 357
  Michael, 309
  Robert, 182(2)
Priscott, Francis, 224
Proctar, Procter, Proctor:
  John, 42
  Richard, 277
  Robert, 207
  Tyomas, 223
Proutyng, William, 123
Prowde, William, 165
Prowe, Robert, 374
Pruse:
  Harrian, 196
  Susana, 196
Prye:
  Jackmine de, 218
  Jacob de, 221
  John de, 6, 218
  Joyce, de, 221
  Mary de, 218
Pryme, —, widow, 211
Pryse, see Price
Puckeringe, Puckerynge:
  Christopher, 228
  Edward, 226
  Francis, 233
Puckle, Puckell:
  Edmund, 378
  Robert, 294, 378
Puddell, Puddle:
  John, 57
  Lawrence, 247
Pudsey, Nicholas, 274
Pulforde, Thomas, 248
Pullet, Mistress —, 4
Pullison, Thomas, alderman, 267
Pullyn, Guillome, 172
Pultrell, William, 60
Purdue, William, 5
Pursell:
  John, 115
  Richard, 56
  William, 389
Purvey, John, 255
Puster, Wynkyn, and wife, 173
Putman, Francis, 288
Puyne, Roger, 165
Puys, Baptiste de, 235
Pyatt, Pyot:
  Charles, 16
  Richard, 255
Pycheford, William, 258
Pycke, see Pike
Pyckmere, George, 282
Pye:
  Gamaliel, 307

395

399

401

403

Index of persons

412

Index of persons

Withenell, William, 269
Withens, Wythens:
Marmaduke, 381
Robert, 244
Withers, Wythars, Wythers, Wytthers:
—, widow, 262
Davy, 275
Edmund, 122
John, 72, 273, 282
Lawrence, 35
Nicholas, 69
Richard, 255
Thomas, 274
William, 241
Wittewrongill, Jacob, 234; see also
Whitfrongell
Woar, Richard, 388
Wodmyster, Charles, 327
Woharpe, Jozephe, 24
Wolcock, Anthony, 309
Wolf, Wolfe, Wollfe, Wulffe:
Mistress —, 75
Agnes, 266
Duram, 266
George, 266
Henry, 154
John, 225
Lambert, 94
Morgan, 100, 549
Wolhouse:
Anthony, 227
Roger, 42
Wollaston, Wollyston (see also
Wolstone):
Henry, 242
Richard, 301
Woller, John, 228
Wolley, Wolleye, Wooley:
Ambrose, 156, 454
Christopher, 151
Henry, 202
Nicholas, 327
Randall, 224
Wollworth, Robert, 401
Wolstone, —, widow, 244; see also
Wollaston
Womst, Derick, 176
Wonters, Haunce, xlix n, 203
Wood, Wodde, Woodde, Woode:
—, widow, 332
[illeg.], cooper, 554
Anne, 85
Antonet, 218
Edward, 170, 179, 183
Francis, 9
Humphrey, 316
Joane, widow, 216
John, 293, 298n, 311, 382
Martin, 353
Michael, 218

Richard, 265, 376
Robert, 12, 25, 34, 46, 310
Thomas, 186, 257, 355
Thomas a, 33, 156
Toby, 365
William, 326, 364, 392
William a, 151
Woodall, Woddall:
Humphrey, 181
Thomas, 181
Woodam, William, 390
Woodborne, Robert, 170
Woodcock, Wodcok, Woodcocke,
Woodcoke, Woodcooke:
Ambrose, 256
Andrew, 149
Hugh, 224
James, 28
John, 379
Nicholas, 3
Ralph, 278
Thomas, 305
Woodfall, William, 342
Woodford, Wodford:
Mr —, 40
Francis, 193
Gamaliel, 276
Stephen, 223
Woodhouse, Wodhowse:
Sir Henry, 327
Hugh, 122
Philip, 175
Thomas, 49, 175
Woodland, Wodland:
Herry, 88
James, 105
Robert, 83
William, 119
Woodlife, Wodlyf, Woodlyff:
Oliver, 238
William, 11, 75
Woodlocke, Woddlak:
Francis, 7
Thomas, 67
Woodman, John, 27
Woodoner, John, 27
Woodroff, Wodrof, Wooderoff,
Woodrofe, Woodroffe:
David, 138, 467, 557
John, 193
Sir Nicholas, alderman, xxiv n, xlviii,
lxv, 166, 168, 362
Woodshawe:
Julian, widow, 105
William, 105
Woodward, Woodwarde:
Alice, widow, 281
John, 270, 354
Nicholas, 146
Richard, 226

416

417

INDEX OF PLACES AND INSTITUTIONS

419

Index of places and institutions

Index of places and institutions

LONDON RECORD SOCIETY

The London Record Society was founded in December 1964 to publish transcripts, abstracts and lists of the primary sources for the history of London, and generally to stimulate interest in archives relating to London. Membership is open to any individual or institution; the annual subscription is £12 ($22) for individuals and £18 ($35) for institutions. Prospective members should apply to the Hon. Secretary, Miss Heather Creaton, c/o Institute of Historical Research, Senate House, London, WC1E 7HU,

The following volumes have already been published:

1. *London Possessory Azzizes: a calendar*, edited by Helena M. Chew (1965)
2. *London Inhabitants within the Walls, 1695*, with an introduction by D. V. Glass (1966)
3. *London Consistory Court Wills, 1492–1547*, edited by Ida Darlington (1967)
4. *Scriveners' Company Common Paper, 1357–1628, with a continuation to 1678*, edited by Francis W. Steer (1968)
5. *London Radicalism, 1830–1843; a selection from the papers of Francis Place*, edited by D. J. Rowe (1670)
6. *The London Eyre of 1244*, edited by Helena M. Chew and Martin Weinbaum (1970)
7. *The Cartulary of Holy Trinity Aldgate*, edited by Gerald A. J. Hodgett (1971)
8. *The Port of Trade of Early Elizabethan London: documents*, edited by Brian Dietz (1972)
9. *The Spanish Company*, edited by Pauline Croft (1973)
10. *London Assize of Nuisance, 1301–1431: a calendar*, edited by Helena M. Chew and William Kellaway (1973)
11. *Two Calvinistic Methodist Chapels, 1743–1811: the London Tabernacle and Spa Fields Chapel*, edited by Edwin Welch (1975)
12. *The London Eyre of 1276*, edited by Martin Weinbaum (1976)
13. *The Church in London, 1375–1392*, edited by A. K. McHardy (1977)
14. *Committees for Repeal of the Test and Corporation Acts: Minutes, 1786–90 and 1827–8*, edited by Thomas W. Davis (1978)
15. *Joshua Johnson's Letterbook, 1771–4: letters from a merchant in London to his partners in Maryland*, edited by Jacob M. Price (1979)
16. *London and Middlesex Chantry Certificate, 1548*, edited by C. J. Kitching (1980)

17. *London Politics, 1713–1717: Minutes of a Whig Club, 1714–17,* edited by H. Horwitz; *London Pollbooks, 1713,* edited by W. A. Speck and W. A. Gray (1981)
18. *Parish Fraternity Register: fraternity of the Holy Trinity and SS. Fabian and Sebastian in the parish of St Botolph without Aldersgate,* edited by Patricia Basing (1982)
19. *Trinity House of Deptford: Transactions, 1609–35,* edited by G. G. Harris (1983)
20. *Chamber Accounts of the sixteenth century,* edited by Betty R. Masters (1984)
21. *The Letters of John Paige, London merchant, 1648–58,* edited by George F. Steckley (1984)
22. *A Survey of Documentary Sources for Property Holding in London before the Great Fire,* by Derek Keene and Vanessa Harding (1985)
23. *The Commissions for Building Fifty New Churches,* edited by M. H. Port (1986)
24. *Richard Hutton's Complaints Book,* edited by Timothy V. Hitchcock (1987)
25. *Westminster Abbey Charters, 1966–c.1214,* edited by Emma Mason (1988)
26. *London Viewers and their Certificates, 1508–1558,* edited by Janet S. Loengard (1989)
27. *The Overseas Trade of London: Exchequer Customs Accounts, 1480–1,* edited by H. S. Cobb (1990)
28. *Justice in Eighteenth-century Hackney: the Justicing Notebook of Henry Norris and the Hackney Petty Sessions Book,* edited by Ruth Paley (1991)
29. *Two Tudor Subsidy Assessment Rolls for the City of London: 1541 and 1582,* edited by R. G. Lang (1993)

Most volumes are still in print; apply to Clifton Books, 34 Hamlet Court, Westcliffe-on-Sea, Essex SS0 7LX. Price to individual members £12 ($22) each, to non-members £20 ($38) each.